GRAMMAR

USAGE

CONTINUED ON BACK END PAPER

English Grammar and Composition

SECOND COURSE

English Grammar and Composition

SECOND COURSE

JOHN E. WARRINER

SHEILA Y. LAWS

HARCOURT BRACE JOVANOVICH, INC.

New York Chicago San Francisco Atlanta Dallas

THE SERIES:

English Grammar and Composition: First Course
English Grammar and Composition: Second Course
English Grammar and Composition: Third Course
English Grammar and Composition: Fourth Course
English Grammar and Composition: Fifth Course
English Grammar and Composition: Complete Course

Test booklet and teacher's manual for each title above

CORRELATED BOOKS OF MODELS FOR WRITING:

Composition: Models and Exercises A
Composition: Models and Exercises B
Composition: Models and Exercises C
Composition: Models and Exercises D
Composition: Models and Exercises E
Advanced Composition: A Book of Models for Writing

AUTHORS: John E. Warriner has taught English for 32 years, in junior and senior high schools and in college. He is also a coauthor of the *English Workshop* series. Sheila Y. Laws has taught English in secondary schools and college. She is a coauthor of the *Harbrace College Workbook:* Forms 6A and 6B.

PRINTED IN THE UNITED STATES OF AMERICA

ISBN 0-15-311926-8

Preface

The most important and most demanding task of the teacher of secondary school English is the improvement of the speech and writing of his students. To this difficult task, the teacher brings his own convictions, based on his training and experience, as to what to teach and how to teach it. Dealing with a particular group of students at a particular time and place, he wisely adapts his motivational schemes to fit the specific situation. To a large degree, his personality and enthusiasm determine class response. Every teacher, however, needs a textbook to supply the subject matter of the course and the indispensable practice materials through which learning is firmly established. The wide acceptance of the *English Grammar and Composition* series in its earlier editions indicates that these textbooks have the qualities teachers want in a textbook.

In general, the series leaves motivation to the teacher, unencumbered by methods imposed by the text. The approach is always businesslike and efficient. Everything that will help the teacher to bring his students to an improved level of competence has been included; everything that will not help has been carefully excluded. The presentation is always direct and clean-cut. Uncluttered by extraneous matter—decorative art, fringe topics of the English curriculum, and discursive, motivational talks to the student—the texts state clearly and exactly what the student is to learn and then provide the abundance of exercise material which is essential to his learning it. Omission of the nonessential leaves more space for the essential.

Texts in the series follow a unit organization. All instructional materials on one topic are placed together in the same chapter or group of chapters. They are not distributed piecemeal throughout the book. For example, all instruction on verb usage is in one chapter; all punctuation rules and exercises are together in a unit of several consecutive chapters. Teachers like the unit organization because it is efficient in permitting concentration on one skill at a time, and because it simplifies the student's problem when he wishes to look up a topic on his own. This type of organization also makes the books completely flexible. With two or three necessary exceptions, the text imposes no sequence; any chapter may be taught as a separate unit without regard for what immediately precedes or follows. This flexibility assures that the books will fit any course of study, whatever its organizing principle. The clarity and conciseness of the rules and explanations are enhanced by the typography: the important rules are printed in red; the tab keys are a reference aid.

With complete units on grammar, usage, sentence structure, composition, mechanics, and oral English, the books cover all important areas of language study, with the natural exceptions of reading and literature.

Grammar

The *English Grammar and Composition* series teaches traditional grammar. The English profession is beginning to feel the impact of linguistic research and to ponder the relative values of several different grammars of English. In the opinion of the authors, the concepts of these new grammars are not yet clearly enough defined for general use in the schools; insofar as a knowledge of grammar is an aid in speaking and writing, traditional grammar's view of the English sentence appears to the authors to be as useful as any other view.

There is little time in the crowded English curriculum for the teaching of grammar as an end in itself. *English Grammar and Composition, Second Course*, covers only that grammar which in simplicity and usefulness is appropriate to students at this level. Typically, a student at this level has been introduced to grammar informally, with varying degrees of thoroughness, in elementary school and more formally in the middle school years. *Second Course* reviews the grammar presented in *First Course* and introduces the concept of subordination through the subordinate clause, the complex sentence, and the participial phrase. The concepts and terms are those which can be applied at this level to the improvement of usage and sentence structure.

Usage

Like all books in the *English Grammar and Composition* series, *Second Course* devotes a large amount of space to establishing good usage habits. Throughout the series, usage is taught in full recognition of the fact that language fashions are constantly changing, that dialects differ in different parts of the country, and that there are usage levels which reflect social and educational backgrounds. The series recognizes also, however, that at any one time there does exist a standard of usage to which the majority of educated people everywhere do conform. The attitude toward usage is sanely liberal but not so permissive as to ignore this standard. The usage habits taught in this book are basic. The series, putting first things first, leaves the genteel refinements of adult English to the upper years of high school.

Sentence Structure and Composition

In the composition section, the student learns the importance of careful planning even in the personal-experience theme. Included in *Second Course* is a supplement, "Topics to Write About." Students are asked to look at cartoons and photographs that tell a story or suggest an idea and then to put these stories and ideas into words. Students are also asked to provide captions and snapshot sentences, to write character sketches, and to describe personal experiences prompted by photographs. Thus, the student learns not only to plan a composition, but to find an abundance of topics by looking around him.

One learns to write through frequent practice. As he practices, the student tries to follow sound composition precepts presented in his text and to imitate the models of good writing provided for him. A general English textbook is necessarily limited, however, in the amount of space it can devote to the reproduction of models. Teachers desiring additional examples of good writing will find them in the series *Composition: Models and Exercises*, which accompanies the *English Grammar and Composition* series. Each book in the *Composition: Models and Exercises* series contains up to 300 pages of carefully selected models, systematically arranged with appropriate analyses and writing assignments.

Mechanics

While *Second Course* concentrates on those punctuation rules which function most in the writing of students, it includes for reference purposes rules governing all marks of punctuation in all uses. Rules for the use of capital letters are presented. The spelling chapter teaches the most useful rules, gives practice in distinguishing common homonyms, and provides a selected list of 250 spelling words, as well as 50 spelling demons—a spelling program for the year.

Speaking and Listening

Chapters on speaking and listening give the teacher material he needs for developing his students' skills in these two areas. The concentration in Chapter 24 is on public speaking: giving announcements and reports, delivering a speech, and evaluating a speech. Chapter 25 attempts to establish good habits in listening in a variety of situations common in the students' experience.

Dictionary, Library, and Vocabulary Development

Under the general heading "Aids to Good English," these chapters provide the teacher with materials for teaching the efficient use of the dictionary and of library and reference tools. The chapter on vocabulary shows the student how to enlarge his vocabulary through context clues, word analysis, a knowledge of common prefixes and suffixes, and the study of companion forms of a word. A list of 240 vocabulary words provides a vocabulary program for the whole year.

Teaching Tests and Manual

A separate booklet of tests is available from the publisher at a small cost. Written by a teacher with extensive experience in preparing English tests, the booklet provides an easily scored test for each testable chapter in *English Grammar and Composition, Second Course*. Best kept in the teacher's possession until the class is ready for a test, these tests provide a sound basis for evaluating student achievement.

A complete *Teacher's Manual*, including a suggested course of study, teaching aids, supplementary material, and an answer key, is available upon request from the publisher.

J. W.

ACKNOWLEDGMENTS The authors and publishers wish to acknowledge the valuable assistance given by many teachers who contributed in many ways to the preparation of this series. Special thanks are due to Mr. Henry Aronson, International School of The Hague, Netherlands; Dr. John Arscott, Coordinator, Senior Division, West Essex High School, North Caldwell, New Jersey; Mrs. Margaret R. Bonney, Lexington High School, Lexington, Massachusetts; Mrs. Louise Brock, Tuckahoe Junior High School, Richmond, Virginia; Mrs. Kenneth Brown, Hand Junior High School, Columbia, South Carolina; Mr. Lewis Browne, Myers Park High School, Charlotte, North Carolina; Mrs. Margaret Christianson, Point Loma High School, San Diego, California; Mr. W. Griffith Couser, Melrose High School, Melrose, Massachusetts; Miss Jean E. Crabtree, Garden City Senior High School, Garden City, New York; Mr. Peter Evarts, Assistant to the Director, Teacher Education Program, Oakland University, Rochester, Michigan; Miss Anna Fort, Deal Junior High School, Washington, D.C.; Mrs. Betty Gray, Abington Junior High School, Abington, Pennsylvania; Mrs. Helen Hiller, Former Chairman of English Department, Macomb's Junior High School, Bronx, New York; Mr. Robert U. Jameson, The Haverford School, Haverford, Pennsylvania; Mr. Raymond Kavanagh, Levittown Memorial High School, Levittown, New York; Mrs. Gladys Kronsagen, Glenbard Township High School, Glen Ellyn, Illinois; Miss Alice Liberto, Miami Edison Junior High School, Miami, Florida; Mrs. Archibald McClure, John Adams High School, South Bend, Indiana; Mrs. Ruth McKinney, A. C. Flora High School, Columbia, South Carolina; Miss Rita Morgan, James Madison High School, Vienna, Virginia; Miss Geraldine Oliver, Fairview High School, Dayton, Ohio; Mr. Orville Palmer, Educational Testing Service, Princeton, New Jersey; Mrs. Helen Slonin, Baldwin Junior High School, Baldwin, New York; Miss Julia Tygart, Miami Edison Junior High School, Miami, Florida; Mr. Arthur Weisbach, Summit High School, Summit, New Jersey.

Contents

PART TWO: USAGE

PART THREE: MECHANICS

PART FOUR: SENTENCE STRUCTURE

PART ONE

Grammar

CHAPTER 1

The Sentence

Subject and Predicate

Suppose that you began to read a story that opened as follows:

> Awakened in study hall John leaped from his seat into the balcony above him came the marching band led by the drum major playing the "Star-Spangled Banner" on his tall hat a great plume nodded to John it was a rude awakening.

Your difficulty in understanding the story comes not from a failure to understand the words but from a failure to understand the writer's units of thought. If the writer told the story to you, he could convey his meaning by the expression in his voice and by pausing at the right places. But writing differs from speaking in that the writer has only his words and punctuation as a method of communication. Thus it is the duty of the writer to use patterns which his reader is familiar with—to write complete sentences that are set off clearly by punctuation.

There is a second important difference between speaking and writing. In speech you often leave a sentence unfinished, and begin over again. You think as you speak. In writing, it is necessary to think *before* you write. You must plan sentences in advance. Writing requires more care than speaking.

1a. A *sentence* is a group of words expressing a complete thought.

A sentence begins with a capital letter and concludes with an end mark: period or question mark or exclamation point. Sometimes a group of words looks like a sentence when it is not. You must examine the group of words closely to be sure that it expresses a complete thought. Reading it aloud will help you.

NOT A SENTENCE	The old tree in the front yard. [This is not a complete thought. What about the old tree in the front yard?]
SENTENCE	The old tree is still standing in the front yard.
NOT A SENTENCE	Upon hearing the good news. [The thought is not complete. Who heard the good news? What did he or they do?]
SENTENCE	Upon hearing the good news, the audience shouted and applauded.
NOT A SENTENCE	After Sandy jumped the fence. [The thought is not complete. What happened after Sandy jumped the fence?]
SENTENCE	After Sandy jumped the fence, the other dogs followed.

● EXERCISE 1. Number your paper 1–20. Read the following groups of words and decide which are sentences and which are not. (Capital letters and end punctuation marks have been purposely omitted.) If a group of words is a sentence, copy it after the proper number, adding a capital letter and end punctuation. If the group of words is not a sentence, write *NS* after the proper number; then add whatever is necessary to complete the thought and make it a sentence.

EXAMPLES
1. living alone in the mountains
1. *NS Living alone in the mountains, the hermit makes his own furniture and clothes.*
2. many islands off the coast of Florida are uninhabited
2. *Many islands off the coast of Florida are uninhabited.*

1. standing in the hall by the fountain
2. at one time China was called Cathay
3. a very mysterious man with a long scar down the side of his face
4. after walking for days across the desert
5. the *Santa Maria* was Columbus' flagship
6. the ship was wrecked off Haiti in December of 1492
7. worked for days on the float for the Christmas parade
8. across the hall from the library
9. do you believe that lightning never strikes the same place twice
10. following closely behind the king
11. study your history
12. for many centuries men believed in witches
13. reading by the light of the fire

14. since the weather was good
15. the rocket was fired
16. when the satellite went into orbit
17. everyone rejoiced
18. during the long winter months when travel was impossible
19. on the lawn in front of the school
20. we made popcorn to take to the drive-in movie

● EXERCISE 2. Number your paper 1–20. Opposite each number on your paper, write *S* if the group of words is a sentence and *NS* if it is not a sentence.

1. In the eighteenth century Jonathan Swift wrote *Gulliver's Travels.* 2. An entertaining travel journal which makes fun of some of the ways of man. 3. In his first voyage Gulliver visits Lilliput. 4. A small island inhabited by people only six inches tall. 5. Gulliver observes some of their customs. 6. While living among the tiny people. 7. He is particularly amused by the way they choose their leaders. 8. Those who are seeking offices do tricks on a tightrope. 9. Such as somersaults and leaps. 10. As the office seekers perform. 11. The king and his court judge their performances. 12. Those who perform best are selected as the political leaders. 13. Although such a system amuses us. 14. The Lilliputians thought that it was a foolproof method. 15. For selecting the best men for public offices.

16. The Lilliputians at one time had a serious quarrel. 17. Which developed over the proper way to break an egg. 18. While some believed the egg should be broken at the big end. 19. Others thought it should be broken at the small end. 20. Thus the two political parties of Lilliput were formed: the Big-Endians and the Small-Endians.

● EXERCISE 3. The following groups of words are not sentences. Add to each whatever is necessary to make an interesting sentence.

1. on the highest peak
2. found only in warmer regions
3. a long black cloak
4. burning brightly in the distance
5. in our tree house
6. the lonely house on the hill
7. which performed many tricks
8. during the tourist season
9. when the storm was over
10. with his hat pulled down over his eyes

THE SUBJECT

You have learned that a sentence is a group of words expressing a complete thought. In order to express a complete thought, a sentence must have a subject and a predicate.

1b. The *subject* of a sentence is that part about which something is being said.

subject
A long line of people | waited at the art museum.

subject
Standing in the line were | several groups of students.

Since the subject is that part of the sentence about which something is being said, you can usually locate it by asking yourself *Who?* or *What?* Who waited at the art museum? Who was standing in the line? Notice that the subject comes at the beginning of the first example above and at the end of the second.

In the subject part of each sentence above, one word stands out as essential: in the first sentence, *line;* in the second sentence, *groups.* These two words, which cannot be removed from the subject parts of the sentences, are called *simple subjects.* The simple subject and the other words that belong with it are called the *complete subject.*

1c. The *simple subject* is the main word in the complete subject.

The simple subjects below are printed in heavy type.

complete subject
My **date** for the dance | arrived late.

complete subject
The long, hard **trip** across the desert | was finally over.

complete subject
Pacing back and forth in the cage was | a black **panther.**

When the subject is only one word or one name, the complete subject and the simple subject are the same.

complete subject
Alvin C. York | was a famous hero of World War I.
He | was decorated many times.

● EXERCISE 4. Number your paper 1–10. After each number, copy the complete subject from the corresponding sentence. Then underline the simple subject.

EXAMPLE 1. The time for the takeoff approached.
1. *The time for the takeoff*

1. A thick fog covered the airport.
2. Many planes had been grounded.

3. The one with the hospital supplies had to get through.
4. The pilot of the plane had a great deal of experience.
5. He taxied slowly down the runway.
6. Everyone in the control tower waited breathlessly.
7. The plane picked up speed.
8. Down the runway sped the fragile craft.
9. It gradually rose from the ground.
10. The plane with its precious cargo was in the air at last.

As has been pointed out, the most important word in the complete subject is the simple subject. Without the simple subject there could be no sentence. From now on in this book, the word *subject* will refer to the simple subject.

● EXERCISE 5. Number your paper 1–20. After the proper number, copy the subject (simple subject) of each sentence. Ask yourself what or whom the sentence says something about.

1. Samuel Coleridge wrote several strange poems. 2. Among them is *The Rime of the Ancient Mariner*. 3. This poem recounts a sailor's terrifying supernatural adventure. 4. The ancient mariner tells of his voyage on a sailing ship. 5. The ship was watched over by an albatross, a huge seabird. 6. For nine days the bird guided the ship through perilous seas. 7. Then, for no reason at all, the mariner killed the albatross. 8. At first the crew was very angry at the mariner. 9. But their good luck continued. 10. Consequently, they praised the mariner for his action. 11. Finally the ship sailed into the Pacific Ocean. 12. Here the wind ceased. 13. The ship stood motionless like a "painted ship upon a painted ocean." 14. Now the

other seamen blamed the mariner for their bad luck. 15. Around his neck they hung the dead albatross. 16. Then in the distance a strange ship appeared. 17. On board the ship was Death with his companion, Life-in-Death. 18. The two weird figures played dice for the crew and the guilty mariner. 19. Death won the crew. 20. And Life-in-Death received the mariner.

THE PREDICATE

The subject is one of the two essential parts of a sentence; the other essential part is the predicate.

1d. The *predicate* of a sentence is that part which says something about the subject.

predicate
A long black limousine | waited at the door.

predicate
Both movies | held my attention to the end.

predicate
On either side of me were | my two best friends.

To find the predicate in a sentence, ask, *What is being said about the subject?* or *What happened?* In the normal order of an English sentence, the predicate follows the subject, but in some sentences the predicate comes before the subject. (See third sentence above.)

The Simple Predicate, or Verb

Just as the simple subject is the most important part of the complete subject, so the simple predicate is the most important part of the complete predicate. The simple predicate is usually called the *verb* of the sentence.

1e. The *simple predicate*, or *verb*, is the main word or group of words in the predicate.

In each of the following sentences the simple predicate, or verb, is in heavy type.

complete subject | *complete predicate*
The movie star | **signed** autographs for hours.

complete subject | *complete predicate*
A whirlwind | **swept** through the town.

complete subject | *complete predicate*
The trees | **sagged** with the weight of the ice.

The simple predicate may be a one-word verb, or it may be a verb of more than one word, such as *have signed, did sweep, will be sagging.* When the simple predicate has more than one word, it is called a *verb phrase*. Note the verb phrases in the following sentences.

In the early days of Rome, cattle **were used** for money.

For many centuries madness **was associated** with the moon.

Your vocabulary **can be increased** by a study of the origins of words.

The complete predicate, which consists of the verb or verb phrase and the other words that belong with it, usually comes after the subject, but it sometimes can appear at the beginning of a sentence as in the following sentences.

complete predicate | *complete subject*
There on its back **was** | a large **tortoise.**

complete predicate | *complete subject*
At the top of the tree **is** | a bird's **nest.**

The subject may come in the middle of the predicate so that part of the predicate is on one side of the subject and the rest is on the other side. In the following examples, the complete predicate is in heavy type:

> **During the winter** many animals **hibernate.**
> **Do** squirrels **hibernate?**

The words *not* and *never*, which are frequently used with verbs, are not verbs. They are never part of a verb or verb phrase.

> She **did** not **believe** me.
> We **had** never **met.**

From now on in this book, the simple predicate will be called the verb.

● EXERCISE 6. Number your paper 1–10. Copy the complete predicates from the following sentences. Then underline the verbs or verb phrases twice.

EXAMPLE 1. The novel *Frankenstein* was written by a woman.
1. *was written by a woman*

1. Jean Nicot introduced tobacco into France.
2. His name has been used as the basis for the word *nicotine*.
3. Many English words, such as *dictate* and *predict*, trace their origins to the Latin word *dicere*.
4. *Dicere* means "say" or "speak."
5. Can you name some other words with a form of *dicere* in them?
6. The Atlas of Greek mythology was the leader of the Titans, a race of giants.
7. For many centuries he has been pictured with the world on his shoulders.
8. The picture of Atlas with the world on his shoulders was used by Mercator in a collection of his maps.

9. Later mapmakers used the same figure.
10. In our time *atlas* refers to a collection of maps.

● EXERCISE 7. Number your paper 1–20. After the proper number, copy the verb or verb phrase in each of the following sentences.

1. At one time the *exemplum* was a popular tale. 2. The *exemplum* is a tale with a moral. 3. One popular *exemplum* is told by the Pardoner in Chaucer's *Canterbury Tales.* 4. According to the story, three young men were looking for Death. 5. During their search they met an old man. 6. He directed them to an oak tree. 7. There they would find Death. 8. The young men hurried to the tree. 9. But the only thing under the tree was a heap of gold. 10. Now the young men no longer looked for Death. 11. Instead they thought of the money. 12. Each wanted all the money for himself. 13. The youngest of the men was sent into town on an errand. 14. On his return he was killed by the other two. 15. Then these two drank a toast to their good fortune. 16. Soon they too died. 17. The youngest man had poisoned their wine. 18. Thus all three men found Death. 19. Greed is the source of much evil. 20. This, of course, is the moral of the *exemplum.*

● EXERCISE 8. Copy the subject and the verb from each of the following sentences. Underline the subject once and the verb twice.

EXAMPLE 1. In 1665 a great plague killed 68,000 people in London alone.
1. *plague killed*

1. The next year a great fire destroyed 13,200 homes.
2. These two catastrophes are recorded in the diaries of the time.

3. Samuel Pepys is one of the most famous diarists of England.
4. A firsthand account of the plague and the fire was given in his diary.
5. Most families in London suffered some loss from the fire.
6. At first the fire seemed very small.
7. In fact, during the first night of the fire, Pepys slept quite peacefully.
8. Why were the people fleeing from their homes and shops?
9. Pepys suggested a plan to the king for stopping the progress of the fire.
10. Houses around the fire were pulled down.

+ ● EXERCISE 9. Find the subject and the verb in each sentence and write them on your paper after the proper number.

1. Our strangest insect is the mosquito.
2. During its early life the mosquito lives in stagnant water.
3. Thus the mosquito can be called an amphibious insect.
4. The eggs are laid by the female mosquito in the water.
5. A nest of mosquito eggs somewhat resembles a small raft.
6. In a few days the mosquito eggs hatch into wriggling larvae.
7. These larvae live in the water.
8. From time to time they come to the surface for air.
9. In the next stage, the mosquito becomes a pupa, or tumbler.
10. Soon "flocks" of winged mosquitoes take to the air.

● EXERCISE 10. Some of the word groups below are complete subjects and some are complete predicates. Add whatever part is needed to make a sentence. Then underline the simple subject once and the verb twice.

EXAMPLE 1. worked throughout the night
1. *The men of the circus worked throughout the night.*

1. the jukebox at the corner drugstore
2. should never be eaten by anyone
3. are mysterious creatures
4. the old house on our block
5. no one in his right mind
6. raced down the track
7. suddenly turned toward us
8. my favorite singer
9. the old woman with the wrinkled hands and the hideous laugh
10. discovered a cave in the hills behind the old, abandoned sawmill

THE SENTENCE BASE

You have been studying the two most important parts of the sentence: the subject and the verb. Because these two parts are essential to the sentence, they are called the *sentence base*. All other parts of the sentence are attached to the sentence base.

SENTENCE BASE **Dogs play.**

SENTENCE BASE WITH OTHER PARTS ATTACHED Every day two frisky **dogs** named Bison and Stark **play** for hours on our front lawn.

The parts that were added give additional information, but they would be meaningless without the sentence base.

● EXERCISE 11. Here are ten sentence bases. Add other parts to them. Notice how the sentence base holds the other parts together.

EXAMPLE 1. Snow covered.
1. *Last night a ten-inch snow covered Nashville.*

1. Wind howled.
2. Plane soared.
3. Dog growls.
4. Group played.
5. Cannon was roaring.
6. Sun set.
7. Man stared.
8. Cat leaped.
9. Guests were waiting.
10. Time has passed.

COMPOUND SUBJECTS AND COMPOUND VERBS

Many times more than one subject is being talked about.

ONE SUBJECT **Kelly** baited his hook.

TWO SUBJECTS **Kelly** and **Roger** baited their hooks.

THREE SUBJECTS **Kelly, Roger,** and **Michael** baited their hooks.

ONE SUBJECT **New York City** is our destination.

TWO SUBJECTS Either **New York City** or **Niagara Falls** is our destination.

Notice that when two or more subjects have the same verb, a connecting word—*and* or *or*—is used between them. The connected subjects are referred to as a *compound subject.*

1f. A *compound subject* is made up of two or more subjects that are joined by *and* or *or* and have the same verb.

> The **Senate** and the **House** are in session. [There are two subjects—*Senate* and *House*—which are joined by a connecting word—*and*—and have the same verb—*are.*]

● EXERCISE 12. Copy the compound subjects from the following sentences, together with the connecting word. Then list the verb or verb phrase which goes with both subjects.

EXAMPLE 1. During World War II destroyers and submarines often engaged in battles.
1. *destroyers and submarines—engaged*

1. Hawaii and Alaska are the newest states in the Union.
2. Both books and money have been donated to our library.
3. The *Pinta*, the *Niña*, and the *Santa Maria* left Spain for the New World.
4. Pencils or pens may be used on this test.
5. Sherlock Holmes and Dr. Watson were created by A. Conan Doyle.
6. At that time the twist and the bossa nova were popular dances.
7. Almost immediately the lightning and the thunder ceased.
8. Either Cal or Ted must pay the bill for the broken slide projector.
9. In the streets were old people, young people, and children.
10. *Re–*, *com–*, and *pro–* are common prefixes.

Just as a sentence may have a compound subject, so it may have a compound verb.

1g. A *compound verb* is made up of two or more verbs that are joined by *and, or,* or *but* and have the same subject.

ONE VERB Surfing **has become** a very popular sport.

COMPOUND VERB The dog **barked** and **growled** at the thief. [There are two verbs—*barked, growled*—joined by *and.* Both verbs have the same subject—*dog.*]

COMPOUND VERB The man **was convicted** but later **was found** innocent of the crime. [There are two verb phrases—*was convicted, was found*—joined by *but.* Both verb phrases have the same subject—*man.*]

● EXERCISE 13. Copy the compound verb from each of the following sentences, together with the connecting word. Then write the subject of the verb.

EXAMPLE 1. The stranded party lighted a bonfire and waved their shirts to the circling plane.
1. *lighted and waved—party*

1. Jane baked the pies and sold them at the fair.
2. Don read *Smoky* and reported on it to the class.
3. According to Greek mythology, Prometheus stole fire from heaven and gave it to man.
4. The female mosquito lays her eggs in the water and then dies.
5. The fire was set by a careless person or was started by lightning.

6. During public hangings, thieves circulated among the spectators and robbed them.
7. We read the book and saw the movie.
8. England was first occupied by the Celts but was later invaded by the Romans.
9. The pompous man slipped on a banana peel and landed in a cart of fish.
10. Many people have gone to Blackbeard Island near Georgia and have searched for treasure.

Sometimes you will see a sentence which has a compound subject and a compound verb. In such a sentence both of the subjects go with both of the verbs.

> s s v
> The **captain** and his **crew** **battled** the storm
> v
> and **prayed** for better weather. [Notice that both *captain* and *crew* perform both actions—*battled* and *prayed*.]

● EXERCISE 14. Copy the following sentences, underlining the subjects once and the verbs or verb phrases twice.

EXAMPLE 1. Many fine poems and novels were written by young men.

1. *Many fine poems and novels were written by young men.*

1. Byron and Keats are famous English poets.
2. They lived short lives but wrote many fine poems.
3. Keats had tuberculosis and died at twenty-five.
4. Byron believed strongly in freedom and wrote several poems on this theme.
5. In one poem a man and his two younger brothers are chained to columns in a dungeon.
6. They neither touch nor see each other.

7. The middle brother weakens from hunger and dies.
8. Eventually death comes and claims the youngest brother.
9. A bird, the spiders in the dungeon, and even his chains become the remaining brother's friends.
10. Years later the man is released from prison but regains his freedom "with a sigh."

● EXERCISE 15. Using titles, words, and characters of songs, books, and poems, write ten sentences, five with compound subjects and five with compound predicates. Underline subjects once and verbs twice.

EXAMPLE 1. *Frankie and Johnny were sweethearts.*

● EXERCISE 16. Make complete sentences by adding predicates to the subjects provided below. Seek sentence variety by using some compound predicates. You may also add to the subjects, making them compound if you wish. Underline the subject once and the verb twice. Capitalize the first word of each sentence.

EXAMPLE 1. the troops
1. *Toward sunset the troops reached camp.*

1. the lively chimpanzee
2. the theater on the corner
3. a crowd of autograph seekers
4. our star basketball player
5. a lazy turtle
6. the star of the show
7. the results of the contest
8. Dorothy
9. five astronauts
10. the reporter

KINDS OF SENTENCES

1h. **Sentences may be classified according to their purpose. There are four kinds of sentences.**[1]

(1) A *declarative sentence* makes a statement. It is followed by a period.

EXAMPLES A violinist played gypsy music while we dined.
Shakespeare was born in 1564.
Curiosity is the beginning of knowledge.

(2) An *interrogative sentence* asks a question. It is followed by a question mark.

EXAMPLES What do you know about glaciers?
Why do we see only one side of the moon?
Who was the chief god of the Greeks?

(3) An *imperative sentence* gives a command or makes a request. It is followed by a period. Strong commands are followed by exclamation points.

EXAMPLES Do your homework each night.
Watch out!
Finish your work, John.

At first glance none of these sentences seems to have any subject. But, of course, the person addressed in each case is the subject. The subject *you*, then, is said to be understood in all these sentences.

(You) do your homework each night.
(You) watch out!
John, (you) finish your work, please.

[1] The classification of sentences according to structure (simple, compound, complex) is taught in Chapter 7.

(4) An *exclamatory sentence* shows excitement or expresses strong feeling. It is followed by an exclamation point.

EXAMPLES What a sight the sunset is!
They're off!
Dan won the portable radio!

Junior high students have a tendency to overuse the exclamatory sentence. Be sure to save your exclamation points for sentences which really do show emotion. If overused, the exclamatory sentence loses its significance.

● EXERCISE 17. Below are ten famous quotations. Number your paper 1–10. After each number, write the kind of sentence it is and give the punctuation mark that should follow the sentence.

EXAMPLE 1. Walk softly and carry a big stick
— THEODORE ROOSEVELT
1. *imperative.*

1. I have nothing to offer but blood, toil, tears, and sweat—SIR WINSTON CHURCHILL
2. The great hope of society is individual character —W. E. CHANNING
3. O, that this too too solid flesh would melt,
Thaw, and resolve itself into a dew
—WILLIAM SHAKESPEARE
4. You can't build a reputation on what you are going to do—HENRY FORD
5. What happiness is there which is not purchased with more or less of pain—MARGARET OLIPHANT
6. What's in a name—WILLIAM SHAKESPEARE
7. Every man has a right to his opinion, but no man has a right to be wrong in his facts
—BERNARD BARUCH

8. Can anything be so elegant as to have few wants and to serve them one's self—RALPH WALDO EMERSON
9. If you do not think about the future, you cannot have one—JOHN GALSWORTHY
10. An expert is one who knows more and more about less and less—NICHOLAS MURRAY BUTLER

DIAGRAMING THE SUBJECT AND VERB

A diagram shows the structure of a sentence as a kind of picture. Making a diagram of the subject and verb is a way of showing that you understand these two parts of the sentence.

PATTERN

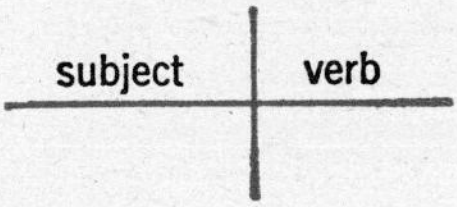

subject | verb

EXAMPLES Lions roar.

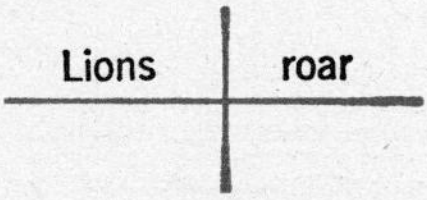

Lions | roar

Men speak.

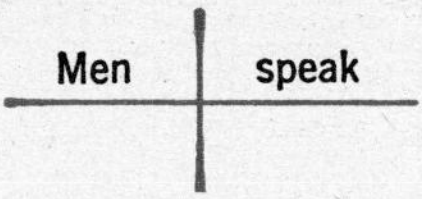

Men | speak

Notice that the parts of the sentence base—the subject and verb—are placed on a horizontal line with a vertical line separating the subject from the verb. The capital marking the beginning of the sentence is used, but not the punctuation.

To diagram a sentence, you first pick out the subject and the verb and then write them on the horizontal line, separated by a crossing vertical line.

EXAMPLES 1. The energetic reporter dashed to the fire.

reporter | dashed

2. Have you been studying for the final test?

you | Have been studying

3. Listen to the beautiful music.

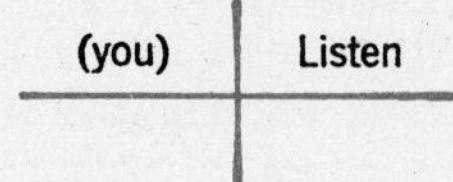

● EXERCISE 18. Diagram the simple subjects and verbs in the following sentences. Omit all other words from your diagram. Use a ruler and leave plenty of space between the diagrams.

1. The nervous radio announcer stammered several times.
2. Many tourists flock to the beach during the hot weather.
3. Our small puppy barked at the postman.
4. The orange and white float won the contest.
5. Tom's old car stopped on every hill.
6. After an hour of frantic searching, the missing child was found.
7. During the night we slept in our sleeping bags.
8. Where are you going for your vacation?
9. Finally, the car in front of us turned left.
10. Open your books to the assignment.

The following example shows how to diagram a sentence with a compound subject. Notice the position of the joining word *and.*

EXAMPLE Vines and weeds grew over the old well.

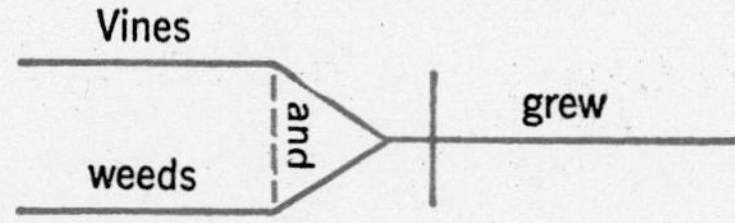

To diagram a sentence with a compound verb, you follow a similar pattern.

EXAMPLE The model walked across the platform and turned around.

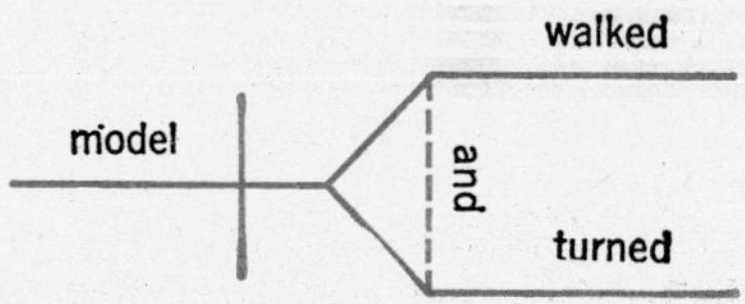

If the sentence has both a compound subject and a compound verb, it is diagramed this way.

EXAMPLE Ken and Dick dived into the water and swam across the pool.

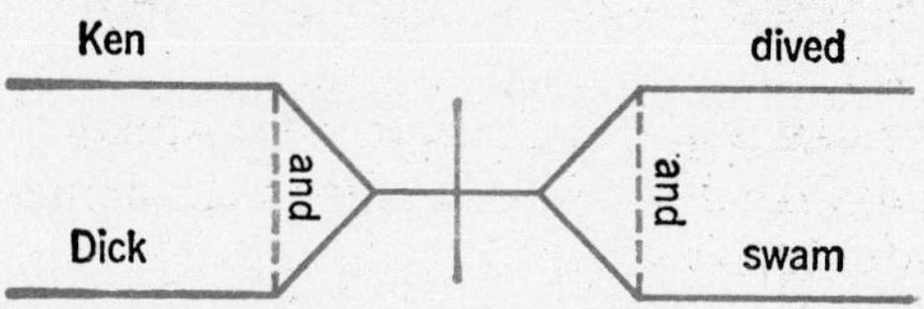

● EXERCISE 19. Diagram the simple subjects and verbs or verb phrases in the following sentences.

1. We ran to the railroad station and barely caught the train.

2. Harriet and Jane rose from their seats and went to the chalkboard.
3. The plane circled above the landing field but did not descend.
4. Pencil and paper are needed for tomorrow's assignment.
5. The knight and his squire prepared for battle.
6. The students either wrote in ink or typed their compositions.
7. Gail and Jeanette polished the silver and set the table.
8. In the evening the crickets and frogs make loud noises.
9. He will write or will call early.
10. The scoutmaster and his troop got out of the bus and hiked up the mountain.

● REVIEW EXERCISE A. *Oral Drill.* One student should identify the complete subject; another, the complete predicate. A third student should point out the simple subject; and a fourth student, the verb or verb phrase. A few sentences have compound subjects and verbs.

1. Robin Hood and his merry band lived in Sherwood Forest.
2. The band of outlaws robbed the rich and gave the money to the poor.
3. On one occasion the Sheriff of Nottingham sent a tinker into the forest with a warrant for Robin Hood's arrest.
4. The tinker met Robin but did not recognize the outlaw.
5. The two went to the Blue Boar Inn.
6. After several glasses of ale, the tinker was drunk.
7. Robin stole the warrant and departed from the inn.

8. Later the tinker and Robin met in the forest and fought.
9. The famous outlaw won the bout.
10. The tinker admitted his defeat and joined Robin Hood's band.

● REVIEW EXERCISE B. Copy the following sentences. Separate the complete subject from the complete predicate with a vertical line. Then underline the simple subject once and the verb twice.

EXAMPLE 1. Collies and German shepherds guard and herd sheep.
1. *Collies and German shepherds | guard and herd sheep.*

1. One German shepherd responded to one hundred commands.
2. Another dog could do about one hundred and fifty things.
3. The people of the Gaines Research Center called Tubby the most useful animal in all of the United States.
4. He herded cattle, gathered firewood, and carried messages.
5. His master would scatter fifteen objects on the floor.
6. The dog would bring each object on command and drop it at his master's feet.
7. He hardly ever missed a command.
8. Other dogs have become famous for their intelligence.
9. Lassie and Rin Tin Tin are known to many television viewers.
10. The trainers of dogs work many hours with them each day.

● REVIEW EXERCISE C. Copy the following sentences, putting in the correct end punctuation. Then underline the simple subject once and the verb twice. (Be able to tell what kind of sentence each one is.)

EXAMPLE 1. Look at the skywriting
1. (*you*) *Look at the skywriting.*

1. My favorite ride at the fair goes very fast
2. How many times does the moon go around the earth in a month
3. Study your spelling each night
4. Despite its huge body, the rhinoceros has a very small brain
5. Can you give a definition for *pandemonium*
6. How exciting the trapeze act was
7. Take your dictionary with you
8. Cats and dogs do not learn by imitation but by participation
9. What animals hibernate in the winter
10. What strange shapes the ice takes

CHAPTER 2

The Parts of Speech

Noun, Pronoun, Adjective

There are many thousands of different words in the English language. But there are only eight different *kinds* of words. These eight kinds, which are called "parts of speech," are the *noun*, *pronoun*, *adjective*, *verb*, *adverb*, *preposition*, *conjunction*, and *interjection*. In this chapter you will study three of these eight parts of speech: the *noun*, the *pronoun*, and the *adjective*.

THE NOUN

One of the first things that happened to you after you were born was that you were given a name. And the first words that you learned to speak were names of things. If you were to travel to a foreign country, where a language other than English is spoken, you would again find yourself inquiring, "What's that called?" Knowing the names of things is basic to communication. A word which names is called a *noun*.

2a. A *noun* is a word used to name a person, place, thing, or idea.

Persons	Robert Frost, Dr. Lacy, child, architect, cowboy
Places	Wyoming, Mexico, Europe, home, city
Things	money, shell, wind, dolphin, desk
Ideas	courage, love, freedom, sorrow, luck

Notice that some kinds of nouns name things which you can see, while others do not. The nouns which name unseen things, like ideas, are more difficult to identify.

• EXERCISE 1. Number your paper 1–13. Pick out the fifty nouns from the following sentences. (*Who*, *which*, *him*, and *all* are not nouns.)

1. Villain and hero met in the dusty street.
2. Forty students asked the librarian for the same book.
3. Many people in the world are still trying to gain independence.
4. Women were given the right to vote over fifty years ago.
5. The fire destroyed 460 homes in California.
6. Both children and adults enjoy the story of the proud emperor who walked down the streets of a village in invisible clothes.
7. The crowd gathered in the arena to see gymnasts from all over the world compete for top honors.
8. In one museum the paintings and drawings of a monkey were exhibited.
9. The newspaper at our school has won many awards.

10. Crowds of reporters soon arrived at the scene of the crash.
11. The koala, an animal found chiefly in Australia, feeds only on the leaves of the eucalyptus tree.
12. The assistant to the magician showed no fear during the performance.
13. All of the crew had confidence in the captain.

● EXERCISE 2. Number your paper 1–10. Pick out the forty nouns from the following famous lines of poetry. List each noun in order after the proper number. (The words *I*, *me*, *you*, *your*, *him*, *it*, and *whom* are not nouns.)

EXAMPLE 1. Sir Patrick Spens is the best sailor
That sails upon the sea.—UNKNOWN
1. *Sir Patrick Spens*, *sailor*, *sea*

1. Friends, Romans, countrymen, lend me your ears;
I come to bury Caesar, not to praise him.
—WILLIAM SHAKESPEARE
2. The best laid schemes o' mice an' men
Gang aft a-gley. . . . [often go wrong]
—ROBERT BURNS
3. My heart leaps up when I behold
A rainbow in the sky. . . .
—WILLIAM WORDSWORTH
4. A thing of beauty is a joy forever. . . .—JOHN KEATS
5. It was many and many a year ago,
In a kingdom by the sea,
That a maiden there lived whom you may know
By the name of Annabel Lee. . . .
—EDGAR ALLAN POE
6. Hitch your wagon to a star.
—RALPH WALDO EMERSON

7. And the night shall be filled with music,
   And the cares, that infest the day,
Shall fold their tents, like the Arabs,
   And as silently steal away.

—HENRY WADSWORTH LONGFELLOW

8. The paths of glory lead but to the grave.

—THOMAS GRAY

9. My object in life is to unite
My avocation and my vocation. . . .—ROBERT FROST

10. The quality of mercy is not strain'd,
It droppeth as the gentle rain from heaven
Upon the place beneath.—WILLIAM SHAKESPEARE

Compound Nouns

Sometimes a single noun is made up of two or more words. These words may be written as a single word (safeguard), as two words (safe deposit), or with a hyphen (safe-conduct). Nouns that are names of particular people or things also often consist of more than one word: Franklin Delano Roosevelt (a three-word noun), Buckingham Palace (a two-word noun), *The Adventures of Huckleberry Finn* (the name of a book; a five-word noun). The only way to be sure how a word is written is to look it up in your dictionary.

Proper Nouns and Common Nouns

There are two main classes of nouns: common nouns and proper nouns. While the common noun names a class of person, place, or thing, the proper noun names a particular person, place, or thing. The proper noun begins with a capital letter; if it consists of more than one word, each important word is capitalized (*Declaration of Independence*).

COMMON NOUNS	PROPER NOUNS
poem	"To a Skylark"
country	Austria
boy	Dale Clark
ship	*Queen Mary*
newspaper	*New York Times*
ocean	Pacific Ocean
street	Fifty-second Street
date	November 6, 1910

● EXERCISE 3. Number your paper 1–13. After each number, list the nouns you find in the corresponding sentence. (Note: *They*, *it*, *Celtic*, *English*, *some*, and *Germanic* are not nouns.) Add capital letters for all proper nouns which are not capitalized.

EXAMPLE 1. The early inhabitants of england were the celts.
1. *inhabitants*, *England*, *Celts*

1. The celts were divided into many tribes.
2. They lived in forts or small villages.
3. Some villages were built on stilts in marshes.
4. The celts used bars of iron for money.
5. They made jewelry out of bronze or gold.
6. Their religious ceremonies involved the oak and the mistletoe.
7. The Celtic influence on the English language is seen in the names of rivers such as the thames.
8. Celtic descendants now live in wales.
9. Over two thousand years ago the romans, under julius caesar, invaded england.
10. The celts absorbed some of the culture and the language of rome.
11. In the fifth century people from several Germanic tribes—the angles, saxons, and jutes—settled in england.

12. The angles were the predominate group; thus the country became known as angle-land or england.
13. The language of the Germanic invaders, which you can see in the long poem *beowulf*, was the ancestor of the modern English language.

● REVIEW EXERCISE A. Make two columns on your paper. Label one column *Proper Nouns* and the other column *Common Nouns*. Under the appropriate heading, list the nouns from the following paragraph. Be sure to capitalize all proper nouns.

Each day several thousand people visit the lincoln memorial in washington. The monument was designed by henry bacon and was dedicated on memorial day. Located in west potomac park, the lincoln memorial consists of a large marble hall which encloses a lifelike statue of abraham lincoln. The figure, which was made from twenty-eight blocks of white marble, by daniel chester french, a distinguished sculptor, is sitting in a large armchair as if in deep meditation. On the north wall is found a famous passage from an inaugural address by Lincoln, and on the south wall is inscribed the gettysburg address.

THE PRONOUN

Once you can recognize nouns, you can learn to identify pronouns. A *pronoun* is a word that stands for a noun. Without pronouns we would be forced to repeat the same nouns again and again.

> When Kelly saw the signal, Kelly pointed the signal out to Terry.
>
> When Kelly saw the signal, **he** pointed **it** out to Terry.

2b. A *pronoun* is a word used in place of one or more nouns.

Name the nouns which the pronouns in the following sentences stand for.

1. Gail read the book and returned **it** to the library.
2. The models bought **themselves** new dresses.
3. "Students," the teacher said, "**you** should keep vocabulary notebooks."
4. Bob and Gene went fishing. **Both** caught six bass.

The noun that a pronoun stands for is called the *antecedent*. This noun is not always stated.

antecedent *pron.* *pron.*
Frederick told **his** mother **he** would be late.

antecedent *pron.*
Josephine, did **you** do the lesson?

You can't sleep now. [no antecedent stated]

There are several kinds of pronouns. The ones you will be studying in this chapter are mainly *personal* pronouns. These are the personal pronouns:[1]

I, me, mine, my, myself
you, your, yours, yourself, yourselves
he, him, his, himself
she, her, hers, herself
it, its, itself
we, us, our, ours, ourselves
they, them, their, theirs, themselves

[1] In this book pronouns that come directly before nouns and show possession (*my*, *his*, *her*, *its*, *your*, *their*) are called *possessive pronouns*. Some teachers prefer to call them *possessive adjectives*. Follow your teacher's directions in labeling these words.

Make sure that you learn to spell *its* and *their.* Never make the serious error of writing *hisself* or *theirselves;* neither of these is acceptable.

Other common pronouns are

who, whom, whoever, whomever
everybody, everyone, someone, somebody
no one, nobody, none, others

The following words are pronouns when they are used in the place of nouns:

what, which, whatever, whichever, whose
this, that, these, those
one, each, some, any
many, more, much, most
both, several, few, all
other, another
either, neither

● EXERCISE 4. Number your paper 1–10. After each number, list the pronouns in the corresponding sentence. After each pronoun, write the noun or nouns that the pronoun refers to.

EXAMPLE 1. The boys decided they would hike up the Appalachian Trail.
1. *they—boys*

1. Ted fired at the distant target until he finally hit it.
2. "I know the answer but can't think of it," explained Jody.
3. Linda, have you prepared the refreshments for the party?
4. After many years of inaction, the time has come for us, the citizens of Grove Community, to build a park.
5. "Listen to me," pleaded Cathy.

6. When the children found the abandoned puppies, they carried them home.
7. The parade was a colorful sight as it moved down the narrow street.
8. The natives decorated themselves with bright colors.
9. Gail looked for Dana at the movie, and after walking up and down the aisle for five minutes, she finally spotted her.
10. After wandering around aimlessly for an hour, the man found himself in a part of the city he did not know.

● EXERCISE 5. Copy the following paragraphs, filling in the blanks with appropriate pronouns. If necessary, refer to the lists of pronouns on pages 35–36.

Let —— tell —— about the strange experience of —— of my friends, Bill Glenn. —— was guiding a group of scientists through Australia. After traveling for hours through wilderness, —— in the group wanted to make camp, but —— insisted that —— continue on. Finally, —— decided to travel for just one more hour.

Soon —— were rewarded for the trip. At the edge of the forest, one human form appeared and then ——. Before long, several strange-looking people had collected in a clearing.

The scientists watched —— from a distance. —— dared not speak a word. The women in the group of strange people began preparations for a meal. —— dug up roots with stones. —— prepared meat with crude implements. —— was trying to make a fire by twirling a stick in charcoal.

The scientists were watching the aborigines, —— are still living as men did during the Stone Age. Although —— of the Australian tribes have become civilized, —— continue to follow primitive ways. —— of the scientists marveled that —— could be living so primitive an existence in the twentieth century.

● EXERCISE 6. There are twenty pronouns in the following paragraphs. Number your paper 1–12. List the pronouns after the proper number. Circle the possessive pronouns.

1. Yesterday Linda and Dotty toured a famous university. 2. Both took notes on the things they saw, and at the end of the tour they discussed the differences between college and junior high school. 3. Each was amazed at the size of the college campus. 4. "College students are given ten minutes to get to their classes," explained Dotty. 5. "Some of them have to ride buses to get from one class to another."

6. "And did you notice," Linda asked, "the students studying in the library? 7. They go to class about three hours a day. 8. Most of their time is spent in private study. 9. Few can afford to waste time."

10. "Dad said we had better prepare ourselves now for hard work if we are going to college," added Dotty. 11. "Someone told him a college student spends at least two hours preparing for an individual class. 12. But I won't mind the hard work because everyone says college life is a lot of fun."

● REVIEW EXERCISE B. Number your paper 1–10. Copy the pronouns from each sentence after the corresponding number. Circle all possessive pronouns.

EXAMPLE 1. What do you know about his life?
1. *What, you, his*

1. All of us hoped to win the skating contest.
2. Almost everyone tends to overestimate the intelligence of the horse.

3. Who would not like to take a gondola ride through one of the canals in Venice?
4. The bitter Scrooge would not share his wealth with anyone.
5. We planned a street dance to celebrate the victory of our team.
6. When the mountain called the proud little squirrel a weakling, the squirrel replied, "If I cannot carry forests on my back, neither can you crack a nut."
7. When someone visits Rome, he sees many of the wonders of ancient times.
8. "These are people who need help," explained our guide.
9. Each of the boys found himself a fishing pole and worms.
10. Several of them drew pictures of the people they had seen on the beach.

THE ADJECTIVE

Allen goes fishing, and after an exciting struggle he reels in a trout over twenty inches long and weighing almost five pounds. He will not be content with describing his catch merely as a trout. Rather, he will call it a *large* trout or even a *huge* trout.

Jan and Sonia are discussing what they are going to wear to a New Year's Eve party. Jan will not be satisfied with saying merely that she is going to wear a dress. Rather, she will say that she is going to wear a *long blue taffeta* dress.

Usually we are not satisfied with just naming things —*trout, dress*. We like to make a noun more definite by describing it in some way. The words which we use to make a noun more definite are called *adjectives*.

When a noun is described by an adjective, it is said to be *modified.* Since a pronoun may be used in place of a noun, it too may be described, or modified, by an adjective.

2c. An *adjective* is a word used to modify a noun or pronoun.

An adjective often answers one of these questions: *What kind? Which one? How much or how many?*

WHAT KIND?	WHICH ONE?	HOW MUCH? OR HOW MANY?
a *tall* man	the *other* one	*five* times
a *steep* mountain	*this* year	*many* mistakes
a *long* hike	the *last* answer	*several* others
an *eager* salesman	*those* people	*no* supplies
a *tired* dog	*that* dress	*few* marbles

The most frequently used adjectives are *a, an, the.* These little words are called *articles.*

● EXERCISE 7. Copy the following sentences, filling in the blanks with adjectives which answer the questions given.

EXAMPLE 1. We bought food for *how many?* guests, but *how many?* people attended our *which one?* party.

1. *We bought food for fifty guests, but ninety people attended our last party.*

1. Although he corrected *how many?* mistakes, he made *how many?* others.
2. *Which one?* night *how many?* boys investigated a *what kind?* house.

3. A *what kind?* donkey carried a *what kind?* load for *how many?* days.
4. We had only a *how much?* amount of gasoline by the time we reached the *which one?* town.
5. During the *what kind?* winter we entertained ourselves by reading *how many?* books.

In Exercise 7 all adjectives preceded the nouns which they modified. Sometimes, however, the adjective follows the word it modifies. Note the position of the adjectives in the following sentences. An arrow is drawn from the adjective to the word it modifies.

> **Each one** of the students brought his **used books** for the auction.
>
> The **books,** although **old** and **worn,** were quickly bought.

● EXERCISE 8. Copy the following sentences, underlining the adjectives. Then draw an arrow from each adjective to the noun which it modifies. Do not underline the articles *a, an,* and *the.*

EXAMPLE 1. It was a rainy day when the tired troops returned from the battle.

1. *It was a rainy day when the tired troops returned from the battle.*

1. A violent storm uprooted a large tree in the front yard.
2. The hot sun beat down on the thirsty animals.
3. The kangaroo has short forelegs and a large, thick tail.
4. A number of famous writers are buried in Westminster Abbey.

5. The traveler, tired and weak, struggled with a heavy bag.
6. The various colors of the spotlight played on the graceful dancer as she performed.
7. The official guides at the United Nations can speak a number of different languages.
8. There will be a gala dance on the last night of the voyage.
9. The charming elderly couple celebrated the fiftieth anniversary of their wedding by performing an elegant waltz at the party.
10. The host, a jovial person, entertained us with exciting stories about his experiences in Iran.

● EXERCISE 9. There are twenty-five adjectives in the following paragraph. Make a list of them as they appear. Do not list articles.

1. The ancient Greeks and Romans worshiped twelve major gods. 2. The one with the most power was Zeus, or Jupiter, who lived on a high mountain, Mount Olympus. 3. From the cloudy peak he surveyed the various affairs of the world. 4. He rode in a great chariot which was drawn by four white horses. 5. Whenever he liked, he called for a great assembly of the gods. 6. At the huge assembly one would find Poseidon, or Neptune, the god of the sea; Hades, or Pluto, the god of the shadowy land of the dead; Hera, or Juno, the beautiful but quarrelsome wife of Zeus; Apollo, the handsome god of the sun; Diana, the swift goddess of the hunt, who in time became known as the goddess of the moon; Hermes, or Mercury, the swift messenger of the gods; Hestia, or Vesta, the goddess of the hearth, who became a special protector of the home; Ares, or Mars, the dreadful god of war; Athena, or Minerva, the favorite daughter of Zeus,

who was noted for great wisdom; Hephaestus, or Vulcan, the ugly god, who was the useful god of fire and of the forge; and Aphrodite, or Venus, the lovely goddess of beauty.

● EXERCISE 10. Except for *a*, *an*, and *the*, the following sentences contain no adjectives. Rewrite them and, wherever possible, add interesting adjectives to modify the nouns and pronouns.

EXAMPLE 1. The dog performed tricks.
1. *The small, short-haired dog performed many unusual tricks.*

1. Todd bought a balloon for his sister.
2. The door opened, and a man was standing there.
3. We rode for miles before we spotted the park.
4. Herb collects pencils and coins.
5. We watched the fireworks from our window.
6. The cold forced people indoors.
7. The lineman picked off the pass and ran yards for a touchdown.
8. The skater glided around the rink.
9. After running for hours, Martin collapsed on the road.
10. The sisters have become stars.

Proper Adjectives

When you speak of the labors of Hercules, you use a proper noun, but when you say *Herculean* labor, you use a proper adjective. A proper adjective is formed from a proper noun, and like a proper noun, it begins with a capital letter.

PROPER NOUN	PROPER ADJECTIVE
Mexico	**Mexican** hat dance
Africa	**African** nations
Shakespeare	**Shakespearean** tragedy

● EXERCISE 11. Number your paper 1–10. If a sentence contains a proper noun, copy the noun after the corresponding number. If the sentence contains a proper adjective, copy both the adjective and the noun it modifies. Some sentences contain both proper nouns and proper adjectives.

EXAMPLE 1. Many French words were added to the English language after the invasion of the Normans in 1066.
1. *French words, English language, Normans*

1. Many soldiers stationed in Japan sent back beautiful Japanese dinnerware to their wives.
2. Many Biblical scholars regard the scrolls found in the caves near Qumran as one of the most important discoveries of the twentieth century.
3. A replica of the Parthenon located in Nashville, a city in Tennessee, faithfully copies the principles of Greek architecture.
4. The remains of several Roman roads can be seen in England today.
5. American tourists in Holland enjoy going to a shoe factory where they can see the traditional wooden shoes being made.
6. The Shakespearean actors were dressed in Elizabethan costumes.
7. The President was uncertain about the Congressional reaction to his proposal.
8. In swimming class this week we are learning to do the Australian crawl.
9. Two Italian dishes which Americans enjoy are pizza and spaghetti.
10. Many writers have based stories and poems on the Arthurian legend.

Changing Parts of Speech

Sometimes nouns are used as adjectives: *Marian's* book, *airplane* ride, *school* mascot. *Marian*, *airplane*, and *school* are nouns, but they act like adjectives when they are put in front of nouns. In parts-of-speech exercises, label as adjectives all nouns used in this way.

Words like *each*, *some*, and *whose* are sometimes pronouns and sometimes adjectives, depending on their use in a sentence. When they are used in place of nouns, they are pronouns; when they modify nouns, they are adjectives. If they are adjectives, they always precede a noun.

PRONOUN **Each** did his own work.
ADJECTIVE **Each** person did his own work.

PRONOUN **Some** have gone to their dressing rooms.
ADJECTIVE **Some** actors have gone to their dressing rooms.

PRONOUN **Whose** are these?
ADJECTIVE **Whose** gloves are these?

● EXERCISE 12. In the following sentences, decide whether the word in italics is used as an adjective or a pronoun. Number your paper 1–10. Beside the number, write *adj.* when the word is an adjective and *pron.* when the word is a pronoun.

EXAMPLE 1. Do *whatever* is best.
1. *pron.*

1. *Both* missed the target.
2. We stuffed a Christmas stocking with candy and toys for *each* one of the children.
3. *Many* high schools emphasize track and field.
4. *One* should study about a state or country before visiting it.

5. *Some* kinds of seaweed are used as ingredients in ice cream.
6. After several days in Paris, *each* of the tourists drove out to Fontainebleau, a favorite residence of Napoleon's.
7. The detective questioned *both* suspects for hours.
8. Sandra found *another* way to work the problem.
9. Last summer *many* of us learned to play tennis.
10. The unicorn is a mythical animal which has only *one* horn.

● REVIEW EXERCISE C. There are twenty adjectives in the following sentences. Write the adjectives in each sentence after the corresponding number on your paper. Do not list articles. Be careful not to confuse adjectives with pronouns.

1. There is an interesting Indian legend which tells how man gained possession of fire. 2. According to this story, fire originally belonged to the bears. 3. Then one day the bears went into a deep forest and left the fire on the ground. 4. Soon there were few flames. 5. And the pitiful voice of the fire cried out, "Feed me, or I will die!" 6. As it happened, there were several people who heard the anxious cry of the fire. 7. They picked up one stick from the north and another stick from the south. 8. They took two others from the east and the west. 9. Then they placed these four sticks on the dying fire. 10. Immediately large flames shot up.

11. When the bears returned, they did not recognize their old friend, the fire. 12. They went away and left it to die. 13. But when some of the people who had cared for the fire saw its great loneliness, they picked it up and took it with them. 14. Since that day fire has belonged to man, who uses it in many ways.

DIAGRAMING NOUNS AND ADJECTIVES

Diagraming, as you recall from Chapter 1, is a way of showing that you understand the relationship between words and groups of words. When you first studied the adjective, you drew an arrow from the adjective to the noun that it modified. This relationship can also be expressed in a diagram.

PATTERN

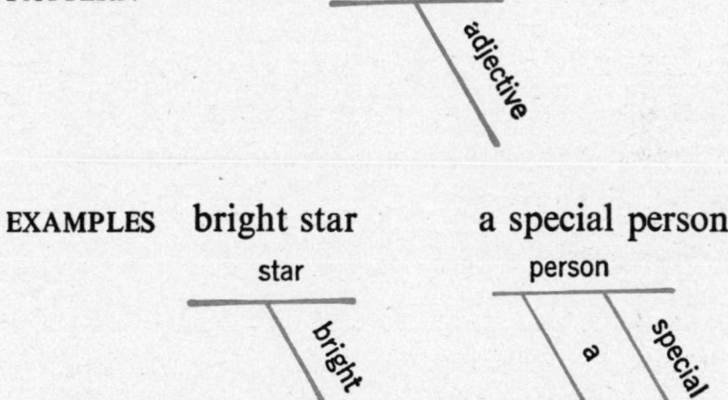

EXAMPLES bright star a special person

Two or more adjectives joined by a connecting word are diagramed this way.

PATTERN

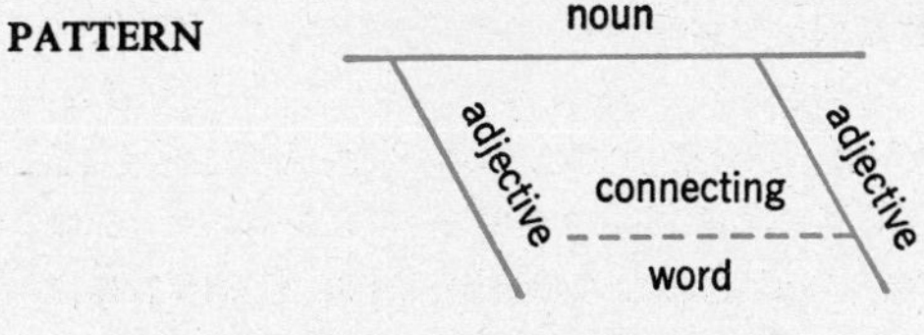

EXAMPLE her red and white boots

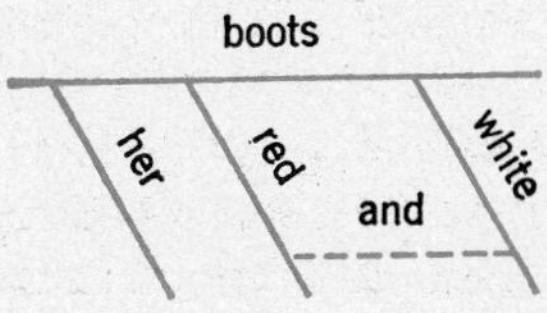

Notice that possessive pronouns are diagramed like adjectives.

● EXERCISE 13. Diagram the following items. Use a ruler and allow plenty of space between diagrams.

1. mighty warrior
2. big blue ox
3. a narrow path
4. long, exciting movie
5. his one purpose
6. the last one
7. blue and silver streamers
8. many others
9. my final offer
10. the slow but persistent turtle

● EXERCISE 14. Diagram the following sentences.

EXAMPLE 1. A funny clown performed.

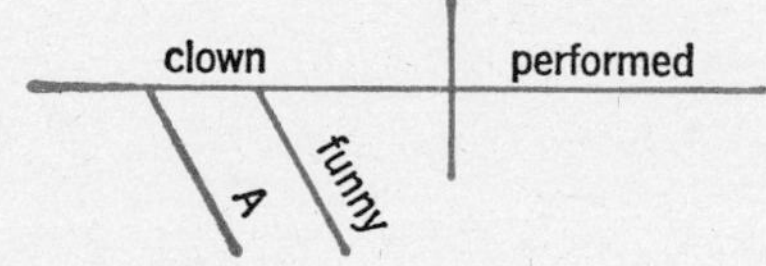

1. Our Swedish visitor arrived.
2. Several answers were given.
3. The angry dog growled.
4. Each one agreed.
5. Our problem has been solved.
6. The small, shy boy won.
7. The poor but generous man helped.
8. A house and a large barn have burned.
9. The noisy crowd jeered and shouted.
10. My favorite candidate will speak.

● REVIEW EXERCISE D. Copy the following paragraph on your paper, leaving an extra line of space between lines of writing. Over each noun, write *n.;* over each pronoun, write *pron.;* and over each adjective, write *adj.* Disregard the articles *a*, *an*, and *the*.

Tantalus tried to make the gods commit a serious sin. He invited them to a great banquet. At this feast he served a special dish made of human flesh. Actually, it was the flesh of his own son, Pelops. The gods recognized the horrible deed of Tantalus. They sent him to the underworld to be punished forever. He was placed in a pool of cool water, but whenever he leaned over to drink, the water drained out of the sandy bottom. And whenever he tried to pluck the delicious fruit above his head, a breeze blew the branch out of reach. From the punishment of Tantalus we have derived our word *tantalize*.

● REVIEW EXERCISE E. Diagram the following sentences.

1. Every minute counts.
2. Many famous actors attended.
3. Five days and five nights passed.
4. The powerful motor shook and roared.
5. The golden clock struck.
6. A few people have left.
7. Several dark clouds can be seen.
8. The ventriloquist and his dummy talked and sang.
9. My favorite comedian is performing.
10. The black and white horses have been sold.

CHAPTER 3

The Parts of Speech

Verb, Adverb, Preposition, Conjunction, Interjection

In Chapter 2 you studied two of the workhorses of the sentence—the *noun* and the *pronoun*—and the part of speech which makes the noun or pronoun more definite—the *adjective*. In this chapter you will learn about the other workhorse of the sentence—the *verb*—and the remaining four parts of speech—*adverb*, *preposition*, *conjunction*, and *interjection*.

THE VERB

You know that a verb is one of the parts of a sentence base. It helps to make a statement about its subject. Some verbs do this by expressing the action of the subject: boy *ran;* monkey *chatters;* sun *sets*. Other verbs help to make a statement without expressing action: I *am* an eighth-grader; this *is* good; he *seems* happy.

3a. **A *verb* is a word that expresses action or otherwise helps to make a statement.**

Action Verbs

The action expressed by a verb may be physical action or mental action.

PHYSICAL ACTION	jump, shout, search, carry, run
MENTAL ACTION	worry, think, believe, imagine

The action verbs in the following sentences are in heavy type.

> The soldiers **rested** in the shade.
>
> Our treasurer **presents** the budget for the year.
>
> A distinguished architect **planned** our school building.
>
> We **listened** to the *New World Symphony* by Dvořák.
>
> Birds **follow** certain migratory routes.

● EXERCISE 1. Number your paper 1–11. Copy after the proper number the verb or verbs in each sentence. They are all action verbs.

1. Cliff finished the eighth grade in June. 2. During the summer months he spent his time with his younger brother Ted. 3. They played together, but they also worked together. 4. Since Ted found mathematics difficult, Cliff helped his brother with some problems. 5. The more Ted thought about addition and multiplication, the less he decided that he knew. 6. But Cliff considered both addition and multiplication easy. 7. He explained to Ted that everyone understands these two kinds of mathematics. 8. Then Ted asked a simple question: "You say that one plus one makes two, but that one times one makes one. 9. Since you

know all about mathematics, show me the reason for the difference." 10. Cliff looked at his brother for several minutes. 11. Finally, he just grinned.

Linking Verbs

Many important verbs do not express action. They do help to make a statement, but they do this by acting as a link between the subject, which normally comes before the verb, and a word in the predicate, which usually follows the verb. They link their subjects with nouns or adjectives in the predicate.

> Her name **is** Carla. [name = Carla]
>
> Marie Curie **became** a famous scientist. [Marie Curie = scientist]
>
> Wild animals **remain** free on the great animal reserves in Africa. [free animals]
>
> The student from Germany **seemed** lonely and unhappy. [lonely and unhappy student]
>
> The watermelon **looks** ripe. [ripe watermelon]

The verb most commonly used as a linking verb is the verb *be*. You should memorize its various forms.

FORMS OF THE VERB BE

am, is, are, was, were, be, being, been

Any verb ending in *be* or *been* is a form of *be: shall be, will be, can be, might be, has been, have been, had been, would have been, might have been*, etc.

In addition to *be*, there are several other verbs which are often used as linking verbs:

seem, appear, look
become, grow
taste, feel, smell, sound
remain, stay

● EXERCISE 2. Copy the following sentences, inserting a linking verb in each blank. Use a different verb for each blank. Be prepared to tell what words the verb links.

EXAMPLE 1. The pilot —— calm during the danger.
1. *The pilot remained calm during the danger.* [*Remained* links *pilot* and *calm.*]

1. An unabridged dictionary —— heavy.
2. *Dracula* —— a weird novel.
3. The pine cones —— festive after they were painted silver and gold.
4. The fudge —— a little too sweet.
5. In many fairy stories a horrible beast —— a handsome prince.
6. After a rain the streets —— fresh and clean once again.
7. Did he —— a prisoner long?
8. The skier —— more daring with each jump he made.
9. We —— quiet during the concert.
10. These roses —— sweet.

Most of the verbs that you studied as linking verbs may also be used as action verbs. Whether a verb is used to express action or to link words depends on its meaning in a given sentence.

LINKING The tiger **looked** tame.
ACTION The tiger **looked** for something to eat.
LINKING The soup **tasted** good.
ACTION **I tasted** the soup.
LINKING He **grew** tired of playing.
ACTION He **grew** into a fine, young man.

● EXERCISE 3. In the sentences below the same verb is used as a linking verb and as an action verb. When the verb is used as an action verb, copy it. When it is used as a linking verb, copy it and the words it links.

EXAMPLE 1. Mr. Hughes appeared quite angry.
1. *appeared, Mr. Hughes—angry*
2. Mr. Hughes appeared suddenly in the door.
2. *appeared*

1. At the king's order, his servant tasted the food.
2. The food tasted safe.
3. The taster looked happy after the experiment.
4. Therefore the king looked upon him with favor.
5. On another occasion the food looked good.
6. The king again looked at his official taster.
7. The poor man felt numb with fear.
8. He felt a sudden chill throughout his body.
9. A dinner bell sounded in the banquet hall.
10. Because the taster knew this food had been poisoned, the bell sounded ominous to him.

● EXERCISE 4. Write two sentences for each of the following verbs. In the first sentence use the verb as a linking verb; in the second, use it as an action verb.

1. smells
2. appeared
3. taste
4. feel
5. looks

● EXERCISE 5. Number your paper 1–16. After the proper number, make a list of the verbs that appear on that line. If the verb is a linking verb, list also the words which the verb links.

1 "Big Bad John" is a modern ballad which every-
2 one likes. According to the song, John wanders
3 into a mining town. No one there knows anything

about his past, although many rumors spread among the people. They think that John was once a bad man; they give him the name "Big Bad John." Still, he seems a hard worker.

Then one day he becomes a hero to the townspeople. The mine caves in, and all hope for the safety of the miners appears futile. But John seems confident. He smells the smoke and the fumes, then braces the broken supports of the mine. The other miners scramble to freedom while John dies below. The miners never forget his sacrifice. They place a marker over the mine shaft: "At the bottom of this mine lies a big, big man."

Helping Verbs

So far in this chapter you have been studying one-word verbs, sometimes called *main verbs.* Without these verbs there could be no sentences. Frequently, though, the main verb is accompanied by other verbs called *helping verbs.* The main verb and the helping verbs make up a *verb phrase.* Each of the main verbs below is made into a verb phrase through the use of helping verbs. Notice that the main verb may change its form when a helping verb is added.

MAIN VERB **crawl**
VERB PHRASE **will crawl**

MAIN VERB **listen**
VERB PHRASE **have been listening**

MAIN VERB **find**
VERB PHRASE **would have been found**

You see that a verb phrase consists of a main verb preceded by one or more helping verbs. Here is a list of the most commonly used helping verbs.

be (am, is, are, etc.)	shall	should	must
has	will	would	do
have	can	could	did
had	may	might	does

The verb *be* in its various forms is the most frequently used helping verb. *Be* used as a helping verb is very easy to distinguish from *be* used as a linking verb. When *be* is used as a helping verb, there is always a main verb used with it; but when *be* is used as a linking verb, it is itself the main verb.

HELPING VERB **are found**
LINKING VERB **are**
HELPING VERB **have been tasted**
LINKING VERB **have been**

The following sentences contain verb phrases. The helping verbs and the main verbs are in heavy type; the main verbs are also underlined.

> Shakespeare **has been <u>quoted</u>** more than any other writer.
> The water **should be <u>heated</u>** to a high temperature.
> The sun **will <u>rise</u>** at six o'clock tomorrow.
> Our squad **is <u>finishing</u>** its pregame practice.

● EXERCISE 6. Copy the verb phrases as they appear in the exercise.

People have been dancing the polka for more than a hundred years. The dance as it is known today has been attributed to a young serving girl from Czechoslovakia whose identity was lost long ago. Because of its grace and beauty, the polka's popularity was established quickly. Soon after it was danced in Prague, people everywhere were doing the polka. The music of the polka can be enjoyed by both the dancers and the listeners. When polka music is being played, no one can remain still.

Sometimes the verb phrase is interrupted by other parts of speech, as in the examples below.

> Because of the dense fog, we **could** not **see** the road.
>
> Parachuting **has** quickly **become** an important sport.
>
> Men **may** someday **communicate** with dolphins.
>
> How much **do** you **know** about the planets?
>
> **Have** you ever **seen** an eclipse of the sun?

● EXERCISE 7. There are twenty verb phrases in the following paragraph. Number your paper 1–20. After the proper number, list the verb phrases that appear on that line. Some of the verb phrases are interrupted by other parts of speech. If a verb phrase begins on one line and ends on another, list it for the line on which it begins.

1 The boomerang has long interested man. It was
2 developed by the aborigines of Australia and may
3 be used for amusement, hunting, or war. A dif-
4 ferent kind of boomerang is used for each pur-
5 pose. We in America have usually misunderstood
6 the boomerang. The kind of boomerang which
7 will return to its owner after it has been thrown
8 is used almost entirely for amusement. This kind
9 of boomerang can hurt an inexperienced thrower.
10 But the aborigines of Australia do not use this
11 type of boomerang for hunting. They have de-

veloped one which will move near the ground for many feet and then suddenly will fly upward at a great speed. With this kind of weapon the natives can surprise the game that they are hunting. The boomerang which is used in war can be thrown only by a strong man. This weapon will easily break the arm of a man who is standing five hundred feet from the thrower. It may even inflict a fatal wound.

● REVIEW EXERCISE A. Number your paper 1–18. After the proper number, list the verbs and the verb phrases that appear on that line. If a verb phrase begins on one line and ends on another, list it for the line on which it begins. After each action verb or verb phrase, write *a.v.;* after each linking verb or verb phrase, write *l.v.*

The term *Viking* was used for all men of the North, whether they were Norwegians, Swedes, or Danes. The Vikings were a fierce people who roamed the seas for about three hundred years. For several centuries people considered them the scourge of Europe because they invaded and pillaged the countries to the south. They worshiped such fierce gods as Thor and Odin, and they believed that they should die in battle. When a Viking died, he went to Valhalla, where he could eternally enjoy battles and banquets. The Vikings thought Valhalla was a very happy place. Each day the warriors would go out to the battlefield and would receive wounds time and time again. But at the end of each day they would all meet back at the banquet hall, where their wounds would promptly heal and they could boast about their great bravery in battle.

● REVIEW EXERCISE B. Number your paper 1–10 and copy the sentences below, writing on every other line of your paper. Some of the words are italicized; underline them. Over each word that you underline, write an abbreviation to show which part of speech it is: *n.* for noun, *pron.* for pronoun, *adj.* for adjective, *a.v.* for action verb, and *l.v.* for linking verb. Treat proper names and verb phrases as one word.

EXAMPLE 1. *Wild Bill Hickok became* a *legend* in his *own* time.

n. *l.v.* *n.*
1. *Wild Bill Hickok became a legend in his*
adj.
own time.

1. Wild Bill's *real name was* James Butler Hickok.
2. During the *War Between the States* he *served* as a *scout* and a *spy* for the Union *army*.
3. He *was captured* on *several occasions*, but *he* always *escaped* from his *captors*.
4. After the *war* he *acted* as a scout for such *famous generals* as Custer.
5. Then he *became* the *marshal* of *Hays City*, *one* of the *roughest* towns on the *frontier*.
6. Once *three* men *attacked* Bill at *one* time, but he *killed them* all.
7. In 1871 the now-famous *gunman* became the marshal of Abilene, another *wild* town in the Old West.
8. In 1872 and 1873 he *toured* the East with *Buffalo Bill*.
9. Finally in 1876 Wild Bill *was murdered* by a *man* named Jack McCall.
10. Wild Bill *may have seemed* a *violent* man, but *he* was actually a very *quiet* person who fought only when *someone* forced him to.

THE ADVERB

3b. An *adverb* is a word used to modify a verb, an adjective, or another adverb.

An adverb usually answers one of these questions: *Where? When? How? To what extent* (*how much or how long*)*?* These are some of the questions a newspaper reporter tries to answer when he covers a story.

WHERE?	WHEN?
The fire started **here.**	The police inspector arrived **promptly.**
The couple was married **nearby.**	**Then** the suspects were questioned.
The thief fell **down.**	The detective takes notes **daily.**

HOW?	TO WHAT EXTENT (HOW MUCH OR HOW LONG)?
The accident occurred **suddenly.**	We should **never** become upset.
The prime minister spoke **carefully.**	The escaped convicts ran **far.**
The train stopped **abruptly.**	He has **scarcely** begun the lesson.

(1) An adverb modifies a verb more often than it modifies an adjective or an adverb.

Notice in the following examples how the adverb makes the meaning of the verb more definite.

> The man crawled **down.** [The adverb tells *where* the man crawled.]
>
> He crawled **slowly.** [The adverb tells *how* he crawled.]

> **Now** we are prepared. [The adverb tells *when* we are prepared.]
>
> The speaker droned on **endlessly.** [The adverb tells *to what extent* the speaker droned.]

Adverbs are sometimes used to ask questions.

> **Where** are you going?
> **How** did you do on the test?

● EXERCISE 8. Number your paper 1–9. Write an adverb for each blank. After each adverb, write what the adverb tells: *Where? When? How?* or *To what extent* (*how much*)*?* the action was done.

Use a different adverb for each blank and include all four kinds.

1. We waved —— and ran ——.
2. The train arrived ——.
3. A clue was found ——.
4. —— the so-called ghost appeared.
5. Our friends could —— wait.
6. —— will the doctor get ——?
7. —— the climbers —— climbed Lookout Mountain.
8. Frank's kite flew —— than the others and rode the wind more ——.
9. The dog moaned —— as the boy —— washed him.

● EXERCISE 9. The following sentences contain twenty adverbs, all modifying verbs. Number your paper 1–8. After the proper number, copy the adverbs in that sentence.

1. We have regularly had four daily flights to Hawaii, but lately we have been scheduling six.
2. Speak now or forever hold your peace.
3. Yesterday Miss Brown thoughtfully assigned two brief exercises for homework.

4. While victims struggled frantically in the water, rescue boats rushed quickly toward them.
5. If you get there before we do, build a fire in the fireplace immediately and then prepare supper.
6. Today, because of the special celebration at our school, the students will arrive early and leave late.
7. Hunters always approach these woods cautiously because they have often been cruelly surprised.
8. She did well on the first test but failed miserably on the second.

(2) An adverb sometimes modifies an adjective.

An adverb is sometimes needed to make the meaning of an adjective more definite. An *extremely* good dancer is quite different from a *fairly* good dancer.

> The skaters put on a **very** exciting show. [The adjective *exciting* modifies the noun *show;* then the adverb tells *how exciting* the show was.]
>
> An **unusually** fast starter, Keith easily won the high hurdles event. [The adjective *fast* modifies the noun *starter;* then the adverb tells *how fast* the starter was.]
>
> Our committee is **especially** busy. [The adjective *busy* modifies the noun *committee;* then the adverb tells *how busy* the committee is.]

● EXERCISE 10. Number your paper 1–10. Copy the adverbs that modify adjectives in each sentence. After each adverb, list the adjective it modifies.

EXAMPLE 1. Kangaroos are extremely fast animals.
1. *extremely, fast*

1. Because there are so many kangaroos in Australia, the kangaroo has become the national animal.
2. Kangaroos seem very graceful when they are leaping about.

3. But they look quite awkward when they are still.
4. Their back legs are extremely long.
5. Their front legs are too short to be of much use in moving about.
6. The baby kangaroo, called a "joey," is hardly longer than an inch at birth.
7. It looks thoroughly contented in its mother's pouch.
8. Some kangaroos are unusually small even after they have reached their full growth.
9. One kind is no larger than a rabbit.
10. The great red kangaroo, the largest variety, is surprisingly tall.

● EXERCISE 11. The adverb *very* is used far too often to modify adjectives. Write an adverb to modify each adjective below. Do not use *very*.

EXAMPLE 1. beautiful
1. *unbelievably beautiful*

1. light
2. narrow
3. happy
4. tidy
5. daring
6. awkward
7. true
8. dishonest
9. tired
10. sweet

(3) An adverb occasionally modifies another adverb.

Alex finished the problem **more** quickly than I did. [The adverb *quickly* modifies the verb *finished* and is, in turn, modified by the adverb *more*, which tells *how quickly* Alex finished the problem.]

Our guest left **quite** abruptly. [The adverb *abruptly* modifies the verb *left* and is, in turn, modified by *quite*, which tells *how abruptly* our guest left.]

● EXERCISE 12. Number your paper 1–10. From the following sentences list opposite the proper number only the adverbs which modify other adverbs. Then, after each adverb, write the adverb that it modifies.

EXAMPLE 1. The fingerprint is most certainly an aid in determining the identity of a person who has committed a crime.
1. *most, certainly*

1. Before 1900, fingerprinting was very rarely used by the police.
2. As a matter of fact, the use of fingerprinting was almost entirely confined to verifying personal identification.
3. A person used his fingerprints quite often to protect himself from forgers.
4. As a means of identification the fingerprint has been fairly consistently used for at least two thousand years.
5. The walls of caves show quite undeniably that primitive man was also interested in the use of fingerprints.
6. So fingerprinting has been used much longer than we ordinarily think.
7. Finally, around 1900, it was established that a fingerprint very clearly distinguishes one individual from all others.
8. The many studies of classifications of fingerprints were most enthusiastically welcomed by Scotland Yard, and, later, fingerprinting was adopted by our own FBI.
9. Today the classification of fingerprints is so well developed that an expert can locate a particular set of prints in minutes by finding the class to which the prints belong.

10. We realize that the expert works quite rapidly when we remember that the files contain millions of fingerprints.

● REVIEW EXERCISE C. Number your paper 1–10. Make a list of the adverbs in the order that they appear in the exercise. After each adverb, write the word or expression that the adverb modifies. Some sentences have more than one adverb.

EXAMPLE 1. The suspect fidgeted quite noticeably.
1. *quite, noticeably*
noticeably, fidgeted

1. After we had finished packing our gear, a terribly violent thunderstorm began in the Amazon Valley.
2. While the storm raged outside, we sat down in our tent to review our research findings on animal life.
3. We found that one very strange frog in the Amazon Valley has a most unusual method of escaping capture.
4. If a snake suddenly attacks him, the frog cleverly expands like a balloon and the snake is not able to swallow him.
5. Another kind of frog has an equally strange escape mechanism.
6. If attacked, it secretes a highly potent poison which completely paralyzes its enemies and allows it to escape.
7. In the Amazon Valley we often found grasshoppers that were surprisingly large.
8. Some were even bigger than our hands.
9. In contrast, some frogs were much smaller than the ends of our fingers.
10. We had been unusually well rewarded during our stay in the Amazon Valley.

DIAGRAMING VERBS AND ADVERBS

The verb, like the noun and pronoun, always appears on a horizontal line. The adverb is diagramed on a slanting line under the word it modifies.

1. An adverb modifying a verb:

EXAMPLES studies hard does not exercise daily

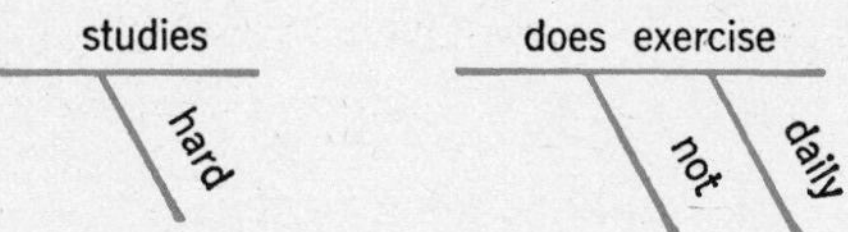

2. An adverb modifying an adjective:

EXAMPLES

extremely hard wind much better swimmer

3. An adverb modifying another adverb:

EXAMPLES tried rather hard flew almost too high

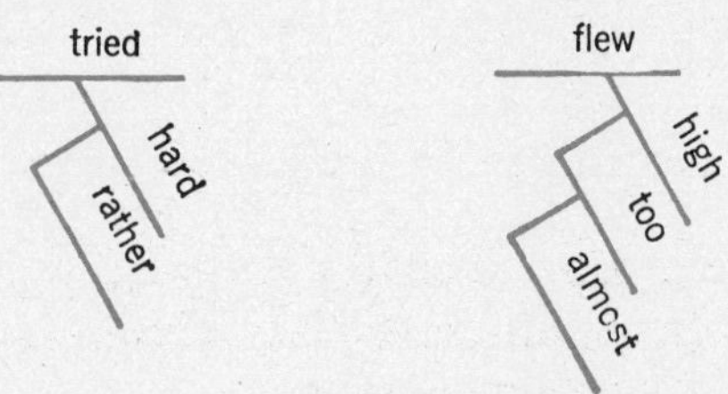

● EXERCISE 13. Diagram the following groups of words. Use a ruler and leave plenty of space between diagrams.

1. answered quickly
2. badly worn sail
3. listened quite intently
4. worked very late
5. dangerously sharp curve
6. never plans very carefully
7. walked proudly away
8. somewhat rickety bridge
9. may possibly come
10. drove rather slowly

● EXERCISE 14. Diagram the following sentences. Use a ruler and leave plenty of space between diagrams.

1. The plane landed smoothly.
2. The guide limped noticeably.
3. The extremely nervous woman collapsed.
4. Our turn finally came.
5. They tried very hard.
6. The shutters rattled quite noisily.
7. Her almost new automobile had been slightly damaged.
8. We are definitely leaving tomorrow.
9. The tired motorist drove much too far.
10. The unbelievably slow turtle got there first.

THE PREPOSITION

3c. A *preposition* is a word used to show the relationship of a noun or a pronoun to some other word in the sentence.

Notice how a change in the preposition changes the relationship between *package* and *tree* in each of the following sentences.

The package **under** the tree is mine.
The package **in** the tree is mine.
The package **near** the tree is mine.

Learn to recognize the following words, which are commonly used as prepositions.

COMMONLY USED PREPOSITIONS

aboard	behind	from	throughout
about	below	in	to
above	beneath	into	toward
across	beside	like	under
after	between	near	underneath
against	beyond	of	until
along	but (except)	off	unto
amid	by	on	up
among	down	over	upon
around	during	past	with
at	except	since	within
before	for	through	without

Occasionally you will find compound prepositions—prepositions of more than one word. A compound preposition may be considered as one word.

COMPOUND PREPOSITIONS

because of	according to
on account of	instead of
in spite of	out of

● EXERCISE 15. Number your paper 1–10. Make a list of the prepositions as they appear in the following sentences. Several of these prepositions will be compound prepositions.

1. In Roman mythology, Vulcan was the god of fire.
2. According to legend he once had a bad fall.
3. His father, Jupiter, kicked him out of heaven.
4. From Mount Olympus, the home of Jupiter, Vulcan fell to the earth.
5. He fell through space like a meteor, and his descent lasted for an entire day.

6. He fell to earth with such force that he broke one of his legs.
7. After his injury Vulcan was called the lame god.
8. He remained on earth and made a new life for himself.
9. Eventually he climbed to the top of Mount Etna in Sicily and established a great forge there.
10. With his forge he created many beautiful golden objects.

A preposition is always followed by a noun or pronoun, which it relates to another word in the sentence. The noun or pronoun following the preposition is called the *object* of the preposition. Words that modify the object may come between the preposition and the object. Taken together, the preposition, its object, and the modifiers of the object are called a *prepositional phrase.*

● EXERCISE 16. Each of the following sentences contains a prepositional phrase. Number your paper 1–10, and after the proper number, copy the phrase. Underline the prepositions.

EXAMPLE 1. Walt Whitman wrote a very moving poem, "O Captain! My Captain!" about Abraham Lincoln.
1. *about Abraham Lincoln*

1. In this poem the ship's captain represents Abraham Lincoln.
2. The ship has just completed a voyage through rough weather.
3. On the shore, people celebrate the ship's safe arrival.
4. One member of the ship's crew addresses his captain.

5. "For you they call, the swaying mass, their eager faces turning. . . ."
6. Everyone except the captain can hear the rejoicing.
7. He has died during the voyage.
8. The ship represents the ship of state.
9. And the ship's voyage across rough seas symbolizes the war.
10. Lincoln, the captain, directed his ship toward a safe harbor.

Sometimes the same word may be used as a preposition or an adverb. In such a case, it is easy to tell the adverb from the preposition if you remember that a preposition must always be followed by a noun or pronoun object.

ADVERB The plane circled above.
PREPOSITION The plane circled above our heads. [Note the object of the preposition—*heads*.]

ADVERB We remained within.
PREPOSITION We remained within the shelter. [Note the object of the preposition—*shelter*.]

● EXERCISE 17. Use each of the following words in a sentence, first as an adverb, then as a preposition. Underline the designated word.

EXAMPLE 1. across
1. "*Why can't I swim across?*" *the child questioned.*
At one time men were afraid to venture across the ocean.

1. below
2. aboard
3. down
4. underneath
5. within

You must also be careful not to confuse a prepositional phrase beginning with *to* (*to town, to her club,* etc.) with a verb form beginning with *to* (*to run, to be seen, to have completed,* etc.). Remember again that a prepositional phrase always ends with a noun or pronoun.

THE CONJUNCTION

3d. A *conjunction* is a word which joins words or groups of words.

Conjunctions joining single words:

brush **and** paint
hot **or** cold
small **but** comfortable

Conjunctions joining groups of words:

through a forest **and** across a river
wanted to notify **but** not to alarm
camping out **or** staying in motels

Conjunctions joining groups of words that are sentences:

The stars seem motionless, **but** actually they are moving rapidly through space.

One queen was very beautiful, **and** the other was very plain.

Larry typed his paper himself, **or** he had his sister type it for him.

Conjunctions are of three kinds: *coordinating, correlative,* and *subordinating.*

The *coordinating conjunctions* are *and*, *but*, *or*, *nor*, *for*, and *yet*.

> The cave explorers carried ropes **and** torches.
>
> You may take the test now, **or** you may wait until later.
>
> Our auction was very successful, **for** every student brought something to be sold.

Notice that when *for* is used as a conjunction, it connects groups of words that are sentences. On all other occasions it is used as a preposition.

CONJUNCTION We wrote to the tourist bureau, **for** we wanted information on places to visit.

PREPOSITION We waited patiently **for** a reply.

Correlative conjunctions are always found in pairs and have other words dividing them: *either . . . or*, *neither . . . nor*, *both . . . and*, *not only . . . but also*.

> Our class will furnish **either** the punch **or** the cookies for the party.
>
> **Both** cats **and** dogs make good pets.
>
> Benjamin Franklin was **not only** a statesman **but also** an inventor.

Subordinating conjunctions occur in complex sentences. They are explained on pages 107–08.

● EXERCISE 18. Number your paper 1–10. Write after each number a coordinating or correlative conjunction to fill the blanks in the corresponding sentence.

1. We will play —— badminton —— volleyball.
2. Paul Bunyan —— Babe, his Blue Ox, are part of American folklore.

3. We read —— —— our texts —— —— the books in the library.
4. Samuel Clemens, —— Mark Twain, wrote *A Connecticut Yankee in King Arthur's Court.*
5. The famous trackman has run a mile —— can easily run another one.
6. —— Los Angeles —— San Diego is the capital of California.
7. My parents are going shopping, —— I am staying at home.
8. —— the seal —— the porpoise enjoy showing off for people.
9. The happy winner of the skating contest waved his hands —— threw his cap into the air.
10. The freshman did not win the race, —— had he expected to win it.

● EXERCISE 19. Make a list of the 20 coordinating and correlative conjunctions as they appear in the exercise below. Be able to tell what words or groups of words each conjunction joins. Treat a pair of correlative conjunctions as one conjunction.

The intelligence of dogs and cats has often been compared. Some people say that the dog is smarter, but others argue that the cat is brighter. Certainly the dog performs tricks more readily than the cat, for he is especially interested in pleasing man. The cat, on the other hand, neither tries nor wishes to please man. The cat is an independent animal, but the dog is dependent on his master for affection and attention. The only work a cat will do for man is to catch mice or rats, and that kind of work is fun for him.

There are many popular misconceptions about both dogs and cats. Most people believe that the mother dog or cat teaches her offspring by showing it how something is done. Actually, the offspring does not learn by imitation but by participation. The mother takes her offspring along and allows it to participate in an activity. Of course, the mother not only puts her offspring into a learning situation but also urges it on.

Another misconception is that a cat instinctively chases and kills mice. We know that this idea is false, for an experiment has shown it so. When a young kitten and a mouse were put into a cage together, the kitten neither chased the mouse nor tried to harm it in any way. In fact, the kitten and the mouse became great friends. They played together happily, and neither was harmed. So *Peter Churchmouse,* the old story about the mouse and the kitten who were friends, is possible after all.

THE INTERJECTION

3e. **An *interjection* is a word which expresses emotion and which is not related grammatically to other words in the sentence.**

> **Oh!** You surprised me.
> **Golly!** Am I tired!
> **Well,** I did my best.

DETERMINING PARTS OF SPEECH

You have now finished a study of the eight parts of speech. Here is a chart which briefly summarizes what you have learned.

Summary

RULE	PART OF SPEECH	USE	EXAMPLES
2a	noun	names	Allen, cave, Africa
2b	pronoun	takes the place of a noun	he, ourselves, who, anyone
2c	adjective	modifies a noun or pronoun	sick, tiny, purple, smooth
3a	verb	shows action or helps to make a statement	play, study, were, become
3b	adverb	modifies a verb, an adjective, or another adverb	very, too, usually, quickly
3c	preposition	relates a noun or pronoun to another word; begins a prepositional phrase	beside [her] to [town] for [John] with [them]
3d	conjunction	joins words	and, but, or
3e	interjection	shows strong feeling	Well! Wow! Oh!

3f. A word's use determines its part of speech.

Although words are given as examples of particular parts of speech in the chart above, you cannot really tell what part of speech a word is until you know how the word is used in a sentence. You've seen in your study of Chapters 2 and 3 that the same word can be used as a pronoun and an adjective or as an adverb and a preposition. Only when you see how a word is used in a sentence can you label it as a particular part of speech.

> **Each** did his part. [pronoun]
>
> **Each** girl baked a cake. [adjective]
>
> The tired shoppers sat **down** for a while. [adverb]
>
> The ball rolled **down** the hill. [preposition]
>
> A member of the crew has spotted **land.** [noun]
>
> The pilot can **land** here safely. [verb]

● REVIEW EXERCISE D. Number your paper 1–20. After each number, copy the italicized word from the corresponding sentence. Then write the part of speech of the word. Be prepared to explain your answer to the class.

EXAMPLES 1. That is a good *date* for the festival.
1. *date—noun*
2. Does Diane still *date* Ted?
2. *date—verb*

1. The package is too heavy *for* her.
2. She had to set the package down, *for* it was too heavy to carry.
3. One night we tried to count the *stars*, but finally we lost count.
4. My favorite actress *stars* in this movie.
5. *Some* have agreed to work in the booths.
6. *Some* booths will feature unusual contests and prizes.
7. The child walked *along* gaily next to his father.
8. Harriet and Jane walked down a path that runs *along* the lake.

9. Do you know where *my* coat is?
10. *My!* What an unusual painting!
11. The *still* water reflected her image clearly.
12. Are you *still* looking for your sister?
13. There are *many* who will help the committee with the project.
14. Tom and I found *many* different shells on the beach.
15. People who do not exercise *tire* easily.
16. My father bought a new *tire* before we left on our vacation.
17. An ice-cream stand is located *nearby*.
18. We are staying in a *nearby* hotel.
19. At the first port twenty-seven passengers climbed *aboard*.
20. While we were *aboard* the ship, we rested and enjoyed ourselves.

● REVIEW EXERCISE E. Write a short sentence for each of the following, using the word as the part of speech that is indicated. Underline the word in your sentence.

EXAMPLE 1. *attempts* as a noun
1. *Man's first attempts at flying ended in failure.*

1. *shade* as a verb
2. *today* as an adverb
3. *all* as an adjective
4. *plans* as a noun
5. *over* as an adverb
6. *tour* as a verb
7. *several* as a pronoun
8. *within* as a preposition
9. *look* as an interjection
10. *for* as a conjunction

● REVIEW EXERCISE F. Number your paper 1–50. From the following paragraphs, copy after the proper number each of the italicized words. After each word, write its part of speech. Be able to explain your answer by giving the *use* of the word in the sentence. Use the following abbreviations:

n.	noun	*adv.*	adverb
pron.	pronoun	*prep.*	preposition
v.	verb	*conj.*	conjunction
adj.	adjective	*interj.*	interjection

(1) *People* have (2) *always* enjoyed playing tricks on (3) *me.* (4) *Yesterday* during (5) *recess* one of my friends (6) *said* that (7) *he* (8) *had* a (9) *difficult* problem (10) *for* me. The problem went something (11) *like* this: "There are (12) *two* (13) *Indians*—a big Indian (14) *and* a little Indian. The (15) *little* Indian (16) *is* the big Indian's son, (17) *but* the big Indian is (18) *not* the little Indian's (19) *father.* What relation are (20) *they?*"

I (21) *thought* (22) *about* the (23) *problem* (24) *throughout* recess. (25) *Later* I thought about it (26) *during* science class. As a matter of fact, I didn't notice when my (27) *teacher* (28) *called* on me to recite. I considered every (29) *possible* answer, but none (30) *seemed* right. (31) *Finally* the (32) *bell* (33) *rang* and I (34) *rushed* over (35) *to* my friend's (36) *desk.* "What's the answer?" I (37) *begged.*

(38) "*Well,* the big Indian is (39) *obviously* the little Indian's mother," my friend knowingly (40) *replied.*

(41) "*What!* (42) *You* mean the answer was that simple!" I (43) *groaned.* "You've (44) *tricked* me for the (45) *last* time." And (46) *no one* did trick (47) *me* (48) *again* (49) *until* the (50) *next* recess.

CHAPTER **4**

The Phrase

Prepositional and Participial Phrases

In Chapters 2 and 3 you studied single-word modifiers: the adjective and the adverb. A whole group of words may also act as a modifier. Just as a verb phrase acts as a single verb, so an adjective phrase acts as a single adjective, and an adverb phrase acts as a single adverb. As modifiers, phrases play an important part in our sentences.

4a. **A *phrase* is a group of related words used as a single part of speech and does not contain a verb and its subject.**

You have already studied the *verb phrase*, which is introduced by a helping verb (*have* bought). You have also been introduced to the *prepositional phrase*. In this chapter you will learn more about the prepositional phrase, and you will meet a new kind of phrase —the *participial phrase*.

THE PREPOSITIONAL PHRASE

4b. A *prepositional phrase* is a group of words that begins with a preposition and usually ends with a noun or pronoun.

In the following examples, the prepositional phrases are in heavy type.

> We prepared treats **for them.**
> **During the night** the horse ran off.
> The children wore white pajamas **with red stripes.**

Of course, a single prepositional phrase may contain two or more objects.

> The dish is filled **with nuts and candy.**
> The group traveled **through Spain and Italy.**

● EXERCISE 1. Number your paper 1–9, using every other line. Write after each number the prepositional phrases in the corresponding sentence. There are twenty-five phrases.

1. Our word *sphinx*, which is often used in the phrase, "a sphinxlike expression," dates back to ancient Greece. 2. Near Thebes, a city in Greece, there supposedly stood a monster which had the head of a woman, the body of a lion, the wings of a bird, and the tail of a serpent. 3. This strange monster posed a riddle for those who passed by: "What walks on four legs in the morning, on two legs at noon, and on three legs in the evening?" 4. If the passerby did not answer, "A man," the sphinx strangled him and flung him from her rock. 5. Finally, the wise Oedipus encountered the sphinx and answered her riddle, whereupon the sphinx threw herself over the cliff and perished. 6. To-

day when we call someone a sphinx, we are saying that his words or actions are puzzling like those of the Theban sphinx. 7. Do you know why "a man" is the correct answer to the riddle of the sphinx? 8. Imagine that morning represents infancy; noon, adulthood; and evening, old age. 9. After a little thought you should solve the riddle and see the relationship between the number of legs and the ages of man.

The Adjective Phrase

Some prepositional phrases are called *adjective phrases* because they act like adjectives; that is, they modify nouns and pronouns.

4c. An *adjective phrase* is a prepositional phrase that modifies a noun or pronoun.

Notice that the adjectives and adjective phrases in heavy type in the following sentences do the same work: they modify a noun.

ADJECTIVE	The **neighborhood** boys formed a baseball team.
ADJECTIVE PHRASE	The boys **in the neighborhood** formed a baseball team.
ADJECTIVE	Their **varsity** players are bigger than our players.
ADJECTIVE PHRASE	The players **on their varsity** are bigger than our players.
ADJECTIVE	I met some **Asian** students.
ADJECTIVE PHRASE	I met some students **from Asia.**

4 b-c

Like the adjective, an adjective phrase is usually located next to the word it modifies. But while the adjective generally precedes the word it modifies, the adjective phrase usually follows the word it modifies.

● EXERCISE 2. Each of the following sentences contains an adjective phrase. Number your paper 1–10. After the proper number, copy the phrase and the noun or pronoun it modifies.

EXAMPLE 1. The snow on the highway was five feet deep.
1. *on the highway, snow*

1. The man with the long beard is a hermit.
2. Many islands in the Pacific are uninhabited.
3. Our days at the beach were very pleasant.
4. We boarded a plane with four jet engines.
5. One of my friends won the poetry contest.
6. The house by the train depot is being torn down.
7. Birds like the pheasant and the peacock have long, beautiful tails.
8. The lights across the bay are visible tonight.
9. Everyone aboard the ship waved and shouted.
10. Philip Nolan was a man without a country.

● EXERCISE 3. Construct sentences using each of the following word groups as an adjective phrase. Underline the noun or pronoun that the adjective phrase modifies.

EXAMPLE 1. on the hill
1. *The single <u>tree</u> on the hill looks lonely.*

1. around the corner
2. near the school
3. like them
4. through the woods
5. under the big tent
6. for our dog
7. with colorful lights
8. in the club
9. under the rock
10. at the dock

Sometimes one adjective phrase follows another. The second phrase usually modifies the object in the first phrase.

Sicily is an island **off the coast of Italy.**

● EXERCISE 4. Each sentence below contains two adjective phrases. Number your paper 1–10, and copy the phrases after the proper numbers. After each phrase, copy the word it modifies.

EXAMPLE 1. Lynn wrote a research paper on monsters in Scotland.

1. *on monsters, paper*
in Scotland, monsters

1. The day of the game with Oak Park finally arrived.
2. Sky diving has become the favorite sport of some students in college.
3. Linda's date for the dance at Bradley should be here.
4. The store near the intersection of Yale and Eighteenth is still open.
5. A man from a country in the Far East visited us.
6. The air in the dungeon under the fort was very damp.
7. Many of the names of our states are Indian words.
8. The drawer on the right-hand side of the bureau contains the pictures.
9. We have tickets to a new show on Broadway.
10. Le Havre is a famous French port across the channel from England.

The Adverb Phrase

When a prepositional phrase is used as an adverb to modify a verb, adjective, or adverb, it is called an *adverb phrase*. Like a single-word adverb, the adverb phrase answers the questions *How? When? Where? To what extent?*

4d. An *adverb phrase* is a prepositional phrase that modifies a verb, an adjective, or an adverb.

> The boys behaved **like gentlemen.** [The adverb phrase modifies the verb *behaved*, telling *how* the boys behaved.]
>
> Her dress is too long **in the back.** [The adverb phrase modifies the adjective *long*, telling *where* the dress is too long.]
>
> We arrived early **in the morning.** [The adverb phrase modifies the adverb *early*, telling *when* we were early.]

Adverb phrases modify verbs more often than they modify adjectives and adverbs.

● EXERCISE 5. Each sentence below contains an adverb phrase. Number your paper 1–10. After the proper number, write the adverb phrase from each sentence. Then write the verb, adjective, or adverb that the phrase modifies.

EXAMPLE 1. The first coffeehouses were built in Egypt.
1. *in Egypt, were built*

1. The first English coffeehouse opened in 1650.
2. Soon coffeehouses were popular beyond belief.
3. Almost everyone went to the coffeehouse.
4. At such a place one learned the latest gossip.
5. Men sat late into the night drinking coffee and talking.
6. They never shied away from a discussion.

7. Instead they argued on every occasion.
8. They were witty in their arguments.
9. For thirty years Will's Coffee House was a favorite.
10. The famous writers John Dryden and Joseph Addison could often be found at Will's.

● EXERCISE 6. Construct sentences in which you use the following phrases as adverbs modifying verbs. Underline the word modified.

EXAMPLE 1. during the night
1. *During the night a bear ate our food.*

1. about a year ago
2. through the storm
3. in the shower
4. down the street
5. beside the policeman
6. outside the shelter
7. by my friends
8. above the clouds
9. after many hours
10. without any books

Like adjective phrases, adverb phrases often appear one after the other, usually modifying the same word.

Animals move **to a warm place during the winter months.**

The adjective phrase almost always follows immediately after the word it modifies, but the adverb phrase may be separated from the word it modifies by other words. Adverb phrases may be moved about in the sentence.

For many centuries men searched **for a way** to make gold.

Men searched **for many centuries for a way** to make gold.

For a way to make gold, men searched **for many centuries.**

4d

● EXERCISE 7. Number your paper 1–7. Write after the proper number the adverb phrase (phrases) in each sentence. After each phrase, write the word it modifies.

1. Mount Vernon is interesting for its history.
2. It is near Washington, D.C.
3. The house was named Mount Vernon by Lawrence Washington, who lived there for many years.
4. Somewhat later, George Washington moved to Mount Vernon.
5. After Washington's death the house passed through several hands.
6. In 1858, it was bought by the Mount Vernon Ladies Association, who restored it.
7. The buildings and grounds are open to the general public.

DIAGRAMING ADJECTIVE AND ADVERB PHRASES

An adjective or adverb phrase is diagramed below the word it modifies. Write the preposition on a line slanting down from the modified word. Then write the object of the preposition (the noun or pronoun following the preposition) in the phrase on a horizontal line leading from the slanting line. Modifiers within a phrase are diagramed in the usual way.

PATTERNS

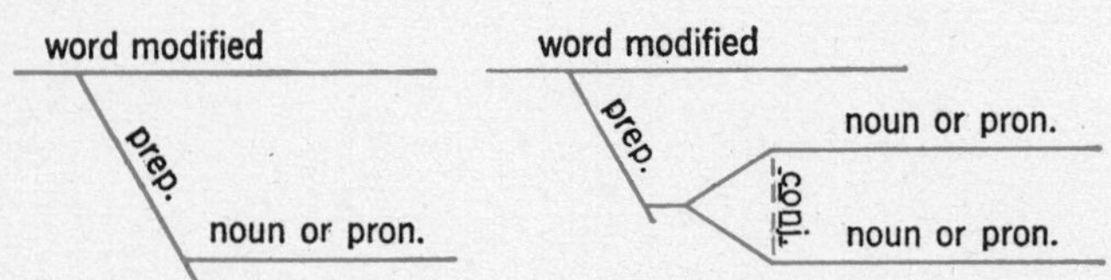

EXAMPLES 1. walked along the road

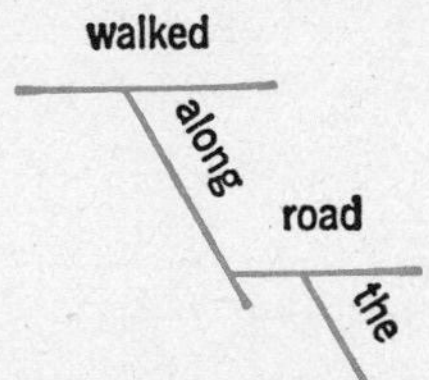

2. paintings by famous artists

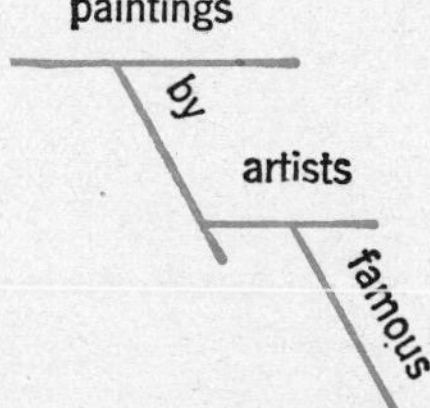

3. went with Hollis and Dave

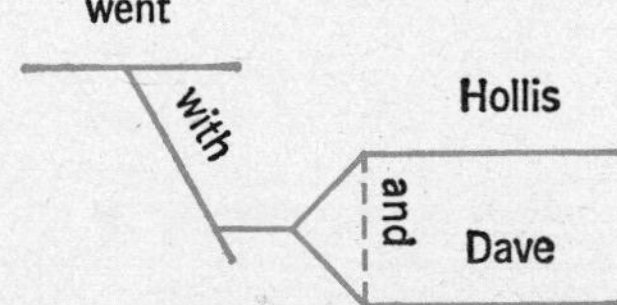

When a prepositional phrase modifies the object of another prepositional phrase, the diagram looks like this:

EXAMPLE camped on top of a mountain

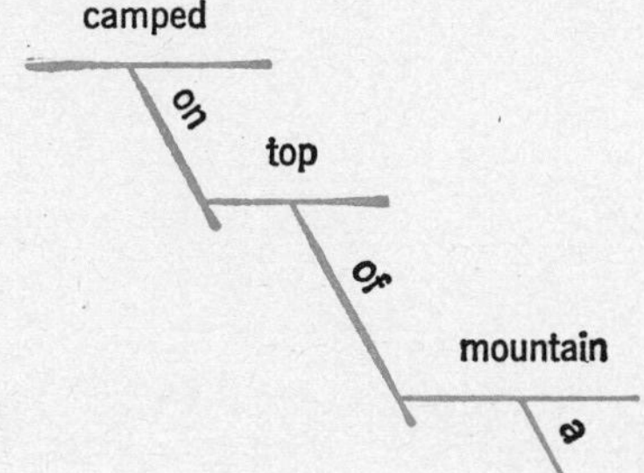

● EXERCISE 8. Diagram the following word groups which contain prepositional phrases. Use a ruler and leave plenty of space between diagrams.

1. invited to the celebrations
2. everyone but him
3. date of the wedding
4. a glimpse of the famous ruler
5. was by my favorite actor and actress
6. hiked for twenty miles
7. one of the people in the room
8. the day before the trial
9. read about King Midas and his golden touch
10. drove to a village near Paris

● EXERCISE 9. Diagram the following sentences, each of which contains an adjective phrase or an adverb phrase or both.

EXAMPLE The company of actors performed in front of a large audience.

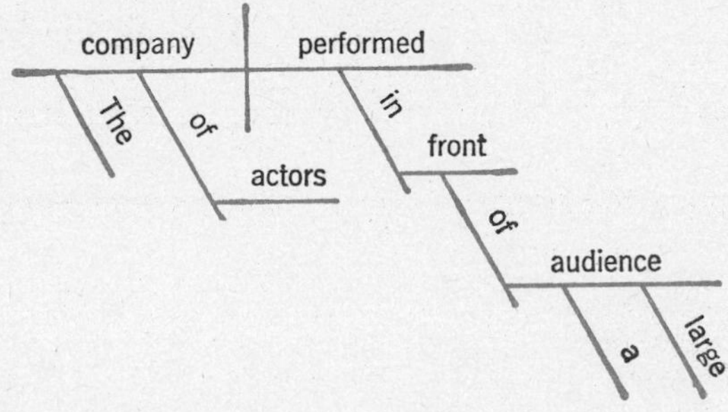

1. The film was made in Spain.
2. The date for our class picnic has been set.
3. Some of the guests stayed late.
4. The parade moved slowly down the street.
5. Pompeii was destroyed by a volcano.
6. Citrus fruits are grown in California and Florida.
7. During the storm we stayed inside the tent.

8. A group from our school is going to Washington.
9. We stopped near a mountain stream.
10. The student in the front row reads well.

● REVIEW EXERCISE A. List in order the adjective and adverb phrases in the following sentences. Before each phrase, write the number of the sentence in which it occurs. After each phrase, write the word or expression it modifies. Be ready to tell whether it is an adjective or an adverb phrase.

EXAMPLE 1. Through the years our understanding of the word *travel* has undergone changes.
1. *Through the years, has undergone*
1. *of the word, understanding*

1. Few of us know that our word *travel* comes from the French term *travailler*, which means "to work hard."
2. Until recent times, *travel* was associated with pain or agony.
3. During your spare time, read a few accounts of the traveling conditions of the past.
4. Before the days of modern transportation, travel was not easy.
5. One might start on a trip to a neighboring state or country and never arrive there.
6. One often faced the dangers of bandits and wild beasts.
7. One certainly met with discouragement from weather and rough terrain.
8. For many centuries a traveler often relied on hospitality in the homes of strangers.
9. The laws of hospitality required that the host be generous with his food and possessions.
10. When a traveler was turned from the house, the host was supposedly punished by the heavens.

THE PARTICIPLE

Besides the eight parts of speech that you have learned, our language contains another kind of word—the *verbal.* A verbal is a word that is formed from a verb but is used in sentences as another part of speech. One kind of verbal is the *participle.*

4e. A *participle* is a verb form used as an adjective.

There are two kinds of participles—present participles and past participles. Present participles end in *-ing*. Past participles often end in *-ed*, *-d*, or *-t*.

> The horses **trotting** past were not frightened by the crowd. [*Trotting*, a form of the verb *trot*, modifies, like an adjective, the noun *horses—trotting horses*.]
>
> **Buried** by pirates, the treasure was undiscovered for centuries. [*Buried*, a form of the verb *bury*, modifies, like an adjective, the noun *treasure—buried treasure*.]

Do not confuse participles used as in the examples above with participles used in a verb phrase.

PARTICIPLE	**Broken,** the toy still ran.
VERB PHRASE	The toy **was broken** but still ran.
PARTICIPLE	**Planning** their trip, the class learned some geography.
VERB PHRASE	While they **were planning** their trip, the class learned some geography.

Think of the participle in a verb phrase as part of a verb, not as an adjective.

● EXERCISE 10. Number your paper 1–12. After the proper number, copy the participle (participles) from each of the following sentences. After each participle, write the noun it modifies. Be prepared to tell whether the participle is a present participle or a past participle.

EXAMPLE 1. We heard the wind howling around the house.
1. *howling, wind*

1. Toys, broken and mutilated, were lying about the room.
2. Grinning broadly, Frank obviously brought good news.
3. The roof, blazing furiously, soon collapsed.
4. His shoes, tattered and stained, had, like their owner, seen better days.
5. For years the shack stood there, quite deserted.
6. Sighing happily, she folded and put away the letter.
7. I watched the dog charging toward me.
8. Singing and dancing, mummers paraded through the streets.
9. The crowd, cheering wildly, applauded the performance.
10. Recently published, this book is not yet available in paperback.
11. The horses, neighing frantically, tried to kick their way out of the burning barn.
12. The cavalry, charging at full speed, scattered the enemy soldiers.

THE PARTICIPIAL PHRASE

When a participle introduces a group of related words that act together as an adjective, this word group is called a *participial phrase*.

4f. A *participial phrase* is a group of related words that contains a participle and that acts as an adjective.

A prepositional phrase often follows the participle. When it does, it is considered a part of the participial phrase. In the examples below all the words in heavy type are part of the participial phrase. An arrow is drawn from each participial phrase to the word that it modifies.

> **Seeing himself in the mirror,** the duck seemed bewildered.
>
> He stood in front of the mirror, **watching his image closely.**
>
> Then, **disgusted with the other duck,** he began to peck the mirror.
>
> Finally, **giving up in dismay,** he backed cautiously away from his strange opponent.

● EXERCISE 11. Number your paper 1–12. After the proper number, copy the participial phrase and the noun or pronoun that it modifies.

1. Lying in the sun, we felt warm and sleepy.
2. The room, painted black and turquoise, is very unusual.
3. The starter, wearing a red armband, signaled that the race was about to begin.
4. Tired from his long and arduous trip, he went to bed early.
5. Breathing fire and smoke, the dragon turned on the Red Cross Knight.

6. Do you recognize the famous actor wearing dark glasses?
7. Seated on his throne, the king listened to those who came to beg favors of him.
8. The detectives investigating the robbery found several clues.
9. Carolyn, rewriting sections of her theme, worked hastily.
10. From the lookout tower we saw a small hut nestled between two large hills.
11. Sprawling lazily on the sofa, he sipped a glass of lemonade and watched television.
12. We waved back at the man waving to us.

● EXERCISE 12. From each of the following sentences, copy the participial phrase. After the phrase, write the word or words that it modifies.

1. Noted for her beauty, Venus was sought by all the gods as a wife.
2. Jupiter, knowing her charms, nevertheless married her to Vulcan, the ugliest of the gods.
3. Bathed in radiant light, Venus brought love and joy wherever she went.
4. Mars, known to the Greeks as Ares, was the god of war.
5. Terrified by Ares' power, the Greeks did not like to worship him.
6. They saw both land and people destroyed by him.
7. Observing his path, they said that Ares left blood, devastation, and grief behind him.
8. The Romans, having great respect for Mars, made him one of their three chief deities.
9. They imagined him dressed in shining armor.
10. Mars, supposed to be the father of the founders of Rome, has a month named after him.

● EXERCISE 13. Use the following participial phrases in sentences of your own. Place each phrase as close as possible to the noun or pronoun that it modifies. If you use a participial phrase to begin a sentence, put a comma after the phrase, and follow it closely with the word that is modified.

EXAMPLE 1. waiting for the train
1. *Waiting for the train, we walked up and down the platform.*

1. published every week
2. standing in the long line for tickets
3. wearing a green silk scarf
4. left by himself for a few minutes
5. taxiing down the runway
6. hidden in a safe place
7. swinging from tree to tree
8. confused by all the questions
9. written in a strange language
10. hearing the clock strike twelve and seeing all the lights go out

● REVIEW EXERCISE B. The following sentences contain prepositional and participial phrases. Number your paper 1–20. After the proper number, copy a phrase, and write the word or words that it modifies. Then write what kind of phrase it is: *prep.* or *part.* List one phrase for each sentence; do not list separately prepositional phrases that are part of participial phrases.

EXAMPLE 1. Seeing him from a distance, I did not recognize my friend.
1. *Seeing him from a distance—I—part.*

1. I read a book about Portugal.
2. Through the long silence everyone seemed uneasy.
3. Carrying a heavy load, the native stumbled home.

4. Our float, decorated with the school colors, won.
5. I gave a report on Pitcairn Island.
6. People once said, "All roads lead to Rome."
7. The wolves running after the sled suddenly turned around.
8. "Miss Sousou," captured by gorilla hunters, was the first adult gorilla to be taken alive.
9. A man with a long, crooked nose is standing outside.
10. The bus, filled with noisy children, finally reached its destination.
11. We ate our lunch near an old water mill.
12. After several minutes the curtain was drawn.
13. The soldiers guarding the tomb never change their expressions.
14. The students in the play are very busy.
15. Receiving no answer, he hung up.
16. The boys left their clothes on the bank.
17. Bart explained the reason for his tardiness.
18. The ship set sail, carrying a valuable cargo.
19. The hikers carried all their equipment on their backs.
20. Do you recognize the man seated next to the principal?

CHAPTER **5**

The Clause

Adjective and Adverb Clauses

In Chapter 4 you studied the phrase, a group of related words without a verb and its subject. In a sentence there may also be groups of related words called *clauses*, that do contain a verb and its subject.

PHRASES **on the ferryboat** [no subject or verb]
have been laughing [no subject]

CLAUSES **as the ferryboat crossed the river** [a verb—*crossed*—and its subject—*ferryboat*]
who have been laughing [a verb—*have been laughing*—and its subject—*who*]

5a. A *clause* is a group of words that contains a verb and its subject and is used as a part of a sentence.

THE INDEPENDENT CLAUSE

5b. An *independent* (or *main*) *clause* expresses a complete thought and can stand by itself as a sentence.

If you can recognize a sentence, you will have no trouble recognizing independent clauses. Independent clauses are sentences when they stand alone. They are usually called independent clauses only when they are part of a sentence.

SENTENCE **I baked her a cake.**
INDEPENDENT CLAUSE Since it was my mother's birthday, **I baked her a cake.**

Study the following sentences, in which the independent clauses are in heavy type. Notice that a sentence may have more than one independent clause. (See the third sentence.)

> If you have worked with the soil, **you are familiar with humus.**
>
> ***Humus* comes from a Latin word** that means "earth."
>
> ***Humilis* means "on the ground,"** and **from this Latin word we derive the word "humility."**
>
> When you are humble, **you are "on the ground."**

THE SUBORDINATE CLAUSE

While an independent clause can stand alone as a complete thought, a subordinate clause cannot stand alone.

SENTENCE The crowds gathered to greet Lindbergh when he landed in Paris.
INDEPENDENT CLAUSE The crowds gathered to greet Lindbergh. [can stand alone]
SUBORDINATE CLAUSE when he landed in Paris [cannot stand alone]

5c. A *subordinate* (or *dependent*) *clause* does not express a complete thought and cannot stand alone.

The word *subordinate* means "lesser in rank or importance." Since a subordinate clause cannot stand by itself, it is considered "below the rank" of an independent clause.

Study the following sentences, which contain subordinate clauses set in heavy type. Notice that the subordinate clauses contain verbs and their subjects, but notice also that they are introduced by words like *since*, *when*, *if*, *as*, *who*, *which*, and *that*, which prevent them from standing alone. A sentence may have more than one subordinate clause. (See the last sentence below.)

s v
Luna, **who was the Roman goddess of the moon,** gave us our word *lunatic*.

s v
Since at one time the moon was believed to cause madness, people avoided moonlight.

s v
Anyone **that slept with the moon shining in his face** might become mad.

s v
Furthermore, the degree of madness changed **when the phase of the moon changed.**

s v s v
Even today many people feel uncomfortable **if the moon shines in on them while they are sleeping.**

Summary

1. A clause has a subject and verb.
2. An independent clause can stand alone as a complete sentence.
3. A subordinate clause cannot stand alone.

● EXERCISE 1. Some of the following expressions are sentences, although they are written without capital letters and periods; some are subordinate clauses; and some are phrases. Number your paper 1–20. If the expression is a sentence, write *S* after the proper number; if a subordinate clause, write *C*; if a phrase, write *P*.

1. we built a swimming pool
2. on the front page
3. after everyone had voted
4. which was sold at the auction
5. after many years
6. during the bad snowstorm
7. the celebrity wore dark glasses
8. although our supplies were giving
9. who escaped without harm
10. in the dolphin's tank
11. when the ship docked at Rotterdam
12. would have been found
13. until the next time we meet
14. down the middle
15. in the meantime everyone can practice his part
16. if the train is not late
17. as I stood on the platform
18. near the zoo
19. everyone cheered
20. because the rain has stopped

● EXERCISE 2. Copy the subordinate clause from each of the following sentences. Underline the subject of the clause once and the verb twice.

EXAMPLE 1. Some historians believe that bowling originated from a religious ceremony.

1. *that bowling originated from a religious ceremony*

1. Many centuries ago people carried clubs for their defense when they went anywhere.
2. While a peasant was visiting a priest for confession, he would stand his club at the end of the cloister.
3. Eventually the clubs came to represent sins that the peasants had committed.
4. After they had finished their confessions, they rolled large stones at the clubs.
5. If one knocked over his club, he was leading a good life.
6. When he failed to knock it over, he needed to attend church more often.
7. Since everyone enjoys competition, before long the peasants made a game out of the stones and clubs.
8. They challenged each other to matches that were not too unlike modern bowling matches.
9. A match was won by the man who could knock down the most clubs.
10. Although there are many other theories about the development of bowling, many historians trace modern bowling back to this origin.

● EXERCISE 3. Add an independent clause to each of the following subordinate clauses, and write the whole sentence on your paper. Draw one line under the subject of each clause and two lines under the verb.

EXAMPLES 1. who came early
1. *He is the man who came early.*
2. when the music stopped
2. *When the music stopped, the party ended.*

1. when I awoke this morning
2. that my class likes best
3. unless you practice each day
4. if it is cold tomorrow
5. who waited in line
6. although the starting quarterback was injured
7. while we performed on stage
8. whose arm is broken
9. since the weather was good
10. that hangs on the wall

THE ADJECTIVE CLAUSE

Like an adjective or an adjective phrase, a clause may modify a noun or a pronoun. In the word groups below you see first an adjective phrase, then an adjective clause.

ADJECTIVE PHRASE the man **in the car**
ADJECTIVE CLAUSE the man **who is in the car**

ADJECTIVE PHRASE a tree **with red blossoms**
ADJECTIVE CLAUSE a tree **which has red blossoms**

ADJECTIVE PHRASE a day **for fishing**
ADJECTIVE CLAUSE a day **that was made for fishing**

5d. An *adjective clause* is a subordinate clause used as an adjective to modify a noun or pronoun.

5d

Observe how the adjective clauses in the following sentences modify nouns or pronouns. Notice that adjective clauses usually follow immediately after the words that they modify.

> Helen was the beautiful woman **who caused the Trojan War.**
>
> Mrs. Jackson showed slides **that she had taken in Iran.**
>
> The ones **whose flight was delayed** spent the night in Detroit.

The Relative Pronoun

Adjective clauses are easy to identify because they are almost always introduced by a special kind of pronoun: the *relative pronoun. Who, whom, whose, which,* and *that* are called *relative* pronouns because they *relate* to another word or idea in the sentence.

> Leonardo da Vinci was the artist **who painted the *Mona Lisa.*** [The relative pronoun *who* begins the clause and relates to the noun *artist.*]
>
> Everything **that could be done** was done. [The relative pronoun *that* begins the clause and relates to the pronoun *everything.*]

● EXERCISE 4. Copy the adjective clauses from the following sentences. Circle the relative pronouns. After each clause, write the word that the pronoun relates, or refers, to.

EXAMPLE 1. Our neighbors have a dog that is called Juno.
1. (*that*) *is called Juno, dog*

1. Antonyms are words which have opposite meanings.
2. Skin diving is a sport that is now becoming very popular.

3. Pluto, which is the farthest planet from the earth, takes 248 years to revolve once around the sun.
4. A scholarship was awarded to the one whose short story was judged best.
5. We invited everyone whom we knew to the round-the-world party.
6. Words in our language which begin with *th* are often hard for foreigners to pronounce.
7. Robert Frost, who for many years was the unofficial poet laureate of America, died in 1963.
8. In her diary Jane kept a record of everything that she did and thought.
9. Achilles was the Greek warrior who could be wounded only in the heel.
10. Here is a picture of the man whom the police want.

Sometimes the relative pronoun is preceded by a preposition. The preposition has actually been moved from the end of the clause to the beginning. Many writers think that the clause sounds better with the preposition at the beginning.

> the day **which we looked forward to**
> the day **to which we looked forward**
>
> my friend, **whom I would do anything for**
> my friend, **for whom I would do anything**
>
> the politician **whose speech the public is interested in**
> the politician **in whose speech the public is interested**

When you are looking for an adjective clause, remember that the relative pronoun may be preceded by a preposition.

● EXERCISE 5. Write the adjective clause from each of the following sentences. Circle the relative pronouns.

1. He is the man for whom the letter is intended.
2. Grendel, the monster that Beowulf slew, had eaten many good men.
3. The fiber glass pole, about which so much has been written, enables vaulters to jump much higher.
4. Monaco, which is one of the smallest countries in the world, is famous for its casino.
5. Christopher Marlowe wrote of Helen of Troy, "Was this the face that launched a thousand ships . . .?"
6. Pygmalion was a celebrated sculptor who supposedly made a woman from stone.
7. In the story of the modern Pygmalion, a man takes an uneducated flower girl and makes her into a woman whom everyone admires.
8. Finally we reached the place toward which we had been traveling for days.
9. Midas, whose touch turned everything to gold, has given us our expression "the Midas touch."
10. The early settlers were brave people to whom we owe a great deal.

● EXERCISE 6. Complete each sentence by supplying an adjective clause for the blank. Remember that a clause must have a subject and a verb. Underline each relative pronoun.

EXAMPLE 1. Gray clouds —— are called stratus clouds.

1. *Gray clouds that form a broad layer are called stratus clouds.*

1. Our class put on a play ——.
2. The ship —— is the largest one I have ever seen.
3. Dogs —— do many things for man.
4. The policeman quickly filled out a ticket for the car ——.
5. The man —— was once a trapeze artist.
6. The paintings —— are very costly.
7. We listened to music ——.
8. Larry's father introduced him to a professional football player ——.
9. Our school newspaper —— is read by all the students.
10. We handed our tickets to the usher ——.
11. The boy —— is my cousin.
12. The man handing out free candy and gum is the same man ——.

● EXERCISE 7. The following paragraphs contain ten adjective clauses. Copy each adjective clause as it appears. After each clause, write the word that it modifies.

EXAMPLE 1. Dogs that are trained carefully at the Seeing Eye Foundation help the blind to lead happy, active lives.

1. *that are trained carefully at the Seeing Eye Foundation—Dogs*

Dogs that are chosen as guide dogs for the blind do not begin their Seeing Eye training until they are mature. From the age of ten weeks to fourteen months, they are cared for by children who are members of a 4-H organization. Then they are taken to the Seeing Eye Foundation, which carefully trains them for three months.

Each week that they are there, they are graded on fifteen items. They are judged on their responses to commands and on their behavior in various situations which might tend to distract them. They must learn not only to be obedient but also to reason well enough to delay obedience in situations which might bring injury to their masters. They must learn to avoid the obstacles that their blind masters cannot see. Dogs are color-blind, and they obviously cannot tell the color of a traffic light; therefore they patiently wait and then move across a street with the crowd that is standing around them.

By the time that the dog and the master have finished their training together, the master is able to have absolute faith in his dog. And the dog is happy because of the affection which he receives from his master.

THE ADVERB CLAUSE

Like an adverb or an adverb phrase, a subordinate clause may modify a verb, adjective, or adverb. Such a clause is called an *adverb clause.*

ADVERB PHRASE **During the cold winter months** many animals hibernate.

ADVERB CLAUSE **When the weather turns cold,** many animals hibernate.

5e. An *adverb clause* is a subordinate clause which is used like an adverb.

An adverb clause may tell *how, when, where, why, to what extent* (*how much* or *how long*), or *under what conditions* the action of the verb is done.

The truck moves **as if it has a heavy load.** [The adverb clause tells *how* the truck *moves.*]

There was a great sea wave **when the volcano erupted.** [The adverb clause tells *when* there *was* a great sea wave.]

We stood **where we could see all of the track.** [The adverb clause tells *where* we *stood.*]

Because the day was very hot, the cool water felt good. [The adverb clause tells *why* the water felt *good.*]

We worked **until we were completely worn out.** [The adverb clause tells *how long* we *worked.*]

If it does not rain tomorrow, we will go to see Crater Lake. [The adverb clause tells *under what condition* we *will go* to see Crater Lake.]

As these examples show, the adverb clause may come at various places in the sentence. When it comes at the beginning, it is usually followed by a comma.

The Subordinating Conjunction

In Chapter 3 you learned to recognize two kinds of conjunctions: coordinating conjunctions, like *and* and *but*, and correlative conjunctions, like *either . . . or* and *neither . . . nor.* There is a third kind of conjunction, called a *subordinating conjunction,* which introduces an adverb clause. Just as a relative pronoun, like *who* or *which*, introduces an adjective clause, so a subordinating conjunction, like *since* or *if*, introduces an adverb clause.

The following words are commonly used to begin adverb clauses: [1]

SUBORDINATING CONJUNCTIONS

after	before	unless
although	if	until
as	in order that	when
as if	since	whenever
as long as	so that	where
as soon as	than	wherever
because	though	while

● EXERCISE 8. Copy the adverb clause from each of the following sentences. Circle the subordinating conjunction and draw one line under the subject and two lines under the verb of each clause. Be prepared to tell what word the clause modifies.

EXAMPLE 1. We read stories before we go to bed.
1. *(before) we go to bed*

1. When divers explore the beds of rivers and lakes, they often find fossils.
2. At the end of seven grueling rounds, the old fighter felt as if hundred-pound weights were chained to his gloves.
3. After Ray had searched for several days, he found just the right gift.
4. The women changed into flat-heeled shoes so that they could walk more easily.
5. The twins had never seen a waterfall until their uncle took them to Niagara Falls.
6. Because Sandra was interested in folk music, she did a research paper on the old ballad "Barbara Allan."

[1] Remember that *after*, *before*, *since*, *until*, and *as* may also be used as prepositions.

7. We sang songs as we rode back from the game.
8. Some animals would become extinct if they were not protected by law.
9. The students collected various kinds of rocks while they were on their field trip.
10. Whenever any kind of danger threatens, the baby kangaroo jumps into his mother's pouch.

● EXERCISE 9. There are ten adverb clauses in the following paragraph. Write the number of the line on which the clause appears. Then write the clause. If the clause begins on one line and ends on another, write it for the line on which it begins. In each clause underline the subject once and the verb twice.

What animals would you name if you were told to make a list of the ten smartest animals in the world? After you had considered the matter for a few minutes, you would probably name the monkey, the dog, and several other animals. Perhaps the horse would also be one of your choices, since you have often heard the expression "horse sense." As you listed the animals, you would probably not think of the donkey. Although everyone considers the donkey a rather dumb animal, his intelligence is superior to that of the brightest horse. When we think of the noble-looking horse, we think of his intelligence. But there are many animals that surpass him in intelligence. He is a high-strung creature that tends to go berserk whenever he is exposed to any strange situation. Because he is so emotional, it is necessary for him to wear blinders so that he will not be distracted from his work. When you make out a list of the brightest animals, don't just list your favorites.

● EXERCISE 10. Add an adverb clause to each of the following sentences (independent clauses). Copy the entire sentence on your paper. Then circle the subordinating conjunctions, and underline the subject of each clause once and the verb twice. Remember that your adverb clauses will tell *how, when, where, why, how much,* or *under what conditions.*

EXAMPLE 1. The rain finally stopped.
1. *After our yard was flooded, the rain finally stopped.*

1. The dog barked.
2. Our team won.
3. The crew on the ship worked hard.
4. Amy speaks German well.
5. We built a sauna, a Finnish bathhouse, in our backyard.
6. The Lawsons have gone to Mexico for a week.
7. Morris finished his homework early.
8. I was almost asleep.
9. Gary wants to be a forest ranger.
10. Everyone enjoyed the banquet.

● REVIEW EXERCISE A. Each of the following famous quotations contains either an adjective or an adverb clause. Copy the clause after the proper number. Write *adj. clause* after each adjective clause and *adv. clause* after each adverb clause.

1. Your own property is concerned when your neighbor's house is on fire.—HORACE
2. If wishes were horses, beggars would ride. —ENGLISH PROVERB
3. All that glitters is not gold.—ENGLISH PROVERB

4. Never answer a letter while you are angry.
—CHINESE PROVERB
5. He who waits to do a great deal of good at once will never do anything.—SAMUEL JOHNSON
6. Everything in nature is a cause from which there flows some effect.—SPINOZA
7. It is foolish to tear one's hair in grief, as if sorrow would be made less by baldness.—CICERO
8. Heaven never helps the man who will not help himself.—SOPHOCLES
9. Every fact that is learned becomes a key to other facts.—E. L. YOUMANS
10. Be courteous to all, but intimate with few; and let those few be well tried before you give them your confidence.—GEORGE WASHINGTON

● REVIEW EXERCISE B. There are twenty subordinate clauses—ten adjective clauses and ten adverb clauses—in the following paragraphs. Write the number of the line in which the first word of the clause appears. Then write the clause. Write *adj. clause* after each adjective clause and *adv. clause* after each adverb clause.

Robert Browning, who was a poet of the Victorian period, wrote a poem about Childe Roland, a daring knight who set out on a dangerous quest for the Dark Tower. Many brave knights had been killed because they had searched for the tower, but Roland was determined not to rest until he found it.

After Roland had searched for years, he came upon an old man who pointed the way to the tower. Following the old man's directions, Roland found himself in a land which was horrible beyond belief. As he passed across the eerie wasteland, he saw all around him the signs of savage struggles that had taken place here in the past. Although Roland now felt doomed, he rode on. He saw sights that would have convinced the bravest of men to turn back. But Roland would not give up while he had strength to continue.

Finally, when he had become discouraged, a large black bird swooped down over his head. As he watched it fly away, he saw in the distance the place for which he was searching. Lying in a valley, the dark tower loomed up before him as a rocky shelf might appear to a sailor at the very moment that his ship crashes into it. While Roland paused to look, he heard ringing in his ears the names of all those who had died in the quest for the tower. Then, on the hillsides, he saw in a sheet of flame the figures of the knights who had perished. But, in spite of the horror, Roland raised his horn to his lips and blew: "*Childe Roland to the Dark Tower came.*"

CHAPTER **6**

The Sentence Base

Direct and Indirect Objects, Subject Complements

As you learned in Chapter 1, every sentence has a sentence base. The sentence base always consists of at least a verb and its subject. In many sentences this subject-verb base is enough.

s v
John shouted.

s v
The squirrels scampered across the campus.

The sentence base usually has another part, in addition to the subject and verb, called a *complement*. The word *complement* means "completer." A complement completes the meaning begun by the subject and verb. Notice that the following word groups are not complete, even though they have subjects and verbs.

s v
Marlene made [what?]

s v
I met [whom?]

s v
His friend is [what?]

Here a complement completes the meaning of each.

S V C
Marlene made a cake.

S V C
I met Troy.

S V C
His friend is a painter.

6a. A *complement* is a word or group of words that completes the meaning begun by the subject and verb.

Jody redecorated her **room.** [*Room* completes the meaning by telling *what* Jody redecorated.]

My uncle sent **me** a **postcard** from Amsterdam. [*Me* and *postcard* complete the meaning by telling *what* was sent and *to whom.*]

I asked **what he wanted.** [The group of words *what he wanted* completes the meaning by telling *what* I asked.]

The early explorers were courageous **men.** [*Men* completes the meaning by telling something about the subject *explorers.*]

The *Mona Lisa* is very **famous.** [*Famous* completes the meaning by describing the subject *Mona Lisa.*]

In the sentences above you see two kinds of complements. In sentences 1, 2, and 3 you see complements which are affected by the action of the verb. In sentences 4 and 5 you see complements which refer to the subject. A noun, a pronoun, or an adjective can serve as a complement. But an adverb can never be a complement.

The bus is **here.** [*Here* is an adverb, not a complement.]

A complement, like a subject, is never in a prepositional phrase.

> Sarah is reading the **dictionary.** [*Dictionary* is a complement; it completes the meaning begun by the subject and verb.]
>
> Sarah is thumbing through the dictionary. [*Dictionary* is in the phrase "through the dictionary"; it is not a complement.]
>
> Helen is an expert **skier** and **skater.** [*Skier* and *skater* are complements; they complete the meaning begun by the subject and verb.]
>
> Helen is in Colorado. [*Colorado* is in the phrase "in Colorado"; it is not a complement.]

● EXERCISE 1. Make three columns on your paper. Label the first *Subject*, the second *Verb*, and the third *Complement*. Write in the appropriate columns these three parts of the base of each sentence.

1. Gorillas are strange animals.
2. They look ferocious.
3. But they are actually shy and affectionate.
4. Of course, they can easily hurt a person.
5. Certainly one should treat a gorilla kindly.
6. Mistreated, he can be dangerous.
7. Scientists have changed the personalities of some animals.
8. They injected special serum into a cat and a mouse.
9. The mouse then chased the cat.
10. The cat seemed very afraid of the mouse.
11. The rhinoceros can be a dangerous animal.
12. Despite his bulk, he is actually very fast.
13. His charge can overturn a car.
14. Hunters fear an angry rhinoceros.
15. Sometimes the reason for his anger is trivial.

● EXERCISE 2. Make three columns on your paper. Label the first *Subject*, the second *Verb*, and the third *Complement*. Find the base of each sentence, and enter the parts in the appropriate columns. Remember that a complement is never in a prepositional phrase.

1. In Shakespeare's time, plays were very popular.
2. Many people attended performances at the Globe Theatre.
3. Shakespeare himself was one of the owners of the Globe.
4. The playhouse looked quite different from our theaters today.
5. It was an octagonal structure with galleries.
6. The galleries surrounded an open court with a large platform at one end.
7. The platform was the scene of most of the action in a play.
8. Many people in the audience did not have seats.
9. They watched the play from standing positions around the platform.
10. Of course, some of the wealthier people purchased seats in one of the galleries or on the stage itself.

● EXERCISE 3. Write five sentences using the following sentence bases. Add enough words to make *interesting* sentences.

SUBJECT	VERB	COMPLEMENT
boy	delivered	telegram
days	are	long
Jay	won	contest
runner	appeared	tired
Venus	is	planet

DIRECT AND INDIRECT OBJECTS

There are two kinds of complements which are affected by the action of the verb: the *direct object* and the *indirect object*.

6b. The *direct object* receives the action expressed by the verb or names the result of the action.

> Beowulf fought Grendel's **mother** in her cave at the bottom of the lake. [*Mother* is the direct object; it receives the action of the verb *fought.*]
>
> Beowulf's men had built a seaworthy **boat.** [*Boat* is the direct object; it names the result of the action *had built.*]

Direct objects follow action verbs only. They answer the questions *What?* or *Whom?* after an action verb. Beowulf, in the first sentence, fought whom? He fought Grendel's *mother;* therefore, ***mother*** **is** the direct object. In the second sentence, Beowulf's men had built what? They had built a *boat;* therefore, *boat* is the direct object.

● EXERCISE 4. Number your paper 1–10. Copy the action verb and its object in each sentence. Say the verb to yourself and ask *What?* or *Whom?* Remember that objects are complements and will never be in a prepositional phrase.

1. The Cherokees carve beautiful objects from oak and cherry woods.
2. We watched a performance of Shakespeare's *A Midsummer Night's Dream.*
3. The whole neighborhood decorated the twenty-foot Christmas tree.

4. Cyrano wore a hat with a large plume.
5. Will you answer the telephone?
6. During the summer months we studied French for an hour every day.
7. Did you invite him to the party?
8. The scientists discovered prehistoric animals buried in the snow.
9. Every evening my father and his friend play chess by the hour.
10. Has your sister set the date for her wedding?

6c. An *indirect object* tells *to whom* or *to what, for whom* or *for what* the action of the verb is done.

> The speaker gave **us** his opinion. [*Us* is the indirect object because it tells *to whom* the speaker gave his opinion.]
>
> My father bought our **boat** a new sail. [*Boat* is the indirect object because it tells *for what* father bought a new sail.]

Notice that the sentences above have a direct object as well as an indirect object. This is usually the case. The indirect object normally precedes the direct object.

> The guide gave **me** clear **directions.** [*Me* is the indirect object; *directions* is the direct object.]

The indirect object, like the direct object, is never in a prepositional phrase.

> She sent her **mother** some of her earnings. [*Mother* is an indirect object, telling *to whom* she sent some of her earnings.]

She sent some of her earnings to her mother. [*Mother* is not an indirect object; it is in the prepositional phrase "to her mother" and is the object of the preposition *to*.]

● EXERCISE 5. Number your paper 1–10. Copy the direct and indirect objects from the following sentences. Write *d.o.* after each direct object and *i.o.* after each indirect object. Not every sentence has an indirect object.

1. His father wired him the money he needed.
2. She directed me to the nearest drugstore.
3. Celia sent the treasurer a check to cover expenses.
4. The guide showed the tourists the best places to eat.
5. Someone deliberately gave us poor advice.
6. Unfortunately, we had lost two of our tickets.
7. We sent our relatives some handmade Christmas cards.
8. Ken answered his pen pal's letter promptly.
9. Becky and Amy made themselves costumes for Halloween.
10. In some European countries, you must have your passport with you to register in a hotel.

● REVIEW EXERCISE A. The following paragraphs contain sixteen direct objects and four indirect objects. Number your paper 1–13. After the proper number, write the objects which appear in the corresponding sentences. Label direct objects *d.o.* and indirect objects *i.o.*

1. Authorities often give us advice which goes unheeded. 2. Consider the public's reaction to seat belts. 3. The National Safety Council has shown the public the need for seat belts, but far too many people still

do not have them in their cars. 4. Many owners of cars with seat belts do not use them.

5. In 1949 Nash Motor Company installed seat belts in its cars, but the motorists tore them out. 6. Ford Motor Company had a similar experience. 7. Ford equipped its cars with seat belts, and its sales dropped appreciably. 8. A safety campaign in 1956 achieved only partial success. 9. The general public did not show any real concern, but some special groups, such as police departments and insurance companies, did respond to the campaign. 10. Even after that campaign, however, less than two percent of American drivers were using seat belts.

11. Today we can see an increase in the public's interest. 12. Statistical reports offer us undeniable proof of the value of seat belts. 13. At long last John Q. Public may buy himself a seat belt and use it.

DIAGRAMING DIRECT AND INDIRECT OBJECTS

All complements except the indirect object are diagramed on the main horizontal line with the subject and the verb as part of the sentence base. The direct object is diagramed on the horizontal line with a vertical line preceding it. The vertical line stops at the horizontal line to distinguish it from the line separating the subject and the verb.

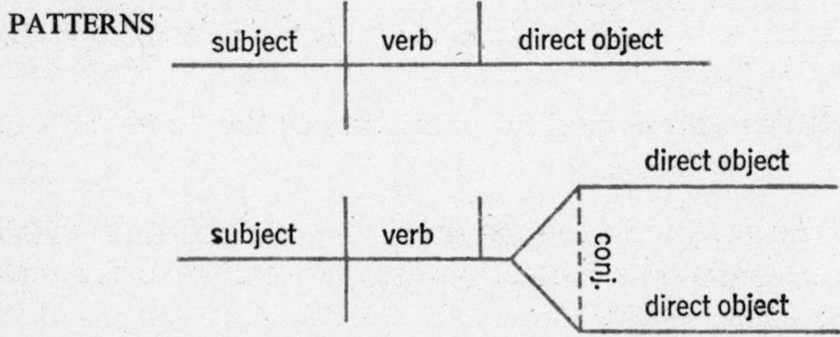

EXAMPLES 1. The rain cleaned the street.

2. We sold lemonade and cookies.

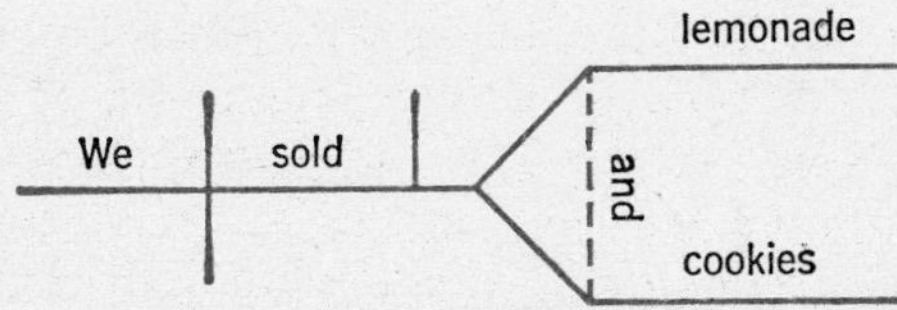

● EXERCISE 6. Diagram the following sentences, which contain direct objects. Use a ruler and leave plenty of space between diagrams.

1. We completed our assignment.
2. The quarterback made the touchdown.
3. The distinguished conductor directed his own composition.
4. Our class collects leaves and rocks.
5. The audience saw a serious one-act play and two amusing skits.
6. The school of fish paid no attention to the diver.
7. I have heard programs from Germany on my shortwave set.
8. Denise read several articles on surfboarding and water skiing.
9. A few people still plant corn by the light of the moon.
10. We grow orchids and chrysanthemums in our greenhouse.

To diagram an indirect object, write it on a short horizontal line below the verb. Connect it to the verb by a slanted line.

PATTERNS

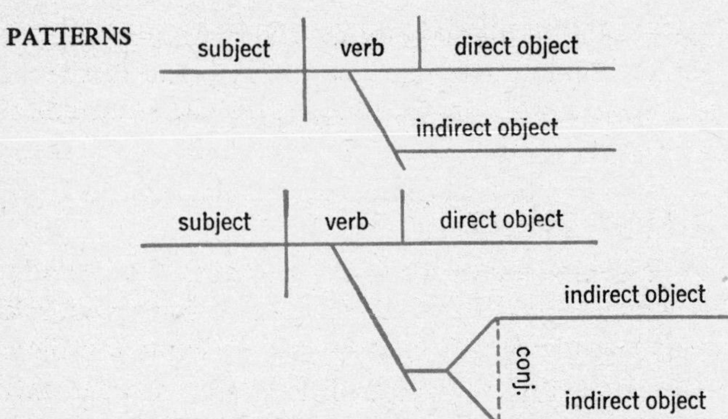

EXAMPLES 1. The artist showed me his painting.

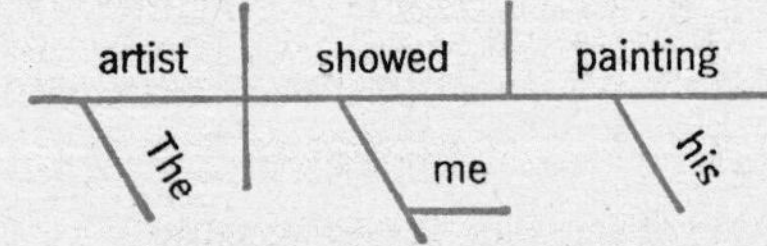

2. The company gave Jan and John summer jobs.

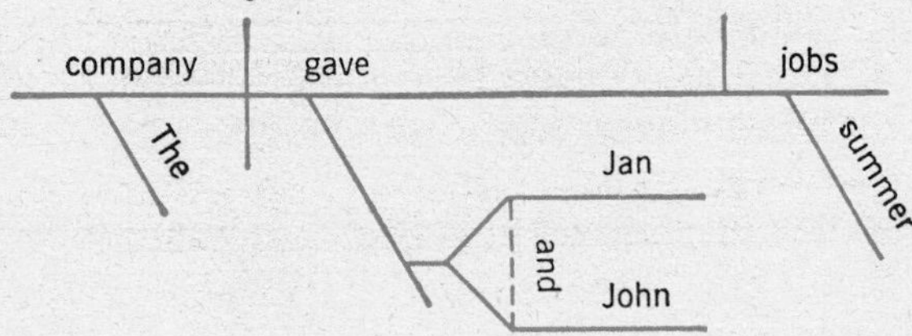

● EXERCISE 7. Diagram the following sentences. Not every sentence has an indirect object.

1. The lifeguard gave us lessons.
2. Don's brother taught him the rules.
3. The cashier handed the children balloons.
4. The judges awarded Jean and Ralph the prizes.
5. Snow gives motorists and pedestrians trouble.
6. At the dime store we bought Japanese lanterns.
7. The policeman sold my parents tickets to the ball.

8. Arnold built a doghouse for his two puppies.
9. Mr. Thompson lent Charles his binoculars.
10. Have you given your report on the pyramids of Egypt?

SUBJECT COMPLEMENTS

Sometimes a complement completes the meaning by explaining or describing the subject. Such a complement is called a *subject complement.* While the direct and the indirect object can follow action verbs only, the subject complement can follow linking verbs only. (If you need to review the list of linking verbs, turn to page 52.)

6d. A *subject complement* is a word which follows a linking verb and refers to (explains or describes) the subject.

> Mr. Fuller is a **teacher.** [*Teacher* follows the linking verb *is;* it explains something about *Mr. Fuller.*]
>
> We are the **ones.** [*Ones* follows the linking verb *are;* it refers to the subject *we.*]
>
> A lemon tastes **sour.** [*Sour* follows the linking verb *tastes;* it describes *lemon*—sour lemon.]
>
> The weather looked **good.** [*Good* follows the linking verb *looked;* it describes *weather.*]

Nouns, pronouns, and adjectives can serve as subject complements.

Predicate Nominatives and Predicate Adjectives

There are two kinds of subject complements—*predicate nominatives* and *predicate adjectives.*

(1) If the subject complement is a noun or a pronoun, it is called a *predicate nominative.*

EXAMPLES Tuesday is my **birthday.** [*Birthday* is a predicate nominative. It is a noun referring to the subject *Tuesday.*]

He is **one** of the best players. [*One* is a predicate nominative. It is a pronoun referring to the subject *he.*]

Like subjects and objects, predicate nominatives never appear in a prepositional phrase.

The result was a **declaration** of war. [The predicate nominative is *declaration,* not *war,* because *war* is part of a prepositional phrase.]

(2) If the subject complement is an adjective, it is called a *predicate adjective.* A predicate adjective modifies the subject.

EXAMPLES An atomic engine is very **powerful.** [*Powerful* is a predicate adjective modifying the subject *engine.*]

This ground looks **swampy.** [*Swampy* is a predicate adjective modifying the subject *ground.*]

● EXERCISE 8. Copy the linking verb and the subject complement from each of the following sentences. If the complement is a predicate nominative (noun or pronoun), write *p.n.* after it. If it is a predicate adjective, write *p.a.* after it.

1. My glasses are dirty.
2. "I am the one who called you," the boy said.
3. Monticello, near Charlottesville, Virginia, is one proof of Thomas Jefferson's versatility.

4. The French Embassy appeared especially busy today.
5. Mr. Tomlinson seems happy with the results of the election.
6. The patient felt heavy to the stretcher-bearers.
7. Antarctica was the scene of intensive investigation during the last International Geophysical Year..
8. The clown's makeup became a mask behind which he hid all of his sorrow.
9. Some words, like *cavern* and *meander*, sound especially melodious.
10. While the mountain lion looked around for food, the young fawn remained perfectly still.

Some verbs, like *look*, *grow*, and *feel*, may be used as either linking verbs or action verbs. They are followed by a predicate nominative or a predicate adjective only when they are used as linking verbs. They are followed by objects only when they are used as action verbs.

LINKING VERB The pitcher **felt happy.** [*Happy* is a predicate adjective after the linking verb *felt.*]

ACTION VERB The pitcher **felt** the **ball.** [*Ball* is a direct object after the action verb *felt.*]

● EXERCISE 9. Six of the sentences in this exercise contain a subject complement—predicate nominative or predicate adjective. If a sentence has a subject complement, copy the complement after the proper number; if not, leave the space blank after the number.

1. After the guests had left, the house seemed very lonely.
2. Seals grow very playful before feeding time.

3. The injured man felt his right leg.
4. The fossil bones discovered by the divers were those of a gigantic bird which once lived in Florida.
5. At first the drums sounded loud.
6. The employer looked carefully at all the applications.
7. Roots of plants grow toward water.
8. The chemistry student looked dumbfounded when he discovered that he had accidentally concocted an explosive.
9. The dictionary is a valuable source for many kinds of information.
10. A picture of the Lake District was on the cover of our literature book.

● REVIEW EXERCISE B. Number your paper 1–12. List after the proper number the subject complement (complements) in each sentence. Be sure your words follow a linking verb and refer to the verb's subject.

1. Many members of the gourd family are popular with amateur gardeners.
2. Some fruits of gourd plants taste sweet, but others seem bitter.
3. Still others, including the decorative gourds sold in curio shops, are not edible at all.
4. The watermelon is a very popular gourd.
5. After selecting a watermelon, we want to see whether it looks ripe inside.
6. If the seeds are black and the flesh is a rich pink, the melon will be good.
7. Nothing could be better.
8. The squash is a less popular member of the gourd family.
9. The pumpkin, a close relative of the squash, long ago became an American favorite.

10. To some people, squash looks strange.
11. Some people will eat acorn squash but will not touch crookneck squash, which is very nutritious.
12. Perhaps someday squash will be a treat like pumpkin pie.

DIAGRAMING SUBJECT COMPLEMENTS

A subject complement is diagramed somewhat like a direct object. But the short vertical line separating it from the verb is slanted toward the subject to show that the complement refers to the subject.

PATTERNS

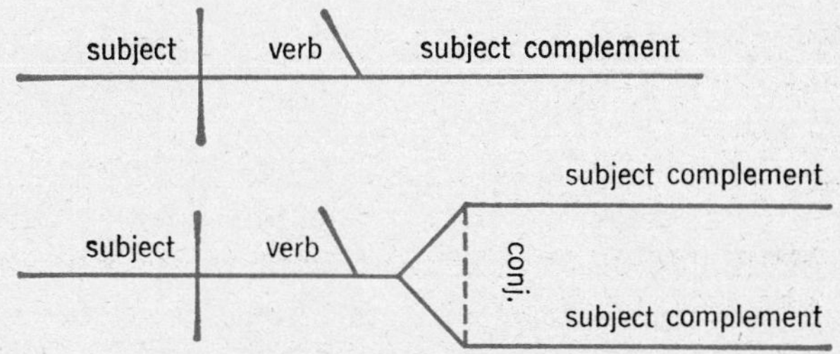

EXAMPLES 1. The dancers are graceful.

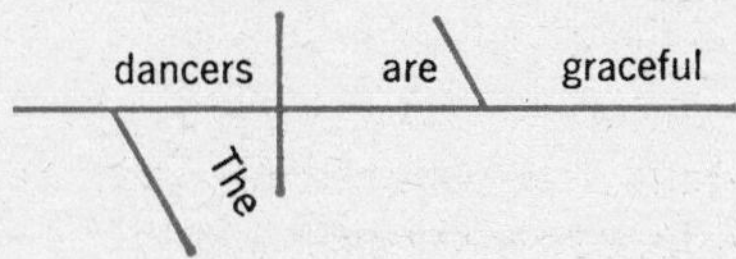

2. The contestants are Joan and Dean.

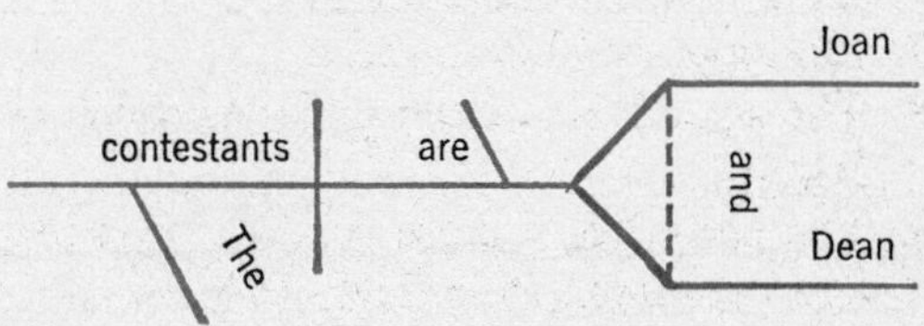

● EXERCISE 10. Diagram the following sentences.

1. The lights were dim.
2. Who are they?
3. The boys became lifeguards.
4. The cave was cold and damp.
5. Our speaker was a teacher and a writer.
6. We felt qualified for the job.
7. One of the most daring explorers of the sixteenth century was Sir Francis Drake.
8. The chimpanzees seem happy in their new environment.
9. My shoes looked worn and dusty after the long walk.
10. John Donne was a famous poet and a great preacher.

● REVIEW EXERCISE C. List the verbs in each of the following sentences. Before each verb, write the number of its sentence. If a verb has one or more objects, write the objects after it. If it is a linking verb, write the subject complement after it. Then write what kind each object or subject complement is: direct object (*d.o.*); indirect object (*i.o.*); predicate adjective (*p.a.*); predicate nominative (*p.n.*).

EXAMPLE 1. I have never seen a bald eagle, but its picture is very common.
1. *have seen, bald eagle d.o.*
1. *is, common p.a.*

1. On one side of a quarter, you will find a bald eagle with outspread wings.
2. The bald eagle is our national symbol.
3. Because bald eagles steal fish from other birds, many people would prefer another symbol.
4. Benjamin Franklin was one of those people.
5. The bald eagle has many good qualities.

6. It is a native of North America, and it looks far nobler than many birds.
7. Its strength seems enormous, and its eyesight is phenomenal.
8. From a distance of three miles, a bald eagle can spot a fish floating on the water.
9. It is one of the few animals that takes only one mate during a lifetime.
10. These are only a few of its good traits.
11. They give the bald eagle some claim to our affection.
12. The bald eagle was once common in many sections of our country, but it has become a fairly rare bird.
13. Today we find bald eagles principally in Florida and Alaska.
14. Certainly we must offer them protection.

● REVIEW EXERCISE D. Diagram the following sentences.

1. The lifeguard gave the rescued boy artificial respiration.
2. We then deposited our money at the bank.
3. You seem very cheerful today.
4. His mother was a leading ballerina with a famous ballet troupe.
5. Don and Maria acted the parts of Romeo and Juliet.
6. The origin of the gypsies remains a great mystery.
7. The girls made themselves bracelets and necklaces for the dress rehearsal.
8. Two of the most important canals in the world are the Suez Canal and the Panama Canal.
9. We proudly displayed our best paintings along the sidewalk.
10. The clown's shoes were long and wide.

● Review exercise E. Fill the blanks in the following paragraph with words which will make a funny or ridiculous story. Copy on your paper the words that you want in the blanks. After each word, write what kind of complement it is: *p.n.*, *p.a.*, *d.o.*, or *i.o.*

Yesterday I looked out my window and thought I saw a ——. But when I got outside I realized that it was a ——. It looked —— and ——. It gave —— a ——. Then I became —— and ran back inside. When I opened the —— fifteen minutes later, it was still there. Finally I decided that it was not ——. I went back outside and offered it a ——. Now it follows me wherever I go.

CHAPTER 7

The Kinds of Sentence Structure

Simple, Compound, Complex, and Compound-Complex Sentences

In Chapter 1 you learned that sentences may be classified according to their purpose: *declarative*, *interrogative*, *imperative*, and *exclamatory*. Another way to classify sentences is according to their construction, the kind and number of their clauses. In this chapter you will study the four kinds of sentences that result from this classification: *simple*, *compound*, *complex*, and *compound-complex*.

THE SIMPLE SENTENCE

From your study of clauses in Chapter 5, you will remember that a clause is a sentence part which contains a verb and its subject. An independent clause expresses a complete thought and may stand alone. A subordinate clause does not express a complete thought and cannot stand alone. When an independent clause stands alone with no other clauses attached to it, it is called a simple sentence.

7a. A *simple sentence* has one independent clause and no subordinate clauses.

In the examples below, the subjects and verbs are printed in heavy type. Notice that a simple sentence may have a compound subject (sentence 2) or a compound verb (sentence 3) or both (sentence 4).

EXAMPLES The hair **stylist gave** Marilyn a new hairdo.

Alaska and **Hawaii are** the newest states in the Union. [compound subject: *Alaska* and *Hawaii*]

Lawrence caught the ball but then **dropped** it. [compound verb: *caught* but *dropped*]

The **astronomer** and his **assistant studied** the heavens and **wrote** reports on their findings. [compound subject: *astronomer* and *assistant;* compound verb: *studied* and *wrote*]

● EXERCISE 1. After the proper number, copy the subjects and the verbs from the following simple sentences. Some of the sentences have compound subjects and verbs.

EXAMPLE 1. The first baseball games were quite different from those of today.

1. *games, were*

1. No system or set of rules governed baseball in the early days.
2. Young men in knickers gathered in lots near the town hall.
3. They used barrel staves for bats.
4. Sometimes stumps or posts served as bases.

5. The number of bases depended on the amount of space available.
6. The first college game was played in 1859 and was won by Amherst College.
7. According to the rules for this first college game, the game ended, not after nine innings, but after the scoring of seventy-five runs by one team.
8. The War Between the States made baseball popular and spread a knowledge of the rules and practices of the game throughout the United States.
9. Soldiers waiting for battle and prisoners waiting for the war to end staged baseball games to break the monotony.
10. After the war, the men, remembering the excitement of the game, continued to play it.

THE COMPOUND SENTENCE

Sometimes two or more independent clauses appear in the same sentence without any subordinate clauses. Such a sentence is called a *compound sentence.*

7b. A *compound sentence* has two or more independent clauses but no subordinate clauses.

The independent clauses are usually joined by coordinating conjunctions: *and*, *but*, *or*, *nor*, *for*.

EXAMPLES **Thad prepared the slides,** and **Jeff examined them under the microscope.** [two independent clauses joined by the conjunction *and*]

The train stopped at the station, but **no one got off.** [two independent clauses joined by the conjunction *but*]

7
a-b

> **The whistle blew, the drums rolled, and the crowd cheered.** [three independent clauses, the last two joined by the conjunction *and*]

● EXERCISE 2. Number your paper 1–10. After each number, write the subject and verb of the first independent clause, the coordinating conjunction, and the subject and verb of the next clause. Insert a comma before the conjunction. Underline subjects once and verbs twice.

EXAMPLE 1. A director of a theater-in-the-round visited our class, and we listened to his humorous stories for almost an hour.

1. *director visited, and we listened*

1. Many strange situations develop backstage during a performance, but the audience usually does not know about them.
2. Audiences at theaters-in-the-round contribute to the headaches of the directors, for they are seated very close to the stage.
3. Members of the audience sometimes use stage ash trays, or they hang their coats on the actors' coat racks.
4. Sometimes these actions are overlooked by the stagehands, and the results can be very unfortunate for the actors.
5. On one occasion the main clue in a mystery play depended on three cigarette butts in an ash tray, but the audience used the ash tray during intermission.
6. During the scene after the intermission, the detective counted fifteen cigarette butts instead of three, but he covered his surprise.

7. A director is not always able to predict the reactions of the audience, nor can he always control the audience.
8. During the performance of another mystery drama, a lady sitting in the front row associated herself too much with the action of the play, for at one point, leaping up on the stage, she tackled the killer.
9. The workers in charge of properties are usually alert and efficient, but they do sometimes make mistakes.
10. In the most dramatic scene of one production of *Romeo and Juliet*, the female lead prepared to kill herself with a dagger, but unfortunately there was no dagger for her to use.

Distinguishing Between Compound Sentences and Simple Sentences with Compound Subjects or Verbs

Although it consists of two or more subjects joined by a conjunction, a compound subject is still one subject. A compound verb is still one verb. A simple sentence, which has only one subject and one verb, is still a simple sentence even when its subject or verb is compound. Do not confuse a simple sentence containing a compound subject or a compound verb with a compound sentence, which has a subject and verb in each of its independent clauses.

SIMPLE SENTENCE	Bill and Joe increased their speed and passed the other runners. [compound subject and verb]
COMPOUND SENTENCE	Bill led half the way, and then Joe took the lead.

● EXERCISE 3. Number your paper 1–10. Copy the subjects and verbs in the following sentences. Underline subjects once and verbs twice. Then write *S.* if the sentence is a simple sentence or *Cd.* if it is a compound sentence.

EXAMPLES 1. Many men have followed the tracks of the abominable snowmen and have published reports on their findings.

1. *men have followed, have published* *S.*

2. Some believe in the existence of the snowmen, and others call the snowmen fakes.

2. *some believe, others call* *Cd.*

1. The snowmen supposedly inhabit the Himalaya Mountains, and they are usually called yetis by the natives of the Himalayan area.
2. Snowmen have been known for centuries in legend and literature, but their existence has never been proved.
3. According to accounts, the Sherpa tribesmen of the lower Himalayas often hear the strange whistle of the yetis at night, and, on going outside in the morning, they find yeti tracks in the snow.
4. One explorer found a so-called yeti hand and offered it as evidence of the snowmen's existence.
5. Other kinds of evidence, such as yeti scalps, have been offered, but many of these things have been proved fakes.
6. Some people have reported encounters with the yetis and have described their appearance.
7. The yeti supposedly resembles a large monkey or ape, and he has a large pointed head with sunken eyes.

8. He is covered with grayish hair, but the hair is definitely not like animal fur.
9. Many of the reports about the snowmen are probably hoaxes, but others come from men of unquestionable honesty.
10. Perhaps someday explorers or Sherpas will capture one of the yetis, and then scientists will unravel the mystery of the abominable snowmen.

DIAGRAMING COMPOUND SENTENCES

If you can diagram a simple sentence, then you can easily learn to diagram a compound sentence, for the independent clauses in a compound sentence are diagramed like simple sentences. The second clause is diagramed below the first and is joined to it by a coordinating conjunction diagramed as shown. The coordinating conjunction is placed on the horizontal line.

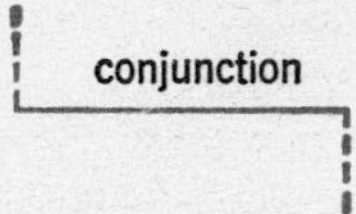

EXAMPLE The quarterback threw a good pass, but the end did not catch it.

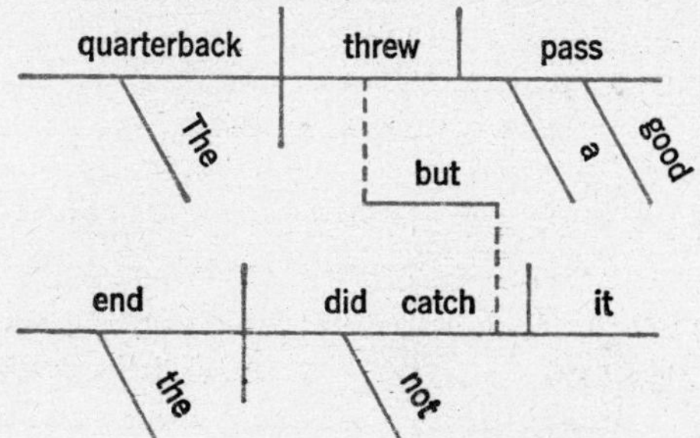

● EXERCISE 4. Diagram the following compound sentences.

1. I want a motorboat, but Jan prefers a sailboat.
2. The bus stopped at the restaurant, and everyone got off.
3. Our club is very small, but it is growing.
4. Shall we meet you at the station, or will you take a taxi?
5. In Arizona the temperature is often high, but the humidity always remains low.

THE COMPLEX SENTENCE

Like a compound sentence, a complex sentence contains more than one clause. But unlike the compound sentence, the complex sentence has at least one subordinate clause.

7c. A *complex sentence* has one independent clause and one or more subordinate clauses.

A subordinate clause may be an adjective clause (see page 101) or an adverb clause (see page 106).

Adjective clauses begin with a relative pronoun: *who, whom, whose, which, that.* Adverb clauses begin with subordinating conjunctions: *after, although, because, if, until, when,* etc.

In the examples below, the subordinate clauses are printed in heavy type.

EXAMPLE **When an important government official dies,** flags are flown at half-mast.

One independent clause flags are flown at half-mast
Subordinate clause When an important government official dies

EXAMPLE Some of the men **who took part in the mutiny on the British ship *Bounty*** settled Pitcairn Island.

One independent clause Some of the men settled Pitcairn Island

Subordinate clause who took part in the mutiny on the British ship *Bounty*

EXAMPLE **Since the ballads that have come down to us are usually sad,** ballad singers often dress in black or other somber colors.

One independent clause ballad singers often dress in black or other somber colors

Two subordinate clauses Since the ballads are usually sad that have come down to us

● EXERCISE 5. Copy the following complex sentences. Draw one line under each independent clause and two lines under each subordinate clause. Circle subordinating conjunctions and relative pronouns. Be prepared to name the subject and the verb in each clause. A sentence may have more than one subordinate clause.

EXAMPLES 1. Antarctica is a continent which is almost twice the size of the United States.

1. *Antarctica is a continent (which) is almost twice the size of the United States.*

2. Although many early voyagers searched for this southern continent, it remained undiscovered until 1820.

2. *(Although) many early voyagers searched for this southern continent, it remained undiscovered until 1820.*

1. Antarctica appeared on many maps before it was actually discovered.
2. Most of the facts that we have about Antarctica were supplied by explorers of the twentieth century.
3. Richard E. Byrd is but one of the men who made expeditions to Antarctica.
4. As explorations progressed, many amazing facts were learned.
5. Scientists discovered several areas that contained ice layers six thousand feet thick.
6. Geologists who were sent to Antarctica discovered some valuable mineral deposits which might be used when the world's supply of minerals runs low.
7. When scientists have finished their study of Antarctica's weather, they may be able to tell us a great deal about our own weather.
8. Although little plant or animal life exists there, a group of zoologists were able to study the penguin and the sea gull.
9. While the men were setting up their stations in Antarctica, the penguins became very friendly.
10. Because Antarctica is largely covered with ice, the men on the expeditions faced many dangers.

DIAGRAMING COMPLEX SENTENCES

The subordinate clause in the complex sentence is diagramed beneath the independent clause. A dotted line is then drawn from the word that is modified in the independent clause to the verb (for an adverb clause) or the relative pronoun (for an adjective clause) in the subordinate clause. If the subordinate clause is an adverb clause, the subordinating conjunction is written on the dotted line.

We had lunch in the student cafeteria when we visited the college. [complex sentence containing an adverb clause]

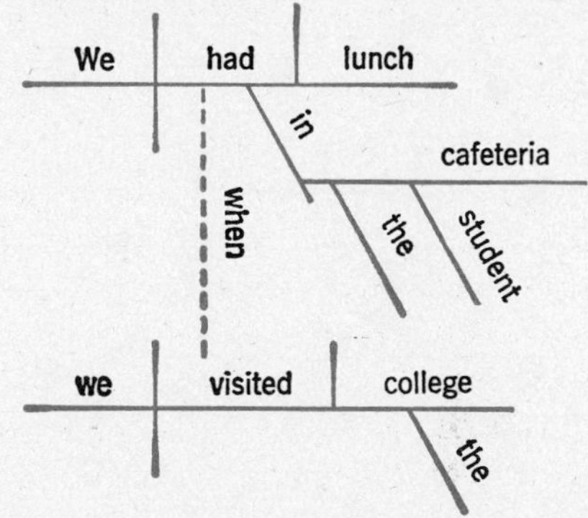

Blair has a ring which belonged to her great-grandmother. [complex sentence containing an adjective clause]

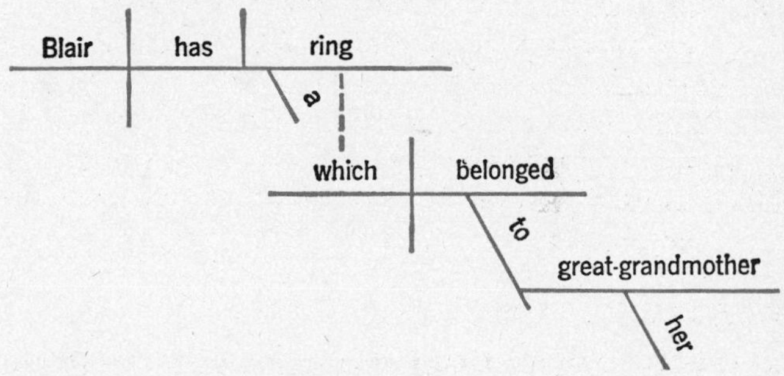

● EXERCISE 6. **Diagram the following complex sentences.**

1. People who visit Holland in the spring see vast fields of tulips.
2. When we stood beside the Washington Monument, we felt very small.

3. The rocket will be launched if the weather remains good.
4. Aeneas was one of the few who escaped from Troy.
5. Alexander the Great, who conquered most of the known world, died at the age of thirty-three.

THE COMPOUND–COMPLEX SENTENCE

A compound-complex sentence, as the name suggests, is a combination of the compound sentence and the complex sentence. Like a compound sentence, it has at least two independent clauses; like a complex sentence, it has at least one subordinate clause.

7d. A *compound-complex sentence* has two or more independent clauses and one or more subordinate clauses.

EXAMPLE Blaine began painting only two years ago, but he has already been asked to hang one of his paintings at the art exhibit that is scheduled for next month.

Two independent clauses Blaine began painting only two years ago, but he has already been asked to hang one of his paintings at the art exhibit

Subordinate clause that is scheduled for next month

● EXERCISE 7. The following sentences are compound-complex. Copy each clause separately, and after the clause, write *independent* or *subordinate.*

1. When we returned from camp, we were very tired, but we had many pleasant experiences to remember long afterward.

2. On our way up to the camp, which is built around a lake in the mountains, we sang songs, and some of the counselors entertained us with stories about past summers at the camp.
3. The minute that the bus stopped at the campsite, we all climbed hurriedly out, for we were anxious to see our cabins.
4. Some cabins were in the woods, and because they were shaded by many trees, they were cool.
5. We were all pleased with our accommodations, and we set to work immediately to find names for our cabins so that we would really feel at home.
6. Later in the day, a committee came around to judge the names, and from the many good ones that were tacked above the cabin doors, the committee finally chose "Linger Longer" as the best name.

● REVIEW EXERCISE. Number your paper 1–20. Identify the kinds of sentences—simple, compound, complex, or compound-complex—in the following paragraphs. Use the abbreviations *S.*, *Cd.*, *Cx.*, and *Cd.-Cx.*

1. A person who is just learning to skin dive usually begins in water that is somewhere between twenty-five and fifty feet deep. 2. At this depth there is no danger from pressure, and there is an abundance of fish and plant life. 3. After the person has been diving in shallow water for several weeks or months, he may go on to deeper water. 4. Below one hundred feet there is the problem of pressure, and one must be especially careful to avoid the hazards of deep diving.

5. One of the most common hazards that threaten the deep diver is caisson disease, or "the bends." 6. Nitrogen builds up in his bloodstream when he dives below one hundred feet. 7. If, when the diver is ready to surface, he ascends too quickly, the nitrogen

expands and then forms bubbles in his bloodstream and body tissues. 8. The nitrogen bubbles cause extreme pain. 9. If the case is very severe, the person may die, but the effects of caisson disease are not usually that serious. 10. Fortunately, a cure was discovered in the late nineteenth century. 11. When a person is put back under pressure, the nitrogen bubbles dissolve, and the person no longer feels pain. 12. Now a recompression chamber is used for a diver who suffers from the bends.

13. Another hazard of deep diving is nitrogen narcosis. 14. The nitrogen that the diver breathes is under pressure and consequently has a strange effect on the brain. 15. When a diver is suffering from nitrogen narcosis, he acts very much like a drunk man. 16. He may do many ridiculous things. 17. On one occasion a diver who was suffering from nitrogen narcosis began to play golf underwater. 18. He used fish for his clubs. 19. Luckily he did not choose a shark for one of his clubs, or the story would not be funny. 20. Like caisson disease, nitrogen narcosis can be fatal to the unwary diver.

PART TWO

Usage

CHAPTER 8

Making Subjects and Verbs Agree

Agreement in Number

Certain words in a sentence are closely related. The verb is closely related to its subject. A pronoun is closely related to the noun it stands for. Such closely related words have matching forms. When the related words are correctly matched, we say that they agree. They may agree in *number*. Rule 8a below explains the meaning of *number*.

SINGULAR AND PLURAL NUMBER

8a. **When a word refers to one person, place, thing, or idea, it is *singular* in number. When it refers to more than one, it is *plural* in number.**

SINGULAR	book, woman, fox, one, I, he
PLURAL	books, women, foxes, many, we, they

● EXERCISE 1. Number your paper 1–20. After each number, write *S* if the word is singular and *P* if it is plural.

1. athletes
2. job
3. foods
4. patios
5. him
6. problem
7. patients
8. feet
9. morning
10. beliefs
11. them
12. strength
13. policeman
14. costume
15. passersby
16. us
17. this
18. gases
19. friendliness
20. cities

● EXERCISE 2. *Oral Drill.* Read the following expressions aloud. Tell whether each is singular or plural.

1. the lion yawns
2. the cubs play
3. we listen
4. no one stays
5. the refugees land
6. he wins
7. the flower blooms
8. I am
9. they have
10. the actors practice
11. the play opens
12. everyone goes
13. the curtain rises
14. all applaud

8b. A verb agrees with its subject in number.

(1) Singular subjects take singular verbs.

EXAMPLES The **candle burns** slowly.

The **car comes** to a sudden stop.

On its return trip the **plane** always **flies** at a low altitude.

[The singular subjects *candle*, *car*, and *plane* take the singular verbs *burns*, *comes*, and *flies*.]

(2) Plural subjects take plural verbs.

EXAMPLES The **candles burn** slowly.

The **prisoners walk** in the exercise yard.

Again and again the **dolphins leap** playfully.

[The plural subjects *candles*, *prisoners*, and *dolphins* take the plural verbs *burn*, *walk*, and *leap*.]

Generally, subjects ending in *s* are plural (*candles*, *prisoners*, *dolphins*) and verbs ending in *s* are singular (*burns*, *comes*, *flies*). The verb *be* is a special case. In the present tense the form *am* agrees with the subject *I;* the form *is* agrees with *he*, *she*, *it*, and all singular nouns; and the form *are* agrees with all other subjects. In the past tense the form *was* agrees with *I*, *he*, *she*, *it*, and all singular nouns; and the form *were* agrees with *you* and all other subjects.

I am	you are	I was	we were
he is	they are	she was	they were
John is	the boys are	Linda was	the girls were

● EXERCISE 3. After the proper number, write the word from the parentheses which agrees with the given subject.

1. this (costs, cost)
2. plants (grows, grow)
3. the batter (swings, swing)
4. we (considers, consider)
5. the men (was, were)
6. he (asks, ask)
7. these (needs, need)
8. those colors (seems, seem)
9. that (lasts, last)
10. days (passes, pass)
11. water (flows, flow)
12. the troop (salutes, salute)
13. they (plays, play)
14. time (heals, heal)

PREPOSITIONAL PHRASES BETWEEN SUBJECT AND VERB

Students often commit agreement errors because they mistake words in prepositional phrases for the subjects of verbs.

WRONG The many lights on the Christmas tree makes it look very festive. [*Lights*, not *tree*, is the subject.]

RIGHT The many **lights** on the Christmas tree **make** it look very festive.

8c. The number of a subject is not changed by a prepositional phrase following the subject.

Remember that a word in a prepositional phrase can never be the subject of a verb. If a sentence confuses you, imagine that the prepositional phrase is enclosed by parentheses, and go directly from the subject to the verb.

The **silence** (in the halls) **is** unusual.

● EXERCISE 4. *Oral Drill.* Read each of the following sentences aloud, stressing the italicized words. Be able to tell whether the subject and verb are singular or plural.

1. Many dogwood *trees* on my street *are* in bloom.
2. His *paper* on communicable diseases *lacks* examples.
3. Your *response* to the questions *gives* the psychologist important information.
4. The *scientists* at Cape Kennedy *work* many extra hours during a launch.

5. Some *students* in the class *volunteer* for outside assignments.
6. *One* of the tests *shows* a flaw in the computer.
7. The *owner* of the factories *asks* for weekly reports from his managers.
8. The *chimes* in the tower *play* every hour.
9. The *temperature* inside the caverns *stays* fifty degrees all year long.
10. A good *book* on minerals *costs* very little.

● EXERCISE 5. Number your paper 1–10. After the proper number, write the subject and then the correct form of the verb. Remember that the subject is never in a prepositional phrase.

1. Many tourists from America (goes, go) to Holland during April or May.
2. The flowers in Holland (reaches, reach) their peak at this time of the year.
3. One of the most beautiful sights imaginable (is, are) the long expanse of flowers from Haarlem to Leiden.
4. For mile after mile a solid carpet of brilliant colors (greets, greet) the eye.
5. Strangely enough, the flowers in this section (is, are) grown for their bulbs rather than for their blossoms.
6. When the flowers are in full bloom, workers in the field (clips, clip) them.
7. Then very large garlands of brilliant blooms (is, are) made and sold to passing travelers.
8. Visitors in a Dutch city (is, are) usually amazed to find flowers everywhere.
9. Many homes in the Netherlands (is, are) filled with vases of flowers.

10. Even the cars of the Dutch often (contains, contain) little vases of flowers.

INDEFINITE PRONOUNS

You should learn the number of all the indefinite pronouns so that you will not make an error in agreement when an indefinite pronoun is the subject of the sentence.

8d. **The following common pronouns are singular and take singular verbs: *each, either, neither, one, everyone, everybody, no one, nobody, anyone, anybody, someone, somebody.***

As the examples below indicate, pronouns like *each* and *one* are frequently followed by prepositional phrases. Remember that the verb agrees with the subject of the sentence, not a word in a prepositional phrase.

EXAMPLES **One** of the chairs **looks** comfortable.
Either of the answers **is** correct.
Everyone with passports **was** accepted.
Neither of these **satisfies** me.
Someone in the stands **has been waving** at us.

8e. **The following common pronouns are plural and take plural verbs: *both, few, several, many.***

EXAMPLES **Many** of the students **walk** to school.
Both of the pies **are** good.
Few of the guests **know** of the robbery.
Several of our states **have** Indian names.

8f. The words *some, any, none, all,* and *most* may be either singular or plural.

This rule is an exception to rule 8c because the number of the subjects *some, any, none, all,* and *most* is determined by a word in the prepositional phrase that follows the subject. If the word the subject refers to is singular, the subject is singular; if the word is plural, the subject is plural.

EXAMPLES **All** of the fans **rush** home.
All of my work **is** finished.
Some of the birds **have** gone south.
Some of the glare **has** disappeared.

● EXERCISE 6. Number your paper 1–15. After the proper number, write the subject and then the correct one of the verbs in parentheses.

1. All of the flags (is, are) on display.
2. Each of the flags (has, have) a special design.
3. Someone in this group (is, are) a litterbug.
4. Some of our artists (uses, use) strange materials.
5. One of our modern painters (places, place) real buttons on the canvas where the buttons on clothes would be.
6. Many of them (works, work) with sawdust, nails, and sand.
7. One of the paintings by Jackson Pollock (measures, measure) three feet by eighteen feet.
8. Several of the group (objects, object) to the increase in dues.
9. Both of the movies (looks, look) exciting.
10. Everyone in the first two rows (wins, win) a prize.
11. Several in the crowd (was, were) admitted early.

12. No one except the officials (is, are) allowed on the field.
13. Few of the lakes (freezes, freeze) in the winter.
14. Neither of us (knows, know) the way.
15. Somebody with binoculars (is, are) watching us.

● REVIEW EXERCISE A. Number your paper 1–20. Read each sentence aloud. If the verb agrees with the subject, write *C* after the proper number on your paper. If the verb does not agree with the subject, write the correct form of the verb on your paper. Some sentences have more than one verb for you to consider.

EXAMPLES 1. One of the men practice medicine.
1. *practices*
2. Both of them work hard.
2. *C*

1. Each of the math problems take twenty minutes to solve.
2. Some of the spectators are already leaving the stadium.
3. Neither of your arguments are very convincing.
4. All of the time-outs have been used.
5. No one on the highways are exempt from traffic rules.
6. Several of the group has taken the trip before.
7. No one without a dictionary is prepared for this assignment.
8. Most of the storm damage was reported along the coast.
9. Only one of the contestants are qualified.
10. Planes with radar are taking off in spite of the fog.
11. Several of the spark plugs need to be replaced.
12. Few of the airlines offers direct service between those cities.

13. All of the trouble between the settlers and the natives were the result of a misunderstanding.
14. Many at the picnic plan to go swimming.
15. Either of those answers are correct.
16. All of the money has been spent.
17. Both of the boys in the family has red hair.
18. Some fans in the grandstand was shouting at the umpire.
19. Everybody in the stadium were amazed at the play.
20. Any one of those three routes are better than the one that goes through the city.

COMPOUND SUBJECTS

Most compound subjects which are joined by *and* name more than one person or thing; therefore, they are plural and require a plural verb.

8g. Subjects joined by *and* are plural and take a plural verb.

EXAMPLES **Galileo** and **Copernicus** **were** famous astronomers. [two were]

Last year a **library** and a **museum** **were** built in our town. [two things were built]

If the items in a compound subject actually refer to only one person or are thought of as one thing, the verb is singular.

EXAMPLES The **captain** and **quarterback** of the team **is** the speaker. [One person is both the captain and the quarterback.]

Chicken and **dumplings** **is** a favorite Southern dish. [Chicken and dumplings is one dish.]

● EXERCISE 7. Number your paper 1–10. Decide whether the subjects of the following sentences are singular or plural. Choose the correct verb form from the parentheses, and write it after the proper number.

1. March and April (is, are) windy months.
2. My father and the mechanic (is, are) discussing the bill.
3. The Yankees and the Indians (plays, play) today.
4. Cake and ice cream (is, are) my favorite dessert.
5. (Does, Do) Carla and Jean take dancing lessons?
6. (Is, Are) the knives and forks in the drawer?
7. Mathematics and science (requires, require) many hours of study.
8. (Here's, Here are) our star and winner of the meet.
9. Where (is, are) the bread and the honey?
10. (Does, Do) an Austrian and a German speak the same language?

8h. Singular subjects joined by *or* or *nor* take a singular verb.

EXAMPLES A **pen or a pencil is** needed for this test.
Neither Miami nor Jacksonville is the capital of Florida.

● EXERCISE 8. Number your paper 1–10. From each pair of verbs in parentheses, choose the one that agrees with the subject.

1. Either lemonade or iced tea (tastes, taste) good on a hot day.
2. French and Italian (is, are) Romance languages.
3. Neither Cathy nor Roger (has, have) ever been to California.
4. Both the mango fruit and the pistachio nut (comes, come) from trees of the sumac family.

5. The length of words (affects, affect) our ability to spell them.
6. Neither California nor Texas (is, are) as big as Alaska.
7. The French horn, the bassoon, and the oboe (is, are) wind instruments.
8. Either a drum major or a drum majorette (leads, lead) the band onto the field.
9. (Does, Do) Toni or Kay know the way to the amusement park?
10. (Has, Have) the president and the vice-president of the class been chosen?

8i. When a singular subject and a plural subject are joined by *or* or *nor*, the verb agrees with the nearer subject.

EXAMPLES Either John or his **friends are** mistaken. [The verb agrees with the nearer subject, *friends*.]

Neither the players nor the **director was** on time to rehearsal. [The verb agrees with the nearer subject, *director*.]

Whenever possible, avoid this kind of construction. The second sentence can be rewritten to read: *Both the players and the director were late to rehearsal.*

● EXERCISE 9. Number your paper 1–10. From each pair of verbs in parentheses, choose the one that agrees with the subject.

1. Either the mayor or the city treasurer (is, are) scheduled to speak at the ceremony.
2. Harry and his brother (has, have) a valuable record collection.
3. The Smiths or their cousin (owns, own) the new house on Elm Street.

4. Neither John nor Herbert (has, have) the slightest interest in table manners.
5. Neither the pitcher nor his teammates (was, were) expecting the batter to knock the ball out of the park.
6. Bread and milk (is, are) a digestible combination.
7. Either the violinists or the clarinet player (has, have) rehearsed the wrong selection.
8. The cellists and the bassoon player (is, are) waiting to find out who is mistaken.
9. The violas or the harp (is, are) out of tune.
10. Neither the audience nor the members of the orchestra (seems, seem) satisfied with the performance.

● REVIEW EXERCISE B. Number your paper 1–20. Then choose from the parentheses the verb that agrees with the subject and write it on your paper.

1. Everyone in the class (wants, want) to learn more about astronomy.
2. The stars and the planets (has, have) always fascinated men.
3. A legend from ancient times (says, say) that two Chinese astronomers were put to death in 2137 B.C. for failing to predict an eclipse correctly.
4. The astronomer in many cases (was, were) also versed in astrology.
5. The court astronomer or astrologer (was, were) highly honored in Babylonia, China, and Europe.
6. Of course, one of the astronomers' main duties (was, were) to predict future events.
7. Many of their records (presents, present) interesting information about the astronomy of the time.
8. Today, almost everyone in the world (is, are) interested in space projects.

9. Yet few of us (knows, know) that in 1609 Johannes Kepler published plans for a voyage to the moon.
10. His ideas on space travel (is, are) found in a book called *Somnium.*
11. Many of the problems of space flight (is, are) suggested in Kepler's work.
12. The effects of gravity (is, are) treated at length by Kepler.
13. Kepler's voyagers in space (faces, face) an unbelievable ordeal during takeoff because they must leave the ground at a speed of 12,000 miles per hour.
14. The scientific problems of a moon voyage (is, are) presented by Kepler, but not the practical means for making the trip.
15. Neither he nor other astronomers of his time (was, were) familiar with aeronautics.
16. However, many attempts at flight (was, were) being made.
17. The writings of Kepler (shows, show) that he looked forward to the day when man would fly in "celestial boats with golden sails."
18. Few in Kepler's time (was, were) as farsighted as he.
19. Many men in Kepler's time (was, were) sure that he was a sorcerer, not a scientist.
20. Today, scientists all over the world (is, are) working to find a practical way of reaching the moon.

OTHER PROBLEMS IN AGREEMENT

8j. Collective nouns may be either singular or plural.

A collective noun names a group of persons or things and is singular in form.

COMMON COLLECTIVE NOUNS

group	family	army	audience
flock	club	fleet	crowd
herd	class	troop	assembly
swarm	team	squadron	public

A collective noun takes a plural verb when the noun refers to the individual parts or members of the group. A collective noun takes a singular verb when the noun refers to the group as a unit.

EXAMPLES The **family were arguing** about where to spend the next vacation. [*Family* here refers to individuals acting separately.]

The **family was** dominated by the grandparents. [*Family* here refers to a group considered as a unit.]

● EXERCISE 10. Select five collective nouns. Use each noun as the subject of two sentences. In the first, the subject should be singular in meaning and call for a singular verb. In the second, the subject should be plural in meaning and have a plural verb.

8k. A verb agrees with its subject, not its predicate nominative.

Sometimes the subject and the predicate nominative of a sentence are of different numbers. In this case the verb agrees with the subject, not the predicate nominative. The subject usually comes *before* the linking verb and the predicate nominative *after*.

EXAMPLES The happiest **time** of my life **was** my boyhood days.

My boyhood **days were** the happiest time of my life.

81. When the subject follows the verb as in sentences beginning with *there* and *here* and in questions, be careful to determine the subject and make sure that the verb agrees with it.

EXAMPLES Here **is** my **seat.**
Here **are** our **seats.**
There **is** an exciting **ride** at the fair.
There **are** exciting **rides** at the fair.
Where **are** the **programs?**

Be especially careful when you use the contractions *here's* and *there's*. These contain the verb *is* and should be used only with singular subjects.

WRONG There's the books.
RIGHT There **are** the **books.**

● EXERCISE 11. Number your paper 1–10. Write the correct verb for each sentence.

1. One problem of commuters (is, are) traffic jams.
2. (Here's, Here are) my crayons.
3. The class (does, do) not agree among themselves on this issue.
4. Here (is, are) the dresses I mentioned to you.
5. (Where's, Where are) the paintings for the exhibit?
6. (Here's, Here are) the winners!
7. My present to you (is, are) these books.
8. (There's, There are) two of my favorite relatives.
9. His herd of cattle (was, were) larger than ours.
10. Here (is, are) the funniest comedians on television.

DON'T AND DOESN'T

Don't and *doesn't* (contractions of *do not* and *does not*) are often used incorrectly.

8m. ***Don't* and *doesn't* must agree with their subjects.**

Use *don't* with plural subjects and with the pronouns *I* and *you.*

EXAMPLES These **gloves don't** fit.
You don't speak clearly.
I don't like that record.

Use *doesn't* with other subjects.

EXAMPLES The **music box doesn't** play.
He doesn't walk enough.
It doesn't matter.

The most frequent errors in the use of *don't* and *doesn't* are made when *don't* is incorrectly used with *he, she,* or *it.* Remember always to use *doesn't* with these singular subjects: *he doesn't, she doesn't, it doesn't.*

● EXERCISE 12. *Oral Drill.* Read the following sentences aloud. By getting your ears accustomed to the correct use of *doesn't* and *don't,* you will get into the habit of using these two words correctly.

1. It doesn't look like a serious wound.
2. He doesn't feel well.
3. One doesn't interrupt a speaker.
4. She doesn't know what to do.
5. Doesn't the television set work?

● EXERCISE 13. Number your paper 1–10. Copy the subject of each sentence and write the correct verb (*doesn't* or *don't*).

1. He —— like rhubarb pie.
2. This —— worry him.

3. One —— get his own way all the time.
4. Many people still —— have enough to eat.
5. My mother —— know how to paint.
6. These —— appeal to him.
7. —— everyone have a pen?
8. They —— need new watches.
9. Cold weather usually —— continue into June.
10. —— anyone in the class know about Julius Caesar?

● REVIEW EXERCISE C. Eight of the following sentences are correct, while twelve have mistakes in agreement. If a sentence is correct, write *C* beside the proper number. If the sentence is incorrect, write the correct form of the incorrect verb.

1. Neither of our school libraries have the books I need.
2. Every one of my friends own a library card.
3. The only library in some communities is in the school.
4. Either the librarian or his assistant helps us continually.
5. Where's the books on sports?
6. The most famous library of ancient times were in Alexandria.
7. Where's the list of recommended books?
8. The modern circulating library, which lends books to readers, was developed in the monasteries of the Middle Ages.
9. Collections of documents in a special room of a palace was probably the earliest kind of library.
10. Today there's more than six thousand circulating libraries in this country.
11. Neither the Alexandrian library nor the Roman libraries were circulating libraries.

12. One of the world's great libraries are the Library of Congress.
13. A magnificent collection of recordings are located there.
14. A shortage of money and librarians handicaps some libraries.
15. There's some books in the library that no one ever reads.
16. Many of our public libraries were financed by Andrew Carnegie.
17. The wide sale of paperback books show that people like to read.
18. How many books is there in your library?
19. From the state library come several of the books we are using.
20. The cost of books have been rising.

CHAPTER 9

Correct Use of Verbs

Principal Parts of Regular and Irregular Verbs

Few errors in speaking or writing are more obvious than verb errors. The student who writes *she done it*, *he begun*, *they drownded*, or *it bursted* immediately tags himself as a person who does not know the standard usages of his language.

THE PRINCIPAL PARTS OF A VERB

A verb shows the time of an action. This expression of time by the verb is called *tense*. To express different times a verb has different tenses, and the tenses are formed from four *principal parts* of the verb.

9a. **The principal parts of a verb are the *infinitive*, the *present participle*, the *past*, and the *past participle*.**

From these four principal parts all the tenses of our language are formed. The four principal parts of *sing* are *sing* (infinitive), *singing* (present participle), *sang* (past), and *sung* (past participle). Notice in the following sentences how the four principal parts are used to express time.

> I **sing** in the school glee club.
> We **are singing** at the Music Festival tonight.
> We **sang** for last year's Music Festival.
> We **have sung** all over the state.

Here are the principal parts of two familiar verbs:

INFINITIVE	PRESENT PARTICIPLE	PAST	PAST PARTICIPLE
work	working	worked	(have) worked
eat	eating	ate	(have) eaten

Notice that the present participle always ends in *–ing*. The past participle is the form used with *has*, *have*, or *had*.

THE SIX TENSES

Through the use of the four principal parts of the verb and various helping verbs, you can form six tenses for the verb. When you give the forms of a verb in its six tenses, you are *conjugating* a verb.

CONJUGATION OF WRITE

Principal parts: write, writing, wrote, (have) written.

PRESENT TENSE

Singular	*Plural*
I write	we write
you write	you write
he writes	they write

9a

PAST TENSE

Singular	*Plural*
I wrote	we wrote
you wrote	you wrote
he wrote	they wrote

FUTURE TENSE

Singular	*Plural*
I will (shall) write	we will (shall) write
you will write	you will write
he will write	they will write

PRESENT PERFECT TENSE

Singular	*Plural*
I have written	we have written
you have written	you have written
he has written	they have written

PAST PERFECT TENSE

Singular	*Plural*
I had written	we had written
you had written	you had written
he had written	they had written

FUTURE PERFECT TENSE

Singular	*Plural*
I will (shall) have written	we will (shall) have written
you will have written	you will have written
he will have written	they will have written

● EXERCISE 1. Conjugate orally the following verbs: *run*, *want*, *throw*, and *fall*.

REGULAR VERBS

9b. A regular verb forms its past and past participle by adding *-ed* or *-d* to the present form.[1]

INFINITIVE	PRESENT PARTICIPLE	PAST	PAST PARTICIPLE
follow	following	followed	(have) followed
date	dating	dated	(have) dated

Few mistakes are made with the present forms of regular verbs. Occasionally mistakes do occur in the use of the past and the past participle. These errors usually result from careless pronunciation. The mistakes in pronunciation may be of two kinds: (1) adding an extra syllable—*drownded* for *drowned, attackted* for *attacked;* (2) not pronouncing the normal *-ed* ending—*ask* for *asked, was suppose* for *was supposed.*

● EXERCISE 2. The following sentences contain regular verbs which are often mispronounced. Read *aloud* every sentence, stressing the pronunciation of the italicized words, especially their endings.

1. The troops *attacked* the fort.
2. Our speaker was *supposed* to arrive at six o'clock.
3. How many people have *drowned* in this lake?
4. Jay has often *used* his knowledge of geography.
5. The accident *happened* at night.
6. The brave man *risked* his life to save his son.
7. You *asked* me that question yesterday.
8. This shampoo has *lasted* for a long time.
9. Australian tribesmen have sometimes *tracked* criminals for the police.
10. Have you *washed* the car?

[1] Some regular verbs have an alternate past form ending in *t: burn, burned* or *burnt; learn, learned* or *learnt.*

● EXERCISE 3. *Oral Drill.* Use the following verbs in sentences. Put each verb in the past tense or use the past participle and the helping verb *have* or *has.*

1. use
2. experience
3. ask
4. attempt
5. suppose
6. drown
7. attack
8. travel
9. rent
10. play

IRREGULAR VERBS

9c. An irregular verb forms its past tense in some other way than a regular verb.

Irregular verbs form their past and past participle in several ways:

1. by a vowel change: *drink, drank,* (have) *drunk*
2. by a consonant change: *make, made,* (have) *made*
3. by a vowel and consonant change: *bring, brought,* (have) *brought*
4. by no change: *burst, burst,* (have) *burst.*

If you do not know the principal parts of irregular verbs, you may make errors like this:

WRONG He has drank all his milk. [*Drunk*, not *drank*, is the past participle.]

To avoid errors, memorize the principal parts of irregular verbs. Include *have* with the past participle because a helping verb is always used with the past participle. When memorizing the parts of the verb, say *choose, choosing, chose, have chosen.*

IRREGULAR VERBS FREQUENTLY MISUSED

INFINITIVE	PRESENT PARTICIPLE	PAST	PAST PARTICIPLE
1. begin	beginning	began	(have) begun
2. blow	blowing	blew	(have) blown
3. break	breaking	broke	(have) broken
4. bring	bringing	brought	(have) brought
5. burst	bursting	burst	(have) burst
6. choose	choosing	chose	(have) chosen
7. come	coming	came	(have) come
8. do	doing	did	(have) done
9. drink	drinking	drank	(have) drunk
10. drive	driving	drove	(have) driven
11. eat	eating	ate	(have) eaten
12. fall	falling	fell	(have) fallen
13. freeze	freezing	froze	(have) frozen
14. give	giving	gave	(have) given
15. go	going	went	(have) gone
16. know	knowing	knew	(have) known
17. lie	lying	lay	(have) lain
18. ride	riding	rode	(have) ridden
19. ring	ringing	rang	(have) rung
20. rise	rising	rose	(have) risen
21. run	running	ran	(have) run
22. see	seeing	saw	(have) seen
23. set	setting	set	(have) set
24. shrink	shrinking	shrank	(have) shrunk
25. sing	singing	sang	(have) sung
26. sit	sitting	sat	(have) sat
27. speak	speaking	spoke	(have) spoken
28. steal	stealing	stole	(have) stolen
29. swim	swimming	swam	(have) swum
30. take	taking	took	(have) taken
31. throw	throwing	threw	(have) thrown
32. write	writing	wrote	(have) written

Caution: Be careful not to confuse irregular verbs with regular ones. Never say *blowed, knowed, throwed,* or *bursted.*

● EXERCISE 4. Your teacher or a classmate may dictate to you the infinitive form of the thirty-two irregular verbs listed above. Write the past and the past participle on your paper.

Merely knowing the principal parts of the irregular verbs is not enough. You should practice using them in sentence patterns. The following patterns will help you practice usage of the irregular verbs.

> Today I **bring** a lunch.
> Yesterday I **brought** a lunch.
> Often I **have brought** a lunch.

● EXERCISE 5. Number your paper 1–20. Choose the correct one of the two verbs in parentheses and write it after the corresponding number. If there are two verbs in a sentence, write them on the same line. When your paper has been corrected, read each sentence *aloud* several times, stressing the correct verb.

1. Students have often (chose, chosen) "The Devil and Daniel Webster" as their favorite short story.
2. The story was (wrote, written) by Stephen Vincent Benét.
3. Jabez Stone, a New Hampshire farmer, had (gave, given) up all hope of succeeding.
4. Everything he (did, done) turned out wrong.
5. Then one day the devil (came, come) to see Jabez Stone.
6. The devil (knowed, knew) that Jabez had (spoke, spoken) some fatal words.

7. In desperation Jabez had one day (began, begun) to curse his luck.
8. He had even (went, gone) so far as to say that he would do anything to improve his lot.
9. The devil had (saw, seen) his chance and so had (came, come) to make a bargain with Jabez.
10. At first Jabez had (shrank, shrunk) from the devil's proposal.
11. Then he had (took, taken) another look at his poor farm.
12. After the devil had (spoke, spoken) to him for a short while, Jabez (did, done) what the devil asked.
13. He (throwed, threw) his soul away in exchange for a period of prosperity.
14. Circumstances had (drove, driven) Jabez to agree to a bargain that he would soon regret.
15. For several years Jabez (drank, drunk) from the well of prosperity.
16. But all too soon the well (ran, run) dry.
17. The time (came, come) for Jabez to deliver his soul to the devil.
18. Before his time was up, though, Jabez had (rode, ridden) to see Daniel Webster, the great lawyer.
19. Luckily, Daniel Webster had (took, taken) Jabez' case.
20. You should read Benét's short story to see what Daniel Webster (did, done).

● EXERCISE 6. Number your paper 1–20. After the proper number, write the past or the past participle form of the verb given at the beginning of each sentence.

1. *blow* The little boy —— too much air into the balloon.
2. *burst* It finally ——.

3. *fall* Only a few large meteorites have ever —— to earth.
4. *throw* The umpire has —— the angry player out of the game.
5. *swim* Marilyn Bell, a seventeen-year-old, —— the English Channel.
6. *steal* Imagine what someone who is not familiar with baseball thinks when he hears that Bobby Richardson has —— home!
7. *ring* Last night the bell in the deserted old tower —— for the first time in twenty-eight years.
8. *bring* The same mailman has —— our mail for ten years.
9. *speak* Have you —— to your classmates about the problem?
10. *choose* The judges —— a German shepherd as the winner.
11. *break* Roger Bannister's four-minute-mile record has been —— many times.
12. *blow* The wind has —— steadily from the north.
13. *know* The spy —— that his mission was dangerous.
14. *ride* The messenger had —— for many miles before he found the right man.
15. *freeze* Our milk has —— solid.
16. *see* Have you —— the movie at the Tower Theater?
17. *write* The poet discovered that he had —— a masterpiece.
18. *begin* After we —— the climb, we realized that the mountain was very steep.
19. *drink* We —— too much lemonade.
20. *burst* After she had —— out laughing, she suddenly realized that her friend was quite serious.

● REVIEW EXERCISE A. Write two original sentences using correctly the past and past participle forms of each verb that you missed in Exercises 5 and 6. After your sentences have been checked for accuracy, read them aloud until you feel that you have mastered the troublesome verbs.

● REVIEW EXERCISE B. Number your paper 1–20. Write *C* after the number of each correct sentence. Write the correct form of the verb after the number of each incorrect sentence.

EXAMPLES 1. We drove up to the house.
1. *C*
2. He come upon something unusual.
2. *came*

1. After we had rode around for a while, we stopped in front of an old house.
2. We saw that the grass had not been cut in months.
3. Many of the windows had been broke by storms.
4. We blowed our horn, but no one appeared to greet us.
5. Then we saw that a "for sale" sign in the front yard had fallen over.
6. We knowed then the house was vacant.
7. We begun to feel afraid the moment we got out of the car.
8. No one had spoken as we walked toward the house.
9. Although we had seen no one, we knocked on the door just to make sure.
10. When no one answered, we give the door a push.
11. The door burst open, and we went inside.
12. We were glad we had brought a flashlight.
13. After we had went through all the rooms downstairs, we decided to take a look upstairs.

14. Nothing at all unusual happen until we started up the stairs.
15. Suddenly we heard a noise that sounded as if a hundred balloons had bursted right in front of us.
16. We freezed in our tracks.
17. Then a loud wailing began.
18. No one ask what to do next.
19. As we run out of the house, I turned my head.
20. Coming down the stairs was a little boy who was grinning broadly at the scare he had gave four high school students.

Sit and Set

Study the principal parts of the verbs *sit* and *set.* Notice that *sit* changes to form the past tense, but *set* remains the same in the past and the past participle.

INFINITIVE	PRESENT PARTICIPLE	PAST	PAST PARTICIPLE
sit (to rest)	sitting	sat	(have) sat
set (to place)	setting	set	(have) set

Sit and *set* are verbs which are often confused. But you will not make mistakes with these two verbs if you remember two facts about them:

(1) *Sit* means "to rest in an upright, sitting position" while *set* means "to put or place (something)."

> Let's **sit** under the tree.
>
> Let's **set** the bookcase here.
>
> The tourists **sat** on benches.
>
> The children **set** the dishes on the table.
>
> We **had sat** down to eat when the telephone rang.
>
> We **have set** the reading lamp beside the couch.

(2) *Sit* is almost never followed by an object but *set* may often be.

> My father **sits** in the large chair. [no object]
> He **sets** the chair in the corner. [Sets what? *Chair* is the object.]
>
> The audience **sat** near the stage. [no object]
> The stagehand **set** a microphone near the performer. [Set what? *Microphone* is the object.]

● EXERCISE 7. *Oral Drill.* Read the following sentences aloud, paying particular attention to the meaning of *sit* and *set*. Pronounce each verb distinctly.

1. Let's sit here.
2. Look at the dog sitting on the porch.
3. Our teacher set a deadline for our term projects.
4. Have you set the clock?
5. I have always sat in the front row.
6. The natives set their goods at the side of the road.
7. He has set a high standard for his work.
8. The man sits by the window every day.
9. The referee is setting the ball on the fifty-yard line.
10. After I set the mop in the closet, I sat down to rest.

● EXERCISE 8. Number your paper 1–10. After the proper number, write the correct one of the two words in parentheses. If the verb you choose is a form of *set*, write its object after it.

EXAMPLE 1. The movers (sat, set) our table down gently.
1. *set, table*

1. We were (sitting, setting) outside watching the cloud formations.
2. Peggy (sat, set) her dictionary on her desk.

3. In the summer the owners of the restaurants (sat, set) their tables outdoors.
4. Have you ever (sat, set) at a sidewalk cafe and watched the people go by?
5. When the hermit needs supplies, he (sits, sets) a lantern in his window.
6. Wordsworth wrote a poem about a boy (sitting, setting) alone in a cemetery.
7. I like to (sit, set) up late, watching television.
8. The twins had not (sat, set) still for long before they were planning another trick.
9. The class had to (sit, set) still for ten minutes.
10. Where were you (sitting, setting)?

● EXERCISE 9. Use correctly each of the following verbs in sentences of your own.

1. sits
2. sets
3. was sitting
4. was setting
5. sat
6. set
7. have sat
8. have set
9. will set
10. will sit

Lie and Lay

Study the principal parts of *lie* and *lay*.

INFINITIVE	PRESENT PARTICIPLE	PAST	PAST PARTICIPLE
lie (to recline)	lying	lay	(have) lain
lay (to put)	laying	laid	(have) laid

Like *sit*, *lie*[1] has to do with resting and it has no object. *Lay* is like *set* because it means "to put something down" and because it may have an object.

[1] The verb *lie* meaning "to tell a falsehood" is a different word. Its past forms are regular: lie, lying, lied, lied.

The cows **are lying** in the shade. [no object]

The workmen **are laying** the foundations for the building. [*Are laying* what? *Foundations* is the object.]

The soldiers **lay** very still while the enemy passed by. [no object—*lay* here is the past tense of *lie*]

The soldiers **laid** a trap for the enemy. [*Laid* what? *Trap* is the object.]

The injured man **had lain** in the cave for weeks. [no object]

The boy **had laid** the newspaper next to his briefcase. [*Had laid* what? *Newspaper* is the object.]

● EXERCISE 10. *Oral Drill.* Read each of the following sentences aloud several times. Be able to explain why the verb is correct.

1. The delegates laid the groundwork for future conferences.
2. She lay in bed until eleven o'clock.
3. Don't lie in the sun too long!
4. You shouldn't lay your papers on the couch.
5. The lion had been lying in wait for an hour.
6. The senator laid his notes aside and spoke extemporaneously.
7. He had lain still for a few minutes.
8. He has laid his books on his desk.
9. Our cat lies on the radiator.
10. She lays the sharp knives on the top shelf.
11. The cook laid the meat on the grill.
12. The exhausted swimmer lay helpless on the sand.
13. Lie down for a few minutes until you feel better.
14. He laid his pen on the edge of the desk.

● EXERCISE 11. Number your paper 1–10. After the proper number, write the correct form of the proper verb (*lie–lay*) for each of these sentences.

1. My father always —— down for a few minutes before dinner.
2. Last night the musician —— his instrument down and joined in the dance.
3. The puppy —— very still as long as we petted him.
4. Because of the heat I have —— in the shade most of the day.
5. After they had —— the carpets in the new house, the owners moved in.
6. The ships were —— in the harbor.
7. The sheriff has been —— plans to catch the bank robber.
8. Have you ever —— in a hammock?
9. From where we ——, we could see the stars very clearly.
10. Whoever —— the brick for your barbecue pit did a good job.

● EXERCISE 12. Use correctly each of the following verbs or verb phrases in a sentence of your own.

1. lies
2. laid
3. was laying
4. has lain
5. lays
6. has been lying
7. lay (past tense of lie)
8. have laid
9. will lie
10. are lying

Rise and Raise

Study the principal parts of *rise* and *raise*.

INFINITIVE	PRESENT PARTICIPLE	PAST	PAST PARTICIPLE
rise (to go up)	rising	rose	(have) risen
raise (to lift up)	raising	raised	(have) raised

The verb *rise* means "to go up" or "to get up." *Rise* like *lie*, never has an object. *Raise*, which means "to lift up" or "to cause to rise," may, like *lay*, have an object.

> My neighbors **rise** very early in the morning. [no object]
>
> Every morning they **raise** their shades to let the sunlight in. [*Raise* what? *Shades* is the object.]
>
> The moon **rose** slowly last night. [no object]
>
> Last year Mr. Tucker **raised** corn and tomatoes in his garden. [*Raised* what? *Corn* and *tomatoes* are the objects.]
>
> The men **have risen** from their seats to show respect for the women. [no object]
>
> The wind **has raised** a cloud of dust. [*Has raised* what? *Cloud* is the object.]

● EXERCISE 13. *Oral Drill.* Repeat each of the following correct sentences aloud several times, stressing the italicized verbs and thinking of the meanings of the verbs.

1. The newsmen *rise* when the President enters the room.
2. The newsmen *raise* their hands to be recognized.
3. The reporter who was recognized *rose* to his feet.
4. He *has raised* an interesting question.
5. Another reporter *was rising.*
6. Several reporters *rose* at the same time.
7. Who *had risen* first?
8. He recognized the one who *rose* first.
9. The reporters *had raised* many questions.
10. Everyone *rises* as the President leaves.

● EXERCISE 14. Number your paper 1–10. After the proper number, write the correct one of the two verbs in parentheses. If the verb you choose is a form of *raise*, write its object after it.

1. The poet Longfellow wrote "The Tide (Rises, Raises), the Tide Falls."
2. When no one paid any attention to the man, he (rose, raised) his voice.
3. The audience (rose, raised) and gave a standing ovation to the singer.
4. At the beginning of the exercise, you (rise, raise) your arms above your head.
5. The hikers (rose, raised) refreshed after a good night's rest in their warm sleeping bags.
6. The temperature has (risen, raised) to an unprecedented high for this time of the year.
7. The announcement has (risen, raised) new hope for the lives of the missing men.
8. Hitler (rose, raised) to power in Germany during the 1930's.
9. At five o'clock our counselor shouted, "(Rise, Raise) and shine."
10. We may have (risen, raised), but we certainly did not shine.

● EXERCISE 15. Number your paper 1–10. After the proper number, write the form of *rise* or *raise* that you would use in each blank in the following paragraphs.

Yesterday we —— early to start our hike to the Chimneys. From our position at the foot of the Chimneys, the mountain looked as though it —— to the heavens.

But we had not —— at daybreak just to look at the high peak. We —— our supply packs to our backs and started the long climb up the mountain. With every step we took, the mountain seemed to —— that much higher. Finally, after several hours, we reached the summit and —— a special flag that we had brought for the occasion. When our friends at the foot of the mountain saw the flag ——, they knew that we had reached the top safely. They —— their arms and shouted.

Although we could not see them, we heard voices that seemed to —— from the valley below. Then we felt glad that we had —— early enough to climb to the top of the Chimneys.

● REVIEW EXERCISE C. Number your paper 1–20. Choose the correct verb from the two in parentheses and write it after the proper number. If a sentence has two verbs, write both of them on the same line in the order they occur. Be prepared to explain your choices in class.

1. The great plane (rose, raised) smoothly from the runway.
2. Everyone should (sit, set) still during the performance.
3. The trail (lay, laid) in front of us.
4. After the parade the band members were glad to (sit, set) down.
5. Zoroastrians (lie, lay) the bodies of their dead in a Tower of Silence.
6. The curtain (rises, raises) on a completely empty stage.
7. Majorca (lies, lays) off the southeastern coast of Spain.
8. To provide food for St. Nicholas' white horse, the children of Holland (sit, set) shoes stuffed with hay or grain on their windowsills.

9. Legend says that when the moon (rises, raises), vampires (rise, raise) from their coffins to perform their fearful deeds.
10. While Eddy is (sitting, setting) in the shade, Marilyn is (sitting, setting) the table for their picnic.
11. He would have (lain, laid) in bed all morning if we had not made him (rise, raise).
12. Smoke was (rising, raising) from the cabin's chimney as the old trapper (lay, laid) his plate and cup upon the table.
13. Last night the parents carefully (lay, laid) their children's presents under the tree.
14. In Antarctica, snow (lies, lays) on the ground all year.
15. The price of gasoline has (risen, raised) in the last month.
16. We had been (sitting, setting) on the porch watching the sun go down.
17. The stream has (risen, raised) so high that it has overflowed its banks.
18. The dignified businessman (rose, raised) his eyebrows when a man in overalls and a top hat (sat, set) down beside him.
19. Our dog (lay, laid) down in front of the door and refused to move.
20. Salaries had not (risen, raised) as much as the cost of living had.

CONSISTENCY OF TENSE

You should never shift tenses needlessly. When you are writing about events in the past tense, you should consistently use the past tense unless there is some reason for you to change tenses. You should not shift without reason to the present tense.

9d. Do not change needlessly from one tense to another.

WRONG After we were comfortable, we begin to do our homework. [*Were* is past tense and *begin* is present.]

RIGHT After we **were** comfortable, we **began** to do our homework. [Both *were* and *began* are in the past tense.]

WRONG Suddenly the great door opened, and an uninvited guest comes into the dining hall. [*Opened* is past tense and *comes* is present.]

RIGHT Suddenly the great door **opens,** and an uninvited guest **comes** into the dining hall. [Both *opens* and *comes* are in the present tense.]

● EXERCISE 16. Read the following paragraph, and decide what tense you should use to tell about the events. Prepare to read the paragraph aloud, making the verb tense consistent throughout.

I got back to camp somewhat later than usual last night. When I walk into my cabin, I thought something is strange. Everyone is in bed. "My roommates went to bed extremely early," I say to myself. But I soon forgot about my roommates' strange behavior and start getting ready for bed. After putting on my pajamas, I turn out the light. By this time I am ready for a good night's sleep. I think about my soft bed as I pulled back the bedspread. Then I lie down, but not for long. My soft bed had suddenly become a very hard bed. When I got up, I hear a very loud giggling from everyone in the cabin. My roommates had replaced my comfortable mattress with several hard boards.

● REVIEW EXERCISE D. Number your paper 1–20. Select from each sentence the correct one of the verb forms in parentheses and write it after the corresponding number on your paper.

1. After I (saw, seen) the movie, I read the book.
2. The inner tube (bursted, burst) when Howard put too much air in it.
3. The men always (sit, set) in the back row.
4. The people have (chose, chosen) a leader.
5. When the oxygen (run, ran) out, the diver was forced to surface.
6. We have (rode, ridden) the Ferris wheel five times.
7. The commander (rose, raised) a white flag over the fort.
8. The ship has (began, begun) to sink.
9. Dolphins have often (swam, swum) behind ships for many miles.
10. The mountain climbers (drank, drunk) some hot coffee.
11. His right shoulder is sore because he (lay, laid) on it all night.
12. In desperation, the quarterback (throwed, threw) a long pass.
13. No one (knowed, knew) how the feud had started.
14. Wars have always (took, taken) the lives of many creative men.
15. They have (broke, broken) the agreement.
16. The turtle has (shrank, shrunk) back into its shell.
17. Several horses have (fell, fallen) on the first turn.
18. A famous jewel was (stole, stolen) last night.
19. The telephone (rang, rung), but no one answered.
20. The policeman (blowed, blew) his whistle at the speeding motorist.

● REVIEW EXERCISE E. Number your paper 1–25. Write after the corresponding number the form of the verb at the left which correctly fills the blank in each sentence. In some instances you must choose the correct verb as well as the correct form.

begin	1. Snow —— to fall early this morning.
bring	2. Who —— you home last night?
eat	3. After I had —— five hamburgers, I was too full for dessert.
rise, raise	4. When prices ——, everyone complains.
come	5. My parents were asleep when I —— in.
sit, set	6. Please —— down for a while.
see	7. I —— an exhibit of his work last year.
rise, raise	8. By noon the fog had ——.
know	9. The firemen should have —— what to do.
lie, lay	10. Bob —— the frying pan on the hot coals.
run	11. We —— into several friends at the movies last night.
give	12. The boys had —— away our secret.
lay	13. Yesterday we —— the new linoleum in the kitchen.
freeze	14. You could have —— to death.
speak	15. Has Jean —— to you about the assignment?
swim	16. When we were children, we —— there often.
write	17. At least he could have —— a postcard.
lie, lay	18. You should have —— there until help came.
throw	19. I tried to find out who had —— the stone.

ring	20. The bell must have —— early.
shrink	21. My new sweater had —— when I washed it.
steal	22. The thieves had —— nothing of value.
ride	23. Unfortunately, I had never —— that horse.
take	24. She might have —— the children with her.
burst	25. As he crossed the waiting room, his suitcase —— open.

CHAPTER **10**

Correct Use of Pronouns

Nominative and Objective Cases

Nouns and pronouns have case. The case of a word depends on how the word is used in the sentence. For example, a word used as a subject is in the *nominative* case; a word used as an object is in the *objective* case; and a word used to show possession is in the *possessive* case.

The case of nouns presents no problem because a noun has the same form in the nominative and objective cases.

> The **man** [nominative] said he saw another **man** [objective] in the park.

The possessive case of a noun usually requires only the addition of an apostrophe and an *s*.

> The **man's** friend has arrived.

The case of personal pronouns, however, does present a problem because they change form in the different cases. To use these pronouns correctly, you must know their various case forms and when to use them.

THE CASE FORMS OF PERSONAL PRONOUNS

Study the following list of pronouns to see how their forms differ in the three cases.

NOMINATIVE CASE	OBJECTIVE CASE	POSSESSIVE CASE
	Singular	
I	me	my, mine
you	you	your, yours
he, she, it	him, her, it	his, her, hers, its
	Plural	
we	us	our, ours
you	you	your, yours
they	them	their, theirs

You can see that the pronouns *you* and *it* can cause few usage problems because their forms remain unchanged in the nominative and objective cases. The possessive case forms, which show ownership, sometimes present spelling problems. (See page 279.)

When *you* and *it* and the possessive pronouns are omitted from the above list, you have the following pronouns with different forms in the nominative and objective cases. Memorize the list for each case and remember which pronouns are nominative and which are objective.

NOMINATIVE CASE	OBJECTIVE CASE
I	me
he	him
she	her
we	us
they	them

The Nominative Case

10a. The subject of a verb is in the nominative case.

EXAMPLES **I** like music. [*I* is the subject of the verb *like.*]

He and **she** sold tickets. [*He* and *she* are the subjects of the verb *sold.*]

They called while **we** were away. [*They* is the subject of *called; we* is the subject of *were.*]

We boys work together. [You can avoid mistakes in this kind of sentence by recognizing that *We* is the subject and that *boys* is an appositive. When you omit the appositive, you can see that *We* is correct: *We* work together. (For an explanation of appositives, see page 247.)]

Pronoun usage errors occur most frequently when the subject is compound. It is very easy to say, "Dave and *me* study together" when you should say, "Dave and *I* study together." "Dave and I" is a compound subject. If you test the pronoun by itself with the verb, you can usually tell which form is correct.

WRONG Me study.
RIGHT **I** study. (Dave and I study.)

● EXERCISE 1. *Oral Drill.* Read the following sentences aloud stressing the italicized pronouns.

1. *He* and *she* collect Indian head pennies.
2. My grandfather and *I* are painting the boat.
3. Both *they* and *we* were frightened.

4. Did Sally or *she* answer the phone?
5. *We* girls are giving a fashion show.
6. *You* and *I* will stay behind.
7. Where are *he* and *she?*
8. My parents and *they* are good friends.
9. *He* and *I* deliver newspapers.
10. Do you and *he* like to fish?

● EXERCISE 2. Number your paper 1–10. Beside the proper number, write a pronoun which will correctly fill the blank. Use a variety of pronouns. Don't use *you* or *it*.

1. She and —— are officers in the club.
2. Our friends and —— want to learn to ski.
3. Neither —— nor Cynthia is here.
4. —— and Diane have pen pals in Austria.
5. Where are —— and —— going?
6. Everyone knows that —— students are proud of our school.
7. No one can say that —— and —— give up easily.
8. Have you or —— ever gone deep-sea fishing?
9. Both —— and —— have entered the contest.
10. Did —— or Stan see the lighthouse?

10b. A predicate nominative is in the nominative case.

A predicate nominative is a noun or pronoun completing the meaning of a linking verb. A pronoun used as a predicate nominative usually follows a form of the verb *be: am, is, are, was, were,* and verb phrases ending in *be* or *been,* such as *will be* and *has been.*

Read the following examples aloud, stressing the words in heavy type.

It may be **he** at the door. [*He* is a predicate nominative following the linking verb *may be*.]

The speakers are **he** and **I**. [*He* and *I* are predicate nominatives following the linking verb *are*.]

Do you think it was **they**? [*They* is a predicate nominative following the linking verb *was*.]

◆ USAGE NOTE You should understand two facts about English usage. First, some usages are acceptable in conversational English, but not in written English. Second, from time to time usage changes so that expressions that were once considered unacceptable may become acceptable. The application of rule 10b is an example of both these facts. The expressions *It's me*, *That's him*, *It was them*, etc., although they violate the rule and were once considered incorrect, have now become acceptable spoken English. In writing, however, standard usage still follows the rule except for *It's me*, which is always acceptable and almost never appears in writing anyway.

SPOKEN No one would believe it was her. (him, etc.)
WRITTEN No one would believe it was she. (he, etc.)

Of course, it would be correct to use *she* in speaking, even though *her* is acceptable.

In doing the exercises in this book, base your answers on the usage of written English.

● EXERCISE 3. Number your paper 1–10. Copy each linking verb and write the correct pronoun.

1. Everyone believed it was (him, he).
2. Many people think I am (she, her).
3. If it was (them, they), their parents will be angry.

4. It might have been (she, her) that he meant.
5. No one could tell that it was (we, us) boys.
6. It could have been (him, he), but I doubt it.
7. Our visitors could have been (them, they).
8. I knew it was (they, them) to whom he referred.
9. If it had been (her, she), I would have known her.
10. Is that Betty or (she, her)?

The Objective Case

10c. Direct and indirect objects of a verb are in the objective case.

EXAMPLES You surprised **us.** [*Us* is the object of the verb *surprised.*]

Our neighbor gave **him** and **me** a job. [*Him* and *me* are indirect objects; they tell *to whom* our neighbor gave a job.]

The ranger guided **us** boys to the camp. [*Us* is the object of the verb *guided.* It will help you if you recognize that *boys* is an appositive. When you omit the appositive, you can see that *us* is correct: The ranger guided *us* to the camp. (See page 247.)]

Most errors in the use of the objective case occur when the object is compound. You can often avoid making an error with a compound object by trying each pronoun separately with the verb.

The representative met (she, her) and (he, him).

WRONG The representative met she.
The representative met he.

RIGHT The representative met **her.**
The representative met **him.**
The representative met **her** and **him.**

● EXERCISE 4. *Oral Drill.* Read the following sentences aloud at least twice, stressing the italicized pronouns. When your ear becomes accustomed to the right sound of pronouns, you will be able to choose the correct forms more easily.

1. The hot chocolate burned Gail and *me.*
2. Frank showed *her* and Allen his home aquarium.
3. The dog followed *her* and *him* to school.
4. Did you expect *us* or *them?*
5. The beautician gave *her* and *me* a shampoo.
6. The president of the club called *us* girls to a special meeting.
7. Let's help Jerry and *him* with their chores.
8. Have you seen the Jacksons or *them?*
9. The mayor thanked you and *him.*
10. The cook made *us* boys a special dessert.

● EXERCISE 5. Number your paper 1–10. Supply correct pronouns for the blanks in these sentences; write the pronouns after the proper numbers. Be sure to use a variety of pronouns, but do not use *you* and *it.* When your answers have been checked, read aloud at least three times the corrected form of each sentence that you missed.

1. The group selected —— and —— as the king and queen of the festival.
2. We asked —— and Mr. Smith for help.
3. Lane finally found Mark and —— at the theater.
4. Do you believe Evans and ——?
5. My grandfather told —— boys what life was like when he was a boy.
6. Mother sent —— and —— for some ice cream.
7. A guide took my sister and —— through the museum.

8. Let's call Mel and ——.
9. Do you know —— or ——?
10. The storm frightened Paul and ——.

10d. The object of a preposition is in the objective case.

A prepositional phrase begins with a preposition and ends with an object, which is always a noun or pronoun. When the object is a pronoun, you must be careful to use the objective case. Below are prepositional phrases with the objects printed in heavy type.

with **me**	near **her**	except **them**
to **him**	by **us**	for **us**

Most errors in usage occur when the object of the preposition is compound. Notice that in the following prepositional phrases all pronouns are in the objective case.

about Dad and **me**	without **them** or **us**
near Gay and **her**	from Doug and **him**

● EXERCISE 6. *Oral Drill.* Read each of the following sentences several times, stressing the correct, italicized pronouns.

1. The safari continued without *him* and *me*.
2. Everyone except *us* counselors had left the camp.
3. We stood beside their families and *them* during the ceremony.
4. Do you have any suggestions for Jane or *me?*
5. The clowns talked to Claire and *him*.
6. Behind *us* boys was a playful bear cub.
7. Give this to either your father or *her*.
8. With the help of Mac and *him*, we built a fire.

9. The group sat in a circle around the Indians and *them* while they danced and sang.
10. There was a spelling bee between *us* and *them.*

● EXERCISE 7. Number your paper 1–10. After each number, write the prepositional phrase in the corresponding sentence, including in it a pronoun that will complete the phrase correctly. Use a variety of pronouns, but do not use *you* or *it.*

1. You can sell tickets to Walter and ——.
2. The big day for you and —— finally came.
3. The dog was walking behind Sally and ——.
4. Everyone except —— and Hazel was resting.
5. Without you and —— we're sure to lose the game.
6. When did you last speak to Sandy and ——?
7. Our team played against both Clarkson High and ——.
8. We were near you and —— when it happened.
9. "Between you and —— and the gatepost" is a familiar expression.
10. Do you have news about your brother and ——?

● REVIEW EXERCISE A. Number your paper 1–20. Opposite the proper number, write the pronoun in the parentheses that will make the sentence correct. After each answer, write an abbreviation showing how the pronoun is used: *subj., p.n., d.o., i.o., obj. prep.*

EXAMPLE 1. I saw (she, her) and Amy at the circus.
1. *her* *d.o.*

1. The speaker addressed (we, us) members of the graduating class.
2. Good citizenship medals were awarded to Gordon and (he, him).
3. The last performer was (she, her).

10d

4. When will you and (I, me) meet again?
5. The dogs barked at (he, him) and Neil.
6. (We, Us) girls voted for Mary.
7. The best speller in the class is (she, her).
8. We passed Bob and (they, them) on the road.
9. The organist at the restaurant played a special song for Jack and (she, her).
10. The guide showed the other tourists and (we, us) around the castle.
11. Catherine and (he, him) will perform next.
12. Did you give the presents to Ralph and (they, them)?
13. Ask your neighbor and (they, them) to the next meeting.
14. She sent Cathy and (I, me) beautiful scarves.
15. The one in the clown mask is (he, him).
16. The farmer gave (we, us) boys a bushel of peaches for our help.
17. The best students in the class are John and (she, her).
18. You and (they, them) may manage the hot dog stand at the school bazaar.
19. The next speaker will be either George or (I, me).
20. I wrote a theme about my grandmother and (he, him).

● REVIEW EXERCISE B. Write ten original sentences using correctly the following pronouns. After each sentence, identify the use of the pronoun or pronouns: *subj., p.n., d.o., i.o., obj. prep.*

1. you and I
2. you and me
3. his friend and he
4. his friend and him
5. him and her
6. Gail and they
7. us students
8. our parents and we
9. Larry and her
10. our teacher and us

● REVIEW EXERCISE C. Number your paper 1–20. After the proper number, write the correct one of the two pronouns in parentheses.

1. Kent and (he, him) are rehearsing their parts.
2. A special report was assigned to Beth and (I, me).
3. The judges will be you and (he, him).
4. The cast of the play includes two boys and (we, us).
5. When the curtain went up, everyone except Jim and (I, me) was on stage.
6. Have you heard from Carolyn or (she, her)?
7. He is teaching (we, us) beginners to swim.
8. It was (they, them) who called you.
9. That must have been (they, them).
10. The Jacksons and (we, us) watched the elaborate display of fireworks.
11. The company sent (he, him) and his wife to Argentina.
12. A friend painted a picture of Jan and (she, her).
13. Our neighbors lent (we, us) boys their cottage.
14. Neither Lawrence nor (she, her) speaks German.
15. The collection of elephant figurines belongs to Bill and (he, him).
16. The two girls in white are (they, them).
17. Do you remember Ginny and (I, me)?
18. Harold and (I, me) are visiting our grandparents.
19. It's only (we, us) girls.
20. Don't leave without (she, her) and Tracy.

CHAPTER **11**

Correct Use of Modifiers

Choice, Comparison, Placement

You know from your study of Chapters 2 and 3 that adjectives and adverbs are called modifiers. A modifier describes or makes more definite the meaning of another word. The adjective modifies a noun or a pronoun, and the adverb modifies a verb, an adjective, or another adverb. You also know from your study of Chapters 4 and 5 that phrases and clauses, as well as individual words, may be used as modifiers. This chapter will help you learn to use modifiers correctly and effectively.

GOOD AND WELL

11a. Distinguish between *good* and *well* as modifiers.

Use *good* to modify a noun or a pronoun. Never use *good* to modify a verb. Use *well* to modify a verb.

WRONG Dean swims good.
RIGHT Dean swims **well.**

WRONG The orchestra played very good.
RIGHT The orchestra played very **well.**

In the following examples, *good* is correct because it is a predicate adjective modifying the subject. Like all predicate adjectives, it follows a linking verb.

RIGHT The pie tastes especially **good.** [good pie]
RIGHT Over the microphone his voice sounds **good.** [good voice]

Well can also be used as an adjective when it refers to a person's health or appearance.

EXAMPLES Doug feels **well** today. [*Well* is a predicate adjective modifying the subject *Doug.*]
You look **well** in red. [*Well* is a predicate adjective modifying the subject *you.*]

● EXERCISE 1. *Oral Drill.* Read aloud each of the following sentences, stressing the italicized words. This exercise will train your ear and check your tendency to use *good* as the modifier of a verb.

1. Everyone did *well* on the test.
2. We work *well* together.
3. Do you sing as *well* as your sister does?
4. I can't water-ski very *well.*
5. How *well* can you write?
6. The pilot landed the plane *well.*
7. Everything was going *well* until the actor forgot his lines.
8. Our class pictures turned out *well.*
9. The second-string quarterback can pass as *well* as the starting quarterback.
10. The plans for the square dance are working out quite *well.*

● EXERCISE 2. Number your paper 1–10. If *good* or *well* is correctly used in a sentence, write + after the corresponding number. If *good* or *well* is not correctly used, write 0.

1. Father did not bowl as good as usual last night.
2. The plans sound good to me.
3. How good can he pass a football?
4. I don't know the new neighbors very well.
5. Although he has been sick, he looks well now.
6. I explained the situation as well as I could.
7. The team played very good.
8. Freshly baked bread smells good.
9. The work did not go so good as we had hoped.
10. How good the cake looks!

COMPARISON OF MODIFIERS

Adjectives and adverbs may be used in comparing two or more things.

Richard is **heavier** than Bob.
This is the **heaviest** box of the three.
Hazel spoke **more clearly** than Alice.
Of all the speakers, Hazel spoke **most clearly.**

When adjectives and adverbs are used to express comparison, they show degrees of comparison. They show the degree to which one word has a quality compared to another word having the same quality.

This building is **tall.**
This building is **taller** than that one.
This building is the **tallest** one in the world.

I ski **frequently.**
I ski **more frequently** than he does.
Of the three of us, I ski **most frequently.**

11b. There are three degrees of comparison of modifiers: *positive, comparative,* and *superlative.*

POSITIVE	COMPARATIVE	SUPERLATIVE
weak	weaker	weakest
ancient	more ancient	most ancient
loud	louder	loudest
loudly	more loudly	most loudly
good	better	best
bad	worse	worst

There are two regular ways to compare modifiers. To form the comparative degree, the letters *er* may be added to the word, or the word *more* may precede it. To form the superlative, the letters *est* may be added to the word, or the word *most* may precede it.

(1) Most one-syllable modifiers form their comparative and superlative degrees by adding *er* and *est*.

POSITIVE	COMPARATIVE	SUPERLATIVE
near	nearer	nearest
meek	meeker	meekest

(2) Some two-syllable modifiers form their comparative and superlative degrees by adding *er* and *est*, but most two-syllable modifiers form their comparative and superlative degrees by means of *more* and *most*.

POSITIVE	COMPARATIVE	SUPERLATIVE
simple	simpler	simplest
drowsy	drowsier	drowsiest
modern	more modern	most modern
pleasant	more pleasant	most pleasant

When you are in doubt about which way an adjective is compared, consult a dictionary.

(3) Modifiers of three or more syllables form their comparative and superlative degrees by means of *more* and *most*.

POSITIVE	COMPARATIVE	SUPERLATIVE
ignorant	more ignorant	most ignorant
hopefully	more hopefully	most hopefully

● EXERCISE 3. Write the forms for the comparative and superlative degrees of the following modifiers.

1. late
2. careful
3. gracefully
4. agile
5. interesting
6. low
7. merry
8. nervous
9. efficiently
10. soft

(4) Comparison to indicate *less* and *least* of a quality is accomplished by using the words *less* and *least* before the modifier.

POSITIVE	COMPARATIVE	SUPERLATIVE
skillful	less skillful	least skillful
delicate	less delicate	least delicate

Irregular Comparison

When adjectives and adverbs do not follow the regular methods of forming their comparative and superlative degrees, they are said to be compared irregularly. You should learn the comparative and superlative degrees of the five modifiers below.

POSITIVE	COMPARATIVE	SUPERLATIVE
bad	worse	worst
good	better	best
well	better	best
many	more	most
much	more	most

● REVIEW EXERCISE A. Write the comparative and superlative degrees of the following modifiers. When in doubt about the words of two syllables, consult a dictionary.

1. foolish
2. quickly
3. many
4. simply
5. polite
6. short
7. dreary
8. frequently
9. good
10. cold
11. well
12. unexpectedly
13. curious
14. much
15. distant
16. enthusiastically
17. easy
18. heavy
19. bad
20. mischievous

Use of Comparative and Superlative Forms

11c. Use the *comparative* degree when comparing two things; use the *superlative* when comparing three or more.

Comparing two things:

> The second problem is **harder** than the first.
>
> He is **more studious** than his brother.
>
> This book is **more interestingly** written than that one.

Comparing three or more things:

> This road is the **narrowest** of the three we've traveled.
>
> Of all the performers, she was the **best.**
>
> This is the **simplest** recipe for fudge that I've seen.

Most mistakes in the use of modifiers are made when two things are being compared. Remember that the comparative degree should be used when two things are compared.

WRONG Of the two cakes, this is the best one.
RIGHT Of the two cakes, this is the **better** one.

WRONG Marie is the youngest of the two girls.
RIGHT Marie is the **younger** of the two girls.

When comparing one thing with a group of which it is a part, do not omit the word *other*.

WRONG He is faster than any boy on his team. [He is a member of his team, and he obviously cannot be faster than himself.]
RIGHT He is faster than any **other** boy on his team.

11d. Avoid the double comparison.

A person uses a double comparison when he adds *er* or *est* to the modifier and, at the same time, precedes the modifier with *more* or *most*. Words are compared in one of two ways; you should never use both ways at the same time.

WRONG Our dog is more smaller than yours.
RIGHT Our dog is **smaller** than yours.

WRONG It was the most beautifulest waterfall I had ever seen.
RIGHT It was the **most beautiful** waterfall I had ever seen.

● EXERCISE 4. Number your paper 1–10. Write a *C* after the number of each correct sentence. After the number of each incorrect sentence, rewrite the sentence correcting the error.

1. The noise of band practice is getting more louder every day.
2. Harold, the star of the play, is better than any member of the cast.
3. The dog's eyes are the most saddest that I've ever seen.
4. After looking at the two hats carefully, Mother bought the largest one.
5. In the seventh grade, work was more easier than it is now.
6. The patient looks worser today.
7. The wallpaper in the kitchen is more interesting than that in the living room.
8. New York is larger than any city in the United States.
9. "I am feeling more better," I replied.
10. He is the most agreeable person in our class.

● EXERCISE 5. Use the first five words as modifiers in sentences comparing two things. Use the second five in sentences comparing three or more things.

1. bad	6. murky
2. happy	7. realistically
3. practical	8. often
4. young	9. stubborn
5. unusual	10. damp

THE DOUBLE NEGATIVE

Words like the following are called negatives: *no, not, none, never, no one, nothing, hardly, scarcely.* (Notice that many negatives begin with the letter *n.*) When such a word is used in a sentence, it makes an important change in the meaning.

I have found the wallet that I lost.
I have **never** found the wallet that I lost.

11e. Avoid the use of double negatives.

In the fifteenth and sixteenth centuries, a writer could freely use two or more negatives for emphasis, as in the sentence "I *never* treacherously slew *no* man." However, fashions change in language, and we can no longer pile up negatives in this way. In modern English, the use of more than one negative in a statement is considered incorrect.

WRONG We don't have no extra chairs.
RIGHT We have **no** extra chairs.
RIGHT We do**n't** have any extra chairs.

WRONG He couldn't hardly talk.
RIGHT He **could hardly** talk.

● EXERCISE 6. Revise the following sentences, eliminating the double negatives.

1. Karen hasn't never been to Florida.
2. Because of the fog we couldn't scarcely see the road.
3. He never has no trouble with spelling.
4. The runners don't hardly have time to rest between races.
5. Don't use no double negatives in sentences.
6. I reached into my pocket for some change and found I didn't have none.
7. I can't hardly believe the report.
8. This doesn't make no difference to me.
9. Don't never use *not* and *hardly* together.
10. The truant hasn't no excuse.

● REVIEW EXERCISE B. Rewrite the incorrect sentences in the exercise below, eliminating the errors in the use of modifiers. Number your revised sentences as they are numbered in the exercise. You should have thirteen revised sentences.

1. Art is the most laziest boy on the team.
2. Which do you like best—apples or pears?
3. Gail works harder than any other student on the debating team.
4. Suddenly the troops marched more faster.
5. I can't hardly communicate with her.
6. Frank and Mark get along good together.
7. Don was the more careful driver of the two.
8. Logan feels worse today than he did yesterday.
9. He is the best looking of the twins.
10. They can't do nothing about it.
11. He did so well on the exam that the college was glad to admit him.
12. Of the two candidates, Jim is the best qualified.
13. Which is the heavier load—yours or mine?
14. Kelley doesn't want none of your advice.
15. The violinist plays extremely well.
16. Which of the four motors is the oldest?
17. Africa is much more larger than Europe.
18. Which of the two television sets costs most?
19. Every time I see her she looks beautifuller.
20. Thad is more stronger than Don.

PLACEMENT OF MODIFIERS

Notice how the meaning of the following sentence changes when the modifying phrase *from Canada* is moved about in the sentence.

> The professor **from Canada** gave a televised lecture on famous writers
>
> The professor gave a televised lecture on famous writers **from Canada.**
>
> **From Canada** the professor gave a televised lecture on famous writers.

The first of the three sentences above says that the *professor* was from Canada; the second sentence, that the *famous writers* were from Canada; the third, that the *televised lecture* came from Canada. As you can see, shifting the position of the modifying phrase has resulted in important changes in meaning.

11f. Place modifying phrases and clauses so that they clearly and sensibly modify a word in the sentence.

Prepositional Phrases

You know that prepositional phrases are used as adjectives and adverbs. To make a sentence clear and sensible, you should place a prepositional phrase near the word modified.

◆ NOTE As was said on page 85, adverb phrases are more flexible than adjective phrases and do not have to come immediately after the modified word. However, to avoid confusion, an adverb phrase should be placed near the modified word. Often, as in the second right sentence below, it can come before the modified word.

WRONG The vase was set in the middle of the table with flowers. [*With flowers* should go with *vase*, not *table*.]

RIGHT The vase **with flowers** was set in the middle of the table.

WRONG I read about the lost puppy that was found in today's newspaper. [The puppy was not found in the newspaper.]

RIGHT **In today's newspaper** I read about the lost puppy that was found.

Be careful to avoid having a prepositional phrase come between two words that it might modify. Instead, place it next to the *one* word that you intend it to modify.

UNCLEAR He said in the morning he was going to Chicago.

CLEAR He said he was going to Chicago **in the morning.**

CLEAR **In the morning** he said he was going to Chicago.

● EXERCISE 7. The meaning of each of the following sentences is not clear and sensible because the modifying phrase is in the wrong place. Decide where the phrase belongs; then rewrite the sentence.

1. The famous explorer told us about running into a tribe of cannibals in today's assembly.
2. Inside the cage I watched a large, melancholy gorilla.
3. The fashion display attracted an enormous crowd in the department-store window.
4. A large crowd was watching a jet plane in the park.
5. The teacher required three articles from magazines on Pike's Peak.
6. My neighbor promised on Sunday he would take me fishing.
7. You are the only one who can do a double somersault on the diving team.
8. The hockey player lost his balance with the red cap.
9. The woman was reading a mystery story in a large hat with a plume.
10. We saw a meteor falling through a large telescope.

Participial Phrases

A participial phrase, like an adjective, modifies a noun or a pronoun. When a participial phrase begins the sentence, it modifies the noun or pronoun immediately following it. Notice that the participial phrases below are separated from the other parts of the sentences by commas. (Review participles, see pages 90–92.)

EXAMPLES **Screaming wildly,** the Indians chased the stagecoach.

Arriving after the others, we waited until intermission to be seated.

When you begin a sentence with a participial phrase, you should be sure that it modifies the noun or pronoun immediately following; otherwise your sentence will have a *dangling participle.*

DANGLING PARTICIPLE Coming in for a landing, the tower contacted the plane. [The participial phrase dangles because the *tower* was not coming in for a landing.]

RIGHT **Coming in for a landing,** the plane was contacted by the tower.

RIGHT The tower contacted the plane **coming in for a landing.**

DANGLING PARTICIPLE Broken in many pieces, I saw my watch lying on the floor. [The participial phrase dangles because *I* was not broken in many pieces.]

RIGHT **Broken in many pieces,** my watch was lying on the floor.

● EXERCISE 8. All of the sentences below contain participial phrases. Some of the sentences are nonsensical or awkward because the participial phrases dangle. If a sentence is correct, write *C* after the proper number. Rewrite all incorrect sentences so that the participial phrases modify the right words. (You may have to supply words.) A participial phrase beginning a sentence should be followed by a comma.

1. Standing on the corner, an accident happened right in front of us.
2. Exploring the cave, the boys found a new entrance.
3. Circling the earth, the men at the control center carried on a conversation with the astronaut.
4. Damaged in an accident, we got our car repaired.
5. Confused by the questions, a period of rest was allowed the prisoner.
6. Stumbling on the curve, the race was lost by the favored horse.
7. After studying for several hours, our lessons were finally finished.
8. Laid aside for cold weather, the heavy sweater was a lifesaver during the unexpected snowstorm.
9. Risking his life, the fireman rescued the small boy from the burning house.
10. Tired from the long walk, food and rest were what we wanted.

● EXERCISE 9. Use correctly the following introductory participial phrases in sentences of your own.

1. Parked on a side street, ...
2. Lying on the beach, ...
3. Waiting for a telegram from his wife, ...
4. Almost destroyed by the storm, ...
5. Leading the way, ...
6. Fishing from the pier, ...

7. Not expecting a party, ...
8. Doomed to roam the sea forever, ...
9. Listening to the special bulletin, ...
10. Encouraged by the good news, ...

Clauses

Like modifying phrases, adjective and adverb clauses should be placed as near as possible to the words they modify. Notice in the following examples how the confusion resulting from misplaced clauses is cleared up when the clauses are placed near the words they modify.

MISPLACED CLAUSE	My parents cleaned the house on Clinch Avenue which they had recently bought. [The sentence suggests that the parents bought Clinch Avenue.]
RIGHT	My parents cleaned the house **which they had recently bought** on Clinch Avenue.
MISPLACED CLAUSE	A man stopped me who was lost. [It was the man who was lost.]
RIGHT	A man **who was lost** stopped me.

● EXERCISE 10. Read each of the following sentences. Decide what word the misplaced clause should modify; then rewrite the sentence, placing the clause near the right word.

1. The men were not far from their homes who had volunteered for the mission.
2. We waded through the water in our bare feet which was ankle deep.

3. The Knights of King Arthur's Round Table rescued many fair ladies who were very fearless and strong.
4. Several of the "Hungarian Rhapsodies" were played at yesterday's assembly that were composed by Franz Liszt.
5. The clean-up campaign was endorsed by Mayor Tibbetts that was sponsored by the Garden Club.
6. The test was postponed by the teachers that was scheduled for Friday.
7. A strange knight entered King Arthur's hall that was dressed entirely in green.
8. When I worked for Western Union, I delivered a telegram to a businessman that was several pages long.
9. My cousin Frank visited me who lives in Detroit.
10. A movie is being made in a Maine fishing village which is based on a best-selling novel.

● REVIEW EXERCISE C. In each of the following sentences, a modifier is used incorrectly. The mistake may result from (1) a confusion between *good* and *well*, (2) comparison, (3) the use of a double negative, or (4) a dangling or misplaced modifier. Rewrite the sentences, correcting the mistakes.

1. During World War II, many installations were protected from being bombed by using decoys.
2. You can't hardly imagine how effective these decoys were.
3. Trying to prevent the bombing of Berlin, a decoy city was built by the Germans.
4. Inflated rubber decoys of ships and tanks worked very good.
5. Decoy construction became one of the most biggest activities of the war.

6. Sometimes a decoy airstrip was constructed near the real one which was made by painting the ground white.
7. The enemy bombardiers couldn't hardly tell the difference between the decoy airfield and the real one.
8. Lighting up a decoy airfield, many British bombardiers were fooled by the Germans.
9. When the British began to suspect the trick, German experts thought up new tricks who were highly skilled at decoy operations.
10. Sometimes the real field would be the most brightly lighted of the two.
11. Warned about highly lighted areas, the darker airfield would be chosen by the bombardiers.
12. No one could never know whether the real field or the decoy field would be lighted.
13. One of the most cleverest decoy operations of the war was used by the Allies just before D day.
14. In full view, the Allies placed decoy ships in a harbor where German planes could see them.
15. They would then pick up the decoy ships and, after deflating them, plant them in another harbor.
16. Seeing many ships in many different harbors, the size of the Allied fleet was overestimated by the Germans.
17. The decoys, among other devices, caused Hitler to make one of the most costliest mistakes of the war.
18. Convinced that the big invasion was coming at Calais, many of the German divisions were ordered there by Hitler.
19. Hitler's miscalculation worked out good for the Allies.
20. Certainly, decoys played a more vitaler role in the war than most people realize.

PART THREE

Mechanics

CHAPTER **12**

Capital Letters

Rules for Capitalizing

Capital letters indicate important words—the beginnings of sentences and quotations, titles, and other words that warrant attention. Most rules for capitalization you have already mastered. Perhaps there are others that you find troublesome. This chapter will help you to use capital letters correctly.

12a. Capitalize the first word in every sentence.

In order to capitalize the first word in a sentence, you must be able to identify the beginning of a sentence. If you are not sure of your ability to do this, the section on run-on sentences (pages 330–34) will help you.

WRONG Nowadays Americans are traveling to other countries in ever-increasing numbers, some of them go as students, some as soldiers, some as tourists, most of them find it thrilling to experience foreign ways of life for a while, in a way, they are all informal American ambassadors.

RIGHT Nowadays Americans are traveling to other countries in ever-increasing numbers. Some of them go as students, some as soldiers, some as tourists. Most of them find it thrilling to experience foreign ways of life for a while. In a way, they are all informal American ambassadors.

The first word of a direct quotation is capitalized, even though it may fall within a sentence. For example: *Mac shouted, "Come on over!"* For a fuller explanation of this rule, see the section on writing quotations, pages 266–68.

◆ NOTE Traditionally, the first word in a line of poetry is capitalized, whether or not the word begins a sentence.

EXAMPLE **A**lone she sits and binds the grain,
And sings a melancholy strain;
O listen! for the vale profound
Is overflowing with the sound.

12b. Capitalize the pronoun *I*.

EXAMPLES Recently **I** have begun to enjoy reading adult books.

May **I** help you?

12c. Capitalize the interjection *O*.

The interjection *O* is most often used on solemn or formal occasions. Notice that it is most often used with a word in direct address and that no mark of punctuation follows it.

12 a-c

EXAMPLES Hear our prayer, **O** Lord.
Protect us in the battle, **O** great Athena!

The interjection *oh* requires a capital letter only at the beginning of a sentence. It is usually followed by a comma.

EXAMPLES **Oh**, wait till you see tomorrow's assignment.
We haven't seen him for some time—**oh**, perhaps two or three months.

12d. Capitalize proper nouns.

The proper noun, which you studied on page 32, names a particular person, place, or thing. It is always capitalized. The common noun is capitalized only when it begins a sentence or is part of a title.

PROPER NOUNS	COMMON NOUNS
Aaron Copland	person
Saturn	planet
Tennessee	state
Bolivia	country

(1) Capitalize the names of persons.

EXAMPLES **J**im **K**jelgaard is my favorite writer.
Is **A**lice coming, too?
According to **M**iss **S**andoz, **J**onas **S**alk would be a good subject for a biography.

(2) Capitalize geographical names.

Cities, Towns **J**amestown, **S**an **D**iego, **A**kron
States **G**eorgia, **I**daho, **H**awaii
Countries **G**hana, **N**icaragua, **T**hailand
Sections of the Country the **M**idwest, the **N**orth

♦ NOTE Do *not* capitalize *east*, *west*, *north*, *south*, or any combination like *southwest* when these words indicate direction; do capitalize them when they indicate a region.

EXAMPLES Walk south for three blocks and turn left. [direction]

Marjorie Kinnan Rawlings' books are usually set in the South. [region]

The fireplace never draws well when there is a strong wind from the east. [direction]

Living in the East, he had never before seen mountains as high as the Rockies. [region]

Islands Isle of Wight, Molokai, Wake Island, Attu, Guernsey

Bodies of Water Danville Reservoir, Tennessee River, Lake Erie, Niagara Falls, Tampa Bay, Indian Ocean, Puget Sound, Bering Sea

Streets, Highways Cherry Lane, Taconic Avenue, Crescent Circle, West Ninety-fourth Street, Route 44, Skyline Drive

♦ NOTE In a hyphenated street number, the second word begins with a small letter.

EXAMPLES East Seventy-eighth Street, South Forty-third Place

Parks Estes Park, White Mountain National Forest

Mountains Big Horn Mountains, Mount Washington, Sawtooth Range, Pikes Peak, Great Smokies

Continents North America, Europe, Africa, Asia, Australia

(3) Capitalize names of organizations, business firms, institutions, and government bodies.

EXAMPLES Debating Club
Air National Guard
Follett's Hardware Store
United Tool and Die Corporation
Cary Memorial Hospital
Hillcrest School
Antioch College
Department of Agriculture
Governor's Council

◆ NOTE Do *not* capitalize words like *school, circus, restaurant, club* unless they are part of a proper name.

Irving Junior High School	a junior high school
Ringling Brothers' Circus	a huge circus
Milbank Garden Club	a women's club

(4) Capitalize special events and calendar items.

EXAMPLES World Series
National Chess Tournament
Rockland Lobster Festival
Fourth of July
Labor Day
Friday
October

◆ NOTE Do *not* capitalize the names of seasons.

We go on fishing trips in spring and fall.

(5) Capitalize historical events and periods.

EXAMPLES Space Age, World War II, Battle of Bunker Hill, Middle Ages, Renaissance, Crusades

(6) Capitalize the names of nationalities, races, and religions.

EXAMPLES Spanish, Egyptian, Negro, Indian, Moslem, Lutheran, Protestant

(7) Capitalize the brand names of business products.

EXAMPLES Cannon towels, Buick convertible, Ivory soap [Notice that only the brand name is capitalized; the common noun following it begins with a small letter.]

(8) Capitalize the names of ships, planets, monuments, awards, and any other particular places, things, or events.

EXAMPLES U.S.S. *Maine* [ship] Fort Dix
Tiros [satellite] Pulitzer Prize

● EXERCISE 1. Number your paper 1–20. For each proper noun, write a corresponding common noun. For each common noun, write a proper noun.

EXAMPLES 1. John Wayne
1. *actor*
2. country
2. *France*

1. baseball team
2. New Year's Day
3. government building
4. ocean
5. *Kidnapped*
6. national park
7. historical event
8. Danny Kaye
9. historical period
10. lake
11. astronaut
12. Asia
13. Lincoln Memorial
14. orchestra
15. business firm
16. story
17. Wheaties
18. Pepsi-Cola
19. national anthem
20. Christianity

● Exercise 2. Copy these expressions, using capital letters where needed. Do not capitalize the first word unless it requires a capital.

1. labor day weekend
2. congress of the united states
3. mountains of virginia
4. will rogers turnpike
5. member of the peace corps
6. hoover dam
7. student at columbia university
8. federal bureau of investigation
9. united states supreme court
10. indians of the southwest
11. member of the u.s. olympic team
12. rocky mountain national park
13. walter farley
14. exercises held on memorial day
15. continental can company
16. two blocks north of st. paul's cathedral
17. 36 east fifty-seventh street
18. aetna casualty insurance company
19. a book about the space age
20. many islands of the pacific
21. the great lakes
22. a methodist
23. heinz's ketchup
24. friday, october 22
25. the battle of bull run

● Exercise 3. Number your paper 1–10. After each number, copy and capitalize all words in the sentence that need capital letters.

1. We crossed the atlantic on the s.s. *united states*, and a month later we returned by pan american airways.

2. orville and wilbur wright made their first successful flight at kitty hawk, north carolina, in 1903.
3. I plan to see as many home games of the detroit tigers as I can this summer.
4. the battle of gettysburg was fought in 1863.
5. I am sure our halloween party will be hilarious.
6. new westinghouse air conditioners are being installed in the apartments.
7. the new charitable organization is jointly supported by protestants, catholics, and jews.
8. it would be fun to be at cape kennedy, florida, when a missile is launched.
9. gerard's father bought a new ford convertible.
10. in the eighth grade we study the spanish-american war.

12e. Capitalize proper adjectives.

A proper adjective, which is formed from a proper noun, is always capitalized.

PROPER NOUN	PROPER ADJECTIVE
China	Chinese doctor
Egypt	Egyptian cotton
Ireland	Irish wolfhound
Middle East	Middle Eastern tour
Brazil	Brazilian artist

● EXERCISE 4. Number your paper 1–10. After each number, copy and capitalize all proper nouns and adjectives in the corresponding sentence.

1. The television program presented an interesting discussion of the new african nations.
2. A belgian farmer and an english miner, both of whom once lived in africa, made the session lively.
3. She thinks copenhagen is the most beautiful of all european capitals.

4. A finnish architect, eliel saarinen, designed a number of buildings in the detroit area.
5. In our study of american literature, we read many works of the new england poets.
6. Speaking in german, the lutheran minister gave a stirring sermon.
7. Much of our salmon comes from alaskan canneries.
8. We hope to see a shakespearean play this winter.
9. Dick is learning to play the french horn.
10. The south american llama is a cousin of the arabian camel.

12f. Do *not* capitalize the names of school subjects, except languages and course names followed by a number.

EXAMPLES I have tests in **E**nglish, science, and **m**ath.

You must pass **H**istory II before taking **H**istory III.

Next year we will have **a**lgebra and **L**atin.

● EXERCISE 5. Copy these phrases, inserting capitals where needed.

1. the study of russian
2. a member of an art class
3. project for science I
4. teacher of english and social studies
5. importance of french and spanish
6. problems in mathematics and european history
7. new interest in astronomy
8. courses in physics, civics I, and american history
9. laboratory period for science II
10. studying history, latin, chemistry, and government II

12g. Capitalize titles.

(1) Capitalize the title of a person when it comes before a name.

EXAMPLES There will be a short address of welcome by **G**overnor **H**alsey.

Report to **L**ieutenant **E**ngstrom, please.

Did you know that **D**r. **P**oliti has a new nurse, a **M**iss **D**avidson?

This is the church in which the **R**everend **H**enry **W**ard **B**eecher preached.

How many terms did **P**resident **C**leveland serve?

Did **Q**ueen **W**ilhelmina reign in the Netherlands or Belgium?

(2) Capitalize a title used alone or following a person's name only if it refers to a high official or to someone to whom you wish to show special respect.

EXAMPLES The **S**ecretary of **L**abor will hold a news conference this afternoon. [*Secretary of Labor* is a high government office.]

Since 1800 the White House has been the official residence of the **P**resident. [The word *President* is ordinarily capitalized when it refers to the President of the United States.]

Calvin Coolidge, **G**overnor of Massachusetts, suppressed a Boston police strike in 1919. [Although it follows the person's name, the title is that of a high office.]

The **t**reasurer of our Scout troop has the measles. [This title is not that of a very high office.]

12 f-g

Ellen Rafferty, chairman of the program committee, reported on plans for the Winter Carnival. [The office is not high enough to warrant capitalization.]

◆ NOTE When a title is used instead of a name in direct address, it is usually capitalized.

EXAMPLES How long must I stay in bed, Doctor?
Can you tell me, Officer, how to find the new high school building?

(3) Capitalize words showing family relationship when used with a person's name but *not* when preceded by a possessive.

EXAMPLES Aunt Christine, Grandfather Smith
Mario's father, our brother, his uncle

EXCEPTION When family-relationship words are *usually* used before a name, so that they are considered a part of the name, they are capitalized even when preceded by a possessive.

EXAMPLES Joe's Uncle Pete

When family-relationship words are used in place of a person's name, they may or may not be capitalized.

EXAMPLE Ask Mother, *or* Ask mother. [Either way is correct.]

(4) Capitalize the first word and all important words in titles of books, magazines, newspapers, poems, stories, movies, paintings, and other works of art.

Unimportant words in a title are *a*, *an*, *the*, and prepositions and conjunctions of fewer than five letters. Such words should be capitalized only if they come first or last in the title.

EXAMPLES My father likes to recite Tennyson's poem, "The Charge of the Light Brigade."

Edward Everett Hale wrote *The Man Without a Country* in 1863.

Curtain Going Up! is a biography of Katharine Cornell.

EXCEPTION When you write the names of newspapers and magazines within a sentence, do not capitalize the word *the* before the name.

EXAMPLES May I borrow your copy of the *Reader's Digest?*

Is that the late edition of the *New York Times?*

(5) Capitalize words referring to the Deity.

EXAMPLES Lord, our Father, the Creator, Son of God

◆ NOTE The word *god* is not capitalized when referring to pagan deities.

EXAMPLE the gods of ancient Rome

● EXERCISE 6. Number your paper 1–10. After the proper number, copy and capitalize the words requiring capitals.

1. Most boys will enjoy reading *the call of the wild.* [a book]
2. Do you subscribe to the *saturday evening post?*
3. Franklin D. Roosevelt died in office during his fourth term as president of the united states.
4. We will visit uncle John and aunt Susan this summer.
5. Every man worships god in his own way.
6. We saw a rerun of Walt Disney's *the living desert.*
7. John is president of the arlington boys' club.

8. The mayor announced that both the governor of Illinois and the secretary of the interior would speak at the political rally.
9. Yes, dr. Carey is a member of the hospital staff, and he is highly respected by the other doctors at the hospital.
10. How is my father, doctor?

● EXERCISE 7. Number your paper 1–10. After the proper number, copy and capitalize the words requiring capitals.

1. The audience rose as the president of the united states entered.
2. I am going to consult the *readers' guide to periodical literature.*
3. We are visiting my uncle Jack.
4. Ancient babylonian families kept clay figurines of their household gods in wall niches.
5. We heard an address by governor Martin.
6. The vice-president and the secretary of state spoke to the reporters about South America.
7. Tom Brown, captain of our football team, is a fullback.
8. Jonathan Swift is the author of *a tale of a tub.*
9. My uncle usually brings home a copy of the *chicago sun-times.*
10. Yes, judge Collins is more sympathetic than the other judge.

Summary Style Sheet

This list gives examples of the rules of capitalization studied in this chapter. Use it as a review by studying each item below and justifying the use of each capital or small letter. The list will also be convenient for quick reference.

1. Johnson **C**ity	a **c**ity in Tennessee
2. Apache **R**eservation	a **r**eservation in New Mexico
3. Second **S**treet	a **s**treet in Pasadena
4. Milton **P**ond	a **p**ond in Milton
5. the **N**ortheast	a **n**ortheast gale
6. **N**orth Dakota	**n**orth of South Dakota
7. the Music **C**lub	a **c**lub for girls
8. Slater **W**oolen **C**ompany	a **w**oolen **c**ompany
9. Topeka **H**igh **S**chool	a **h**igh **s**chool in Topeka
10. the Korean **W**ar	a **w**ar in Korea
11. the John Hancock **B**uilding	an insurance **b**uilding
12. Washington's **B**irthday	Henry's **b**irthday
13. the Industrial **R**evolution	a **r**evolution in manufacturing
14. **G**od, our Father	the **g**ods of pagan Europe
15. the **W**inter **P**rom	a **p**rom in the **w**inter
16. the **S**ophomore **C**lass	a **c**lass of **s**ophomores
17. **F**rench, **E**nglish, **R**ussian	**m**athematics, **m**usic, **g**eography
18. **S**cience **II**	a lesson in **s**cience
19. **P**rincipal Harris	Mr. Harris, the **p**rincipal
20. the **P**resident of the United States	the **p**resident of the company
21. Will you call **M**other (or **m**other)?	My **m**other is here.
22. **A**unt Marie	her **a**unt
23. the *__A__merican __G__irl*	a monthly **m**agazine
24. the *__C__hicago __D__aily __N__ews*	a **n**ewspaper
25. *__T__he __W__ar __o__f __t__he __W__orlds*	
26. customs of the **In**dians	
27. an **E**piscopalian	
28. **C**anadian **b**acon	
29. **F**ord **t**ruck	

● REVIEW EXERCISE A. Number your paper 1–10. After the proper number, copy and capitalize the words requiring capitals.

1. larry price, the secretary of our club, could not be at the meeting.
2. admiral edward smith will speak this june at the graduation ceremonies of the united states naval academy at annapolis, maryland.
3. he studied spanish and ancient history at harvard university.
4. will you tell your father to meet me at the davidson building?
5. one of thomas hardy's most famous novels is *the return of the native.*
6. when you go to the store, uncle george, will you get me a package of wrigley's spearmint gum?
7. john has a summer job as a lifeguard at the beach in harrison park.
8. yesterday principal edwards conducted a meeting of the student body.
9. mr. carlson is a vice-president of the logan trucking company.
10. if you want to find third street, go south for three blocks.

● REVIEW EXERCISE B. Number your paper 1–10. After the proper number, copy and capitalize the words requiring capitals.

1. We bought beautiful indian pottery and rugs while we were in the southwest.
2. What a thrilling time tom had on grandfather morse's ranch in wyoming!
3. Do you plan to study latin and french, together with mathematics and civics II, next year?

4. The fifth day of the week, thursday, gets its name from thor, the norse god of thunder.
5. One of our most important american holidays is thanksgiving.
6. Hawaii, the newest one of the united states, is a group of islands in the pacific ocean 2,000 miles west of california.
7. A forum of young people representing the jewish, catholic, and protestant faiths met last evening at central high school on main street.
8. The supreme court's ruling against required religious exercises in public schools did not imply a lack of belief in god.
9. The swedish writer, selma lagerlöf, is the author of *the story of gösta berling* and of the children's classic, *the wonderful adventures of nils.*
10. At the hampton supermarket there is a window display of kleenex napkins, kellogg's cereals, and campbell's soups.

● REVIEW EXERCISE C. Write ten short sentences, using one of the items in the following list in each sentence. Use capital letters correctly, according to the rules you have studied.

1. name of a magazine
2. a business
3. a range of mountains
4. title of a person
5. title of a book
6. geographical section of country
7. a street
8. a language and two other school subjects
9. a historical event
10. a continent

● REVIEW EXERCISE D. Number your paper 1–20. For each sentence, write the words that should be capitalized, capitalizing them, and the words that are incorrectly capitalized, omitting the capitals.

1. The president's news conferences in the state department auditorium were very popular.
2. In science class we are studying about such Scientists as sir isaac newton, samuel f. b. morse, and alexander graham bell.
3. the languages in which i'm most interested are french, spanish, and russian.
4. In sutherland junior high school we have classes in English and Mathematics.
5. Members of Morse Junior High hiking club climbed mt. chicorua.
6. The new prudential building in Boston, Massachusetts, is fifty-two stories high.
7. Someday you should visit the shakespeare festival in Stratford, Ontario.
8. The Period of Time between july 1957 and january 1959 was known as the international geophysical year.
9. The DEW line, whose initials stand for *d*istant *e*arly *w*arning, consists of a string of radar stations across the Northernmost part of the north american continent.
10. dr. jonas salk developed a successful polio vaccine.
11. The names of african and asian countries are becoming more familiar to us.
12. John Stacey, President of our Club, has received an appointment to the u.s. naval academy at annapolis.
13. Are you familiar with my favorite magazine the *american girl?*
14. our journey will take us through the northwest.

15. We are anxious to see the great Fir trees of Oregon.
16. our new High School is being built on pleasant street.
17. Over two million people are stockholders in the american telephone and telegraph company.
18. Recently, our Junior High School was visited by indian and african teachers who are studying in this country.
19. The st. lawrence seaway, built by the Governments of canada and the united states, provides a channel from Montreal to lake ontario for seagoing vessels.
20. Every boy should be familiar with mark twain's famous classic *the adventures of tom sawyer*.

CHAPTER **13**

Punctuation

End Marks and Commas

In spoken language the voice indicates the pauses and the stops, but in written language punctuation does the work. While English might seem easier to write without periods or commas or other marks of punctuation, it would be very difficult to read. This chapter and the next one will help you to master punctuation so that your writing will be correct, clear, and easier to read.

END MARKS

13a. A statement is followed by a period.

EXAMPLES The lens is the most important part of a camera**.**

One of the greatest animal photographers was a woman named Ylla**.**

13b. A question is followed by a question mark.

EXAMPLES Have you ever used a wide-angle lens**?**

Is photography a science or an art**?**

13c. An exclamation is followed by an exclamation point.

EXAMPLES What a good time we had!
Wow! What a view!

13d. An imperative sentence is followed by either a period or an exclamation point.

EXAMPLES Please give me the scissors. [making a request]
Give me the scissors! [showing strong feeling]

● EXERCISE 1. In the following paragraphs, sentences have been run together without end marks. Copy the last word of every sentence and the first word of the next sentence, inserting the proper end mark. There are twenty end marks to supply.

Have you ever visited New Salem Park in Illinois There you will find a reproduction of the little village of New Salem, just as it was when Abraham Lincoln lived there If you do visit this village, you will find that life in Lincoln's time was much harder than it is today

What tiny, crude cabins the people lived in The twenty-three cabins include ten shops, a school, and a sawmill There is also a carding mill, where wool fibers were cleaned and straightened before they were spun into cloth

The cabin of Mr. Onstat is not a reproduction but the original cabin where Lincoln spent many hours In that living room, on that very floor, young Abe Lincoln studied with Isaac Onstat The rest of the

Onstat family was also there It was the cabin's only room

Across the way a big kettle hangs under a porch This is the original kettle used by Mr. Waddell for boiling wool Mr. Waddell, the hatter of the village, made hats of wool and fur

If you looked into the various cabins, you would see rough floors and walls and uncomfortable-looking furniture You might wonder how you would enjoy living in such a home In almost every cabin there is a ladder running up to the loft where some of the family slept How cold it was up there in winter and how hot in summer

Do any of you feel you would like to go back to those days What endurance those people must have had Could we manage to live as they did

13e. An abbreviation is followed by a period.

EXAMPLES	min.	minute	Neb.	Nebraska
	St.	Street	in.	inch
	Dr.	Doctor	Mr.	Mister
	Aug.	August	Co.	Company

Note that *Miss* preceding a woman's name is not an abbreviation and is not followed by a period. On the other hand, initials used with a name are abbreviations of names and should be followed by periods.

EXAMPLES Miss Ellsworth
A. B. Guthrie

COMMAS

A comma does not indicate a full stop, as a period does, but divides a sentence into readable parts by indicating pauses. If you master the use of the comma, your written work will improve in clarity. One word of warning: don't use commas carelessly. Have a reason for every comma you put into a sentence.

Items in Series

13f. Use commas to separate items in a series.

Words, phrases, and clauses in a series should be separated by commas so that they will be clear to a reader.

(1) Use commas to separate words in series.

EXAMPLES We have read poems by Longfellow, Whittier, and Emily Dickinson this week.

The Big Dipper, the Little Dipper, Orion, and the Pleiades are four constellations that are easy to recognize.

In the early morning, the lake looked cold, gray, and uninviting.

◆ NOTE You should form the habit of using a comma before the *and* joining the last two items in a series. Although many writers omit this comma, it is sometimes necessary to make your meaning clear.

EXAMPLE Next year we will study algebra, civics, French and American history. [No comma used; are we to study the French language or French history?]

(2) Use commas to separate phrases in series.

EXAMPLES We found seaweed in the water, on the sand, under the rocks, and even in our shoes.

It makes no difference whether that hamster is in a cage, on a string, or under a net—he always escapes.

(3) Use commas to separate subordinate clauses and short independent clauses in a series.

EXAMPLES Everyone wondered who had been in the house, what he had wanted, and where he had gone.

We worked, we played, and we rested.

(4) If all items in a series are joined by *and* or *or*, do not use commas to separate them.

EXAMPLE Have you read *Huckleberry Finn* or *Tom Sawyer* or *A Connecticut Yankee in King Arthur's Court?*

● EXERCISE 2. Number your paper 1–10. After the proper number, show where commas are needed in each sentence by copying the words before a necessary comma and adding the comma. Two sentences do not require commas.

1. We had lessons in swimming canoeing archery and handicrafts.
2. Mary and Frances and Ted dashed out of the car down the beach and into the water.
3. Our school has organized clubs for music art radio and chess.
4. One representative on the Student Council should be the senior class president or the secretary or the treasurer.
5. The high school orchestra includes violins cellos bass viols clarinets saxophones trumpets and drums.
6. I've planted seedlings fertilized them carefully and watered them each day.
7. The children played happily on the swings on the slides and in the pool.

8. Science and Latin and algebra are all included in next year's course of study.
9. Do you know anything about how to pitch a tent how to build a campfire or how to cook out-of-doors?
10. I enjoy swimming boating and surf-riding more than skiing sliding or skating.

● EXERCISE 3. Number your paper **1–10**. After the proper number, show where commas are needed in each sentence by copying the words before a necessary comma and adding the comma.

1. Find out who is going to the picnic what we must take and when we have to leave.
2. We reviewed what we have learned about verb forms what pronouns must be used as subjects and what pronouns are always used as objects.
3. This morning Tom will wash the car Mary will pack the lunch and then we'll go on a picnic.
4. In spite of bad weather predictions, the fog lifted the sun shone and everyone was happy.
5. *The Red Badge of Courage Anna and the King of Siam The Virginian* and *Sea Gulls Woke Me* are all good books for junior high students.
6. William and Lynn are anxious to water-ski to learn to sail and to do some skin diving.
7. Science teaches us how to conserve our forests how to prevent erosion of our land and how to control our water supplies.
8. Iron copper aluminum lumber coal and oil are some of our natural resources.
9. I would like to visit England France Spain and Norway, the Land of the Midnight Sun.
10. Soccer basketball and football are all strenuous games.

13g. Use a comma to separate two or more adjectives preceding a noun.

EXAMPLES An Arabian stallion is a fast, beautiful horse.
The early cowboy often depended on the small, tough, surefooted mustang.

When the final adjective is so closely connected to the noun that they seem to form one expression, do not use a comma before it.

EXAMPLE Training a frisky colt to become a gentle, dependable riding horse takes great patience. [No comma is used between *dependable* and *riding* because the words *riding horse* are closely connected in meaning and may be taken as one term.]

A comma should never be used between an adjective and the noun immediately following it.

WRONG The palomino is distinguished by its golden coat and long, flowing, mane and tail.

RIGHT The palomino is distinguished by its golden coat and long, flowing mane and tail.

● EXERCISE 4. Copy the following sentences, inserting commas where needed.

1. John was the popular efficient president of the senior class.
2. The cold dry northern air is very exhilarating.
3. We loved running barefoot over the cool wet sand.
4. What a stern dignified manner that soldier has!
5. The dark dingy musty attic seemed spooky.
6. The noisy carefree spectators cheered when they saw the bright new uniforms and instruments of the marching band.

7. Have you read about the strong courageous men who climbed the sheer icy slopes of Mt. Everest?
8. An alert businesslike and popular leader is needed.
9. A squat dark cooking stove stood in one corner of the old kitchen.
10. Alfred Hitchcock fascinates us with his thrilling blood-curdling yarns.

Compound Sentences

13h. Use a comma before *and, but, or, nor, for,* and *yet* when they join independent clauses.

EXAMPLES The musical comedy originated in America, and it has retained a distinctly American flavor.

Grand opera is a popular form of entertainment in Europe, but few Americans have an opportunity to see live productions of operas.

Singers must devote many years to training and practice, for a musical career is a demanding one.

If the clauses in a compound sentence are very short, the comma before the conjunction may be omitted.

EXAMPLE Hammerstein wrote the words and Rodgers wrote the music.

To follow comma rule 13h, you must be able to distinguish a compound sentence from a simple sentence with a compound verb.

COMPOUND SENTENCE Herb likes tennis and golf, but he doesn't enjoy soccer. [comma between independent clauses joined by a conjunction]

13 g-h

SIMPLE SENTENCE WITH COMPOUND VERB Herb likes tennis and golf but doesn't enjoy team sports. [no comma between parts of compound verb joined by a conjunction]

● EXERCISE 5. Number your paper 1–10. After the proper number, copy the words in the sentence that should be followed by commas. Add the commas. Several sentences do not require commas.

1. There are many beautiful beaches along the New England coast but one has to get used to the very cold water.
2. Henry came but Tom stayed at home.
3. I used steel traps to catch muskrats but my friends said I was cruel.
4. Astronomy is an old science yet it is now one of the most exciting.
5. Our teacher is using films and slides in our English class and we find them most interesting.
6. She tried on eight pairs of shoes but didn't buy any of them.
7. A robin has a nest in a tree near our porch and we watch her feeding the baby birds.
8. Harry lived on a farm and had to get up early in the morning to do his chores.
9. I will explain this theory once more but you must listen carefully.
10. The teacher explained the project and we went to work.

Phrases and Clauses

Participial phrases, as you learned on page 210, act as adjectives to modify nouns or pronouns. Subordinate clauses may also act as adjectives (see page 101).

In some sentences, the participial phrase or adjective clause is essential to the thought. It cannot be removed without destroying the meaning.

EXAMPLES All farmers **growing hybrid corn** owe a debt to an Austrian monk named Gregor Mendel. [The participial phrase in heavy type tells which farmers. It is essential to the meaning of the sentence.]

Mendel's discoveries about inherited traits in plants became a key **that unlocked many doors.** [The adjective clause modifies *key*. It cannot be removed without destroying the meaning.]

In other sentences, the participial phrase or adjective clause is *not* essential to the thought. Such a phrase or clause can be removed without changing the basic meaning.

EXAMPLES Sometimes seeds and nuts, **forgotten by the squirrels that hid them,** germinate far away from their parent plants. [The participial phrase can be removed without changing the basic meaning of the sentence: *Sometimes seeds and nuts germinate far away from their parent plants.*]

Migrating birds, **which often fly hundreds or thousands of miles,** are one of the main carriers of seeds. [The adjective clause can be removed without changing the basic meaning of the sentence: *Migrating birds are one of the main carriers of seeds.*]

13i. Use commas to set off participial phrases and adjective clauses that are not essential to the basic meaning of the sentence. Do not use commas with phrases or clauses that are essential to the meaning.

To *set off* with commas means to separate from the rest of the sentence. If the phrase or clause comes in the middle of the sentence, a comma is needed before and after it. If it comes at the end, a comma is needed before it; if it comes at the beginning of the sentence, a comma is needed after it.

EXAMPLES A new spider web**, shining in the morning light,** is an impressive example of engineering. [nonessential participial phrase; commas needed]

Anyone **who finishes early** may start on tomorrow's assignment. [essential adjective clause; no commas needed]

If a participial phrase or adjective clause is preceded by a proper noun, a comma is ordinarily needed to separate it from the noun.

EXAMPLE Tom reported on *Insects and Plants*, which was written by Elizabeth Cooper.

● EXERCISE 6. Number your paper 1–20. Write *C* after the numbers of sentences that are correctly punctuated. After the numbers of other sentences, write the words that should be followed by commas and add the commas.

1. The pitcher thinking the runner was out started off the field.
2. Here is my cousin whom you met yesterday.

3. Mary who enjoys her course in home economics will be a good homemaker.
4. Louis Pasteur striving to save a little boy from death by rabies used the vaccine which conquered that dread disease.
5. The man and woman who discovered radium were Pierre and Marie Curie.
6. Ernest Thompson Seton who was a famous artist-naturalist was born in England in 1860.
7. *Wild Animals I Have Known* which is one of his most popular works was his first book.
8. The boy or girl who enjoys reading usually does well in school.
9. The boy playing left end is our best tackle.
10. The two runners breathing hard and visibly tired broke the tape at the same time.
11. Lake Superior which covers an area of 30,000 square miles is the largest of the Great Lakes.
12. The girl with whom you worked is my sister.
13. The sun shining brilliantly on the ski slopes gave us a good winter tan.
14. The children, having gorged themselves on hot dogs, ice cream, and soda, called the picnic a huge success.
15. The Mexican jewelry which we bought made fine Christmas presents.
16. Mary prized very highly the bicycle which she had bought with her own money.
17. John cramming for the next day's history exam wished he had studied his lessons each day.
18. Our new school library which has just been opened is a valuable asset to our school.
19. The birds flying over the water made a pretty picture.
20. Autumn which is New England's most colorful season is enjoyed by many tourists.

13j. **Use a comma after a participial phrase or an adverb clause that begins a sentence.**

> **Forced onto the sidelines by his torn ligament,** Harris was restless and unhappy. [introductory participial phrase]
>
> **When March came,** the huge ice pack began to melt and break up.

An adverb clause that comes at the end of a sentence does not usually need a comma.

> The huge ice pack began to melt and break up **when March came.**

● EXERCISE 7. Number your paper 1–10. If a comma is needed in a sentence, supply it by copying the word before it and adding the comma. If no comma is needed, write *C* after the number.

1. Hitting a home run when the bases were loaded Tom saved the game for his school.
2. While the wind was howling outside we sat by the fire watching the flames leaping up the chimney.
3. We were not allowed to go to the party because we had not done our homework.
4. Fanned by a high wind the fire spread quickly.
5. The hypnotist came on stage after the dancers had finished their performance.
6. Bursting into the room Mary shouted that her team had won.
7. When the tide was coming in we had great fun in the surf.
8. John would have won the archery contest if he had shot as well as usual.
9. Unless you are willing to work hard you might as well give up that project.

10. Springing up and down on the trampoline the boys performed many acrobatic stunts.

Interrupters

When an expression like *of course* or *well* or a person's name interrupts a sentence, commas are needed to set off the interrupter. If the interrupting expression comes in the middle of the sentence, two commas are needed. If it comes first or last, only one comma is needed.

13k. Use a comma after a word such as *well*, *yes*, *no*, *why*, when it begins a sentence.

EXAMPLES Why, everyone knows what happened in 1776!

Yes, Olympia is the capital.

Well, it could be worse.

♦ NOTE Such words are not followed by a comma if they do not interrupt the sentence; that is, if no pause follows them.

EXAMPLES Why are you late?

Well along in the second game, there was a double play.

13l. Use commas to set off an expression that interrupts a sentence.

(1) Appositives and appositive phrases are usually set off by commas.

An *appositive* is a word which means the same thing as the noun it follows; usually it explains or identifies the noun. An appositive phrase is an appositive plus the words that go with it.

EXAMPLES Have you ever been in Texas, **the Lone Star State?** [*The Lone Star State* is an appositive meaning the same thing as *Texas.*]

The Rio Grande**, one of the major rivers of North America,** forms part of the border between Texas and Mexico. [*One of the major rivers of North America* is an appositive phrase meaning the same thing as the *Rio Grande.*]

♦ NOTE When an appositive is closely related to the word it follows, no comma is needed. Such appositives are usually one word.

EXAMPLES my brother Tom
the author Stevenson

● EXERCISE 8. Copy the sentences which require commas. Insert the commas.

1. Jackie my little cousin still likes nursery rhymes.
2. My friend Ann will visit us soon.
3. Howard Pease the author of the Tod Moran stories is a popular writer.
4. Have you met Jane Bradshaw my best friend?
5. Science my favorite subject gets more fascinating each year.
6. The Brantingham twins members of the football team have to report for practice soon.
7. Archimedes the Greek physicist supposedly made one of his discoveries while taking a bath.
8. The boys had great fun working on their car a dilapidated old model.
9. Only two of the animals a horse and a cow were saved from the fire.
10. A black funnel-shaped cloud sign of a tornado sent everyone running for shelter.

(2) Words used in direct address are set off by commas.

When someone speaks directly to another person, using that person's name, commas precede and follow the name.[1]

EXAMPLES Would you rather go to Africa or South America, **Hazel?**

Mrs. Clarkson, I just want to get to the beach this weekend.

Can you tell me, **sir,** when the next bus is due?

● EXERCISE 9. Number your paper 1–10. After the proper number, copy the words in the sentence that should be followed by a comma and add the comma.

1. Mr. Chairman may I ask the speaker a question?
2. Are you leaving tomorrow for your vacation John?
3. Can you tell us Mr. White where we can find the information we need?
4. You need more practice Ted if you are to become a good catcher.
5. Helen and Marie come here at once if you want to go with us.
6. You scoundrel what do you mean by trying to cheat your friends?
7. May we go now Mother or must we wait for the others?
8. Be sure to dress warmly boys; the weather is really cold.
9. Let's get out of here Sue; it's too spooky for me.
10. Girls are you ever going to be ready on time?

[1] For rules governing the use of commas in dialogue, see pages 269–70.

(3) Parenthetical expressions are set off by commas.

Occasionally a sentence is interrupted by an expression like *to tell the truth, in my opinion, in fact.* Such expressions are called *parenthetical* because like words enclosed in parentheses, the expressions are not grammatically related to the rest of the sentence. These expressions are set off by commas.

EXAMPLES The President said**, off the record,** that he was deeply disappointed.

To be honest, I thought the movie was fairly good.

It wasn't very good**, in my opinion.**

These expressions are often used parenthetically:

in fact	however
mind you	for example
as I was saying	to tell the truth
of course	nevertheless
on the contrary	I suppose (*or* know *or* believe *or* hope)
for instance	
in my opinion	if you ask me

◆ NOTE Such expressions are not always parenthetical. Be careful to use commas only if they are needed.

What**, in his opinion,** is the best closing hour? [a parenthetical expression set off by commas]

I have no faith **in his opinion.** [not a parenthetical expression; no commas needed]

Traveling by boat may take longer**, however.** [a parenthetical expression, preceded by a comma]

However you go, it will be a delightful trip. [*however* not used parenthetically; no commas needed]

● EXERCISE 10. Number your paper 1–10. After the proper number, copy the words in the sentence that should be followed by commas and add the commas.

1. Well we should get started by six o'clock.
2. You too can learn to play golf if you are willing to practice.
3. The story in my opinion is much too long and complicated.
4. Yes that is the longest covered bridge in the world.
5. Modern turnpikes for example are marvelous feats of engineering.
6. You will stay I hope as long as you possibly can.
7. No you will not enjoy that book unless you like mysteries.
8. Mathematics I'm afraid is my hardest subject.
9. The weather to tell the truth was much too hot.
10. Why what a surprise this is!

13m. Use a comma in certain conventional situations.

The conventions of English usage require that commas be used in dates, in addresses, and after the salutations and closings of letters.

(1) Use a comma to separate items in dates and addresses.

EXAMPLES The delegates to the Constitutional Convention signed the Constitution on September 17, 1787, in Philadelphia, Pennsylvania.

Spring vacation begins on Friday, April 12, this year.

My friend has just moved to 6448 Higgins Road, Chicago, Illinois.

The ZIP code number should be written several spaces after the state (unless you are writing it in a sentence). No comma should come before it.

Jackson Heights, New York   11372

◆ NOTE If a preposition is used between items of an address, a comma is not necessary: He lives at 144 Smith Street *in* Moline, Illinois.

(2) **Use a comma after the salutation of a friendly letter and after the closing of any letter.**

EXAMPLES Dear Aunt Margaret,
Sincerely yours,
Yours truly,

● EXERCISE 11. Copy the following items on your paper, inserting commas wherever needed.

1. 443 North University Avenue Ann Arbor Michigan   48103
2. 1900 Lower Road Linden New Jersey   07036
3. Monday August 5 1973
4. after January 1 1975
5. 379 Scott Avenue Salt Lake City Utah 84115
6. Michigan Avenue at Twelfth Street Chicago Illinois
7. Thanksgiving Day 1973
8. from June 23 1972 to January 2 1973
9. either Tuesday September 3 or Saturday September 7
10. Box 147F Wisconsin Dells Wisconsin   25367
11. the building on the corner of Market Street and Highland Avenue in Akron Ohio
12. Sincerely yours
13. Dear Jean
14. Friday July 9 in Roanoke Virginia

● REVIEW EXERCISE A. Number your paper 1–20. If a comma is needed in a sentence, supply it by copying the word before it and adding the comma. If a sentence is correctly punctuated, write a *C* after its number.

1. Since Susan's visit was to be a short one we wanted to do something special each day.
2. A beach party was planned for the first day but the weather was bad.
3. Disappointed we went to the movies instead.
4. At the movies we met Mary Tom Jane and Harry.
5. Since no one had plans for the evening, we arranged to have a party in our playroom.
6. Mother helped us get food and drinks together, and everyone brought records for dancing.
7. Susan who was a very appreciative guest said she had never had so much fun.
8. On Saturday July 18 we all went to the beach together.
9. Yes we swam rode surfboards and played ball on the sand.
10. After enjoying a long afternoon of play, everyone tired and hungry ate an enormous supper.
11. Completely exhausted by our day out-of-doors we were very happy to tumble into our beds at an early hour.
12. Susan lived on a farm, and she invited us to visit her on another weekend.
13. Although we had seen many farms, visiting one was a new experience.
14. It was great fun in my opinion to see all the cows, horses, pigs, and chickens.
15. When the roosters began to crow at dawn the farm seemed to come to life.

16. Breakfast was very early so that we could get to the barn to see the milking machine help feed the pigs and scatter grain for the chickens.
17. Dinner was at noon and we had never seen such heaping platters of mashed potatoes fried chicken fresh peas and homemade blueberry biscuits.
18. After we had eaten our dessert of apple pie and homemade ice cream, we stretched out under a big tree and went to sleep.
19. Since it was a warm humid afternoon we were glad later that we had the chance to go down to the river for a cool refreshing swim.
20. Getting ready for bed that night we decided that the farm which we were visiting was a perfect place for a vacation.

● REVIEW EXERCISE B. Number your paper 1–20. After the proper number, supply commas and end marks in the following sentences by copying the word before a mark of punctuation and adding the comma or end mark.

1. Yes Mary you and Alice may go with us
2. If the weather permits we will leave Saturday morning September 7 at six o'clock
3. You should take your bathing suits girls as the weather will still be warm
4. Since he's such a well-behaved dog Rusty will certainly go along Joe
5. Dad will drive Joe will take charge of Rusty and Mary and Alice will help Mother
6. What a wide smooth highway this is
7. If one is not in a hurry the quiet tree-lined roads are very inviting
8. However the turnpikes help us get to our destination quickly

9. Do you prefer fresh water or salt water for swimming Joe
10. Well we may get a chance to try both lakes and ocean
11. We are not sure when we'll stop or just how long we'll stay
12. What fun it will be to be vagabonds for a while
13. If we plan well we need take only a few clothes on the trip
14. The temptation I know is to take too much with us
15. If we took everything we thought we needed what a crowded uncomfortable car we'd have
16. Father much to my surprise does not plan to do any fishing
17. However he does plan to play golf and he will take his clubs
18. Planning our route getting together the things we need and packing carefully will take some time
19. Mother who has so much to do for us will be busiest of all
20. No this is not our first long trip

● REVIEW EXERCISE C. Number your paper 1–20. After the proper number, supply commas and end marks in the following sentences by copying the word before a mark of punctuation and adding the comma or end mark.

1. Constituting one third of the land area of the earth Asia is the world's largest continent
2. If both North and South America were fitted into Asia there would be a little space left over
3. Asia contains some of the coldest the hottest the wettest and the driest areas of the world
4. The Himalayas the highest mountains in the world are covered with mighty glaciers

5. The Himalayan range contains Mt. Everest K2 and a number of the world's other major peaks
6. Asia however also contains one of the world's most unusual bodies of water the Dead Sea
7. Mt. Everest is 29,028 feet above sea level and the Dead Sea is 1,290 feet below sea level
8. What a wonderful view one must have from the high peaks
9. On May 29 1953 a New Zealand mountain climber Sir Edmund Hillary stood on the summit of Mt. Everest highest point on the earth's surface
10. Then on May 22 1963 Jim Whittaker became the first American to reach this point
11. Probably many young men who love climbing have been inspired by these feats
12. Isn't it interesting to read about other countries and other people
13. Because you live in America your life is different from that of a boy or girl who lives in Burma or India
14. The geography of a country whether we enjoy studying it or not greatly affects the life of the people
15. Now that we can travel from one country to another so quickly we need to understand all we can about one another
16. We should know how other people live what their homes are like and what kinds of problems they may have
17. We study French Spanish German Russian and I'm sure other languages
18. There is a Spanish girl living at 122 Main Street Ashburnham just a few miles from the regional school we all attend
19. Yes she has some difficulty with the language but it is amazing how fast she is learning

20. When we know people from different countries how thrilling our study of geography is

● REVIEW EXERCISE D. Number your paper 1–20. If a sentence has been punctuated correctly, write *C* after the proper number. Supply commas and end marks in the other sentences by copying the word before a mark of punctuation and adding the comma or end mark.

1. Unless I notify you otherwise please send your letters to my summer address 15 Cedar Avenue Plymouth New Hampshire.
2. Sally, are you ever going to get that job done?
3. The ski lodge a large attractive building was very comfortable.
4. We enjoyed, too, meeting the many young people who were there.
5. What a perfect day we have had
6. No Jane you may not stay any longer.
7. Our vacation extends from Friday June 22 to Thursday September 5
8. We will soon learn what is to be done, how long it will take, and how best to accomplish the job.
9. The book which you are reading is considered a classic.
10. Dick, who is the leader of the group, has been ill.
11. We don't know in fact just how many young people will be here.
12. Running hurriedly down the stairs, Marie caught the heel of her shoe and fell.
13. William Bob Jerry and Ken the coach wants to see you all after school
14. Determined to win the prize Helen practiced for many hours

15. The girl who is determined to win must work very hard.
16. The storm our first real hurricane came suddenly.
17. Why Jane what do you intend to do with that
18. The snowstorm is over, the wind has died down, and we are going out to shovel the walk.
19. Well, what a good job you've done, boys!
20. Do you think you know all the answers now, Tom?

CHAPTER **14**

Punctuation

Semicolons, Colons, Italics, Quotation Marks, Apostrophes, Hyphens

Just as we use many kinds of expression and intonation to convey our meaning when we speak, we need several different marks of punctuation to make clear the meaning of our written language. In this chapter you will study the use of six marks of punctuation.

SEMICOLONS

The semicolon, as you can tell from its appearance, is part period and part comma. It signals a pause stronger than a comma but not so strong as a period.

14a. Use a semicolon between independent clauses in a sentence if they are not joined by *and, but, or, nor, for, yet.*

EXAMPLES On his last voyage Henry Hudson was accompanied by his son John**;** both men were victims of their crew's mutiny.

The survivors of Hudson's mutinous crew were brought to trial in England**;** the outcome of that trial is unknown.

14a

A period (and capital) between the independent clauses would change these examples into two sentences. This would be correct, but it would not show how closely related the ideas are.

◆ NOTE Very short independent clauses without conjunctions may be separated by commas.

EXAMPLE The leaves whispered, the brook gurgled, the sun beamed benignly.

14b. Use a semicolon between independent clauses joined by such words as *for example, for instance, that is, besides, accordingly, moreover, nevertheless, furthermore, otherwise, therefore, however, consequently, instead, hence.*

EXAMPLES Benjamin Franklin is remembered as one of the founders of our nation; moreover, he is remembered as an author and a scientist.

Mary Jane decided not to go to the game; instead, she stayed home and read.

Certain animals combine surprising characteristics; for example, the duck-billed platypus is a mammal with a ducklike beak, dense fur, and a wide, flat tail.

The early Christians refused to worship the Roman emperor as a god; therefore, they were persecuted by the Romans.

Algebra was Harold's most difficult subject; accordingly, he gave it more time than any other subject.

14c. A semicolon (rather than a comma) may be needed to separate the independent clauses of a compound sentence if there are commas within the clauses.

The mark of punctuation that is ordinarily used to indicate a separation between independent clauses is a comma. But if commas are used within the clauses, it may be difficult to distinguish between these commas and a comma indicating the end of a clause. In such a case, a different, more emphatic signal—the semicolon—is needed.

EXAMPLE A tall, swarthy man entered the large, drafty room**;** and a short, slight, blond man followed him.

● EXERCISE 1. Number your paper 1–10. After the proper number, indicate that the sentence requires a semicolon by writing the words before and after the semicolon and inserting the mark of punctuation. If the sentence does not require a semicolon, write *C* after the proper number. Seven of the following sentences require semicolons.

1. Giuseppe Verdi composed many famous operas, among the most popular are *Aida* and *La Traviata.*
2. His operas are performed throughout the Western world, and millions of people go to see them and enjoy his music.
3. Millions of others do not go to see operas however, many of them are familiar with melodies by Verdi, such as the "Anvil Chorus."
4. A chorus from one of Verdi's operas reflected the desire of the Italian people to be free of Austrian rule, this chorus inspired many anti-Austrian demonstrations.

5. The letters of Verdi's name came to stand for *V*ittorio *E*manuele *R*e *d'I*talia, or Victor Emmanuel, King of Italy, a leader of the struggle, and the name VERDI written on walls referred both to the composer and the king.
6. Giuseppe Verdi was born on October 10, 1813, Le Roncole, Italy was his birthplace.
7. Verdi's life was marked by tragedy. In 1836 he married Margherita Barezzi, but some time later his wife and their two small children died.
8. Verdi's most popular opera, *Aida*, has an Egyptian setting, moreover it had its premiere at Cairo, Egypt, in 1871.
9. When everyone thought that the seventy-four-year-old Verdi had ceased composing, he surprised the world by completing his opera *Otello*.
10. Verdi's last opera, *Falstaff*, is based on a play by Shakespeare, it is an adaptation of *The Merry Wives of Windsor*.

COLONS

The colon says, in effect, "Note what follows."

14d. Use a colon before a list of items, especially after expressions like *as follows* or *the following*.

EXAMPLES Minimum equipment for camping is as follows: bed roll, utensils for cooking and eating, warm clothing, sturdy shoes, jackknife, coil of rope, and flashlight.

This is what I have to do on Saturday: clean my room, shop for a birthday present for my sister, baby-sit for Mrs. Magill for two hours, do my Spanish homework, and make a cake for dinner.

14e. Use a colon in certain conventional situations.

(1) Use a colon between the hour and the minute when you write the time.

EXAMPLES 11:30 P.M.
4:08 A.M.

(2) Use a colon after the salutation of a business letter.

EXAMPLES Gentlemen:
Dear Mr. Gonzalez:
Dear Sir:

◆ NOTE The friendly letter requires a comma, not a colon, after the salutation.

● EXERCISE 2. Number your paper 1–10. Supply necessary semicolons, colons, and commas by copying the word before a mark of punctuation and adding the punctuation.

1. Spectators were arriving early at the stadium already eager vendors were hawking their wares up and down the aisles.
2. Some of the music was gay some was somber.
3. We have seen the following birds this summer blue jays robins cedar waxwings Baltimore orioles chickadees and nuthatches.
4. Mother knows nothing about baseball she is bewildered by the game.
5. Anyone coming late will not be admitted.
6. The gym is on the ground floor the classrooms are above it.
7. Next year we will study these subjects French algebra science history and English.

8. The first day at camp June was homesick but sports and crafts and new friends soon cured her of feeling lonely.
9. The following schedule will be observed breakfast at 7 30 A.M. classes from 8 30 A.M. until 12 00 noon lunch at 12 30 and the rest of the day free for recreation.
10. Children like to read about dinosaurs most adults do too.

UNDERLINING (ITALICS)

Italics are printed letters that lean to the right, *like this.* In handwritten or typewritten work, italics are indicated by underlining. If your composition were to be set in type, the typesetter would use italics for underlined words. For example, if you wrote—

Born Free is the story of a lioness who became a pet.

the printed version would look like this:

Born Free is the story of a lioness who became a pet.

14f. **Use underlining (italics) for titles of books, periodicals, works of art, and so on.**

EXAMPLES *Big Red* is a book about an Irish setter.

Tchaikovsky's *Nutcracker Suite* is perfect music for a ballet.

The *Chicago Tribune* has one of the largest circulations of any newspaper in the country.

Did you see my copy of *Popular Mechanics?*

The *Gripsholm* is a Swedish ship.

◆ NOTE When writing the title of a newspaper or a magazine within a sentence, underline the title. Do not underline or capitalize the word *the* with the name of a newspaper or magazine. The name of a city in a newspaper title is usually, but not necessarily, underlined.

EXAMPLE My father subscribes to two newspapers published in other cities: the St. Louis Post-Dispatch and the San Francisco Chronicle.

● EXERCISE 3. Number your paper 1–10. After the proper number, copy and underline the words in the sentence that should be in italics.

1. Seventeen is a very popular magazine for girls, while Popular Mechanics appeals to the boys.
2. We always read the Sunday edition of the New York Times.
3. Are you familiar with George Gershwin's Rhapsody in Blue?
4. James Fenimore Cooper, one of our earliest writers about American life, wrote The Last of the Mohicans and The Deerslayer.
5. Guernica is a famous painting by Picasso.
6. Two of my favorite books are Call It Courage, by Armstrong Sperry, and Who Rides in the Dark? by Stephen W. Meader.
7. Peter and the Wolf is a musical composition that tells a story.
8. The Queen Elizabeth 2 is a luxurious ocean liner.
9. William S. Gilbert and Arthur Sullivan wrote many popular light operas, including The Mikado and The Pirates of Penzance.
10. Our family subscribes to Life, the Saturday Review, Newsweek, the National Geographic, and the Christian Science Monitor.

WRITING QUOTATIONS

Quotations are words spoken or written by someone and reported directly. In your writing you will often find it necessary to tell what someone has said, whether you are describing a true happening or writing an imaginary story. You will need to know several rules of punctuation in order to write quotations.

14g. Use quotation marks to enclose a direct quotation—a person's exact words.

Quotation marks before and after a person's words show exactly what he said.

EXAMPLES "Has anyone in the class swum in the Great Salt Lake?" asked Mr. Cahill. [Mr. Cahill's exact words]
"I did last summer," said June. [June's exact words]

Do not confuse a person's exact words with a rewording of his speech. If you tell what someone said without repeating his exact words, you are using an *indirect* quotation. No quotation marks are needed for an indirect quotation.

INDIRECT QUOTATION Pauline asked for **my interpretation of the poem.** [not Pauline's exact words; no quotation marks needed]

DIRECT QUOTATION Pauline asked, **"What is your interpretation of the poem?"** [Pauline's exact words; quotation marks needed]

INDIRECT QUOTATION I told her that **I thought the poet was expressing awe at the power of nature.**

DIRECT QUOTATION **"I think the poet is expressing awe at the power of nature,"** I said.

14h. A direct quotation begins with a capital letter.

EXAMPLES Jimmy shouted, "The first man has landed on the moon!"

"Is it true?" gasped Sandra.

Mike groaned, "And I wanted to be the first myself!"

14i. When a quoted *sentence* is divided into two parts by an interrupting expression such as *he said* or *Mother asked,* the second part begins with a small letter.

EXAMPLES "What are some of the things," asked Mrs. Perkins, "that the first man on the moon found out?"

"He found out," answered Jack, "that the moon is covered by a layer of dust."

"I would like," said Alice, "to meet the man in the moon."

If the second part of an interrupted quotation starts a new sentence or if it begins with a word that ordinarily requires a capital, it should start with a capital letter, of course.

EXAMPLES "Anything that is dangerous is exciting, too," remarked Mrs. Perkins. "Space travel is no exception." [The second part begins with a capital because it is a new sentence.]

"In my opinion," Tony said, "Mars would be more fun than the moon." [The second part begins with a capital, because Mars, a proper noun, is always capitalized.]

● EXERCISE 4. Copy the following sentences, supplying whatever capitals and marks of punctuation are needed. Two sentences require no changes and should not be copied.

1. how long will it be, asked Jack, before you are ready to go?
2. if it can be arranged, the teacher announced, we will visit the United Nations next Thursday.
3. read this book, said Charles you'll enjoy it.
4. we must hurry to the beach, said Ed, for the tide will be high in an hour.
5. Mr. Thornton, our science teacher, says he has a new telescope that we may use tonight.
6. that will be fun, said Jim I've never used a telescope.
7. maybe we can see more of the surface of the moon Alice suggested it's very strange-looking.
8. yes, Jim answered, but we'll soon be able to go there and see it.
9. Alice replied that looking at the moon through a telescope would be enough for her.
10. You girls, answered Jim, just don't have the adventurous spirit.

14j. A direct quotation is set off from the rest of the sentence by commas or by a question mark or exclamation point.

EXAMPLES "I've just finished reading a book about Narcissa Whitman," Ellen said.

"Was she one of the early settlers in the Northwest?" asked Janet.

"What an adventure!" exclaimed Carol.

14k. A period or a comma following a quotation should be placed inside the closing quotation marks.

EXAMPLES Maria said, "I think women should have more chances to be pioneers."

"They have the chances—they just don't take them," jeered Ray.

14 l. A question mark or an exclamation point should be placed inside the closing quotation marks if the quotation is a question or exclamation. Otherwise it should be placed outside.

EXAMPLES "What is the time difference between California and Chicago?" asked Ken. [The quotation is a question.]

Bob exclaimed, "I thought everyone knew that!" [The quotation is an exclamation.]

Is the right answer "two hours"? [The whole sentence is a question, but the quotation is not.]

If a sentence contains two questions, you still use only one question mark: Who said, "What's your name?"

● EXERCISE 5. Copy the following sentences, supplying whatever marks of punctuation and capitals are needed.

1. Mother may we go to the movies this afternoon asked Mary Ann
2. Yes Mary Ann replied Mother if you will come directly home after the show
3. Please lend me some money John said Frank I've spent my allowance
4. Did you say I'm out of stamps
5. What a fine lesson we've had today exclaimed the teacher
6. Play ball shouted the umpire
7. John's question was What is helium
8. Did Bob answer A gaseous element
9. Fire Fire cried the boys the whole kitchen is on fire
10. Christopher called his sister Mother wants you right away

14m. When you write dialogue (two or more persons having a conversation), begin a new paragraph each time you change speakers.

EXAMPLE "What did you think of that movie about Japan?" Sara asked Ron as they left the school building.

"I was surprised at the scenes in Tokyo. I didn't know it was so modern and Westernized."

"I guess a lot of the young people don't wear traditional Japanese clothes nowadays," Sara said. "I hope the kimono doesn't disappear completely—it's so pretty."

"How would you like to wear one to school tomorrow?" asked Ron. "You'd be the center of attention."

14n. **When a quotation consists of several sentences, put quotation marks only at the beginning and at the end of the whole quotation, not around each sentence in the quotation.**

WRONG "Memorize all your lines for Monday." "Have someone at home give you your cues." "Enjoy your weekend!" said Mr. Goodwin, knowing very well we couldn't do it.

RIGHT "Memorize all your lines for Monday. Have someone at home give you your cues. Enjoy your weekend!" said Mr. Goodwin, knowing very well we couldn't do it.

● EXERCISE 6. Rewrite the following dialogue, punctuating and paragraphing correctly.

Well Tom how did you enjoy reading *Treasure Island* asked Miss Cranston I thought it was great Miss Cranston Fine Tom Can you tell us one or two things you liked especially There was plenty of excitement Tom replied and I guess I like lots of that Anything else Well Jim seemed like a real boy and it's fun to read about adventures like his even though you know they just couldn't happen What chapter did you think was most important The chapter where

Ben Gunn came into the story he was very important to the plot Good Tom you've really thought about the story Now let's hear from someone else

14o. Use single quotation marks to enclose a quotation within a quotation.

EXAMPLES "I said, 'The quiz will cover Unit 2 and your special reports,' " repeated Miss Allyn.

"What poem begins with the line, 'I'm going out to clean the pasture spring'?" Jim asked.

14p. Use quotation marks to enclose titles of chapters, articles, short stories, poems, songs, and other *parts* of books or magazines.[1]

EXAMPLES Irwin Shaw's "Strawberry Ice-Cream Soda" is a story of an older and a younger brother.

Our assignment for tomorrow is the first part of Chapter 11, "Americans Create New States out of the Wilderness."

Helen can still recite several stanzas of "Paul Revere's Ride," which she memorized last year.

The poetry of Elizabeth Madox Roberts is the subject of an article called "A Tent of Green" in the *Horn Book Magazine*.

[1] For the use of italics for titles, see rule 14f on page 264.

● EXERCISE 7. Copy the following sentences, inserting punctuation marks and quotation marks where needed and underlining words that should be in italics.

1. Today we are studying the chapter Settlers Move into the West.
2. Doris says that she read a magazine article entitled Along the Oregon Trail.
3. Do you know the poem All Day on the Prairie?
4. Who wrote the story To Build a Fire asked the teacher.
5. I know said Phil. It's from a book called Lost Faces, by Jack London.
6. Do you remember the battle cry of the Texans Remember the Alamo asked John.
7. The magazine American Heritage has thrilling stories from American history.
8. How many trips to the moon have U.S. astronauts made asked Beth.
9. Did you read asked Mr. White the article Space Shuttle Problems in the Miami Herald.
10. My lunch hour has been changed Dick said now I don't have lunch until 1230.

● REVIEW EXERCISE A. If a sentence is punctuated correctly, write *C* after its number on your paper. Copy the incorrect sentences and make all necessary corrections.

1. Mother warned us "Be sure to have these things with you a first-aid kit a compass plenty of matches and a can opener.
2. "Are you going away now," Alice said, "we haven't had dinner yet."
3. "Why, Jim," cried Sam, "you've cut your finger badly!"

4. There's a spider on my dress screamed Peggy
5. The girls want to know if we really know how to handle a boat.
6. "Jack, do you know who said Give me liberty or give me death" asked the teacher.
7. We should get started by 10 30 A.M. it will take us at least two hours to get there
8. "Come on in," shouted Dick. "The water's fine!"
9. Let us get our work done now I suggested. It will seem much harder if we leave it.
10. "What a job this has been!" exclaimed Tom.
11. Oh dear sighed Cheryl isn't the umpire ever going to say Play ball
12. Laura asked, which team are you cheering for Cheryl
13. Father asked if we wanted to go to the movies.
14. Mary said she and Sally would be over this evening, but it's raining so hard that they may not come.
15. These are the things you'll need on the picnic sandwiches lemonade pickles cookies fruit and anything else edible.
16. I don't know where Jane can be, Gladys She distinctly said I'll meet you here in an hour.
17. Rudyard Kipling's If is a good poem for anyone to know.
18. "That was a lot of homework, Miss Ames. It took two hours," said Marsha.
19. "What a fine rider James is!" exclaimed his instructor.
20. "Come, come, Dick," said his teacher, you can do better than that."

● REVIEW EXERCISE B. Write a brief dialogue between two classmates. Show that you understand the use of quotation marks and the paragraphing of dialogue.

APOSTROPHES

The *apostrophe* has two uses: to show ownership or relationship, and to show where letters have been omitted in a contraction.

The Possessive Case

The possessive case of a word shows ownership or relationship.

EXAMPLES Harold's boat
Mother's job
book's title
an hour's time

◆ NOTE Personal pronouns in the possessive case require no apostrophe: Is this bat *ours*, *yours*, or *theirs?*

14q. To form the possessive case of a singular noun, add an apostrophe and an *s*.

EXAMPLES Betty's typewriter
dog's collar
a country's natural resources
a moment's thought
one cent's worth

EXCEPTION A proper name ending in *s* may add only an apostrophe under the following conditions:

1. The name consists of two or more syllables.
2. Adding *'s* would make the name awkward to pronounce.

EXAMPLES Mr. Rogers' house
Marjorie Kinnan Rawlings' novels
Hercules' feats

● EXERCISE 8. Number your paper 1–10. After the proper number, copy from each sentence the nouns that are in the possessive case and supply the necessary apostrophes.

1. The dogs leash is too short.
2. That cars tires are badly worn.
3. Mortimers homework is on the table.
4. I was surprised at Franks answer.
5. The roar of one planes engines was deafening.
6. To have a locket like her oldest sisters was Anns greatest desire.
7. You may be able to borrow Henrys book for the review.
8. Have you seen my mothers hat?
9. A chairmans job is to keep order.
10. Put your fathers briefcase and Alices bag in the car, please.

14r. To form the possessive case of a plural noun ending in *s*, add only the apostrophe.

EXAMPLES friends' invitations
citizens' committee
pupils' records

The few plural nouns that do not end in *s* form the possessive just as singular nouns do, by adding an apostrophe and an *s*.

EXAMPLES men's suits
mice's tracks
children's voices

◆ NOTE Do not use an apostrophe to form the *plural* of a noun. The apostrophe shows ownership or relationship, not number. It is usually followed by a noun.

WRONG The new car's are sporty this year.
RIGHT The new cars are sporty this year. [plural]
RIGHT The new car's styling is sporty this year. [possessive]

● EXERCISE 9. Ten plural expressions are listed below. Write the possessive for each one.

EXAMPLE 1. artists paintings
1. *artists' paintings*

1. boys hats
2. women magazines
3. neighbors houses
4. girls friends
5. three weeks losses
6. Joneses car
7. men clothing
8. children toys
9. cities slums
10. oxen pens

● EXERCISE 10. Draw lines, making three columns on your paper. Label the columns *Singular Possessive*, *Plural*, and *Plural Possessive*. In each column, write the form of the noun which the column calls for.

1. house
2. baby
3. pilot
4. enemy
5. calf
6. valley
7. mouse
8. child
9. citizen
10. student
11. wolf
12. piano
13. customer
14. decoy

Contractions

14s. Use an apostrophe to show where letters have been omitted in a contraction.

A contraction is a word made by combining or shortening two or three words. An apostrophe takes the place of the letters that are omitted.

EXAMPLES **Where is** the exit?
Where's the exit?

We will have gone by then.
We'll have gone by then.

He **might have** let us know.
He **might've** let us know.

The word *not* is contracted to *n't*. This is often added to a verb to form a contraction. Usually the spelling of the verb is unchanged.

is not	isn't
are not	aren't
does not	doesn't
do not	don't
was not	wasn't
were not	weren't
has not	hasn't
have not	haven't
had not	hadn't
should not	shouldn't
would not	wouldn't
could not	couldn't

But:

shall not	shan't
will not	won't
cannot	can't

Contractions may also be formed with nouns or pronouns and verbs:

I am	I'm
you are	you're
she would	she'd
you will	you'll
they are	they're
Ann is	Ann's

Its and It's

The word *its* is a pronoun in the possessive case. It does not have an apostrophe.

The word *it's* is a contraction of ***it is*** or ***it has*** and requires an apostrophe.

EXAMPLES **Its** right front tire is flat. [*Its* is a possessive pronoun.]

It's wet paint. [*It's* means *it is*.]

It's been a long time. [*It's* means *it has*.]

Whose and Who's

The word *whose* is a pronoun in the possessive case. It does not have an apostrophe.

The word *who's* means ***who is*** or ***who has***. Being a contraction, it requires an apostrophe.

EXAMPLES **Whose** idea was it? [*Whose* is a possessive pronoun.]

Who's been in my room? [*Who's* means *who has*.]

Your and You're

The word *your* is a possessive pronoun. It does not have an apostrophe.

You're is a contraction of ***you are***. It requires an apostrophe to show where the letter is omitted.

EXAMPLES **Your** paper shows great improvement, Henry. [*Your* is a pronoun in the possessive case.]

You're going to get a better mark this term. [*You're* means *you are*.]

In Plurals

14t. Use an apostrophe and *s* to form the plural of letters, numbers, and signs, and of words referred to as words.

EXAMPLES Doesn't he know the *ABC*'s?
Your *2*'s look like *5*'s.
Don't use &'s in place of *and*'s.

● EXERCISE 11. Number your paper 1–10. Copy from the following sentences the items that require an apostrophe. Supply the apostrophes.

1. The girls wont say where theyll be.
2. Lets go watch the baseball game.
3. Jill gets all *A*s and *B*s on her report card.
4. It is incorrect to use &s in a theme.
5. Everything depended on the number of 10s and 20s we had.
6. Get your books; theyre in the library.
7. Do you know what youre doing?
8. Whos going skiing tomorrow?
9. Dont forget to put in your +s and −s.
10. Always cross your *t*s and dot your *i*s.

● EXERCISE 12. Write six sentences in which you use the following words correctly: *its, it's; whose, who's; your, you're.*

HYPHENS

14u. Use a hyphen to divide a word at the end of a line.

Often when you write, you find there is not enough space for a whole word at the end of the line. When this happens, you may divide the word, using a hyphen to indicate the division.

EXAMPLES How long has the building been under construction?

If you want to know, look it up in the almanac.

You must be careful to divide words only between syllables. For more information about the rules for dividing words, see page 315.

14v. Use a hyphen with compound numbers from twenty-one to ninety-nine and with fractions used as adjectives.

EXAMPLES There were twenty-one ducks in that flock.

A two-thirds majority will decide the issue, and the other one third will have to abide by the decision. [In the first use, *two-thirds* is a compound adjective modifying *majority;* in the second use, *third* is a noun modified by the single adjective *one.*]

● EXERCISE 13. Number your paper 1–10. After the proper number, write the words from the following expressions which require hyphens. Supply hyphens.

1. a three fourths majority
2. one half of the room
3. one hundred twenty five people
4. ninety eight
5. Fifty ninth Street
6. twenty four eggs
7. one third of a game
8. three fourths of the population

9. one and two thirds inches
10. one quarter of the distance

● REVIEW EXERCISE C. Form contractions from the following groups of words:

1. will not
2. there is
3. who will
4. they are
5. who is
6. is not
7. it is
8. should not
9. let us
10. cannot
11. you are
12. does not
13. he will
14. shall not
15. we are
16. I am
17. was not
18. she is
19. you will
20. would not

● REVIEW EXERCISE D. Number your paper 1–20. After the proper number, copy the words in the following sentences that require apostrophes or hyphens. Supply these apostrophes and hyphens.

1. Heres where we get off.
2. Whose coat is that on the chair, Billys or Tommys?
3. Wholl get the tickets for tonights game?
4. The Blaine sisters Irish setter won first prize at the dog show.
5. I wonder if theyre ready; we have forty three miles to drive.
6. Two fifths of Johns allowance will be deducted until he has paid for the broken window.
7. Shouldnt you inquire about directions for getting there?
8. Standing on the corner of Seventy ninth Street and Walker Avenue, I saw thirty two large women walking small pets.

9. He just cant seem to understand.
10. Ive seen Andys project, but wheres yours?
11. Youve no idea how hard weve worked!
12. Twenty five students (almost four fifths of the class) raised their hands to show that theyd taken long trips during their vacation.
13. If Mary wants the job, shed better come now!
14. The measure received the two thirds majority necessary to pass.
15. When questioned, the suspect claimed that he hadnt broken into his neighbors house.
16. Harveys going away tomorrow, but Im remaining at home.
17. Its name is Brainy, but its not really very smart.
18. Please see whos at the door.
19. Lets find out whats happening at your house.
20. My ancestors first settled in this state ninety eight years ago.

● REVIEW EXERCISE E. Copy the following sentences, supplying semicolons, colons, italics, quotation marks, apostrophes, and hyphens where needed.

1. Ill meet you promptly at 7 20 at Fifty eighth Street and Regal Court, said Roger Be sure youre there on time.
2. The Lafayette Chronicle, the Smiths home town newspaper, has an article about them its very informative.
3. The following students scored over ninety five on last weeks test Linda, Tom, Ken, and Priscilla.
4. I dont think said Mark that youve read The Ransom of Red Chief. [a short story]
5. When I asked the time, did you say 5 40 or 5 45?
6. Joe said that his father owned two thirds of the company while Mr. Perry had a one fifth share.

7. Tony said he would attend the meeting however, Fred announced, I won't go.
8. My favorite painting is Van Gogh's Sunflowers in a Vase.
9. Hogans face shone as he announced Ive found the deers tracks moreover Ive caught sight of the deer.
10. He listed the planets nearest the sun as follows Mercury, Venus, Earth, and Mars.

CHAPTER 15

Spelling

Improving Your Spelling

English is a language that is not consistent in its representation of sounds. For this reason, learning to spell in English is a challenging task. You have already learned to spell many thousands of words, but there are probably others that give you trouble. You can increase your ability to spell provided you approach the task slowly and easily—and provided you have the will and patience to learn.

GOOD SPELLING HABITS

These are a few of the things you can do to improve your spelling:

1. Keep a list of your own errors.
2. Use the dictionary as a spelling aid.
3. Spell by syllables.
4. Avoid mispronunciations that lead to spelling errors.
5. Revise your papers to avoid careless spelling errors.

1. *Keep a list of your own errors.*

As your ability to spell improves, you will notice that some words seem to be especially difficult for you.

But don't be discouraged; make your own spelling book. The best way to master your own hard words is to make a notebook list of them and review them frequently.

2. *Use the dictionary as a spelling aid.*

A dictionary is a writer's best friend. Get the habit of consulting a dictionary whenever you have a spelling problem. It's much easier, of course, to guess at spelling; but, if you want to do good work, learn to use the dictionary.

3. *Spell by syllables.*

If you have trouble spelling long words, break them up into syllables. A syllable is a part of a word that can be pronounced by itself. The word *remember* has three syllables: *re-mem-ber.* Most syllables have no more than three or four letters, and certainly you can learn that many. A long word then becomes a group of short parts, and you can learn it syllable by syllable.

4. *Avoid mispronunciations that lead to spelling errors.*

If you listen and speak carefully, you will be less likely to misspell words because you are not pronouncing them correctly. Be sure that you say *chimney* not *chimbly*, *library* not *liberry*, *modern* not *modren.*

5. *Revise your papers to avoid careless spelling errors.*

Half the trouble in spelling comes from careless haste. Whenever you do any writing, reread your paper to correct the spelling not only of difficult words but also of the ordinary, easy words that you may have misspelled through carelessness.

SPELLING RULES

The following rules are helpful, even though there are exceptions to them. If you learn them thoroughly, you will find it easier to spell correctly.

ie and ei

15a. Write *ie* when the sound is long *e* except after *c*.

EXAMPLES believe, relief, field, deceive, ceiling
EXCEPTIONS neither, leisure, seize, weird

Write *ei* when the sound is not long *e*, especially when the sound is long *a*.

EXAMPLES reign, weight, eight, freight, height, sleight
EXCEPTIONS friend, mischief

-cede, -ceed, -sede

15b. Only one word in English ends in *–sede*—*supersede;* only three words end in *–ceed*—*exceed, proceed,* and *succeed;* all other words of similar sound end in *–cede*.

EXAMPLES concede, recede, precede

● EXERCISE 1. Write the following words, supplying the missing letters (*e* and *i*) in the correct order. Be able to explain how the rules apply to each word.

1. fr. . .nd
2. p. . .ce
3. rec. . .ve
4. c. . .ling
5. w. . .ght
6. bel. . .ve
7. br. . .f
8. h. . .ght
9. n. . .ghbor
10. fr. . .ght

● EXERCISE 2. Write the following words, supplying *–ceed*, *–cede*, or *–sede*.

1. pre...
2. pro...
3. con...
4. inter...
5. super...
6. ex...
7. suc...
8. re...

Adding Prefixes

A prefix is one or more letters added to the beginning of a word to change its meaning.

EXAMPLES un + able = unable
pre + arrange = prearrange

15c. **When a prefix is added to a word, the spelling of the word itself remains the same.**

EXAMPLES il + logical = il**logical**
in + elegant = in**elegant**
im + perfect = im**perfect**
un + selfish = un**selfish**
dis + trust = dis**trust**
mis + apply = mis**apply**
re + turn = re**turn**
over + see = over**see**

● EXERCISE 3. Number your paper 1–25. Write correctly the words formed. Then choose ten of the words and use each of them in a sentence.

1. il + legal
2. in + exact
3. im + migrant
4. in + equality
5. dis + order
6. mis + inform
7. re + enter
8. over + rule
9. il + liberal
10. un + natural

11. in + active
12. mis + use
13. over + rated
14. re + establish
15. dis + similar
16. mis + interpret
17. im + probable
18. over + run
19. il + legible
20. mis + sent
21. semi + annual
22. in + numerable
23. dis + array
24. un + necessary
25. im + material

Adding Suffixes

A suffix is one or more letters added to the end of a word to change its meaning.

EXAMPLES care + less = care**less**
walk + ed = walk**ed**
comfort + able = comfort**able**

15d. When the suffixes *–ness* and *–ly* are added to a word, the spelling of the word itself is not changed.

EXAMPLES mean + ness = mean**ness**
casual + ly = casual**ly**

EXCEPTIONS Words ending in *y* usually change the *y* to *i* before *–ness* and *–ly*: misty—mist**iness**; happy—happ**ily**. One-syllable adjectives ending in *y* generally follow rule 15d: shy—shy**ly**.

15e. Drop the final *e* before a suffix beginning with a vowel.

EXAMPLES line + ing = lin**ing**
approve + al = approv**al**
desire + able = desir**able**

EXCEPTIONS In some words, the final *e* must be kept to keep the soft sound of a *c* or *g*: notice + able = notic**eable**; courage + ous = courag**eous.**

15f. Keep the final *e* before a suffix beginning with a consonant.

EXAMPLES hope + less = hop**eless**
care + ful = car**eful**

EXCEPTIONS true + ly = tru**ly**
argue + ment = argu**ment**
judge + ment = judg**ment**

● EXERCISE 4. Number your paper 1–20. Write correctly the words formed as follows:

1. mean + ness
2. final + ly
3. love + able
4. shine + ing
5. true + ly
6. one + ness
7. notice + able
8. outrage + ous
9. pretty + ly
10. advantage + ous
11. change + able
12. please + ing
13. hope + ful
14. place + ing
15. remove + al
16. study + ing
17. happy + ness
18. come + ing
19. sudden + ness
20. cordial + ly

15g. With words ending in *y* preceded by a consonant, change the *y* to *i* before any suffix not beginning with *i*.

EXAMPLES cry + ed = c**ried**
lovely + ness = love**liness**
bury + al = bu**rial**

but

cry + ing = **crying**

Note that words ending in *y* preceded by a vowel generally do not change their spelling when a suffix is added.

EXAMPLES pray + ing = praying
pay + ment = payment
boy + hood = boyhood

15h. With words of one syllable ending in a single consonant preceded by a single vowel, double the consonant before adding *-ing*, *-ed*, or *-er*.

EXAMPLES sit + ing = sit**t**ing
swim + ing = swim**m**ing
drop + ed = drop**p**ed
mop + ed = mop**p**ed

15i. With words of more than one syllable ending in a single consonant preceded by a single vowel, double the consonant before adding *-ing*, *-ed*, or *-er*, if the word is accented on the last syllable.

EXAMPLES occur′ + ed = occur**r**ed
begin′ + er = begin**n**er
permit′ + ing = permit**t**ing

If the word is *not* accented on the last syllable, the final consonant is not doubled before a suffix.

EXAMPLES tra′vel + er = traveler
can′cel + ed = canceled
sten′cil + ing = stenciling

● EXERCISE 5. Number your paper 1–20. Write correctly the words formed as follows:

1. study + ed
2. hurry + ed
3. study + ing
4. hurry + ing
5. bid + ing
6. quiz + ing
7. drop + ed
8. fit + ed
9. race + ing
10. stop + ed
11. cry + ed
12. joke + ing
13. deploy + ing
14. prefer + ed
15. permit + ed
16. beg + ed
17. plan + ed
18. admit + ing
19. run + er
20. bat + er

THE PLURAL OF NOUNS

Plurals are formed in several ways, most of them covered by rules. To learn irregular plurals, you should enter them in your private spelling list and memorize them.

15j. Observe the rules for spelling the plural of nouns.

(1) The regular way to form the plural of a noun is to add an *s*.

EXAMPLES desk, desks
idea, ideas

(2) The plural of some nouns ending in *s*, *x*, *z*, *ch*, or *sh* is formed by adding *es*.

EXAMPLES pass, passes
fox, foxes
buzz, buzzes
clutch, clutches
dish, dishes

● EXERCISE 6. Number your paper 1–10. Write the plurals of the following words:

1. wish
2. pilot
3. machine
4. match
5. automobile
6. porch
7. dance
8. mechanic
9. reflex
10. box

(3) The plural of nouns ending in *y* preceded by a consonant is formed by changing the *y* to *i* and adding *es*.

EXAMPLES army, armies; country, countries; city, cities; pony, ponies

(4) The plural of nouns ending in *y* preceded by a vowel is formed by adding *s*.

EXAMPLES journey, journeys
key, keys

(5) The plural of most nouns ending in *f* is formed by adding *s*. Some nouns ending in *f* or *fe*, however, form plurals by changing the *f* to *v* and adding *s* or *es*.

EXAMPLES grief, griefs
belief, beliefs

shelf, shelves
knife, knives
thief, thieves

(6) The plural of nouns ending in *o* preceded by a vowel is formed by adding *s*; the plural of nouns ending in *o* preceded by a consonant is formed by adding *es*.

EXAMPLES *o* following a vowel:
radio, radios
curio, curios
patio, patios

o following a consonant:

Negro, Negroes
tomato, tomatoes
echo, echoes

EXCEPTIONS Eskimos, silos, pianos, sopranos, altos

Note that many nouns ending in *o* and pertaining to music are exceptions to this rule.

(7) The plural of a few nouns is formed in irregular ways.

EXAMPLES child, children ox, oxen woman, women tooth, teeth goose, geese mouse, mice foot, feet

● EXERCISE 7. Write the plurals of the following nouns:

1. city
2. chimney
3. company
4. foot
5. donkey
6. valley
7. lily
8. goose
9. library
10. galley
11. calf
12. knife
13. leaf
14. belief
15. roof
16. rodeo
17. volcano
18. mosquito
19. soprano
20. echo
21. child
22. tooth
23. mouse
24. hero
25. woman

(8) The plural of compound nouns consisting of a noun plus a modifier is formed by making the noun plural.

EXAMPLES passerby, passersby
maid of honor, maids of honor
brother-in-law, brothers-in-law

(9) The plural of a few compound nouns is formed in irregular ways.

EXAMPLES drive-in, drive-ins
fourteen-year-old, fourteen-year-olds

(10) Some nouns are the same in the singular and plural.

EXAMPLES trout, salmon, sheep, Sioux, deer, moose

(11) The plural of numbers, letters, signs, and words considered as words is formed by adding an apostrophe and *s*.

EXAMPLES	1900	1900's
	ABC	ABC's
	+	+'s
	and	*and*'s

● EXERCISE 8. Write the plurals of the following nouns:

1. sheep
2. weekend
3. trout
4. daughter-in-law
5. *a*
6. teen-ager
7. guard of honor
8. deer
9. cupful
10. 1800

● EXERCISE 9. Write the plurals of the following items. After each plural, write the number of the subrule under rule j (1–11) that applies.

EXAMPLE 1. proof
1. *proofs* (5)

1. child
2. ox
3. 100
4. *t*
5. shelf
6. belief
7. cry
8. monkey
9. brother-in-law
10. sheep

11. piano
12. spoonful
13. Eskimo
14. knife
15. clutch
16. radio
17. potato
18. lass
19. alto
20. *and*
21. baby
22. chef
23. arpeggio
24. pulley
25. wax

WORDS OFTEN CONFUSED

The words grouped together in the following lists are frequently confused with each other because their pronunciation or spelling is the same or similar. Study them carefully and learn to distinguish both their meaning and their spelling.

---

accept *to receive with consent; to give approval to*
Many of his contemporaries did not *accept* Copernicus' theory that the earth moves around the sun.

except *leave out from a number; with the exclusion of; but*
Copernicus' theory was accurate *except* that he thought the planets' paths were circles rather than ellipses.

---

advice *a recommendation about a course of action*
Good *advice* may be easy to give but hard to follow.

advise *to recommend a course of action; to give advice*
I *advise* you to continue your music lessons if you possibly can.

---

affect *to influence; to produce an effect upon*
Copernicus' discovery *affected* the work of all astronomers who followed him.

effect *the result of an action; consequence*
It has long been observed that the phases of the moon have an *effect* on the tides of the earth's oceans.

---

all right *everything is right* or *satisfactory;* two words. The spelling *alright* is never correct.
Stan did *all right* in the track meet.
Was my answer *all right?*

---

all ready *all prepared* or *in readiness*
The players are *all ready* for the big game.

already *previously*
Our class has *already* taken two field trips this year.

● EXERCISE 10. Number your paper 1–10. After the proper number, write the word given in the parentheses that makes the sentence correct.

1. Everyone likes to give (advice, advise).
2. The (affect, effect) of the victory was startling.
3. Why did you (accept, except) Charles from the class ruling?
4. The scientists were (all ready, already) to watch the launching of the rocket.
5. The coach (advices, advises) everyone to stick to his training.
6. His weeks of practice certainly (affected, effected) his final game.

7. Most of the rebels were offered a pardon and (accepted, excepted) it, but the leaders were (accepted, excepted) from the offer.
8. John has (all ready, already) learned how to water-ski.
9. Do you think my work is (all right, alright)?
10. Whose (advice, advise) are you going to take?

---

altar — *a table for a religious ceremony*
The *altar* was banked with lilies.

alter — *to change*
The outcome of the election *altered* the mayor's plan.

---

all together — *everyone in the same place*
The director called us *all together* for one final rehearsal.

altogether — *entirely*
Your story is *altogether* too late for this issue.

---

brake — *a device to stop a machine*
Can you fix the *brake* on my bicycle?

break — *to fracture, to shatter*
The winner will be the one who *breaks* the tape.

---

capital — *a city, the seat of a government*
Olympia is the *capital* of Washington.

capitol — *a government building* (usually capitalized)
The *Capitol* is one of the handsomest buildings in Washington.

choose [present tense, rhymes with *lose*] *to select*
Will you *choose* speech or civics as your elective next year?

chose [past tense, rhymes with *grows*] *selected*
Janet *chose* to play in the band rather than the orchestra.

● EXERCISE 11. Number your paper 1–10. After the proper number, write the word given in parentheses that makes the sentence correct.

1. The building with the dome is the (capital, capitol).
2. By working (all together, altogether) we can do the job easily.
3. Because she loved dramatics, Alice (choose, chose) a difficult part in the school play.
4. Be careful, you might (brake, break) those dishes.
5. That book is (all together, altogether) too complicated for you to enjoy.
6. The candles on the (altar, alter) glowed beautifully.
7. We don't know whether to (choose, chose) band or orchestra next year.
8. A car without a good emergency (brake, break) is a menace.
9. Will Joan's accident (altar, alter) her plans?
10. Albany is the (capital, capitol) of New York.

clothes *wearing apparel*
One can learn a lot about a historical period by studying its fashions in *clothes*.

cloths *pieces of cloth*
You'll find some cleaning *cloths* in the drawer.

---

coarse *rough, crude*
The beach is covered with *coarse* brown sand.

course *path of action; planned program or route; also used in the expression of course*
The wind blew the *Gretel* slightly off its *course.*

---

consul *a representative of a government in a foreign country*
Who is the American *consul* in Nigeria?

council *a group of people who meet together*

councilor *a member of a council*
The king called a meeting of his *council* and informed his *councilors* that the royal treasury was nearly empty.

counsel *advice,* or *to give words of advice*

counselor *one who advises*
When choosing a career, seek *counsel* from your teacher.
Who is your guidance *counselor?*

---

desert [des′ert] *a dry, sandy region*
The Sahara is the largest *desert* in Africa.

desert [de·sert′] *to abandon, to leave*
Most dogs will not *desert* a friend in trouble.

dessert [des·sert′] *the final course of a meal*
Apple pie is my favorite *dessert.*

● EXERCISE 12. Number your paper 1–10. After the proper number, write the word or words given in the parentheses that will make the sentence correct.

1. Each class has four representatives on the student (council, counsel).
2. The guide threatened to (desert, dessert) us as we crossed the (desert, dessert).
3. Most eighth-grade girls are very much interested in (clothes, cloths).
4. Your guidance (councilor, counselor) will be of great help to you.
5. The (coarse, course) for the twenty-five-mile race is a rugged one.
6. The cleaning (clothes, cloths) must be washed after each use.
7. Do we have a Canadian (consul, council) in this city?
8. (Coarse, Course) pebbles made the beach difficult to walk on.
9. The meal didn't seem complete without (desert, dessert).
10. The members of the losing team looked to their coach for (council, counsel).

---

formally *with dignity, following strict rules or procedures*
The Governor delivered the speech *formally.*

formerly *previously, in the past*
Formerly, I knew the Jackson family very well.

---

hear *to perceive sounds by ear*
Dogs can *hear* some sounds that are inaudible to people.

here *in this place*
The campsite is right *here.*

---

its — [a personal pronoun showing possession] *pertaining to it*
Mount Fujiyama is noted for *its* beauty.

it's — [a contraction of *it is* or *it has*]
It's an extinct volcano.

---

lead [lēd] — [present tense] *to go first, to be a leader*
A small town in New Hampshire often *leads* the nation in filing its election returns.

lead [lĕd] — *heavy metal*
A *lead* pencil actually has no *lead* in it.

led — [past tense] *went first*
The Governor *led* his slate with an impressive majority.

---

loose — *not securely attached; not tight fitting*
If a tourniquet is too *loose*, it will not serve its purpose.

lose — *to suffer loss*
Vegetables *lose* some of their vitamins when they are cooked.

● EXERCISE 13. Number your paper 1–10. After the proper number, write the word or words given in parentheses that will make the sentence correct.

1. (Its, It's) a long way from (hear, here) to the park.
2. The plumber is removing the (lead, led) pipes and putting in brass ones.
3. We don't want to (loose, lose) you in the crowd.
4. Before the club takes up new business, the secretary (formally, formerly) reads the minutes of the previous meeting.

5. (Its, It's) too bad that the tree has lost (its, it's) leaves so early.
6. Do you (hear, here) me, Ann? Come (hear, here) this minute!
7. The Yankees were ten runs behind, and it seemed certain that they were going to (loose, lose).
8. The marshal (lead, led) the class into the chapel.
9. Had Ted ever done any running (formally, formerly)?
10. That (loose, lose) bolt can cause trouble.

---

passed [past tense of *pass*] *went by*
The Earth *passed* close to the planet Venus in 1962.

past *that which has gone by; beyond*
Old people sometimes live in the *past.*
They moved *past* the dozing sentry.

---

peace *security and quiet order*
Peace to men of good will.

piece *a part of something*
Some people can catch fish with a pole, a *piece* of string, and a bent pin.

---

plain *simple, common, unadorned; a flat area of land*
A *plain* jackknife is often as useful as one with several blades.
What is the difference between a prairie and a *plain?*

plane *a tool; an airplane; a flat surface*
The *plane* is a mark of the carpenter's trade.
The hangar will accommodate four single-engine *planes.*
Rhoda says she likes *plane* geometry.

principal *the head of a school; main or most important*
The *principal* is the chief officer of a school.
What are the *principal* exports of Brazil?

principle *a rule of conduct; a main fact or law*
He listed some of the *principles* of economics.

quiet *still and peaceful; without noise*
A *quiet* room is needed for concentrated study.

quite *wholly or entirely; to a great extent*
Winters in the New England states can be *quite* severe.

● EXERCISE 14. Number your paper 1–10. After the proper number, write the word given in parentheses that makes the sentence correct.

1. A bright smile often makes a (plain, plane) face attractive.
2. The summer was (quiet, quite) over before the beginning of school gave Mother a (quiet, quite) household once more.
3. This is an important (principal, principle) in mathematics.
4. On July 20, 1963, the moon (passed, past) between the earth and the sun, causing a total eclipse.
5. A (plain, plane) is a useful tool.
6. Save us a (peace, piece) of that blueberry pie, Mother.
7. Our (principal, principle) is leaving the school this year.

8. We should try to learn from (passed, past) experience.
9. The nation was working hard to attain (peace, piece).
10. Cattle were grazing over the (plain, plane).

---

shone [past tense of *shine*]
They polished the silver until it *shone*.

shown [past tense of *show*] *revealed*
A model of the new school will be *shown* to the public next week.

---

stationary *in a fixed position*
Most of the furnishings of a space capsule must be *stationary*.

stationery *writing paper*
I need a new box of *stationery*.

---

than [a conjunction used for comparisons]
The Amazon River is longer *than* the Mississippi River.

then *at that time*
If the baby is awake by four o'clock, we will leave *then*.

---

there *a place* [also used to begin a sentence]
Go *there* in the fall when the leaves are turning.

their [a possessive]
Their team seems very skillful.

they're *they are*
They're taller than most of our players.

threew [past tense of *throw*] *hurled*
Our pitcher *threw* four balls in succession.

through [a preposition]
Have you ever seen a ship go *through* the locks of a canal?

● EXERCISE 15. Number your paper 1–10. After the proper number, write the word given in parentheses that makes the sentence correct.

1. We go (there, their, they're) often, for the children can get (there, their, they're) instruction in swimming, and we can see how (their, there, they're) progressing.
2. She has more (stationary, stationery) than she'll ever use.
3. The stars (shown, shone) brilliantly.
4. The city was so much larger (then, than) I expected.
5. The new desks for our art room are not (stationary, stationery).
6. We often hear the planes break (threw, through) the sound barrier.
7. Sue will have the first ride; (than, then) it will be your turn.
8. The goalposts on the football field have been made (stationary, stationery).
9. We were (shone, shown) all the points of interest in the downtown area.
10. The pitcher (threw, through) a wild ball that almost hit the batter.

---

to [a preposition, also used with a verb]
A visit *to* Chinatown is an exciting treat.
Many small nations are eager *to* become independent.

too *also; more than enough*
We have lived in North Dakota and in Alaska, *too*.
It is *too* cold for rain today.

two *one plus one*
Americans can visit *two* foreign countries without leaving the continent.

---

weak *not strong; feeble*
My mother likes to drink *weak* tea.

week *seven days*
Your pictures will be ready in about a *week*.

---

weather *condition of the air or atmosphere*
Weather prediction is an important branch of meteorology.

whether [a conjunction]
Miss Gordon is wondering *whether* the bond issue for the new school will be approved.

---

whose [a possessive]
Whose report are we hearing today?

who's *who is*
Who's representing the yearbook staff?

---

your [a possessive]
Your work in math is improving.

you're *you are*
You're right on time!

● EXERCISE 16. Number your paper 1–10. After the proper number, write the word given in parentheses that makes the sentence correct.

1. Lack of exercise made the runner's legs (weak, week).
2. (Weather, Whether) we'll go or not depends on the (weather, whether).
3. (Whose, Who's) books are you carrying?
4. Find out (whose, who's) going if you can.
5. Allen thought algebra was (to, too, two) difficult for him (to, too, two) master.
6. (Your, You're) a long distance off your course, captain.
7. We took (to, too, two) (weaks, weeks) for our trip across the country.
8. The (weather, whether) was cloudy so we could see very little from the plane.
9. Would you enjoy a trip (to, too, two) Mars, Ned?
10. Aren't you using (your, you're) compass?

50 SPELLING DEMONS

ache	country	knew
again	doctor	know
always	does	laid
answer	don't	meant
blue	early	minute
built	easy	often
busy	every	
buy	friend	once
can't		ready
color	guess	said
	half	says
cough	hour	shoes
could	instead	since

straight
sugar
sure
tear

though
through
tired
tonight
trouble

wear
where
which
whole
women

250 SPELLING WORDS

abandon
absolutely
acceptance
accidentally
accommodate

accompany
accomplish
achieve
acquaintance
acquire

actually
advertisement
against
aisle
amount

analysis
anticipate
anxiety
apology
apparent

appearance
application
appreciation
approach
arguing

argument

article
assistance
authority
basis

beginning
believe
benefit
boundary
bouquet

bulletin
business
canceled
capacity
careless

carrier
ceiling
challenge
choice
choir

chorus
circuit
colonel
column
coming

commercial

committees
competition
completely
conceive
condemn

congratulations
conscience
conscious
control

convenience
courteous
criticism
cylinder
dealt

deceit
decision
definite
definition
describe

description
desirable
despair
develop
difficulties

disappointment
discipline

discussion
diseased
distinction

distribution
doctrine
duplicate
economic
eligible
embarrass
engineering
enthusiasm
equipped
eventually

exactly
exaggerate
excellent
existence
experience
experiment
explanation
fascinating
favorite
February

finally
flu
forty
fourth
friendliness
generally
governor
grammar
gratitude
guarantee

guardian
gymnasium
hatred
height
heroine
hesitate
humorous
hypocrite
ignorance
imagination

immediately
incidentally
individual
inferior
initial
inspiration
intelligence
interfere
interrupt
involve

judgment
knowledge
laboratory
leisure
lengthen
lieutenant
loneliness
luncheon
majority
manufacture

marriage
mechanical
medieval

military
mourn
multiplication
muscular
mystery
naturally
necessary

Negroes
nickel
nonsense
numerous
obvious
occasionally
occurrence
opinion
opportunity
orchestra

originally
paid
parallel
parliament
patience
performance
personal
personality
persuade
philosopher

picnicking
planned
pleasant
possess
precede
preferred

prejudice
privilege
probably
procedure

professor
pursuit
qualified
realize
receipt
recognize
recommend
referring
regularly
relieve

repetition
research
response
rhythm
satisfied
saucers
schedule
scissors
sense
sentiment

separate
sergeant
shepherd
similar
simply
solemn
source
sponsor
straighten
subscription

succeed
success
sufficient
suggest
suppress
surprise
surrounded
suspense
suspicion
tailor

temperament
tendency
theories
therefore
thorough

tobacco
tonsils
tradition
tragedy
transferred

tries
truly
unanimous
unnecessary
unsatisfactory
until
useful
using
utilized
vacuum

variety
various
vein
view
villain
violence
warrant
weird
wholly
writing

CHAPTER 16

Manuscript Form

Standards for Written Work

A manuscript is any typewritten or handwritten composition, as distinguished from a printed document. In your schoolwork this year and during the years ahead, you will be writing more and more manuscripts. You should learn correct form for your written work now and follow it in all your papers.

16a. Follow accepted standards in preparing manuscripts.

Your teacher will find it easier to read and evaluate your papers if they are properly prepared. There is no single correct way to prepare a paper, but the rules below are widely used and accepted. Follow them unless your teacher requests you to do otherwise.

1. Write compositions on standard size ($8\frac{1}{2} \times 11$ inches) lined paper.
2. Follow the school policy concerning use of both sides of the paper. In general, it is preferable to write on only one side of the sheet.
3. Write in blue or black ink or use a typewriter. If you type, double-space the lines.

4. Leave a margin of about two inches at the top of the page and margins of about one inch at the sides and bottom. The left-hand margin should be straight. The right-hand margin should be as straight as you can make it.

5. Indent the first line of each paragraph about one-half inch from the left.

6. Write your name, the class, and the date on the first page. Follow your teacher's instructions on the placement of these items. You may put them on three separate lines in the upper right-hand corner of the sheet, or write them in one line across the top of the page. Either way, they should begin about one inch down from the top of the page.

7. If your paper has a title, write it in the center of the first line. Skip a line between the title and the first line of your composition.

8. If the paper is more than one page in length, number the pages after the first, placing the number in the center of the line, about one-half inch down from the top.

9. Write legibly and neatly. If you are using unlined paper, try to keep the lines straight. Form your letters carefully, so that *n*'s do not look like *u*'s, *a*'s like *o*'s, and so on. Dot the *i*'s and cross the *t*'s. If you have to erase, do it neatly.

16b. Learn the rules for using abbreviations.

In your writing, you should spell out most words rather than abbreviate them. A few abbreviations, however, are commonly used and are considered acceptable in written work.

The following abbreviations are acceptable when used with a name: *Mr.*, *Mrs.*, *Dr.*, *Jr.*, and *Sr.* If they do not accompany a name, spell out the words instead of using the abbreviations.

EXAMPLES Mr. Hastings Dr. Eustace
Mrs. Galzone Frank B. Nolan, Jr.
Have you called the doctor?
Paul is a junior partner of the firm.

The abbreviations A.M. (*ante meridiem*—before noon), P.M. (*post meridiem*—after noon), A.D. (*anno Domini*—in the year of our Lord), and B.C. (before Christ) are acceptable when they are used with numbers.

EXAMPLES The meeting is called for 3:30 P.M.
Augustus Caesar lived from 63 B.C. to A.D. 14. [Notice that the abbreviation A.D. precedes the number, while B.C. follows it.]

Abbreviations for organizations are acceptable if they are generally known.

EXAMPLE That man is wanted by the FBI. [Abbreviations for government agencies are usually written without periods.]

16c. Learn the rules for writing numbers.

Numbers of more than two words should be written in numerals, not words. If, however, you are writing several numbers, some of them one word and some more than one, write them all the same way. Always spell out a number that begins a sentence.

EXAMPLES Dick and I set out **twenty-three** strawberry plants this morning.

From Malvern take Route **202.**

Jerry started with **120** baby chicks, but now he has only **90.**

Two hundred and fifty-seven seniors graduated from Franklin High School this morning.

Write out numbers like *seventh*, *fifty-third*, and so on. If they represent the day of the month, however, it is customary to use numerals only.

EXAMPLES I was the **first** [not 1st] customer at the bank this morning.

Flag Day is **June 14.**

16d. Learn the rules for dividing words at the end of a line.

Dividing a word at the end of a line in order to keep an even margin should generally be avoided, but sometimes it must be done.

1. Divide a word between syllables (pronounceable parts) only. If you are in doubt about the syllables in a word, look it up in the dictionary. Never divide a one-syllable word.

WRONG	screa- med	(*Screamed* is a one-syllable word.)
WRONG	buil- ding	(The syllables of *building* are *build* and *ing*.)
RIGHT	build- ing	
WRONG	bewitch- ed	(We do not pronounce the word bewitch-ED.)
RIGHT	be- witched	

2. Do not divide a word so that only one letter is left on a line.

WRONG . . . man- . . . i-
y . . . magine . . .

16e. Learn the standard correction symbols.

In marking your papers, your teacher may use some or all of the symbols given below. If you memorize these symbols, you will understand at once what is wrong in your paper. If you are not sure how to correct your error, use the index of your book to find the section that you need to review.

ms error in manuscript form or neatness
cap error in use of capital letters
p error in punctuation
sp error in spelling
frag sentence fragment
ss error in sentence structure
k awkward sentence
nc not clear
rs run-on sentence
gr error in grammar
w error in word choice
¶ You should have begun a new paragraph here.
t error in tense
^ You have omitted something.

Instead of doing exercises for this chapter, apply what you have learned here to every paper that you write. Remember that the appearance of your written work makes an impression on the reader. If your papers show evidence of orderly care, your teachers will give you credit for it and will be better able to evaluate the content of your writing.

PART FOUR

Sentence Structure

CHAPTER **17**

Learning "Sentence Sense"

Fragments and Run-on Sentences

When you speak, you signal the end of a sentence by making your voice rise or fall and by pausing between sentences. When you write, the signals you use are end marks: periods, question marks, and exclamation points. If you use these marks incorrectly, you give your reader the wrong signals. Using written signals requires more attention than using spoken ones, but the two kinds are related. You can eliminate many of your punctuation problems by reading what you have written aloud and listening for the signals your voice makes.

Two frequent errors that occur in written sentences are the *sentence fragment* and the *run-on sentence.* When you put a period, question mark, or exclamation point after a group of words that is not a complete sentence, you have made the error of writing a sentence fragment. When you omit end marks between two or more separate sentences, you are writing a run-on sentence. To avoid these errors, apply the "sentence sense" you use when you speak.

FRAGMENTS

A sentence expresses a complete thought. When only a part of a sentence is written as a complete sentence, the resulting error is a sentence fragment. A fragment almost always belongs with the sentence that precedes it.

17a. A *fragment* is a separated sentence part that does not express a complete thought.

To decide whether or not a group of words is a sentence, ask yourself these two questions: (1) Does it have a verb and its subject? (2) Does it express a complete thought? If the answer to either question is "no," the group of words is not a sentence but a fragment of a sentence.

In each example below, a sentence is followed by a fragment printed in italics. Note that all the fragments, except the one in the third example, do not contain verbs and their subjects. The third one, which is a subordinate clause, has a verb and its subject, but it does not express a complete thought.

> The newspaper staff worked late. *Putting out a special edition.* [The fragment contains no main verb or subject.]
>
> We looked forward to meeting Miss Case. *Our new English teacher.* [The fragment contains no verb or subject.]
>
> *As the countdown continued.* The excitement increased. [The fragment contains a verb and a subject, but it does not express a complete thought. It leaves the reader wondering what happened "as the countdown continued."]

Since these fragments all belong to the sentences they precede or follow, you can correct them by joining them to these sentences.

> The newspaper staff worked late **putting out a special edition.**
>
> We looked forward to meeting Miss Case, **our new English teacher.**
>
> **As the countdown continued,** the excitement increased.

● EXERCISE 1. Seven of the italicized groups of words below are fragments, while three are complete sentences. Indicate a complete sentence by placing a *C* after the proper number. Correct each fragment by copying the entire item and making the fragment part of the sentence.

EXAMPLES 1. Dolphins are intelligent animals. *That are being closely studied today.*

1. *Dolphins are intelligent animals that are being closely studied today.*

2. The study of this aquatic mammal may have surprising results. *The dolphin may eventually be trained as man's sea-going partner.*

2. *C*

1. The man who has done the most research on the dolphin is Dr. John C. Lily. *Who is attempting to devise a method of communication between men and dolphins.*
2. *By putting a partially paralyzed dolphin into a tank with other dolphins.* Dr. Lily discovered the dolphin's distress call.
3. The disabled dolphin emitted its distress call. *When it began to sink.*

4. It was immediately assisted by two other dolphins. *They lifted it to the surface for air.*
5. Dolphins usually stay together in groups. *Helping each other out in times of trouble.*
6. A baby dolphin is looked after by two adults. *Its mother and an assistant mother serve as nurses.*
7. Even the deadly shark is no match for two angry mothers. *Circling and striking at their foe with their hard, beaklike noses.*
8. *In addition to having unusual ability to mimic the human voice.* The dolphin is of extreme interest because of its streamlined body structure and its amazing built-in sonar system.
9. The latest nuclear-powered submarines have the same general shape as the dolphin. *It is the most perfectly streamlined animal known.*
10. The dolphin possesses a built-in sonar apparatus. *Which is more accurate than any devised by man.*

● EXERCISE 2. Copy the following paragraph, joining fragments to the sentences to which they belong. You might have to leave out several words as you rewrite a sentence to correct the fragment.

Everyone is interested in the Pony Express. Which operated for eighteen months and during that time lost only one saddlebag. There were 308 runs made by the Pony Express. One of the fastest runs that was made by the riders. It was made in 1861. When Lincoln's first inaugural address was carried across the country. The trip covered 1,966 miles. And required seven days and seventeen hours for the riders to go from St. Joseph, Missouri, to Sacramento, California. Do you think postal rates are high today? Compare our rates today with those of the Pony Express. Which first charged five dollars per half-ounce of mail but later reduced its rate to one dollar per half-ounce.

Three Kinds of Fragments

The *subordinate clause*, the *verb phrase*, and the *appositive phrase* are three kinds of fragments that often appear in student writing. Once you recognize that these three word groups cannot stand alone as complete sentences, you will have gone a long way toward eliminating fragments from your writing.

The Subordinate Clause

17b. A *subordinate clause* must not be written as a sentence.

As you learned on page 97, a subordinate clause has a verb and its subject but does not express a complete thought. It cannot stand by itself but must always be attached to an independent clause. *As he turned the corner* is a subordinate clause. If you read this word group aloud, you will hear at once that it is not a complete sentence. Read the follow ng subordinate clauses aloud. Do they sound like complete sentences? Then notice the difference when they are joined to independent clauses.

> When it rains during a football game [What happens then?]
>
> Who directed us to our seats [If a question is intended, then the word group is a sentence. If not, it is a fragment.]
>
> **When it rains during a football game,** the stadium looks like a patchwork quilt of umbrellas.
>
> We gave our tickets to an usher **who directed us to our seats.**

Remember that relative pronouns (*who*, *whom*, *whose*, *which*, *that*) or subordinating conjunctions (see the list on page 108) introduce subordinate clauses. These are very important words, for they can change a sentence into a fragment.

SENTENCE It rains during a football game.
FRAGMENT When it rains during a football game

SENTENCE An usher directed us to our seats.
FRAGMENT An usher who directed us to our seats

● EXERCISE 3. The following paragraphs contain ten fragments. Each fragment is a subordinate clause incorrectly written as a sentence. Copy the paragraphs, attaching the fragments to the related independent clauses.

Mrs. Collins opens her home to foreign students. Who are visiting on the college campus. Many humorous situations have developed during the years. That Mrs. Collins has been boarding the students. They tend to make some very funny mistakes. Because they are unfamiliar with our language and customs. Mrs. Collins tells a story about an Iranian student. Who was staying with her. Once while she was away at the beauty parlor. Her sister called long distance from Washington, D.C. The Iranian student answered the phone. Since there was no one else in the house. When the operator asked for Mrs. Collins. He replied in a very clear voice, "He go to beauty parlor."

After she had recovered from that response. The operator explained that she wanted to know about *Mrs.* Collins, not *Mr.* Collins. Still the Iranian student replied, "I say that he go to beauty parlor."

Although the poor operator tried again and again to make herself understood. The Iranian student continued to give the same answer. Because in his language one personal pronoun can be used for all genders.

● EXERCISE 4. Make each of the following fragments into a complete sentence by adding an independent clause to go with the subordinate clause. Write each sentence on your paper

EXAMPLE 1. Because I missed the bus by seconds.
1. *I was twenty minutes late to school because I missed the bus by seconds.*

1. who broke her glasses
2. because the lights on the stage went out during the performance
3. while Joan was rehearsing her part
4. after the fish got away
5. who is president of the Student Council
6. that are working on a clean-up campaign for the school
7. if you want to own a pet
8. which were racing across the lake
9. because the library closes at six o'clock
10. whom I met at your party

The Verbal Phrase

17c. A verbal phrase must not be written as a sentence.

A verbal is a word formed from a verb but used as another part of speech. One kind of verbal, the participle, is often mistaken for a verb, particularly when it begins a phrase. *Reading comic books all the time* is such a phrase. It is not a complete sentence, as you can tell by reading it aloud. Although the participle *reading* is a verb form, it is not a verb since it cannot be used with a subject: *I reading, he reading.* Only when accompanied by a helping verb is a participle used as a verb: *I am reading, he is reading.*

As you know from the *–ing* ending, *reading* is a present participle. Similarly, a past participle cannot be used as a verb unless it is accompanied by a helping verb.

PHRASE built of bamboo

SENTENCE A house **built of bamboo** cannot withstand a heavy wind. [*Built* begins a participial phrase.]

SENTENCE The house **was built** of bamboo. [*Built* is accompanied by a helping verb; it is part of a verb phrase.]

Notice how the fragments below, which are verbal phrases, are corrected by the addition of independent clauses.

FRAGMENTS Lying lazily on the beach
Written by O. Henry

SENTENCES **Lying lazily on the beach,** I completely forgot to notice the time.
"The Ransom of Red Chief" is a delightful short story **written by O. Henry.**

● EXERCISE 5. Below are verbal phrases incorrectly written as sentences. Write ten complete sentences by adding an independent clause to each of the verbal phrases. Underline the participle in each sentence.

1. Standing alone.
2. Seeing the exit sign.
3. Expecting guests.
4. Waiting for the bus.
5. Painted bright colors.
6. Flashing in the sunlight.

7. Firing the rockets.
8. Chosen as the captain of the debating team.
9. Walking on the hot pavement.
10. Working on the project for weeks.

● EXERCISE 6. The following paragraphs contain ten verbal phrases incorrectly used as sentences. Rewrite the paragraphs, joining the fragments to the proper independent clauses.

Alice in Wonderland is a literary classic. Read by college students as well as grammar school students. Every child enjoys this story. Missing some of the fun but laughing at many of the comic incidents. When the child grows up, he reads the story again. Finding more humor in it this time.

In one of the most famous episodes in the book, Alice goes to a tea party. Given by the Mad Hatter. The Mad Hatter and his companions, the March Hare and the Dormouse, have allowed dirty dishes to pile up everywhere. Being very lazy. Alice finds herself at no ordinary tea party. The Dormouse tells a long story. Falling asleep in the middle. The March Hare offers her wine. Alice is told that there is no wine. After accepting his offer. For a while the three creatures ask her riddles. Having no answers. Then they ignore her completely. Carrying on a ridiculous conversation among themselves. Finally, Alice manages to escape from her companions. Thoroughly exhausted.

The Appositive Phrase

17d. An appositive phrase must not be written as a sentence.

An appositive phrase, an appositive with its modifiers, identifies or explains the noun or pronoun it follows (see page 247). Neither an appositive nor an appositive phrase can stand alone as a sentence; it should be set off from the rest of the sentence by a comma or commas.

FRAGMENT The eighteen sailors rowed 3,618 miles to Timor. An island near Java.

SENTENCE The eighteen sailors rowed 3,618 miles to Timor, **an island near Java.** [*An island near Java* is an appositive phrase explaining *Timor* and should be joined to the rest of the sentence.]

FRAGMENT We had dinner at the Banana Tree. An interesting restaurant near Key West.

SENTENCE We had dinner at the Banana Tree, **an interesting restaurant near Key West.** [*An interesting restaurant near Key West* is an appositive phrase explaining *Banana Tree.*]

● EXERCISE 7. Rewrite the following expressions, attaching the appositive phrases to the independent clauses from which they have been separated. Change punctuation and capital letters wherever necessary. Some of the appositive phrases belong in the middle of sentences.

1. We enjoy playing parcheesi. A game from India.
2. The entrance to the Mediterranean is guarded by Gibraltar. A rocklike peninsula two and three-fourths miles long and three fourths of a mile wide.
3. Astronomers have long been intrigued by Saturn. The planet with rings.
4. Thursday was named for Thor. The Norse god of thunder.

5. We went to a double feature. A science fiction show and a western.
6. The famous novel *Frankenstein* was written by Mary Wollstonecraft Shelley. The wife of the great English Romantic poet.
7. The Battle of Marathon was won by the Greeks. One of the most famous battles in the history of the world.
8. At his death in A.D. 54, Claudius was succeeded as Roman emperor by Nero, who cruelly persecuted the Christians. His stepson.
9. The water in the Cypress Gardens near Charleston, South Carolina, is black because it contains titanic acid. A secretion of the cypress trees.
10. It was Confucius who said: "Learning without thought is labor lost." A famous Chinese philosopher of the fifth century B.C.

● REVIEW EXERCISE A. Rewrite the following items, eliminating fragments by attaching them to independent clauses. Then write whether each fragment is a *subordinate clause*, *verbal phrase*, or *appositive phrase*.

1. As I was driving home. I saw a turtle in the middle of the highway.
2. It had been rolled over on its back by a car. While trying to cross the road.
3. Now it was lying there in the middle of the highway. Helplessly moving its feet back and forth.
4. Because I remembered that a turtle cannot get off its back on a smooth surface. I stopped the car and picked the animal up.
5. It immediately drew its feet and head under its shell. So that I could see no more than two eyes. Staring at me from inside the shell.
6. The turtle that I had found was a box turtle. A very shy land dweller.

7. I took it to Tall Oaks. My parents' cottage in the mountains. Since I wanted to observe it for a while.
8. Arriving there, I put the turtle down on a rug. Which covers most of the living room floor.
9. The turtle slowly began to stick its feet and head out from its shell. After being still for almost ten minutes.
10. As soon as it felt safe, it crawled very awkwardly but quickly across the rug. Heading for a corner of the room.

● REVIEW EXERCISE B. Some of the following groups of words are sentences; others are subordinate clauses, verbal phrases, or appositive phrases incorrectly written as sentences. Number your paper 1–23. Write *S* after the corresponding number of each complete sentence. Write *F* after the corresponding number of each fragment. Be prepared to tell how you would correct each fragment by making it a part of a related sentence.

1. Almost every book on art includes a reproduction of the *Mona Lisa.* 2. One of the most famous paintings in the world. 3. The *Mona Lisa* was painted by Leonardo da Vinci. 4. Who worked on it for four years (1503–06). 5. The painting was never quite finished. 6. After working for several hours. 7. Leonardo would sit down in front of the *Mona Lisa* to quiet his nerves. 8. Some people say that Leonardo did not finish the painting. 9. Because he wanted an excuse to keep it with him.

10. There is a mysterious smile on the face of the woman in the painting. 11. Which has intrigued people for centuries. 12. Although no one knows the true explanation of the smile. 13. Several different legends have grown up about it. 14. One story says that the

woman was smiling sadly when she sat for the portrait. 15. Because her child had died. 16. Another story, however, goes on to say that Leonardo hired musicians to play during the sittings. 17. Flutists and violin players. 18. So that he could capture the young woman's rapt expression.

19. When Leonardo left Italy and moved to France. 20. He took the painting with him. 21. The French king persuaded him to sell the painting. 22. Which now hangs in the Louvre. 23. An art museum in Paris.

RUN-ON SENTENCES

Another common writing fault that you can avoid by using your sentence sense is the *run-on sentence.* Run-on sentences occur when the writer fails to recognize the end of a sentence and runs on into the next sentence without proper punctuation or, sometimes, without any punctuation at all.

17e. A *run-on sentence* consists of two or more sentences separated only by a comma or by no mark of punctuation.

RUN-ON The boy peered into the cave he saw two green eyes staring at him.

CORRECTED The boy peered into the cave. **H**e saw two green eyes staring at him.

RUN-ON May we stay up late tonight, we're not sleepy.

CORRECTED May we stay up late tonight**? W**e're not sleepy.

Remember that a comma marks a break in a sentence, not the end of the sentence. Thus a comma should not be used between two sentences.

● EXERCISE 8. Correct the following run-ons. Number your paper 1–10. After the proper number, write the last word in the first sentence and place a period after it; then write the first word of the next sentence, beginning it with a capital letter.

EXAMPLE 1. Please turn off the light, it's much too bright.

1. *light. It's*

1. Kelly should not attend auctions she has an uncontrollable urge to buy whatever the auctioneer holds up.
2. Our car had two flat tires this morning, I imagine we'll buy new tires.
3. The player with the ball could not understand why he was not being pursued, then he discovered that he was racing toward the wrong goal.
4. Doug hung a bulletin board in his room each day he posted interesting facts that he wanted to learn.
5. Annette collects music boxes she has almost thirty different kinds.
6. When Dan finally located the turtle, he found that it had crawled under the couch, it seemed quite contented there.
7. Our class sponsored a fortune-telling booth, a talent show, and an ice-cream stand, we made enough money to buy a movie projector.
8. The lifeguard was watching the new swimmer, when he saw that the lad was in trouble, he swam out to help him.
9. Jack asked for a second helping of sweet potatoes, he thought they were very good.
10. A well-known poet came to our school he showed us how to improve the poems which we had written as a class assignment.

● EXERCISE 9. Each of the following passages contains several run-on sentences. You will find the passages hard to read because run-on sentences always interfere with the clear expression of ideas. After you have decided where each sentence should end, write the last word of each complete sentence on your paper. Place the appropriate end mark after the word; then write the first word of the next sentence, beginning it with a capital letter.

EXAMPLE 1. *Jest* once had a different meaning than it does today, in medieval times the English used the word to refer to a brave deed or the story of such a deed, by the sixteenth century it meant "to jeer or mock" now, of course, a *jest* is a joke.

1. *today. In*
deed. By
mock." Now,

1. Our word *humor* has an interesting history, it comes from Latin in that language *humor* meant "a liquid," people believed that a person's body contained four liquids which determined his disposition, thus a man might be quite odd or eccentric if he had too much of one humor.
2. From the French word *papier* we get our word *paper*, the French word, in turn, can be traced back to the Greek *papyros*, which is the name of an Egyptian plant, the pith of this plant was sliced into strips and then soaked in water, finally it was pressed and pasted into a writing material which was used by the ancient Egyptians, Greeks, and Romans, the kind of paper that we are familiar with, however, came originally from China.

3. The comma can be traced back to the Greek language, our word *comma* comes from the Greek word *komma*, which means "a piece cut off" when you use a comma, you cut off an expression from the rest of the sentence.
4. "Do you know how our word *rigmarole* originated?" asked Bill. "It came from documents called *ragman roll*, which were presented to Edward I in 1291, the *ragman roll* proved the allegiance of Scottish lords to Edward since there were many different kinds of papers and signatures included in the *ragman roll*, it was natural to associate confusion with the documents, as a result we have our word *rigmarole*, which refers to a series of confused or foolish statements."
5. Have you ever wondered about the origin of the word *sandwich*, it came into use during the eighteenth century, John Montagu, the Earl of Sandwich, was addicted to gambling, so addicted that he often would not stop for his meals, during one of his twenty-four-hour gambling sessions, he instructed someone to bring him slices of bread with roast beef inserted between them because the Earl of Sandwich did not want to stop gambling long enough to go to dinner, the world gained the sandwich.

● EXERCISE 10. Of the following sentences, five are correct and five are run-ons. After the proper number, copy only the run-ons, making whatever corrections are necessary.

1. The Amazon is the second longest river in the world, it flows through South America for 3,900 miles.
2. When the runner broke the world's record, everyone in the stadium stood up to cheer him.

3. There is an old belief that birds begin to choose their mates on February 14 perhaps this legend is responsible for our association of romance with Valentine's Day.
4. Have you ever heard of Six Mile that's a strange name for a town.
5. Each girl made her own dress, which she modeled at the fashion show.
6. My grandfather says that we will have six more weeks of winter because the groundhog saw his shadow on February 2.
7. Each of us made a kite, we had a contest to see whose kite would fly the highest.
8. Before the airplane was invented, many men made wings, but they did not succeed in flying.
9. Aladdin had a magic lamp, and when he rubbed it, two jinn appeared to do his bidding.
10. "The albatross is a bird which is popular in legend and literature," our teacher explained, "it is the largest of the seabirds."

● REVIEW EXERCISE C. Some of the following expressions are sentences. Others are fragments or run-ons. Number your paper 1–20. After the proper number, write *S* (sentence), *F* (fragment), or *R* (run-on). Be prepared to tell how you would correct the fragments and run-ons.

1. Medusa and her two sisters were three horrible monsters who, at one time, had been beautiful women.
2. Medusa, the most beautiful of the three, was very proud, she boasted that she was even more beautiful than the goddess Athena.
3. Because of her pride, she and her two sisters were turned into monsters.

4. Who had hissing serpents for hair.
5. No one dared look upon Medusa and her sisters.
6. Because anyone who did turned to stone.
7. Lying all about them were stones that had once been men.
8. Medusa and her two sisters menaced the land for years finally they were challenged by Perseus.
9. A young, handsome warrior.
10. Having been given magic weapons by the gods.
11. Perseus set out to kill Medusa.
12. The only mortal one of the three sisters.
13. When he approached the area in which the monsters lived.
14. Perseus put on a magic cap which made him invisible, he held up a shield that had been given him by Athena.
15. Studying the reflection of Medusa and her sisters in his shield.
16. Perseus slowly approached the monsters.
17. Luckily, they were sleeping.
18. Still using the shield as a mirror, he cut off Medusa's head with a single stroke he put the head into a special pouch.
19. Which had also been given to him by Athena.
20. The other sisters awoke but could not see him, therefore he escaped with the head of Medusa.

● REVIEW EXERCISE D. Pretend that you are writing to a person who has never seen a comic strip. Write a paragraph in which you describe one of the main characters in your favorite comic strip. After you have finished writing the paragraph, read each sentence orally, one by one, to be sure that you have not carelessly written a fragment or a run-on. Make the necessary corrections on your paper.

CHAPTER **18**

Sentence Structure and Variety

Correcting Choppy and Monotonous Styles of Writing

Experienced writers rarely stop with a first draft. First, they get what they have to say on paper. Then they carefully revise what they have written, correcting grammatical errors and improving poorly written passages.

As you continue in school and your writing assignments become more demanding, you too should develop the habit of writing at least two drafts of a composition. In the first draft, express what you have to say. In the revised draft, concentrate on writing clearly and well and on eliminating any faults in style. Watch especially for groups of choppy, abrupt sentences and for rambling sentences held together by a string of conjunctions. Such sentences, while occasionally effective, become monotonous and tiresome if used too often. This chapter will show you how to recognize such poorly written sentences and how to revise them.

COMBINING CHOPPY SENTENCES

Short sentences are often effective in a composition, but a long series of short sentences tends to irritate the reader. They slow him down and make it difficult for him to focus on what is being said. Such choppy sentences are often similar in construction and thus are monotonous in their effect. The following passage of choppy sentences would irritate most readers:

> Dr. Jonas Salk developed the famous Salk vaccine. He was born in New York City on October 28, 1914. He graduated from the City College of New York in 1934. He received a medical degree in 1939. He worked on a vaccine against influenza from 1942 to 1947. This experience helped him develop the vaccine against poliomyelitis.

In addition to being choppy, the second, third, and fourth sentences are monotonously similar in construction. This passage might be rewritten as follows:

> Dr. Jonas Salk, who developed the famous Salk vaccine, was born in New York City on October 28, 1914. He graduated from the City College of New York in 1934, and he received a medical degree in 1939. From 1942 to 1947 he worked on a vaccine against influenza. This experience helped him develop the vaccine against poliomyelitis.

Several methods have been used in revising the passage. One method is combining two short sentences into one compound sentence. Sentences 3 and 4 in the original version have been combined in this way.

18a. Combine short related sentences by making them into a compound sentence.

A *compound sentence* (see page 133) is really two or more simple sentences joined together, usually by the conjunction *and*, *but*, *or*, or *nor*. When simple sentences are joined together in a compound sentence, they are called *independent clauses*. The following sentence has two independent clauses, each with a verb and its subject.

EXAMPLE Tractor drivers (s) bulldozed (v) a barrier along the flanks of the forest fire, and helicopter crews (s) drenched (v) the fire with chemicals.

A comma is needed between the independent clauses of a compound sentence. Do not forget to use commas when you join simple sentences into a compound sentence.

EXAMPLES Alan brought his new water skis. Tom borrowed his brother's ski boat.

Alan brought his new water skis**, and** Tom borrowed his brother's ski boat.

The friendly Pimas welcomed white hunters. The hostile Sioux warned them to stay away.

The friendly Pimas welcomed white hunters**, but** the hostile Sioux warned them to stay away.

A compound sentence tells the reader that the ideas in the independent clauses are closely connected. If you attempt to correct a choppy passage by connecting unrelated ideas, the result will be even worse than the original, choppy version. Be sure that the ideas that you connect in the compound sentence are closely related and equal in importance.

EXAMPLE The quarterback threw a long pass. The opposing team intercepted the ball.

The quarterback threw a long pass, but the opposing team intercepted the ball. [The ideas in these clauses are closely related and equal in importance.]

That television program is very exciting. I like westerns better than comedies. [The ideas in these sentences are not closely related and should not be joined in a compound sentence.]

Bob was elected class president. Pete didn't vote. [The ideas in these sentences are not of equal importance and should not be joined in a compound sentence.]

● EXERCISE 1. Combine the following groups of sentences into compound sentences. Use the conjunctions *and*, *but*, and *or*.

1. The girls unpacked their box lunches. The boys gathered wood to build a fire.
2. Eskimos live under harsh conditions. They are a happy, energetic people.
3. The mothers of the class sewed the costumes. The fathers built the stage set.
4. Our land was once richer in wildlife than many other parts of the globe. Today wildlife is scarce in the United States.
5. You think hiking is fun. I don't. Pete doesn't.
6. Overcrowded European nations did not seek immigrants. America, with its small population, welcomed them.

7. Lightning causes many forest fires. Most forest fires are caused by man.
8. We could use the money in the club treasury to decorate the clubroom. We could give a party.
9. Men rushed to California to find gold. Instead they often found hunger, thirst, and disease.
10. Mr. Grover may have your lawn mower. Perhaps George Lennox has it.

● EXERCISE 2. Most of the following items consist of two closely related ideas. Number your paper 1–10. After the proper number, write the conjunction (*and*, *but*, *or*) you would use in combining the pair of sentences in one compound sentence. If an item contains unrelated or unequal ideas, write *U* after its number.

1. All American Indians in the United States are citizens. The men are subject to military service.
2. When Columbus discovered America, Indians numbered about one million. Columbus was seeking a shorter route to the Indies.
3. Many people believe that the Indians are "vanishing." The Indian population increased from a quarter million in 1900 to more than half a million in 1960.
4. Almost all Indians of school age go to school. The family income of rural Indians averages less than half the national average.
5. The U.S. Public Health Service has set up many hospitals, health centers, and field clinics on reservations. The life expectancy of the Indian has increased.
6. Many Indians still live on tribally owned reservations. Only a few elderly people remember the tribal rites and songs.

7. Indian reservations total more than 53 million acres in area. In some tribes, only a few people are full-blooded Indians.
8. About four percent of Indian tribal land is suited to farming. Most tribes accept as members only people who are at least one-quarter Indian.
9. Many Indians have been shepherds. The United States government is teaching these shepherds how to farm.
10. Navajos are especially good at making jewelry. They are now selling their jewelry throughout the country.

Combining short sentences into a compound sentence is one method of avoiding a choppy style. Another method was applied to the first two sentences of the sample paragraph on page 337. As you may discover by comparing the original and revised versions of the paragraph, these sentences were combined as a complex sentence connecting two related but unequal ideas.

18b. Combine short, choppy sentences into a complex sentence. Put one idea into a subordinate clause.

A *complex sentence* (see page 138) has an independent clause and one or more subordinate clauses.

(1) Make a complex sentence out of short simple sentences by putting one of the ideas into an adjective clause.

An *adjective clause* is a subordinate clause which, like an adjective, modifies a noun or pronoun. Most adjective clauses begin with relative pronouns such as *who, whose, whom, which,* and *that.* In the following example, the adjective clause is in heavy type.

EXAMPLE The boy **who just waved to me** is my first cousin. [The adjective clause modifies *boy.*]

The following groups of short sentences have been combined into complex sentences. One idea in each group has been subordinated by putting it into an adjective clause, printed in heavy type.

EXAMPLES Nora wore her favorite dress. I had given it to her.

Nora wore her favorite dress, **which I had given her.**

Mr. Allen hired Tom. Tom is the strongest boy in our class.

Mr. Allen hired Tom, **who is the strongest boy in our class.**

She gave him an answer. It was an abrupt and definite *no.*

The answer **that she gave him** was an abrupt and definite *no.*

Often when you write complex sentences, you will face a choice: which idea should be expressed in the independent clause and which in the subordinate clause? The choice will depend on which idea you consider more important or wish to emphasize. The more important idea will receive greater emphasis in the independent clause.

EXAMPLE James J. Corbett was the first boxer to become heavyweight champion of the world in a match fought under the Marquis of Queensberry rules. He defeated John L.

> Sullivan in a title bout in New Orleans on September 7, 1892.
>
> James J. Corbett, who defeated John L. Sullivan in a title bout in New Orleans on September 7, 1892, was the first boxer to win the heavyweight championship of the world in a match fought under the Marquis of Queensberry rules. [This version emphasizes the conditions under which the championship was won.]
>
> *or*
>
> James J. Corbett, who was the first boxer to win the heavyweight championship of the world in a match fought under the Marquis of Queensberry rules, defeated John L. Sullivan in a title bout in New Orleans on September 7, 1892. [This version emphasizes the facts of the bout.]

Often the relative importance of the ideas will be determined by the passage in which your sentence appears. For example, the first two sentences of the sample choppy passage on page 337 present ideas of unequal importance:

> Dr. Jonas Salk developed the famous Salk vaccine.
>
> He was born in New York City on October 28, 1914.

The idea that Dr. Salk developed the Salk vaccine may seem more important than the date and place of his birth. However, this passage continues to give other important dates in his life. Therefore, the two sentences should be combined as follows to place emphasis on the second idea:

Dr. Jonas Salk, who developed the famous Salk vaccine, was born in New York City on October 28, 1914.

● EXERCISE 3. Combine each of the following groups of sentences into a single complex sentence by putting one of the ideas into an adjective clause. If necessary, review the rules for using commas with essential and nonessential clauses (see page 244).

EXAMPLE 1. Tom Nelson won the championship. He is a great athlete.

1. *Tom Nelson, who is a great athlete, won the championship.*

1. The boy spoke to me. I did not know him.
2. Johnny rode the bike. I had sold it to him.
3. Mr. Bellack is our new minister. He finished divinity school last year.
4. Jim dived in to help Andy. Jim is the best swimmer in our crowd.
5. Ellen was jealous of Nora. Nora had won a scholarship.
6. Emily was the best dancer at the party. She studies professionally.
7. Mr. Adams swims the year around, summer and winter. He does not look like an athlete.
8. *The Call of the Wild* is my favorite book. It was written by Jack London.
9. Sue showed us a locket. She had received it as a Christmas present.
10. He gave her some advice. It hindered more than it helped.

● EXERCISE 4. Rewrite the following pairs of sentences as complex sentences. For the first five pairs, emphasize the idea of the first sentence. For the second five pairs, emphasize the idea of the second sentence.

EXAMPLE 1. Presidential electors are chosen by the voters of each state. The electors elect the President.

1. *Presidential electors, who elect the President, are chosen by the voters of each state.* [This version emphasizes the idea of the first sentence by placing it in the independent clause.]

1. The President can never escape from his job. He must deal with crises at any time of the day or night.
2. Secret Service guards protect the President wherever he goes. They accompany him at all times.
3. The President has a yacht, a private railroad car, various aircraft, and a naval ship at his disposal. He has to travel frequently.
4. The Constitution makes the President responsible for enforcing federal laws and supervising federal agencies. It gives the President many powers.
5. The President has the responsibility for planning overall strategy during wartime. He is commander in chief of the armed forces.
6. The Senate has the traditional role of approving or disapproving the President's acts of foreign policy. It must confirm all treaties by a two-thirds vote.
7. The President bears many social responsibilities. He must give dinners and receptions for visiting dignitaries and foreign diplomats.
8. The President has various emergency and special powers. He can grant pardons and reprieves to persons convicted of crimes against the United States.

9. The Executive Office has a staff of more than a thousand members. It helps the President perform his duties.
10. The position of President is the highest honor our nation can bestow on a citizen. It is probably the most difficult responsibility on earth.

(2) Make a complex sentence out of short, simple sentences by putting one of the ideas into an adverb clause.

As you know, an adverb clause is a subordinate clause which, like an adverb, modifies a verb, adjective, or adverb. In these sentences the adverb clauses are printed in heavy type.

EXAMPLES She sings **whenever she is alone.** [The adverb clause modifies a verb.]

The conductor stopped the orchestra **because the violins were not in tune.** [The adverb clause modifies a verb.]

Her voice is better **than mine is.** [The adverb clause modifies an adjective.]

She practices more regularly **than I do.** [The adverb clause modifies an adverb.]

An adverb clause begins with a subordinating conjunction. In the sentences you have just read, *whenever*, *because*, and *than* are subordinating conjunctions. Study the following list.

SUBORDINATING CONJUNCTIONS

after	before	than	whenever
although	if	unless	where
as	since	until	wherever
because	so that	when	while

Below are three groups of short simple sentences that have been combined into complex sentences by putting one idea into an adverb clause (printed in heavy type). Notice that a comma is used after an adverb clause placed at the beginning of a sentence.

EXAMPLES My Uncle Jerome suffered from high blood pressure. He refused to read the political news in the paper.

Because my Uncle Jerome suffered from high blood pressure, he refused to read the political news in the paper.

Bob saw the fox near the chicken yard. He shot at it.

When Bob saw the fox near the chicken yard, he shot at it.

Her head ached. She continued dancing.

Although her head ached, she continued dancing.

When you subordinate a short sentence by changing it into an adverb clause, be careful to choose the correct subordinating conjunction. (The common subordinating conjunctions are *because*, *although*, *since*, *if*, *unless*, *when*, *before*, *after*.) A subordinating conjunction shows the relationship between clauses, and a poorly chosen conjunction will show a false or meaningless relationship. For example, a number of subordinating conjunctions could be used to join these two sentences, but not all of them would show a relationship that makes sense:

EXAMPLE John is an industrious student. He receives high grades.

INCORRECT Although John is an industrious student, he receives high grades. [This sentence means that John receives high grades despite his industry.]

INCORRECT Unless John is an industrious student, he receives high grades. [This sentence suggests that being industrious keeps John from receiving high grades.]

CORRECT **Because** John is an industrious student, he receives high grades.

CORRECT **When** John is an industrious student, he receives high grades.

● EXERCISE 5. Combine each of the following groups of sentences into a single complex sentence by putting one idea into an adverb clause. Refer to the list of subordinating conjunctions on page 346.

1. His ankle pained him sharply. He kept on playing.
2. Doris did not go to the movie. She had a headache.
3. He saw the truck rolling down the hill toward him. He jumped onto the curb.
4. The return signal was fired. John kept right on hunting.
5. Jane's mother motioned to her. Jane put down the telephone.
6. The baby screamed and threw his plate on the floor. Mary rushed to the kitchen.
7. Miss White was just about to start the test. Bob ran into the room.
8. His eyes were so tired that the print he was reading danced and faded. He did not stop studying.
9. She was in a gay mood. She said hello to Sam, although he had been rude to her.
10. We were late. Emma had forgotten to tell us that the party would start at seven.

• EXERCISE 6. Combine each of the following groups of sentences into a complex sentence by using adjective or adverb clauses. Use the kind of clause which will make the smoothest, clearest sentence.

1. Mr. Adams chopped down the tree outside his bedroom window. He wanted more light.
2. Miss Leeds loves to hike. She walks the hill trails every Sunday afternoon.
3. The wise rancher lets his pasture remain ungrazed at intervals. Grass must have a chance to recover growth.
4. Andy Towne plays the accordion skillfully. He will appear on television next week.
5. I reached over the side of the boat to pull in the fish. A wave knocked me off balance.
6. The children asked me to read to them. They had been waiting up for almost an hour.
7. The pilot's engine caught fire. He disobeyed orders to maintain radio silence.
8. The phone rang. Jane did not stop reading. She was absorbed in the story.
9. A plane roared overhead. The players had to stop speaking. The play was being performed in an outdoor theater.
10. Mr. O'Malley was blushing as he came forward to accept the prize. He is a very shy man.

• EXERCISE 7. Combine each of the following groups of sentences into a complex sentence using both an adjective clause and an adverb clause.

EXAMPLE 1. Esther took the job as baby-sitter. The pay was poor. She liked baby-sitting.

1. *Esther, who liked baby-sitting, took the job as baby-sitter although the pay was poor.*

1. Dorothy was tired. She did not stop sewing. She is a determined person.
2. A knock developed in the engine. It had been overhauled. He sold the car.
3. Ellen did not eat the candy. She was overweight. Her mother had reminded her to avoid sweets.
4. The snowstorm finally stopped. It had been the heaviest of the year. We went skiing.
5. We were late for dinner. The traffic held us up for an hour. It was unusually heavy.

CORRECTING A MONOTONOUS STYLE

If you look back at the two sample passages on page 337, you will see that the first two sentences in the choppy passage were revised by joining them as a complex sentence and that the third and fourth sentences were revised by combining them into a compound sentence. Still another method was used in revising the fifth sentence. To avoid a monotonous style, the prepositional phrase *from 1942 to 1947* was moved from the end of the sentence to the beginning.

18c. Correct a monotonous style by varying the beginnings of sentences.

A series of sentences that begin in the same way produces a monotonous style. Young writers often write a paragraph of sentences all of which begin with the subject. To avoid such monotony, you can rewrite some sentences to begin with a modifier: an adverb, an adverb clause, a prepositional phrase, or a participial phrase. When you are making such revisions, remember that your purpose is to get more variety into your sentences—you will not need to revise them all. If all the sentences were changed to begin with an adverb, for example, the passage would be as monotonous as before. Above all, you should not write an unclear or awkward sentence merely for the sake of variety. If a sentence sounds best with the subject first, you should leave it that way and try to revise some of the sentences near it, if necessary.

(1) Vary sentences by beginning them with adverbs.

EXAMPLES He paid his debts willingly.
Willingly he paid his debts.
She said sorrowfully, "He's gone."
Sorrowfully she said, "He's gone."

(2) Vary sentences by beginning them with adverb clauses.

EXAMPLES The pain eased after the tooth was pulled.
After the tooth was pulled, the pain eased.

He was not afraid to fight, although he was small.

Although he was small, he was not afraid to fight.

● EXERCISE 8. Revise the following sentences by beginning them with either an adverb or an adverb clause.

1. She agreed to his proposal reluctantly.
2. The puppy started whining instantly.
3. He went fishing whenever work permitted.
4. He carefully sharpened the carving knife.
5. She lived in Mexico before she moved here.
6. Tim was polite although they had angered him.
7. He will wash the car if you wish.
8. She wisely pretended not to hear.

9. He will go to college if he gets a scholarship.
10. She gave him a fine present although she had little money to spare.

(3) Vary sentences by beginning them with *prepositional phrases.*[1]

EXAMPLES A portrait of his mother hung on the wall.
On the wall hung a portrait of his mother.

A policeman sat in the car.
In the car sat a policeman.

Sometimes when you move a prepositional phrase, you will need to change the position of the verb also.

EXAMPLE A kettle hung above the fire.
Above the fire hung a kettle.

(4) Vary sentences by beginning them with *participial phrases.*[2]

A participial phrase is usually separated from the rest of the sentence by a comma.

EXAMPLES He sang for the crowd, **accompanying himself on the piano.**

Accompanying himself on the piano, he sang for the crowd.

The fielder, **running back,** leaped high to catch the ball.

Running back, the fielder leaped high to catch the ball.

They stared at each other in bewilderment, **stunned by the news.**

Stunned by the news, they stared at each other in bewilderment.

[1] If you need to review the prepositional phrase, turn to page 80.
[2] If you need to review the participial phrase, turn to page 91.

● EXERCISE 9. All of the following sentences begin with the subject. For the sake of variety, rewrite them with an adverb, a phrase, or a clause at the beginning.

1. Alice practices the piano after she does the dinner dishes.
2. Sandy ate the whole bag of popcorn as he sat through the movie.
3. The rainmaker, jumping from his chair, smiled with satisfaction as he pointed at the dark clouds massing overhead.
4. The mechanic will repair your car if you tell him what you want done.
5. Tom stared in wordless wonder at the box of mechanic's tools.
6. The general wore a Medal of Honor on his chest.
7. The scouts were singing loudly and happily as they were hiking back to camp.
8. He kept score, watching the players intently.
9. His father said, finally, that he could go fishing on Saturday afternoon if he finished painting the fence.
10. Aunt Martha took the twins to the new swimming pool on the very next day.

● EXERCISE 10. Use the following adverbs and adverb clauses to begin sentences of your own.

1. Carefully
2. Proudly
3. Happily
4. Unwillingly
5. Suddenly
6. After she thought it over,
7. Because he felt tired,
8. As soon as Jimmy heard the news,
9. As if he had plenty of money,
10. Whenever my grandparents visit us,

● EXERCISE 11. Use the following prepositional and participial phrases to begin sentences of your own.

1. On her day off
2. Resisting temptation,
3. Strolling around the zoo,
4. In shocked surprise
5. Wrapped around his arm,
6. Inside the old valise
7. At the bottom of the well,
8. Delighted with his new bike,
9. Picking up the marbles,
10. Turning toward the class,

● REVIEW EXERCISE A. Revise choppy and monotonous sentences in the paragraphs below by using the following methods:

1. Combine short sentences into compound sentences.
2. Combine short sentences into complex sentences.
3. Vary the beginnings of sentences.

It may not be necessary to revise every sentence. Your aim should be a series of paragraphs that are clear and show variety, and thus are pleasing to read.

A lens is different from an ordinary pane of glass. A pane of glass has a flat surface. A lens is curved. Rays of light go through a pane of glass without much change. Rays of light are bent, or refracted, in a lens. This refraction may change both the shape and the size of an image. The curve of the lens determines the size of the image. A concave lens curves inward. It is called a reducing glass. A convex lens curves outward. It is a magnifying glass. Lenses often combine the qualities of a concave and convex lens. Lenses may be concave on one side and convex on the other. A lens may also have one flat surface. A planoconcave lens is flat on one side and concave on the other, for example.

An optical lens must be made from glass of high quality. It must be manufactured by highly trained workmen. Optical glass is first tested for flaws. It is then molded into disks. A disk is first ground roughly, then precisely, to give it the correct shape. It is finally polished with ferric oxide. This substance is called "rouge" by glassmakers.

Two or more lenses are combined in a microscope so that we can see very small objects. One lens is called the objective. It produces the primary image. The second lens is the eyepiece, or ocular. It magnifies the primary image. A microscope is judged not only by its magnifying power. It is also judged by its resolving power. This is its power to show separation between things that are very close together.

CORRECTING RAMBLING SENTENCES

Sometimes you may try to avoid a choppy style by stringing many short sentences together, using the conjunctions *and*, *but*, and *so* to join them. Such rambling sentences are just as irritating and monotonous to read as short, choppy sentences.

18d. Correct rambling sentences by combining ideas and avoiding the overuse of *and*, *but*, and *so*.

Since rambling sentences are usually choppy sentences joined by conjunctions, the methods of correcting choppy sentences may also be applied to rambling sentences. Think of a rambling sentence as a series of choppy sentences as you revise it. Combine some of the clauses as compound or complex sentences. Vary the beginnings of other sentences. Study the following rambling sentence to see how it was revised.

RAMBLING I saw a television program last night, and it was about invaders from another planet and my younger brother Ted became frightened so my father calmed him down and informed him that there is little evidence of life on other planets but there may be life on Mars but it is probably at a very primitive stage of development.

REVISED Last night I saw a television program which was about invaders from another planet. When my younger brother Ted became frightened, my father calmed him down. He informed Ted that there is little evidence of life on other planets. There may be life on Mars, but it is probably at a primitive stage of development.

As with choppy sentences, the first step in revising a rambling sentence is to recognize it as bad writing. When you revise your compositions, watch for long sentences in which the conjunctions *and*, *but*, or *so* are used a great deal. Usually you will find that the independent clauses are not very closely related. These clauses should be rewritten to show a closer relationship, or, sometimes, they should be allowed to stand as complete sentences. The final step in revising rambling (or choppy) sentences is to read aloud what you have written. If the passage does not sound right, you have more revising to do.

● EXERCISE 12. Revise the rambling style of the following passages. Break the sentences down into clauses, and combine some clauses into compound or complex sentences. Let other clauses stand as complete sentences. To avoid a monotonous style, vary the beginnings of some sentences. Then read the passages aloud to see if they flow smoothly and have sentence variety.

1. Sally bought some skis, and she decided she must learn to ski systematically, and so she asked herself what to do first. The answer was to consult an expert, and the expert pointed out that it was dangerous to ski if you didn't know how to fall down properly, and so Sally thanked him, and she went home, and she dressed in her new ski togs, and she went out on the slopes and practiced falling down all day. She sprained her wrist at three o'clock, and she twisted her leg at 4:36, and she left the slopes at 4:38, and now the skis are mine. I bought them from Sally for a song, and so tomorrow I plan to take my first fall at 9:30 sharp.
2. Phil thinks he can speak French, but he made a silly mistake the other day when Herb came limping into class with a bandage on his ankle, and he had sprained it while playing football, so Phil thought he would show off his French. He meant to say *c'est dommage*, and it means "that's too bad," but he said *c'est fromage* instead, and it means "that's cheese," but Phil was quite proud of himself until Mrs. Stevens pointed out his mistake.

● Review exercise B. There are both choppy and rambling sentences in the following passage. Revise it so that the sentences are clear, well written, and varied. Read your revised version aloud to see if it flows smoothly.

The dam is not a modern invention. It was used in ancient times. It was used very early in Egypt. It was used to dam the Nile River. The first dam recorded in history was built about 2600 B.C. It was a large stone dam. It was located about eighteen miles south of Memphis. This dam was an engineering failure. Other Egyptian kings built other dams to store water. Their dams created Lake Moeris.

The Babylonians also built dams to control the Tigris and Euphrates Rivers, and the Romans built dams, and the dams lasted for centuries. The Emperor Nero directed the building of a dam, and it lasted for 1,300 years, but the Arabians built a dam that lasted over a thousand years, and it was two miles long and 120 feet high so it was the greatest dam ever built.

One of the largest dams in the world today is in the United States. It is the Hoover Dam, and it is on the Colorado River, and it is 1,244 feet long and 726 feet high. It took five years to construct. It was dedicated by President Franklin Delano Roosevelt on September 30, 1935. It is an important source of electrical power. It has a power plant that serves a hundred cities in the United States.

PART FIVE

Composition

CHAPTER 19

Writing Narratives

Planning a Story; Using Vivid Details, Dialogue, and Description

Have you ever heard anyone described as a "natural storyteller"? Do you know someone who can hold everyone's attention when he relates a personal experience? Such persons use gestures, facial expressions, and tone of voice to make their stories vivid and interesting, but they are also careful to organize their stories. They make sure that their stories lead somewhere and end with a definite point, and that what they say is clear to their listeners. They are skilled in the art of *narration.*

Not all of them, however, can write a story as well as they can tell it. They may not be as skilled in using words as they are in using gestures and facial expressions. Someone writing a story does not have personal contact with his audience; he must rely on words to make contact. Yet, as you know from your reading, written stories can be as interesting, as funny, or as thrilling, as a story that is told.

Over the years, many fine writers have made us aware of how much can be done with words alone. They have shown that even the simplest story must have a plan behind it, and they have used many effective devices in writing their stories. In this chapter, you will learn the basic principles of planning a story and some of the devices which make a story vivid and interesting.

PLANNING A STORY

What do you write about in a letter to a friend? Mostly, you tell about the things that have been happening to you: about coming down with the measles just before you were to start an exciting trip, about the new dress you accidentally ripped on the first day you wore it, about the fun you had in summer camp—after getting over poison oak. Such incidents can be the basis of many interesting stories. But you must plan such a story more carefully than a letter to a friend. A friend knows much about you, but the reader of your story may be a complete stranger. You must be sure to give all necessary information.

19a. Plan your story before writing it.

Before writing a story of a personal experience, work out a rough plan to guide your thinking and to help you to include all the necessary details.

Such a plan should list the necessary information. If you list the information under the categories of *When*, *Where*, *What happened*, and *How you felt*, you will usually find that you have included all the important information, as in the following story plan.

1. *When:* I was five years old.
2. *Where:* I was alone in my father's car.
3. *What happened:* I tried to drive the car. I released the brake. Car rolled. Hit a fence, a tree, smashed into a house.
4. *How you felt:* Very surprised.

A story about a personal experience need not end with an explicit statement of how you felt about the events described. Often your story will be more effective if you merely suggest your feelings rather than state them. You will find it helpful, however, to include such a statement in your story plan.

● EXERCISE 1. Draw up a story plan for the following story. Remember the items of the plan: *When, Where, What happened, How you felt.* In this case, imagine that you are the writer of the story.

Several years ago my friend Joey and I tried to go to the moon, but some apples and pears got in our way. Both Joey and I had seen a television program about man's efforts to reach the moon. When we talked about the program, we agreed that the important thing was to get up enough speed to overcome the earth's gravity. The rest would be easy. We decided to make an experiment. There was a long block in our neighborhood that ran downhill and then uphill. If we took Joey's wagon and got up enough speed going downhill, we might be able to leave the earth going uphill.

The next morning we got up very early. We wanted to reach the block before people started coming out of their apartment houses to go to work. I sat in the front of the wagon. Joey gave a push and jumped on behind me. The wagon went faster and faster. Joey and I cheered. We were sure that we would leave the earth's gravity and would be on our way to the moon. I began to daydream about newspaper headlines and being interviewed on television.

Suddenly Joey yelled, "Watch out!" Going uphill had made our wagon change direction. We were headed straight for Mr. Loomis' fruit stand. I grabbed the handle of the wagon to steer, but it was too late. We crashed into the fruit stand and almost hit Mr. Loomis. Mr. Loomis shouted. The fruit spilled in all directions.

The story has a sad ending. Out of our allowances we paid $3.40 for the fresh fruit that Mr. Loomis lost. Joey's wagon had a big dent in it. I was spanked for sneaking out of the house in the early morning. Joey and I postponed our plans for the next moon shot indefinitely.

● EXERCISE 2. As a small child, did you ever try to imitate somebody you admired? Do you know anyone who did? Write, in 100 to 150 words, the story of such a personal experience. Make a plan first. If you do not remember such an incident, an item in the following list may suggest an experience that you can write about.

1. You tried using your mother's cosmetics.
2. You used your big brother's razor.
3. You tried a backflip off a high diving board.
4. You tried a stunt on a bicycle or trapeze.
5. You tried to press pleats in a skirt.
6. You tried to use a sewing machine.
7. You tried to diaper your baby sister.
8. You tried to fix your hair in a grown-up style.
9. You tried to milk a cow.
10. You tried to ice-skate for the first time.

● EXERCISE 3. Write a story of about 150 words on the topic "The First Money I Ever Earned." Prepare a story plan first. If you cannot think of an incident, the following list may help you to invent one.

1. Not crying when the barber cut my hair
2. Running an errand
3. Mowing a lawn
4. Picking berries or fruit
5. Baby-sitting
6. Cleaning up the yard or courtyard
7. Walking a dog
8. Selling Christmas wreaths
9. Washing windows or a car
10. Pulling weeds or clipping a hedge
11. Delivering papers, groceries, packages
12. Selling tin foil, bottles, bales of paper, magazine subscriptions
13. Raising and selling chickens or rabbits
14. Helping paint a fence or a barn
15. Serving and dishwashing for a party

19b. Learn the basic parts of a story.

Often, when you write a letter, you refer to an incident only briefly; but when you write a story, you assume the reader knows nothing and supply all necessay information. There is another basic difference between writing about an incident in a letter and writing a story. In a letter, the incident may be just a small part of the news you are sending to a friend. In a story, the incident is *all* you are writing about. You must organize the details so that they will interest and entertain your reader.

Most good stories include five basic story elements. **It will help to remember these elements as you write.**

1. Interesting start
2. Beginning explanation
3. Action
4. Climax
5. Ending

The story in Exercise 1 contains these five elements. The first sentence is the *interesting start*. It tells the reader what the story is about but in such a way that his curiosity is aroused. The rest of the paragraph is the *beginning explanation*. Notice that the paragraph does not supply *unnecessary* information. It does not tell how Joey and the writer became friends, nor does it give all the details of their talk about the program. It tells only enough to show why they decided to make the trip.

Furthermore, this paragraph avoids a common error in story writing: beginning in the wrong place. The real beginning of the story is the decision of Joey and the writer to make the trip. The story should not begin with getting up that morning or going to school or even with Joey meeting the writer. Similarly, a story about an actor forgetting his lines in a school play should begin with the incident that makes the actor nervous, not with the drama club deciding to put on the play.

The step-by-step events that happen after the beginning explanation make up the developing *action*. In the story about the trip to the moon, the second paragraph gives such a step-by-step account. It tells very specifically what happened the morning of the attempted trip to the moon.

The *climax* is the high point of a story. In this story the climax, in the third paragraph, is the wagon crashing into Mr. Loomis' fruit stand. The way in which this climax is made vivid by the use of specific details and effective verbs will be discussed later in this chapter.

The *ending* of a story ties up the loose ends. In this story, the ending tells what happened after the wagon hit the fruit stand. The ending may state in so many words how the writer felt about the events of the story, or his feelings may merely be suggested. Although we are not told directly, the details about the spanking, the dented wagon, and paying for the damaged fruit give us a good idea how Joey and the writer must have felt. We are not surprised that they did not plan another trip to the moon for a while.

Sometimes a story may not contain all these elements. An interest-arousing opening and a strong climax are, of course, assets to a story, but they are not necessities. Many good stories lack them. But keeping the five basic elements in mind as you write will help you to organize your story.

● EXERCISE 4. Identify the five basic story elements in the following story. How do these elements correspond to the preliminary story plan: *When, Where, What happened, How you felt.*

I wasn't sure whether it was a good idea to take my little sister with me last Halloween. Instead of trick-or-treating for candy, I was collecting money for the Orphan's Fund. My collection box had a message on it printed in big letters: TREAT A NEEDY ORPHAN FOR HALLOWEEN. Since my little sister can't read, I don't think she got the message.

I tried a large apartment house first. After I rang the first bell, I told my little sister, "Now remember. We're here to collect money for charity. Don't ask for any candy." She just nodded and smiled.

A man appeared. He didn't look very happy. "Can't you kids give me a little rest? You're the tenth bunch ringing my doorbell."

I tried to explain that I was collecting for charity, but he got more and more impatient. Then my little sister sidled up and held one of his fingers. "I'm not an orphan," she said, "but I'd like some candy." The man looked at my little sister and smiled. "All right. Come on in." After telling us to sit down, he gave my little sister candy, and he put some money in my collection box.

I have decided that taking my little sister along was a good idea, after all. She can't follow orders, but she can certainly raise money.

● EXERCISE 5. Write a story of 150 to 200 words about a personal experience which embarrassed you at the time it happened, but which you can laugh about now. Before you write the story, make a preliminary plan. (See pages 361–62.) Include the five basic story elements in your story.

WRITING VIVID STORIES

Vivid means "clearly seen and lively." A reader responds to a vivid story because the writer's skill has made the story come alive. Your story may not be as clear and lively as one by a professional writer, but you can learn certain principles that will improve your stories.

Choosing Details

19c. Choose details to make the action vivid.

Reread the story in Exercise 1 (page 362). Notice how the second and third paragraphs tell exactly what happened. Suppose the following paragraph were substituted. Would the story be as effective?

> The next morning we got in the wagon and went downhill. Then the wagon got out of control, and we ran into a fruit stand. Some of the fruit was spilled.

The use of effective details makes a story vivid. If such details are missing, the reader will lose interest in the story.

(1) Choose specific details.

Compare the following two paragraphs. Which is the more interesting?

> When the canoe touched the river bank, I told John to push us away with his paddle. Instead he panicked. He got up and tried to climb to the shore. In his efforts, he overturned the canoe. I fell into the water.

> The canoe glided toward the river bank. I felt a bump as it touched land. "Use your paddle. Push us away," I told John. He put his hand on the side of the canoe and pushed himself to his feet. I yelled at him to sit down, but he wasn't listening. His hands trembled. Awkwardly he teetered on one foot as he tried to climb to the bank. The canoe began to sway. "Sit down!" I yelled. The canoe rocked vio-

lently. Suddenly I was thrown from my seat and hit the water with a splash.

Most readers would agree that the second paragraph is the more effective. The first paragraph gives only general information about what happened. The second paragraph tells how John used his hand to push himself up and how he looked (teetering awkwardly) as he tried to leave the canoe. Instead of the general statement *I fell into the water*, the second paragraph gives two specific details: being thrown from the seat and the splash of hitting the water. Also, the second paragraph does more than tell what happened; it *shows* what happened. There is no direct statement about John panicking. A detail, the trembling of John's hands, implies this fact.

To sum up, the second paragraph is superior in two ways: (1) It gives specific details to make the action vivid. (2) It avoids general statements and lets the reader draw his own conclusions from the details.

● EXERCISE 6. Rewrite one of the following paragraphs. Use specific details to make your reader feel that he is participating in or witnessing the action.

1

There was one minute to go in the last quarter. I caught the pass and ran sixty yards for a touchdown. The crowd cheered.

2

There was a very long line in front of the ticket office as I arrived. I was impatient at first. Then I began to think about something else. When the man behind the window asked me how many tickets I wanted, I was very much surprised.

3

When the chairman called on me, I was very nervous. I grew calmer as I explained why our club should donate to the Community Fund. At the end of my speech, the members applauded.

4

The two boys clenched their fists and threatened each other. Each of them wanted to appear brave but did not really want to fight. After the crowd watching them had gone, each muttered a final insult and left.

● EXERCISE 7. Write a paragraph of 50 to 75 words about one of the following situations. Assume that your paragraph is to be part of a longer narrative. Before you begin to write, think of as many details as possible that would be appropriate for this scene and action. Then select the most vivid ones for inclusion in your paragraph.

1. Sliding on the ice and bumping into a lady carrying packages
2. Hitting a long, high ball that you think is a home run until the center fielder catches it
3. Being caught in a hailstorm
4. Winning (or losing) a three-legged race at a picnic
5. After riding for twenty minutes, discovering you are on the wrong bus
6. Trying to keep a little boy from crossing the street against the traffic light
7. Helping move furniture during spring cleaning
8. Saving someone from drowning
9. Making a report to the class
10. Taking part in a pie-eating contest

(2) Use specific verbs.

Some verbs describe actions more specifically than others. The verb *walk*, for example, gives a general idea of an action; the verbs *amble*, *stroll*, *swagger*, and *shuffle* give a more specific impression. When used appropriately, such verbs can help the reader form a clear picture of the action. Of course, you should not try to use a vivid verb in every possible situation. If you are simply telling how you get to school in the morning, it would be better to use *walk* than *stroll* or *amble*. If the point is *how* you walk, a more specific verb may be the thing.

● EXERCISE 8. Some of the verbs in the following paragraph are specific and some are not. List the specific verbs, and be prepared to explain how these verbs make the action vivid.

The circus was a blend of movement, color, and noise. In the center ring, a bareback rider performed. As his horse pranced around the ring, the rider tensed, whirled in the air, and landed neatly on the horse. In another ring, a seal held a large ball in its flippers. A clown dressed in orange, green, and purple tiptoed up and reached out for the ball. The seal yelped. The clown staggered back, threw up his hands, and flopped to the sawdust floor. Above the crowd, aerialists performed their dangerous work. A man swung out on a trapeze, holding a girl by the wrists. Suddenly he released her. As she plunged into space, a third aerialist swooped down just in time and caught her.

(3) Omit unnecessary details.

As you write, you may think of many details to include in your story, but not all of them may belong.

Consider each detail before you make the final copy. Ask yourself: Does this detail, interesting as it may be, give information that is unnecessary to understanding the story? Does it distract attention from what is happening in the story? If the answer to these questions is *yes*, eliminate the detail.

The following story contains one unnecessary sentence. It is in heavy type.

> Last August I was initiated into the Secret Order of Screaming Serpents. Bill Johnson, the Chief of the Serpents, and Joe Riley, the Medicine Man, blindfolded me and took me to the clubhouse. Bill asked, "Are you ready for your initiation? Can you stand terrible pain?"
>
> I said, "Yes."
>
> I heard the Serpents whispering among themselves. Once I heard Joe say, "No, no, that would be too horrible!" The whispering seemed to last for hours. **I also recognized the voice of Olin Bauer, who works in the grocery store.**
>
> Finally, Bill took off my blindfold. He said, "You have been very brave to withstand this mental torture. Here is your membership card."
>
> As he handed it to me, he dropped it. I bent to pick it up, and Joe whacked me with a paddle!

The detail about Olin Bauer gets in the way of the story's action. At this point the reader is anxious to find out what happened, not learn who was present. Only three persons are really necessary to the story; Bill Johnson, Joe Riley, and the writer. Olin Bauer plays no important part in the action, and mentioning him only distracts and confuses the reader.

In your own stories, be careful to stick to the point. Suppose you are writing a story about the last few minutes of a basketball game in which you scored the winning points. You may think of many incidents that happened during the game, but some of them have little to do with your story. For example, one of the players may have collided with the referee and knocked him down. Unless this incident is closely related to your triumph, you should not include it in your story.

● EXERCISE 9. In the following story there are five sentences containing unnecessary details. Copy these sentences on your paper.

The day of the Halloween party, Marilyn Freeman told me she was sure that she would win the prize for the best costume. She was coming as Marie Antoinette, and her mother had bought her an authentic eighteenth-century costume, including a wig. Marilyn's father is a dentist. "What are you coming as?" she asked.

I said, "Oh, you'll see." I didn't have much chance of winning the prize, but I didn't want Marilyn to know that. All I had was a ghost costume that my mother and I had made out of a sheet. Janet Goodrich was coming as a pirate.

That evening we had lamb chops for dinner. At the dinner table, my mother asked me why I looked so gloomy. I told her about Marilyn's costume. "We'll have to do something about that," said mother.

First she got some of father's medals and pinned them on the sheet. Then she pasted on some gold stars. After I put on the costume, she got my brother Billy's western outfit, took off the holster, and put the cartridge belt around my waist. Billy can be nice, but he is usually a pest. Finally, mother took a black crayon and drew a beard on the sheet.

Rita, Tony, Joyce, Elsie, and Greg were at the Halloween party. To Marilyn's surprise and my own, I won the prize for the best costume—as the ghost of a dead general!

● EXERCISE 10. Write a story of about 200 words. Use good details and specific verbs to make the action vivid. Before writing the final copy of your story, reread it and remove unnecessary details. If you cannot think of a topic, use one of the following suggestions.

1. An unexpected gift
2. A quarrel with your best friend
3. Meeting relatives you never knew you had
4. An illness that spoiled a trip
5. An accident that you saw happen
6. How you became friends with a person you had disliked at the start
7. How you learned to swim (or skate or dance, etc.)
8. How you helped somebody in trouble
9. How you got unexpected help when you needed it
10. Conscience pangs after disobeying your parents

DIALOGUE

Conversations in stories are called *dialogue*. Using dialogue is one method of making a story vivid.

19d. Use dialogue to make your stories lively and convincing.

If you present the direct speech of people, your writing will be livelier and more realistic than if you merely describe their thoughts and feelings indirectly. Direct speech can vividly reveal the personalities of the speakers. Conversation makes a story seem more lifelike and exciting.

In the following passage, the characters are engaged in conversation, but what they say is described—it is not reported directly. The result is a dull, uninteresting paragraph.

> My friends Sam and Eddie went abalone fishing at Hondo Beach. When I met them, I asked where they had been. They told me. I asked what an abalone was. Sam said it was a shellfish. I asked how they caught abalone. Sam said they waded out into the water and pried them off the rocks. Eddie said the water was very cold, and that the abalone were hard to pry off the rocks. I wanted to know if the abalone were good to eat. Sam said yes, if properly cooked; but Eddie said they were awfully tough.

In the following paragraphs, the conversation is written as dialogue. Notice how much more interesting this second version is. Notice also that it is much more convincing. The dialogue not only adds liveliness; it also indicates the personalities of the speakers. Sam and Eddie sound like real people, each with a distinct personality, and the dialogue shows their personalities.

> I ran into Sam and Eddie on the street.
>
> "Where'd you go yesterday?" I asked them.
>
> "Abalone fishing at Hondo Beach," Sam said.
>
> "What's abalone?" I wanted to know.
>
> "A shellfish."

"Like oysters?"

"No more like oysters," Eddie snorted, "than a wheelbarrow is like a motorcycle."

Sam explained, "An abalone has just one top shell, like a snail. It's open at the bottom."

"You fish for 'em with hook and line?"

"Gosh, are you ignorant!" Eddie said.

"They stick to the rocks, under water," Sam said, "and you wade out—"

"In water that's so cold you turn blue," Eddie interrupted.

"—and you pry them off the rocks. It's easy."

"Yes, sure," Eddie said, "as easy as prying names off plaques."

"What do you do with them?" I asked.

"Eat them," Sam said.

"If you're crazy enough," Eddie said. "By rights, you should use them for shoe soles."

"They're not tough if you remember to tenderize them by pounding before you fry them."

"Personally," Eddie insisted, "I prefer slabs of old automobile tire fried in axle grease."

One of the problems in writing conversation is to keep the reader aware of who is talking. There are many ways to do this. How many different ways of revealing who is speaking are shown in the passage above? Notice where the speaker is identified—at the beginning, at the end, or in the middle of his speech. With several speeches, there is no identification, yet the reader knows easily who the speaker is because the author has been careful to make it clear.

Before you write a story with conversation in it, review the rules for punctuation of dialogue on pages 266–72. Remember these three rules:

1. Place quotation marks before and after words that anyone speaks.
2. Use commas to separate a person's speech from the rest of the sentence.
3. Start a new paragraph to indicate a change of speaker.

● EXERCISE 11. The following story is told without direct quotations. Rewrite it, putting the appropriate lines into direct quotations.

A mean, bullying man borrowed a plow from his meek neighbor and failed to return it. Finally the owner of the plow asked for it. The big man said sorrowfully that he could not return it; rats had eaten it up. When the little man left without his plow, the big man laughed and laughed.

Some days later, the big man found that the buzz saw he used to cut up logs had been ruined by somebody. Furious, he went to his little neighbor and shouted that someone had knocked big chunks out of his fine new saw. The little man suggested that the damage must have been done by cats. Wildly, the big man protested that it couldn't have been cats, that it would take mighty tough cats to bite pieces out of a buzz saw. This was so, the little man agreed; in a country where the rats feed on iron, the cats have to be tough.

● EXERCISE 12. Select two of the following situations and write a short conversation to fit each of them. Let the dialogue show the personalities of the speakers.

1. Two motorists have had a collision; each is saying that the accident is the other's fault.
2. Two small boys are bragging about their dogs.
3. Two boys argue about a baseball hero.

4. A girl insists to her mother that she is old enough and capable enough to be a baby-sitter.
5. A girl tries to persuade her mother to let her skip piano practice that day.
6. Two girls try to persuade a third girl to invite two particular boys to a party she is giving.
7. A boy tries to make his mother see why it is impossible for him to go to a girl cousin's birthday party.
8. A boy tries to convince his father that his allowance must be increased.
9. A girl is talking about sewing to a boy who would rather talk about sports.
10. An uncle treats his nephew like a baby; the boy tries to convince his uncle that he has grown up.

DESCRIPTION

19e. Use description to make your stories vivid and convincing.

A good description makes the reader see, hear, or otherwise experience something. You have already learned how good details and specific verbs can make the description of action vivid. Description can also improve a story in other ways. A description of a scene can make a reader feel that he is present at the scene. A description of a person may almost make a reader think that he knows that person. Properly used, description can convince the reader that what is happening in a story is real because the details seem real.

The longer your story, the more description you will probably employ. There is no place for a long description of a person or scene in a very short story, but even here a sentence or two of vivid detail can make the story more effective. In this part of the chapter, you will learn how to use description to improve your stories.

(1) Use details that appeal to the senses.

Before you can write a good description, you must learn to be a good observer. Notice the things around you, and make a mental list of them. For example, what might you observe in the halls when classes are passing at your school? First, you would *see* the students on their way to their classes. Next, you would *hear* them talking with each other or shouting to students across the hall. Finally, you would *feel* some of them jostling you as you passed them. You would have been aware of all these details through your senses.

Just as you learn about life around you through your senses, so you can make a story lifelike by using details that appeal to the senses. The senses you will use most often are *sight* and *hearing*, but many times you will also use *touch*, *taste*, and *smell*. The more senses you appeal to, the more convincing your description will be.

Sometimes you can write a description appealing to all the senses. Suppose you were describing a river cruise that you took last fall. You would include details about *seeing* your fellow passengers at the boat's rail and trees with beautiful orange, red, and purple leaves on the river bank; *hearing* the chatter of the passengers, the lapping of the waves, and the breeze rustling the leaves; *feeling* the gentle motion of the boat and the slight, pleasant chill in the air; *smelling* the clean, fresh odor of the autumn air mingled with smoke from the boat's engine; and perhaps *tasting* a salty lunch of ham sandwiches and potato chips.

● EXERCISE 13. Test your powers of observation on your way home from school. How many details can you observe? To which senses do they appeal? List at least ten details.

● EXERCISE 14. Write a description of about 150 words based on the list you made for Exercise 13.

● EXERCISE 15. The following paragraphs might belong to stories in which long descriptions would be out of place. The addition of several vivid sentences would improve these stories. Rewrite two of the four paragraphs, following the directions in parentheses.

1

The room was dark as we entered. I turned on the light. As we looked around the room, John said, "My gosh!" I was too surprised to reply. (Write two or three sentences telling how the room looked.)

2

At the end of the debate an old man stood up. "I've attended many town meetings," he said, "and I've never heard such nonsense as I've heard tonight." Angrily he banged his cane on the floor. (Insert several sentences to follow the first. Describe how the old man looked and spoke.)

3

My uncle had worked on the model boat for months. It had occupied most of his spare time. Lovingly he had carved, sanded, and painted it. Now he held it proudly in his hand, displaying it before us. (Write two or three sentences about the boat.)

4

It was a very unpleasant trip. I was relieved when the train finally arrived at the San Francisco station. (Insert several sentences after the first. Show how the trip was unpleasant. Appeal to at least three of the senses.)

(2) Select adjectives and adverbs carefully, and use them sparingly.

As you remember, an adjective describes a noun or a pronoun and tells *What kind, Which one, How many.* An adverb describes a verb, an adjective, or another adverb and tells *When, Where,* or *How.*

A lazy writer will not try to find the adjective or adverb that gives an exact description. He will rely on a dull, tired word that has already been used too often. For example, he may write:

> We had a swell time, because the speaker was very interesting. He made some tremendously good remarks. After he finished, the applause was absolutely fabulous. We all agreed that he was a terrific speaker.

The writer of this passage indicated that the speaker was *interesting* and *terrific,* but these tired words tell little about the speaker or his speech. Was he *stimulating? thought-provoking? witty? persuasive?* Similarly, the applause is described as *absolutely fabulous,* a phrase which has almost no meaning. Was the applause *enthusiastic? deafening?*

Get into the habit of avoiding such words as *swell, terrible,* and *terrific.* When you encounter these words in your own writing, cross them out and find adjectives and adverbs that are more interesting and more exact in meaning.

Some vague, dull, and overused adjectives and adverbs are

nice	grand	tremendous
swell	terrible	really
horrible	cute	wonderful
neat	fabulous	great
cool	awful	very
funny	absolutely	terrific

● EXERCISE 16. Number your paper 1–10. After the proper number, replace the overused adjectives and adverbs in italics with words that you think are fresher and more exact. Use your dictionary, if you need to.

EXAMPLES 1. After Joe sprained his ankle, he walked in a *funny* way.

1. *peculiar*

2. Since Marsha was elected secretary of the club, she has become *terribly* efficient.

2. *extremely*

1. Harriet, your birthday party was *nice*.
2. I had an *absolutely terrible* time at the dentist's.
3. She is a *cute* little girl and often makes *cute* remarks.
4. Bongo Brady has recorded a *terrific* new song.
5. Just as we ran out of ideas, John Keller made a *neat* suggestion.
6. Frank gave a *swell* performance in the class play.
7. Margie's hair looks *horrible* this morning.
8. The homework Miss Smith assigned is *really* difficult.
9. Frank plays the clarinet *awfully* well.
10. We had an *awfully wonderful* weekend at your home.

● EXERCISE 17. Write the following sentences. For the first five, fill in each blank with as fresh and exact an adjective as you can. Supply fresh and exact adverbs for the second five sentences. Use the dictionary if you need to.

1. She refused to give him a(n) —— answer.
2. In spite of his —— suit, he looked shabby.
3. They ate an enormously —— dinner.
4. The actress wore a strikingly —— evening gown.
5. The general handled his troops with —— skill.
6. A frightened child —— asked a question.
7. My new sweater is —— scarlet.
8. After cleaning house, I flopped —— on my bed.
9. The wind was whistling outside, but the March family sat —— around the fire.
10. Breathing ——, I began to unwrap the presents.

Adjectives and adverbs are like spices in food. They are necessary for seasoning, but too many of them will spoil the dish. Do you feel that the following passage is overseasoned?

> The lithe, reddish-brown, long-eared dog sagged mournfully and wearily at its oblivious master's feet. The huge man with the bushy, black beard had hunted tirelessly and enthusiastically all that cool, sunny day. Now he had fallen blissfully asleep in the soft but threadbare easy chair.

This passage would be more effective if some of the modifiers were eliminated:

> The long-eared dog sagged at its master's feet. The huge man had hunted enthusiastically all day. Now he had fallen asleep in the soft easy chair.

Sometimes you may be tempted to include a great many adjectives and adverbs in your own stories in the hope that such a practice will make your writing more professional, more like the stories you read in books and magazines. Most experienced writers do not overload their sentences with modifiers but use them where they will do the most good. They have learned how to avoid too many modifiers.

One method is simply to eliminate modifiers that do not contribute much to a description. In the passage about the hunter and the dog, the elimination of many adjectives and adverbs resulted in a much stronger description. Another method is to use comparisons. Sometimes a comparison is the most vivid and exact way to describe a person or an object. One writer does not describe a woman as fat. He writes that her figure "was like a barrel with a belt around it." Another writer compares a person to "a military procession with a brass band, the way he always set the pace for anyone who accompanied him." Comparisons are often effective, but a reader may tire of them even sooner than he will tire of modifiers. Use comparisons sparingly and save them for important moments in your stories.

A third method is to rewrite some sentences so that nouns and verbs do the work of describing. The sentence *He was a joyous, smiling boy* can be changed to *His smile showed his joy*. In the second sentence, the adjectives *smiling* and *joyous* have been changed to nouns. Verbs with descriptive adverbs may be replaced by more exact verbs. The sentence *Suddenly he ran forward and quickly pulled the letter from her hand* can be changed to *He darted forward and jerked the letter from her hand.* The verb *darted* replaces *suddenly ran,* and the verb *jerked* replaces *quickly pulled.*

● EXERCISE 18. The passage below has too many adjectives and adverbs. Rewrite it according to the following directions:

1. Eliminate unnecessary modifiers from the first two sentences.
2. Use a comparison in the third sentence (perhaps to a little dog cautiously approaching a big dog).
3. Rewrite the last sentence so that an exact verb will replace a verb and an adverb.

The shabby, pathetic-looking little man shuffled timidly and fearfully along the dingy, cracked, uneven sidewalk. His old, battered hat jiggled precariously on his head. When he saw Mr. Abercrombie, the banker, coming up the street, he cautiously sidled up to him. Mr. Abercrombie walked haughtily past.

● EXERCISE 19. Write a story about a time you enjoyed a big success. If you prefer, invent such a story. Be sure to plan before you write, bearing in mind the basic parts of a story. Try to use fresh and exact adjectives and adverbs. The following list of ideas may help you think of a story.

1. You won a merit badge.
2. You won a contest and got a prize.
3. You pitched a winning game.
4. You baked a prize-winning cake.
5. You were in a talent show.
6. You built a radio set that worked.
7. You won the lead in a class play.
8. You found something of value: money, jewelry, etc.
9. You hit a home run.

10. You shot a deer or caught a big fish.
11. You won an election for patrol leader, class president, cheerleader, etc.
12. You made a very pretty dress.

(3) Use description to make characters and setting vivid.

The persons in a story are called the *characters*, and the place where a story happens is called the *setting*. A story gains conviction if the reader knows something about the characters and setting. If a character is to play an important role in a story, a description will focus attention on him. At the beginning of *Treasure Island*, Robert Louis Stevenson focuses attention on one important character:

> I remember him as if it were yesterday, as he came plodding to the inn door, his sea chest following behind him in a handbarrow; a tall, strong, heavy, nut-brown man; his tarry pigtail falling over the shoulders of his soiled blue coat; his hands ragged and scarred, with black, broken nails; and the saber cut across one cheek, a dirty, livid white.

Setting may also play an important role in a story. If you were writing about a night spent in a supposedly haunted house, the house itself would be an important factor and a description of it would make your story more effective. In *Green Mansions*, most of the action takes place in the forest wilderness of Venezuela. The author, W. H. Hudson, describes the enchanting beauty of this wilderness:

> The rare loveliness of the scene touched and lightened my heart. Away back in the east the hills of Parahuaria . . . loomed with a strange

> glory against the gray rainy clouds. . . . On that side, also to the north and south, there was open forest, but to the west a different prospect met the eye. Beyond the stream . . . spread a brown savanna [treeless plain] sloping upward to a long, low, rocky ridge. . . . As the sun went down . . . the whole western sky changed to a delicate rose-color that had the appearance of rose-colored smoke blown there by some far-off wind, and left suspended. . . .[1]

● EXERCISE 20. Pretend one of the following persons is a character in a story, and write a description of 75–100 words. Let physical details show the personality of the character. You might also show the character performing some typical action.

1. An aunt or uncle
2. A policeman
3. The president of your class
4. Your best friend
5. A public official you have seen on television
6. The librarian at your local library
7. Your older brother or sister
8. A saleslady in a department store
9. A waiter or waitress
10. A character you invented

● EXERCISE 21. Write a description of a setting (no longer than 100 words) which might be used in a story. Perhaps you can make your setting suggest a feeling or mood; mystery, dreariness, brilliance, gaiety, fear, and so on.

● REVIEW EXERCISE. Write a story of about 400 words. Use dialogue if it is appropriate.

[1] From *Green Mansions* by W. H. Hudson, published by Alfred A. Knopf, Inc.

CHAPTER 20

The Paragraph

Developing and Writing Paragraphs

Dividing a piece of writing into paragraphs serves two purposes. Unbroken lines of type stretching down a page have a difficult and forbidding look, while a page broken into paragraphs of varying lengths looks interesting and inviting. More important, division into paragraphs helps the reader grasp the organization of a piece of writing. Each paragraph deals with one main idea and no more. The beginning of a new one is a signal that the writer is moving on to his next idea.

THE STRUCTURE OF A PARAGRAPH

20a. A *paragraph* is a series of sentences developing one topic.

The main idea or topic in the following paragraph is stated in the first sentence. The rest of the paragraph consists of a series of sentences that give details to support this idea.

> Throughout the Middle Ages, most of the people in Europe were extremely poor. They were called peasants, and they had to work hard

all their lives for the nobleman on whose land they were born. Their homes were small, miserable huts with thatched roofs, dirt floors, and crude furniture. No lamps or candles lighted the peasants' huts. At sundown the peasants dropped onto their beds of straw, exhausted after the long day's labor. They lived mainly on coarse, dark bread. The little meat they had was often partly spoiled, for refrigeration was unknown.[1]

All the details in this paragraph are about the life of the poor farm people, or peasants. If the author of this paragraph were to write about the life of the rich people, or nobles, he would have to write a new and different paragraph.

The Topic Sentence

20b. The topic of a paragraph is stated in one sentence. This sentence is called the *topic sentence.*

If a paragraph has one main idea, it should be possible to state that idea in a sentence. Such a sentence is called the *topic sentence*. In the following paragraphs the topic sentence is in heavy type.

1

Hot water ruined the rich silver mines of the old Comstock Lode in Nevada. The tunnels and shafts were so hot and damp from the steaming water which seeped into them

[1] From *Story of the American Nation* by Mabel B. Casner, Ralph H. Gabriel, Edward L. Biller, and William H. Hartley. Reprinted by permission of Harcourt Brace Jovanovich, Inc.

from underground sulphur springs that miners had to work stripped to the waist and take frequent rests. Occasionally streams of boiling water shot into the tunnels, forcing men to run for their lives. This water collected in sumps, and men who fell into them died in agony. The hot water accumulated, gradually filling the tunnels and bringing all mining to a halt.

2

Experienced shoppers know that price is not always a good guide to quality. Comparative tests have shown many times that the highest-priced product among a number of competing brands is not necessarily the one with the highest quality. Even when the most expensive brand is the best, it may happen that other brands will give more quality per dollar. That is, the expensive brand may not be enough better than its competitors to justify the difference in price.[1]

In these paragraphs, the topic sentence is the first sentence. This is its usual position, and often its most effective position. At the beginning it tells the reader what the paragraph is going to be about. Knowing this, the reader is able to follow the writer's idea easily.

However, the topic sentence may come elsewhere in the paragraph. In the paragraph below it comes last and summarizes the preceding sentences.

In the old days, coal miners worked with pick and shovel and hand drill. Today, hand tools

[1] From *Our American Economy*, Second Edition, by Richard W. Lindholm and Paul Driscoll. Reprinted by permission of Harcourt Brace Jovanovich, Inc.

are replaced by power cutters, drilling machines, mechanical loaders, timbering machines, and roof bolters. Electric locomotives, replacing mules, pull larger cars that carry heavier loads. Belt conveyors, too, move coal in a continuous flow through mine tunnels to the cleaning, washing, and loading machines. **In every way, mechanization has vastly increased the efficiency of coal mining.**

● EXERCISE 1. Find the topic sentence in the paragraphs below. Number your paper 1–5 and copy the topic sentence of each paragraph after its number.

1

Playfulness is a characteristic of most animals. Kittens wrestle and spar with each other. Puppies chase their tails, and bear cubs slide down mud banks. Sailors know that porpoises often race with vessels.

2

Not only did the pioneer mother spin yarn, weave cloth, and sew garments, but she also made soap with fat and lye and made candles with tallow. She churned butter, grew fruits and vegetables, and tended a family cow. Since there was rarely a doctor available, she acted as nurse and doctor both. Often she taught her children to read and write and to love music. On occasion she even fought off Indians with her husband's rifle. The pioneer mother had to have many skills.

3

A number of American place-names taken from Indian tongues are painfully difficult to spell. Indian names that have undergone changes present few spelling problems. Mauwauwaming has become, and is easily spelled, Wyoming. Machihiganing has been simplified to Michigan. Rarenawok and Asingsing are now Roanoke and Sing Sing. But the spelling of other names, which seeks to reproduce the sound of the original words, must present travelers with a few uneasy moments. Pity, for example, the wretched tourist who is spending several weeks in Maine and must write home that he has seen Lake Magaguadavic and Lake Mooselookmeguntic and passed through the towns of Oquossoc, Passadumkeag, Mattawamkeag, and Wytopitlock.

4

For the first time in generations our forests are growing more wood each year than we are cutting. This does not mean that fewer trees are cut; on the contrary, each year more logs are hauled out of the forests than were removed during the preceding year. It is the rate of growth of new wood that is rising annually. This increase is due to wise forest management. Trees that are mature or diseased are cut out to allow room for growth of healthy or younger trees. Loggers leave seed trees to make sure that new growth gets started, or they plant seedlings where there are not enough seed trees.

5

Many people think that the rocket is a recent invention. Although the rocket has received its greatest development within the last fifty years, it was used as a primitive weapon many centuries ago. The Chinese had rockets in the thirteenth century and called them "arrows of fire." In the fifteenth century, the Italians used rockets which traveled over the ground on rollers and were made in the shapes of animals. Neither the Chinese nor the Italian rockets were probably very destructive. They were designed to frighten the enemy, not to kill him.

The Concluding, or Clincher, Sentence

Sometimes a paragraph may be long and complicated or may include details that the writer wants to emphasize. Such a paragraph may end with a concluding sentence. This sentence clinches the point made in the paragraph.

The concluding sentence restates the idea of the topic sentence, summarizes details in the paragraph, or does both. It is helpful at the end of a long paragraph but usually seems out of place in a short paragraph. Do not use the concluding sentence unless it really contributes to a paragraph's effectiveness. The concluding sentence in the following paragraph appears in heavy type.

> Agricultural experts attacked the problems of the dairy farmer. In 1890, Professor S. M. Babcock invented a simple method to test the butterfat content of milk. This butterfat test encouraged dairy farmers to build up herds whose milk was rich in butterfat. Another expert, W. A. Henry, found out that cows give more and better milk when they are fed a balanced diet. In the meantime a German scientist, Robert Koch, had discovered that germs caused tuberculosis. H. L. Russell, an American scientist, visited Koch in Germany and brought back the knowledge that led to the testing of cows for tuberculosis. **These three men—Babcock, Henry, and Russell—helped supply the scientific knowledge upon which the dairy industry is based.**[1]

[1] From *Story of the American Nation* by Mabel B. Casner, Ralph H. Gabriel, Edward L. Biller, and William H. Hartley. Reprinted by permission of Harcourt Brace Jovanovich, Inc.

● EXERCISE 2. Choose three of the topics below and write a topic sentence for each. Then write a paragraph of about 100 words developing the idea of one of your topic sentences.

1. The most useful (or lovable) animal
2. Your favorite holiday
3. How large a weekly allowance should be
4. Why a party was (or was not) enjoyable
5. A movie or TV program you liked
6. Baking a pie
7. A place you would like to visit
8. An experience that taught you responsibility
9. Your daily (or weekly) chores
10. How television helps (or hinders) your education

DEVELOPMENT OF A PARAGRAPH

20c. Plan your paragraph before you write it.

The topic sentence states the general idea of a paragraph, but other sentences are needed to develop and support the topic sentence. To be sure that these other sentences provide effective support, plan your paragraph in advance. Write your topic sentence. Then make a list of the supporting ideas that will develop this sentence. Discard those that are not related to the main idea of the paragraph.

Notice that the writer of the following paragraph made a plan before writing the paragraph.

TOPIC SENTENCE	Prospecting for oil in California in the early days was often a strange and risky business.
SUPPORTING IDEAS	1. telltale explosion 2. prospecting by nose 3. the oilcloth test

Prospecting for oil in California in the early days was often a strange and risky business. Oil seekers got a wonderful clue one day when a cowboy lit a cigarette and tossed his match to the ground. It fell into a ground-squirrel burrow—and an explosion resulted that stampeded the cowboy's stock. The burning match had fallen into a hole full of natural gas which was the vapor from a petroleum seep. Prospectors began to look for other such telltale signs. They would sniff at holes in the ground to detect the odor of petroleum gas, and, if they caught a whiff, would drop a match into the hole. If a loud bang resulted, an oil seep had been located. The test was refined to detect fainter accumulations of gas: the prospector would erect a man-high tent of oilcloth over a hole and stick a goose quill in the top of the tent. A few days later he would apply a match to the quill. If a flame burned, it proved that gas from an oil seep was present, and the prospector would file a mineral claim on the land.

● EXERCISE 3. Choose one of the following topic sentences. By answering the questions that follow it, find supporting ideas that will develop the topic sentence. Make a plan for your paragraph and then write it.

1. The helicopter is a workhorse of the air. (What can a helicopter do that a fixed-wing plane cannot? How can these abilities be used in farming? rescue work? fighting forest fires? traffic control? inspecting power lines and pipelines?)
2. Vacationing at the seashore is fun. (What sports and activities can you participate in at the beach? What can you do if you just feel like loafing?)

3. A young person can earn money after school. (Have you ever mowed lawns? delivered for a drugstore or grocery? gardened? baby-sat? clerked?)
4. It is important to learn to be a good loser. (Can anybody win all the time? What are the harmful results of fretting and fuming about defeat? What are the advantages of taking a loss good-naturedly?)
5. Living in a small family has advantages. (How about problems of sharing gifts, books, toys, radio or television programs in a large family? How about baby-sitting for smaller brothers and sisters? How about accompanying parents on trips or to movies and parties? How about privacy?)
6. Living in a large family has advantages. (Is it sociable? Do you get help from an older sister in fixing your hair? or help from an older brother in repairing a bike? Can you share chores?)
7. A best friend must have certain qualities. (What about loyalty? a sense of humor? the ability to sympathize when you are in trouble? What is the most important quality in a best friend?)
8. A new baby in the family certainly changed my life. (Did you have additional chores to do? Did you have to baby-sit? Did you have to share a room with a brother or sister? Were there any compensations?)

20d. Develop a paragraph by giving details or examples to support the main idea.

The topic sentence of a paragraph is always a general statement. It must be supported by a number of more specific statements which give additional information to make the main idea more meaningful. This information may take many forms: facts, examples, incidents, or reasons.

If your topic sentence were *In their attack on Pearl Harbor, the Japanese inflicted severe damages on the United States armed forces*, you would need specific supporting facts. You could mention the 19 ships that were damaged or sunk and the 80 naval aircraft that were destroyed. You might also give facts about military casualties. In the following example about the American Revolution, numbers have been added to help you see the supporting details.

Most of the young soldiers had very little schooling. They wrote the way they talked, and it is amusing today to see how they spelled. They wrote [1] bums for bombs; [2] warter for water; [3] git for get; [4] sartin for certain; [5] arams for arms; [6] Dullerway for Delaware; [7] cateridges for cartridges; [8] Salletoga for Saratoga; and [9] jest or jist for just. The names of French officers must have been responsible for many troubled moments. We can almost see the young soldier scratching his head as he tries to figure out how to write the name of the Marquis de Lafayette. [10] In at least one instance, this puzzler came out as Markis Delefit.[1]

topic sentence

(1)–(10) Supporting details

[1] From *Story of the American Nation* by Mabel B. Casner, Ralph H. Gabriel, Edward L. Biller, and William H. Hartley. Reprinted by permission of Harcourt Brace Jovanovich, Inc.

Examples are often used to support a topic sentence. In the following paragraph, the writer uses three examples to develop his topic sentence. Notice that each of these examples is developed more fully than any of the details in the paragraph on page 397.

You'll see a block and tackle being used especially where heavy weights must be lifted or moved. [1]Cranes, power shovels, and hoists make use of the block and tackle because it reduces the force that the engine must develop. [2]Of course, on sailing ships pulleys and block and tackle have been used for thousands of years for hoisting the sails and "trimming" them—pulling them into the right position. Perhaps the movable pulley was invented by a sailor! [3]You may see painters or bricklayers at work, standing on a scaffold that is hung by a block and tackle at each end. When the men want to raise their platform a bit higher, a small force put into the block and tackle at each end allows them to raise themselves, the platform, and their equipment.[1]

topic sentence

(1) cranes and power shovels

(2) on sailing ships

(3) scaffolds

[1] Adapted from *You and Your Resources* by Paul F. Brandwein et al. Reprinted by permission of Harcourt, Brace & World, Inc.

● EXERCISE 4. Develop one of the following topic sentences and its supporting facts or examples into a paragraph. You may add facts and examples if you wish. If you prefer and your teacher approves, you may make up a topic sentence of your own, find your own facts or examples to support the topic sentence, and then write a paragraph.

1. We remember and honor great events in our history by having national holidays.
   a. Lincoln's Birthday
   b. Washington's Birthday
   c. Memorial Day
   d. Fourth of July
2. Children are protected by safety regulations from the dangers of fast-moving traffic.
   a. crossing guards
   b. traffic signals at pedestrian crossings
   c. rules against jaywalking
   d. speed laws
3. The American public is deeply interested in sports events.
   a. Newspapers have sports sections.
   b. Newsreels show sports events.
   c. Television and radio broadcast regular and special sports events.
   d. Baseball parks and football stadiums are crowded.
4. Thomas Alva Edison, who patented over a thousand inventions, provided us with many of our daily conveniences and pleasures.
   a. the electric light bulb
   b. the phonograph
   c. telephone improvements
   d. the moving-picture camera and projector

5. Our country has many kinds of climates.
   a. hot desert of Death Valley
   b. snow peaks of the Rockies
   c. warm beaches of Florida
   d. cool forests of Maine
6. Home accidents are often caused by children's carelessness.
   a. dropping pins or needles on the floor to be stepped on by bare feet
   b. pushing fingers or hairpins into electric outlets or television sets
   c. leaving skates on stairways
   d. playing with matches
7. We take for granted today many conveniences which were unknown fifty years ago.
   a. television
   b. automatic washers
   c. the speed of air travel
   d. no-iron fabrics
8. Many skills contribute to a winning football team.
   a. accurate passing
   b. speed and evasiveness
   c. determined blocking
   d. quick thinking
9. Through the centuries, man has found a number of ways to preserve food for long periods of time.
   a. pickling and preserving with spices
   b. curing and smoking meats
   c. canning a wide variety of foods
   d. freezing fresh fruits and vegetables
10. A person living in a city has many places to visit in his leisure time.
    a. public parks
    b. libraries
    c. theaters
    d. museums

● EXERCISE 5. Write a paragraph of about 100 words in which you use one or more examples to explain or support the idea of the topic sentence. If you cannot think of a topic, here are some suggestions.

1. The power of an invention to change our way of living (the printing press, the cotton gin, the airplane, television, etc.)
2. The treasures that money cannot buy
3. The ways a rainy day can be enjoyable
4. The reward of constant and consistent effort (Use an athlete's daily training as an example.)
5. How wood may be used in different ways

20e. Develop a paragraph by telling an incident.

Sometimes a brief story, that is, an incident or an anecdote, can be used to support the idea of the topic sentence.

All his life, Julius Caesar was a proud and implacable enemy. As a youth, he was captured by pirates. When he learned that they demanded twenty talents [units of money] for his release, he jeered at them for underestimating the value of their prisoner and set the ransom at fifty talents. During his stay on the pirates' island, he treated his captors as servants. He joined in their games and read poems and speeches, which he composed, to

topic sentence

incident

them. When they failed to appreciate his work, he called them savages and threatened to have them hanged. After the ransom was paid, Caesar organized a force of men, sailed against the pirates, and captured them on their island. True to his promise, he executed them all.

● EXERCISE 6. Select one of the following topic sentences to develop into a paragraph. Prove the point it makes with a good incident or anecdote. Make up your own topic sentence if you prefer.

1. My dog is a smart animal.
2. Some television programs teach you to expect good in people.
3. Unexpected company can be embarrassing.
4. Sometimes promises are hard to keep.
5. Mistakes are worthwhile if you learn from them.
6. Occasionally you make friends in unexpected ways.
7. Sometimes I am very lucky.
8. It is a mistake to lose your temper.
9. Cooking isn't as simple as it looks.
10. The first day at a new school can be unhappy.
11. Postponing one's homework is not a good idea.
12. A good friend is a help when you are in trouble.

20f. Develop a paragraph by giving reasons to support your main idea.

When your topic sentence states an opinion, give reasons to support the opinion. Persuading others that your opinion is correct depends a great deal on how convincing your reasons are. Suppose your topic sentence were *Our neighborhood needs a new swimming pool.* A reason like *I'm tired of going to the old swimming pool* would convince few people, if any. But if you pointed out that the neighborhood had grown and that the old pool was too small to accommodate everyone who wished to use it, then you would stand a good chance of persuading others.

The following paragraph begins with an opinion. Not everyone would agree with the writer, but he has given some persuasive reasons to support his opinion.

Tennis is a sport with many advantages. [1] It can provide plenty of exercise for the most energetic person, or it can be played in a more relaxed way and be just as much fun. [2] Tennis is an interesting game because you can always work to improve your skill. Every opponent has different weaknesses, and it is challenging to figure out how to take advantage of them. [3] Tennis requires very little equipment and money. [4] Unlike some sports, it is a game you can play when you are older if you stay in good physical condition.

topic sentence

reasons (1)–(4) supporting topic sentence

● EXERCISE 7. Develop one of the following topic sentences and its supporting reasons into a paragraph. If you prefer and your teacher approves, make up a topic sentence of your own and write a paragraph, developing the topic by giving reasons.

1. Young people should be given a regular allowance.
   a. self-respect
   b. amount of allowance sets limit on spending
   c. permits planning and saving
   d. removes need of coaxing
2. Boys should learn cooking in school.
   a. useful when camping
   b. to help out at home when mother ill
   c. when grown, to help out when wife ill
   d. to appreciate wife's cooking more intelligently
3. Baby-sitting is a job that requires training.
   a. ability to treat cuts and bruises
   b. change and bathe a baby
   c. amuse a young child
   d. soothe a frightened child
   e. handle occasional emergencies
4. Young people should be responsible for a pet.
   a. to learn about needs, habits, character of some other living thing
   b. to develop concern for another's comfort
   c. to enjoy the love and companionship of a pet
5. A person my age should have a paying job.
   a. to earn own spending money
   b. to develop self-confidence
   c. to develop a sense of responsibility and worth
   d. to learn a little about some line of work
   e. to contribute a little to the family living costs
6. Boy Scout (or Girl Scout) training is not only fun but also preparation for good citizenship.
   a. helps develop concern for others
   b. helps develop ideals of behavior
   c. helps develop self-reliance
   d. helps acquire useful knowledge

● EXERCISE 8. Write four topic sentences, and make a plan for each. (See page 394.) The first plan, or outline, should develop the topic sentence by giving details; the second should develop by using examples; the third, by telling an incident; and the fourth, by giving reasons.

● EXERCISE 9. Choose one of the plans you made for Exercise 8 and write a paragraph based on it.

UNITY IN PARAGRAPHS

20g. Every sentence in a paragraph should support the main idea expressed in the topic sentence.

All sentences in a paragraph should develop, explain, or prove the paragraph's main idea. A sentence that departs from the main idea is dead weight; it contributes nothing to the paragraph. Furthermore, by wandering from the central topic, it confuses the reader.

Each of the following paragraphs contains a sentence, in heavy type, that wanders from the central topic.

1

A device has recently been developed to enable a blind person to detect objects by sound. Many blind people use canes to probe for obstacles; this device uses a beam of sound instead. The blind person wears a transmitter, which sends out the beam, and a receiver, which gives a signal. If there is no obstacle in front, the blind person hears only a steady hum. If the beam of sound hits an obstacle, the hum grows

20g

louder. If the obstacle is very near, the hum becomes a screech, warning the blind person to stop or turn aside. **Books printed in braille also help blind people to overcome their handicap.**

2

A new kind of mountain, the guyot, has been discovered at the bottom of the sea. Professor Harry H. Hess, the discoverer of the guyot, named it after Arnold Guyot, the geologist and geographer. **Arnold Guyot was born in Switzerland in 1807 and died in Princeton, New Jersey, in 1884.** Guyots have flat tops and gently sloping shoulders, and sometimes stand as high as two or three miles above the ocean floor. Nevertheless, their tops are at least half a mile beneath the surface of the ocean. Professor Hess believes that guyots are over 600,000,000 years old and were originally volcanic mountains.

● EXERCISE 10. In each of the following paragraphs there is a sentence that wanders from the main idea. Write the number of the paragraph. Then copy the unnecessary sentence.

1

The miners of Panamint faced the problem of how to prevent the silver bullion they shipped out on the stagecoaches from being seized by highwaymen. How, the miners debated, could they stop these holdups? It was impossible to send an army of guards along with each coach. Bill Stewart worked out a cheap, simple answer to the problem. Bill had made his first fortune in the Comstock mines. He sent his bullion out in an open wagon attended only by the driver, who carried no weapons of any kind. The plan worked. Thieves disgustedly let the bullion pass. For what could men on horseback do with silver bullion that had been melted and formed into a huge ball so heavy that they could not lift it?

2

The problem of water supplies, a concern all over the world, is related to the problem of food supplies. Millions and millions of acres that could produce crops to feed men and animals lie idle for lack of moisture. Millions of people go to bed hungry every night. Yet millions of gallons of water flow unused to the sea every second. Fast-flowing water deepens and widens riverbeds; slow-flowing water drops silt to fill the channels. The United States spends a billion dollars a year on soil and water projects. Other nations, too, must spend money and energy to bring water to unused land if the problem of growing enough food for their people is to be solved.

3

The United States is the greatest industrial nation in the world because of a combination of factors. The ingenuity and energy of her people are basic assets, and a fortunate closeness of rich natural resources to natural means of transportation is another advantage. Americans are generous and fun-loving. The Lake Superior region provides the nation with an abundance of iron ore and the adjacent Great Lakes enable the ore to be moved by boat to the vicinity of the major coal deposits, which provide the coking coal necessary for making steel.

4

One of the dangers that a crew must guard against when drilling an oil well is a "blowout"—a sudden explosive rush of oil and gas up the drill pipe. Blowouts can hurl the heavy drilling tools out of the ground as if shot from a mile-long cannon, smashing the derrick, killing workers, and starting oil-well fires that may burn for months and waste much precious oil. The Lakeview #1, a famous California gusher, fortunately did not catch fire. To prevent blowouts, a device called a "blowout protector" is installed at the top of the drill hole. At the first warning rumble in the drill pipe, the crew can quickly shut the drill pipe at the top, sealing the oil and gas within the hole and protecting machinery and workers.

COHERENCE IN PARAGRAPHS

A paragraph is hard to read if the sentences do not follow each other in logical order. Each individual sentence may be good, and all the sentences may be directly related to the paragraph's main idea. But unless the sentences are arranged according to a logical plan, the reader will have no clear idea of what the paragraph is about. Paragraphs with a logical plan have the quality of *coherence*.

Arrangement of Ideas

20h. Arrange the sentences in a paragraph according to a definite plan.

There are a number of ways of arranging the sentences in a paragraph. Three of the most useful plans are *chronological order*, *spatial order*, and *order of importance*.

(1) Sentences in a paragraph may be arranged *chronologically*.

Chronological order—the order of time—is used most frequently in stories, where events are told in the order they happened. But chronological order is also useful in other kinds of writing. A paragraph explaining how to sew a hem or build a model plane will divide the explanation into steps and give these steps in the order they should be done. In the following paragraph, the steps for making a plaster figure are given in chronological order. Notice how the underlined words help you to follow the steps in order.

A plaster figure can be made with modeling clay and plaster of Paris. Use a small china figure as your model—a dog or a cat, for example. [1] Press the china figure into the modeling clay [2] and then carefully remove it. The clay will now serve as a mold for your plaster figure. [3] Mix about three teaspoonfuls of plaster of Paris with water to make a thin paste. [4] Next, fill the clay mold with the paste, and let it set for two hours. [5] Carefully remove the clay. [6] You will now have a plaster figure similar to the part of the china figure that was pressed into the clay.[1]

topic sentence

steps (1–6) arranged in order of time

[1] Adapted from *You and Your Resources* by Paul F. Brandwein et al. Reprinted by permission of Harcourt Brace Jovanovich, Inc.

(2) Sentences in a paragraph may be arranged *spatially*.

When you describe objects, the most useful plan is to deal with the objects in terms of their position. In describing a room, you might begin with the objects nearest you—the lamp, the sofa—and finally describe the objects farthest from you—the painting on the wall, the plants on the windowsill. If you were describing the parts of an object, you would also deal with them in terms of position. For example, a description of a car might begin with the front bumper, headlights, and fenders, pass on to the dashboard and seats, and conclude with the fins, taillights, trunk, and rear bumper. When you arrange your sentences according to the position of the objects, you are using *spatial order.*

The following description of the earth's composition proceeds from the outer layers of the earth to the inner layers.

Earth scientists have discovered that the earth is composed of a number of layers. [1]The outside layer, called the crust, is hard rock, which varies in thickness. In many places it is twenty or thirty miles thick, but beneath some parts of the sea it has a thickness of only three miles. [2]Inside the crust, there is a layer about 1,800 miles deep called the mantle, which is composed of flow-

topic sentence

details (1–4) arranged in order of position (spatially)

ing rock. [3]Beneath the mantle is the outer core, a layer about 1,300 miles thick and thought to be liquid iron. [4]Finally, there is the inner core, which is a ball of hot, solid metal.

(3) Ideas in a paragraph may be arranged in *orde importance.*

Items in a paragraph that do not involve time or position can often be arranged in order of importance. This plan is especially useful when the topic sentence is a statement of opinion and the other sentences present supporting reasons. You may use the order of least important to most important or of most important to least important. Either plan helps your reader to see the connection between sentences and so to understand your paragraph.

The following paragraph uses the order of least important to most important.

Our eighth-grade class needs a student newspaper. [1]A newspaper can entertain the class by printing interesting news and gossip about students. [2]It can announce important events like a basketball game or Halloween party. [3]The money raised from sales can be donated to a worthy cause or used to buy a gift for the school. [4]Most important, a

— topic sentence

reasons (1–4) in order of increasing importance

student newspaper can provide valuable training for eighth-graders by letting them write for readers their own age.

● EXERCISE 11. Choose three of the following topics and write a topic sentence and paragraph plan for each. Your first plan should use chronological order; your second plan should use spatial order; and your third plan should use order of importance.

1. A typical morning at your house
2. How to iron a dress
3. Why an after-school job is a valuable experience
4. The appearance of your assembly hall
5. The thrilling conclusion of a basketball (or baseball or football) game
6. Raising a farm animal
7. The importance of physical fitness
8. How a particular bicycle looks (your own or a friend's)
9. The advantages of living on a farm (or in a big city)
10. Your reasons for choosing a particular career

Transitional Words and Expressions

20i. Use transitional expressions to make clear the organization of a paragraph.

Well-planned sentences follow one another naturally in a paragraph. Sometimes, however, it is wise to provide the reader with clues that help him to follow your train of thought more easily. Words that show the relation of one sentence to another within the paragraph are called *transitional expressions.* The underlined words in the paragraphs on pages 409, 410, and 411 are examples.

Transitional expressions can be classified according to the kind of relationship they show.

CHRONOLOGICAL

first	later	formerly
then	soon	after
meanwhile	now	finally

SPATIAL

outside	near	above
inside	behind	to the right (left)
beyond	ahead	in the distance

BETWEEN IDEAS

furthermore	in fact	therefore
moreover	in conclusion	on the other hand
similarly	however	as a result
in addition	consequently	on the contrary

The transitional expressions in the following paragraph are printed in heavy type. Notice how they help the reader understand the plan behind the paragraph and the relationship between the sentences.

> The first plastic is said to have been invented as the result of a contest. After the War Between the States, the game of billiards became very popular, and a great demand arose for billiard balls, which had always been made of ivory. Now there was not nearly enough ivory to meet the demand. **Consequently,** one firm offered a prize of ten thousand dollars for a good substitute. A young printer, John Wesley Hyatt, mixed cellulose, nitric acid, and camphor, and

produced a substance which he called "celluloid." This new substance did not prove to be suitable for billiard balls, and Hyatt did not win the prize. **However,** his invention turned out to be worth a great deal more than ten thousand dollars. **Soon** many articles were being made from this plastic. **As a result,** Hyatt became a wealthy man.

● EXERCISE 12. Write a paragraph based on one of the paragraph plans you prepared for Exercise 11. Underline the transitional expressions you use.

● REVIEW EXERCISE. Write a paragraph of 100 words or more on a topic from the list below or on some other topic of your choice. Follow a definite plan of organization—chronological, spatial, or order of importance, whichever is appropriate. Be sure that you have a good topic sentence and that you support it with sufficient details or examples, with an incident, or with reasons.

1. A sport I would rather watch than play
2. If I could travel anywhere I wished
3. Baking an angel food cake
4. A person I admire
5. How to make a bird feeder, bookends, magazine rack, etc.
6. How to tune a violin
7. The layout of the front page of a newspaper
8. What I dislike (or like) about television commercials
9. The fictional character I would most like to be
10. My favorite holiday

CHAPTER 21

The Composition

Planning and Writing an Expository Composition

Although compositions may be of varying lengths—some no longer than a paragraph—the word *composition* usually means a piece of writing of at least 250 to 300 words that is divided into several paragraphs. Of course, the right length for any particular composition depends on the subject and the amount of information presented about it. The minimum of 250 to 300 words is intended only to give you a general idea.

The *expository* composition, which you will be studying in this chapter, is one that presents a certain amount of information about a subject. All writing presents some information; a narrative about a family incident may well contain some incidental facts about your house or neighborhood, the members of your family, and so on. In expository writing, however, the information is the main thing. The object is to tell the reader something he may not know and to tell him in a way that he will understand. You can see that exposition is a very important kind of writing. Most of the things we know we learn from other people, and a great many of these things we learn through reading. In your lifetime you have accumulated a great deal of information that will be interesting or helpful to others. To present it clearly and well, you will need the skills that are discussed in this chapter.

SELECTING A SUBJECT

Some of the compositions you write this year will be on subjects assigned by your teacher. For these, you will simply have to be sure that you understand the assignment and know how to find the information that you will need. At other times, you will probably be able to choose a subject of your own. Such a choice may be the most important decision you make in planning and writing your composition. It requires careful thought.

21a. Choose a subject that you know something about.

The best subject is one that you know well. Nuclear submarines and rocket engines are interesting, but the chances are that you are not an expert on either. On the other hand, you may know a lot about stamp or coin collecting—how to start a collection, where to obtain specimens, what pleasures and advantages this hobby offers. Such a subject, which you can write about from your own experience, is an excellent possibility for a composition. If you stop to think about it, there are a number of things that you know about. Your whole experience is raw material for compositions.

A good composition, of course, need not always be about things you have done yourself. Much of what you know has come to you at second hand from books and other sources. If you have done considerable reading about the War Between the States, the Pony Express, the Gold Rush, or the early days of aviation, you have information that could be the basis of a good composition. As a rule, however, such a subject should be one that you know already, not one that you have to read up on extensively before you write.

● EXERCISE 1. Think of two subjects from your own experience that you could use for compositions and two more that you know about mainly from books, magazine articles, or other sources. List the four subjects, indicating which are from your experience and which are from other sources. Choose your subjects carefully. You will be working with one or more of them in later exercises. See the Supplement, "Topics to Write About," pages 587–611.

21b. Limit your topic.

If you have to write 300 words or more, you may think that a broad, general subject will do better than a smaller one. It is true of course that there is more to say about "The History of Aviation" than about "The Wright Brothers' First Flight." The trouble is, there is too much that *has* to be said about a large subject. Whole books have been written about the history of aviation. All that a short composition on this subject can do is make a number of general statements without the supporting details that would make such statements meaningful. Exposition calls for precise, detailed information. The larger the topic, the more details you have to deal with.

Probably more student compositions turn out badly because their subjects are too broad than for any other reason. When you have thought of a subject, therefore, it is essential that you consider whether it is manageable in the number of words you have in mind. For example, stamp collecting may provide you with an idea for a composition, but the whole subject is too large. On the other hand, a composition telling how to get started with a stamp collection may be just right.

● EXERCISE 2. Five of the subjects listed below are too general to make good composition topics. Five are limited enough to be suitable. Write *S* after the number of each suitable topic. For the broad general topics, write a smaller but related topic that would do for a short composition.

EXAMPLES 1. Spring cleaning at our house
1. *S*
2. Sports
2. *Our neighborhood baseball team*

1. The boyhood of an American President
2. Preparing for an overnight hike
3. Industries of our state
4. Agriculture in Africa
5. A historical landmark in our town
6. Pioneer life
7. The steel industry
8. Starting a vegetable garden
9. The joys of cooking
10. Causes of the Second World War

21c. **Remember the purpose of your composition.**

In general, all expository compositions make explanations. However, the specific purpose you have in mind should guide you first in limiting your topic and then in selecting details and planning the composition. Suppose you have decided to write about fish. If your purpose is to show that fish are an essential part of man's diet, you will limit your topic in one way. If it is to show how to catch a trout, you will limit the topic in another way. Before you settle on a definite topic to write about, be sure that you can state your purpose.

● EXERCISE 3. Write a statement of purpose for each of the topics that you listed in Exercise 1. You may revise the original topics if you wish.

EXAMPLE 1. *Keeping goldfish as pets* [topic]
To explain the proper methods of feeding and caring for goldfish [statement of purpose]

● EXERCISE 4. Write a composition of 250–300 words on one of the topics from Exercise 1. Include, at the top of your paper, the statement of purpose that you worked out for Exercise 3 above. As you write, keep this purpose in mind and consider whether what you are saying really carries it out.

PLANNING A COMPOSITION

21d. **Plan your composition before writing.**

You have already had some practice in making a plan for a paragraph. Since a composition is usually longer and more complicated than a paragraph, there is even more need for a careful plan. The final result of the planning you do for a composition will be a topic outline (shown on page 428), but there are several important steps that come first.

(1) Make a list of ideas.

Once you have chosen a topic, jot down ideas as they occur to you. At this stage, do not try to organize the ideas. Simply list any details or ideas that may be related to your topic.

When you have completed your list, eliminate any ideas that are not closely related to the topic. In exposition, as in most other kinds of writing, what you leave out can be as important as what you put in. By crossing a poorly related idea from your list, you can often improve your paper greatly.

TOPIC Beginning a stamp collection
PURPOSE To explain how to collect and display stamps

educational value
family mail
hobby stores
removing stamps from envelopes
fun of watching collection grow
learning locations of countries
appreciating beauty of stamps
~~history of postage stamps~~ [eliminated because it does not contribute to purpose of composition]
learning about people and customs of foreign lands
mounting stamps in album
supplies: tongs, hinges, album
post office
stamp packets
approval sheets
~~valuable stamps~~ [eliminated because a beginning collector would not ordinarily try to acquire valuable stamps]

● EXERCISE 5. The following list contains several unnecessary ideas. Copy them on your paper. Be prepared to give reasons for your choices.

TOPIC Learning to swim
PURPOSE To show how a person can become accustomed to water and learn to stay afloat.

overcoming fear of water	safety in the water
basic swimming strokes	racing strokes
treading water	artificial respiration
learning to float	surfing
motion of the tides	water temperature

● EXERCISE 6. Prepare a list of about ten ideas on a topic of your own choice. You may use one of the topics from Exercise 2, if you wish. At the top of your list, write a title and statement of purpose. Later on you will be asked to write a composition on this subject.

(2) Group your ideas under headings.

Now that you have listed your ideas and eliminated the unsuitable ones, you are ready to begin grouping closely related ideas together. To do this, you must consider whether two or more ideas have something in common—whether there is a larger idea that includes them. For example, here are six of the ideas from "Beginning a Stamp Collection" (page 420):

1. fun of watching collection grow
2. removing stamps from envelopes
3. learning about people and customs of foreign lands
4. appreciating beauty of stamps
5. learning locations of countries
6. educational value

A quick glance tells us that some of these ideas are related and some are not. There is an obvious connection between numbers 1 and 4, both of which involve pleasure or enjoyment. A similar connection exists between 3, 5, and 6, all of which have something to do with the educational aspect of collecting stamps. Only 2 does not combine with a related idea.

Once you have grouped your ideas by finding a larger idea that they have in common, it is an easy step to give each group a heading. You simply express the central idea of the group in a word or phrase. For example, we grouped the following items together because they both had to do with pleasure, or enjoyment:

1. fun of watching collection grow
4. appreciating beauty of stamps

We need only choose between *pleasure* and *enjoyment*, and we have a heading for the group. Suppose we choose pleasure:

Pleasure

fun of watching collection grow
appreciating beauty of stamps

It will be easier to find a heading for the group including 3, 5, and 6:

3. learning about people and customs of foreign lands
5. learning locations of countries
6. educational value

Obviously, 3 and 5 describe specific educational values of collecting. Therefore, the heading for this group is ·upplied by one of the ideas from the list itself:

Educational value

 learning about people and customs of foreign lands

 learning locations of countries

By following the same general process of grouping ideas and adding heads, the complete list of ideas for the composition on stamp collecting would look like this:

Pleasure

 fun of watching collection grow

 appreciating beauty of stamps

Educational value

 learning about people and customs of foreign lands

 learning locations of countries

Sources of stamps

 family mail

 hobby stores

 post office

 stamp dealers

Displaying stamps

 removing stamps from envelopes

 supplies: tongs, hinges, album

 mounting stamps in album

Perhaps the process of grouping is not quite finished. Our first two headings have more similarity than we noticed at first—they are, in fact, the reasons for collecting stamps. Therefore we can combine our first two groups into one:

Reasons for collecting stamps

 Pleasure

 fun of watching collection grow

 appreciating beauty of stamps

Educational value

learning about people and customs of foreign lands

learning locations of countries

Notice that indention is used to show that ideas are part of larger ideas. The outline form described on the following pages will indicate other ways of showing the relationship between ideas.

● EXERCISE 7. Each of the following lists of ideas can be grouped under two general topics. Write the two general topics and place the ideas under them.

EXAMPLE 1. Baking a cake: Mixing ingredients; flour; shortening; rolling dough; setting oven temperature; sugar; eggs.

1. *Baking a cake*

Ingredients

flour *sugar*

shortening *eggs*

Procedure

mixing ingredients

rolling dough

setting oven temperature

1. School activities: Glee club; football; baseball; science club; drama club
2. How to make a model plane: Balsa wood; sharp knife; cutting out parts; gluing parts together; blueprints; paint; painting; glue
3. Training a dog: "Heel"; patience; "sit"; firmness in giving commands; "lie down"; importance of rewarding the dog
4. Using an encyclopedia: Using the index to find information on a topic; gaining additional information from maps and charts; finding topic alpha-

betically by title; skimming to find needed facts; taking notes on the article

21e. Make an outline.

Making an outline is the final step in planning a composition. It has the same relation to the composition you will be writing as an architect's blueprint has to the finished building. You have already limited your topic and listed supporting details, crossing out those that have no real bearing on the purpose of your composition. You have grouped related ideas under suitable headings.

The purpose of your outline is to show all of the ideas and headings that will go into the composition in the order you will take them up and in the relation they have to each other. It is possible that you may find a reason for changing your plan slightly once you have started writing. In that case, revise your outline accordingly. Preparing an outline is not just an extra job. The planning you do at this stage will make the actual writing much easier.

There is a conventional form for outlines which you should learn to use. The main ideas in the composition are indicated by Roman numerals (I, II, etc.). These will usually be the heads under which you grouped related ideas earlier (see page 422). In the outline for a composition on "Beginning a Stamp Collection," for example, the first Roman numeral head might be

I. Reasons for collecting stamps

Notice that the heading itself begins with a capital and that it is not a complete sentence. This will be true of all of the heads in the kind of outline (*topic outline*) you are working with.

The idea expressed in the first head indicates that several reasons will be given. If each of the reasons is taken up separately, each will become a subheading under the main heading. These divisions of the main idea are indicated on an outline with capital letters:

I. Reasons for collecting stamps
   A. Pleasure
   B. Educational value

Notice that the subheadings are indented to show that they are divisions of the idea marked with the Roman numeral. Since the subheadings are divisions, there must obviously be at least two of them. An outline should never have one subhead under a main head:

WRONG I. Reasons for collecting stamps
   A. Pleasure
II. Sources for the collector

If the only reason for starting a collection is pleasure, then the Roman numeral heading should be revised and the isolated subheading eliminated:

BETTER I. The pleasure of collecting stamps
II. Sources for the collector
etc.

If either or both of the subheadings can be further divided, a further indention is made and the new and smaller ideas are marked with Arabic numerals (1, 2, etc.):

I. Reasons for collecting stamps
   A. Pleasure
      1. Fun of watching collection grow
      2. Appreciating beauty of stamps

   B. Educational value
      1. Learning about people and customs of foreign lands
      2. Learning locations of countries
II. etc.

For most short papers, these levels of headings and subheadings will be sufficient. If you wish to make still smaller divisions, the following skeleton outline shows how it is done:

I.
   A.
      1.
      2.
         a.
         b.
   B.
II. etc.

Arranging groups of related ideas in outline form will help you to find a clear and logical order of presentation. Often the ideas themselves suggest the proper method of arrangement. For example, the topics in an outline for a composition about producing a play might follow the order of time: choosing the play, casting the play, rehearsing the play. A composition on "Our Obligations," on the other hand, might call for topics arranged from the most general to the most specific: obligations to our country, obligations to our community, obligations to our family.

The major topics for "Beginning a Stamp Collection" may be arranged in order of time. Certainly the idea of "acquiring stamps" belongs before that of "displaying stamps," and "reasons for collecting stamps" comes before either. The complete topic outline on this subject would look something like this:

TITLE Beginning a Stamp Collection [title not part of outline]

PURPOSE To give reasons for collecting stamps and to show how to get started

I. Reasons for collecting stamps
   A. Pleasure
      1. Fun of watching collection grow
      2. Appreciating beauty of stamps
   B. Educational value
      1. Learning about people and customs of foreign lands
      2. Learning locations of countries
II. Sources for the collector
   A. Family mail
   B. Post office
   C. Hobby stores
   D. Stamp dealers
      1. Packets
      2. Approval sheets
III. Stamp display
   A. Supplies
      1. Album
      2. Hinges
      3. Tongs
   B. Procedure
      1. Removing from envelopes
      2. Mounting in album
IV. Specialization

Notice that a fourth main idea has been added to provide a conclusion for the composition. The writer has told how to start a collection; he wants to end by giving the reader some idea of a more advanced kind of collecting. The problems of writing a conclusion are discussed later in this chapter.

● EXERCISE 8. Copy the incomplete outline at the left. Then fill in the blanks with the topics given at the right.

OUR SCIENCE CLUB

PURPOSE To explain how our science club began and to show its activities

I. Formation of club
 A.
 B.
 C.
  1. Campaigning for office
  2.
 D. Writing the club constitution
II.
 A.
  1. Government laboratories
  2.
 B. Projects
  1.
  2.
 C. Talks by eminent speakers
 D.

Holding elections
Tours of laboratories
Recruiting members
Discussions of current scientific developments
Raising an ant colony
Choosing a name
Industrial laboratories
Electing officers
Club activities
Studying a bacterial mold

● EXERCISE 9. Arrange the following ideas and details into an outline. Your outline, like the one on page 428, should have three levels.

TAKING A CAMPING TRIP

Major ideas

Camp health and safety
Planning
Setting up camp

Supporting ideas and details

Selecting equipment	Dry ground
Making a fire	Safety when hiking
Safety tips	Arranging the wood
Setting up tents	Tents
Presence of fuel	Purifying water
Knives, hatchets, and axes	Safety in the water
	Choosing a camp ground
Chopping wood	Bedding
Selecting clothing	Food, pans, plates, spoons, etc.
Personal health	

● EXERCISE 10. Convert the list of ideas which you made for Exercise 6 into an outline. Later you will use this outline to write a composition. Be sure your outline has a title, a statement of purpose, at least two main headings, and supporting ideas for each main heading.

WRITING THE COMPOSITION

21f. Learn the basic parts of a composition: introduction, body, conclusion.

An expository composition has three basic parts.

The *introduction* should prepare the reader by indicating the general purpose and subject of the composition. Notice that the sample composition on pages 432–34 begins, "Stamp collecting is a very popular hobby for several reasons." This sentence not only gives the basic idea of the paragraph, it also leads to the basic purpose of the composition—to tell how to begin a stamp collection.

The *body* is the longest part of a composition and contains most of the information. It carries out the purpose indicated by the introduction. In the sample composition, the body consists of the second, third, fourth, fifth, and sixth paragraphs, which develop ideas given in parts II and III of the sample outline.

The *conclusion* brings the composition to a definite close, and should not be long or complicated. One way of ending a composition is to sum up some of the points made earlier. Notice that the last sentence of the sample composition restates the main idea of the first paragraph.

In a short composition, the introduction and the conclusion need not be longer than one or two sentences.

21g. Use transitional expressions to connect paragraphs.

In Chapter 20, you studied one use of transitional expressions—connecting sentences within a paragraph. Transitional expressions are also used to make a smooth connection between successive paragraphs in a composition. As the following list indicates, most transitional words can join paragraphs as well as separate sentences.

first	furthermore	besides
then	moreover	thus
next	therefore	for example
in addition	nevertheless	in fact
even more	on the other hand	finally

BEGINNING A STAMP COLLECTION

introduction

Stamp collecting is a very popular hobby for several reasons. The collector gains pleasure from the varied colors and designs of the stamps, while he enjoys the fun of watching his collection grow. In addition, stamp collecting has educational value. Stamps often tell the collector much about a country's important customs, events, and famous men. Furthermore, a collector soon learns to find out the exact location of a country. Often he is interested enough to find out other important facts about that country.

(reasons for collecting stamps—I, A–B in outline)

body

A beginning collector can start with family mail. A variety of stamps can be collected from the letters and packages the average family receives. If a relative or family friend happens to be serving overseas in one of the armed services, another valuable source is available.

(acquiring stamps—II, A in outline)

In addition, the collector can get domestic stamps at the post office. Some large post offices have special windows for new stamps, but all

(II, B–C in outline)

post offices have the new stamps. Foreign stamps can often be bought in hobby stores or ordered from stamp dealers.

(II, D in outline)

In fact, stamp dealers who advertise in magazines (often in magazines popular with young people) are an important source of stamps for all collectors. Most dealers offer beginners a packet of assorted stamps at a low price. After a collector has acquired many common stamps, he may be interested in dealers' approval sheets. Stamps on an approval sheet are usually less common than those in the packets; each is mounted and priced separately. The collector keeps any stamp he wants and sends his money and the remaining stamps back to the dealer.

(displaying stamps—III, A in outline)

Most collectors display their stamps in albums. Albums for beginners usually have sections for the different countries and pictures of some of the stamps. Besides an album, a collector needs stamp tongs—a sort of tweezers—and hinges, small bits of paper that connect the stamp to the album page.

(outline III, B)

Stamps taken from the family mail, as well as many included in the packets that come from dealers, have to be removed from the part of the envelope to which they are still sticking. To remove the stamp, the collector first places it face down on a blotter and moistens the envelope paper with warm water. After the paper is thoroughly soaked, he can usually remove the stamp easily. By working slowly and carefully with the tongs, he can avoid tearing or otherwise damaging the stamp. To mount the stamp in his album, the collector allows it to dry, then folds a hinge with the gummed side out, moistens it and attaches the stamp to the page.

conclusion

(specializing—IV in outline)

After the beginner has had a taste of the pleasure of collecting, he is likely to want to specialize. For example, he may wish to concentrate on stamps of a particular country, or on those that have ships or certain animals on them. Whether he specializes or not, however, he is certain to gain much enjoyment and knowledge from his hobby.

21h. Revise your composition.

When you have completed the first draft of your composition, take the time to read and revise your paper carefully. You will be looking for omitted words, grammatical errors, and mistakes in spelling, of course; however, you should also be looking for ideas that are not as clearly expressed as they could be, sentences that have an awkward sound, paragraphs that do not adequately develop their topic sentences, and so on. Be sure to read the composition aloud and to listen for sentence completeness and variety.

The following checklist will serve as a guide to revision:

Revision Checklist

1. Rewrite confusing sentences and paragraphs.
2. Omit unnecessary details.
3. Omit unnecessary words and phrases.
4. Check all punctuation.
5. Look for common spelling errors.

● EXERCISE 11. Write a composition based on the outline you made for Exercise 10. If you have second thoughts about the subject for your composition, you may revise your outline now. Use the checklist above as a guide to revision before you hand in your composition.

CHAPTER 22

Writing Summaries and Reports

Gathering and Organizing Information

All through school and in your later life as well, you will be called upon to find information and report on it in your own words. No skill that you study this year will be more useful—not just in English classes, but in all of your other courses as well. Skill in gathering information and reporting on it is not difficult to acquire if you keep a few simple steps in mind.

SUMMARIES

The simplest kind of report is the *summary*, an account in your own words of a longer piece of writing.

22a. In writing a summary, give in your own words the main ideas of the original article.

The main point of a summary is to provide a short, handy account of a longer piece of writing. To be useful, a summary should be no longer than one third the length of the original.

To write a summary, first read the article or other piece of writing carefully. Then go through it again, this time jotting down the main ideas. Now write your summary, restating the main ideas briefly. Be sure to state the ideas in your own words. At the end of your summary, give the source of the original article.

Study the following article and the summary of it.

ORIGINAL ARTICLE

The *Bounty* II, a seagoing sloop that has a length of 40 feet and a beam of 10 feet, is made almost entirely of a plastic composed of fiberglass and resin. The only wood aboard is used in cabin bulkheads (walls) and furnishings. Even the mast, 36 feet, is of hollow plastic and is just half as heavy, though three times as strong, as a similar mast made of wood.

This plastic yacht cost half of what it would cost if made of wood; yet, in many respects, the plastic yacht is better than a wooden one. The plastic is stronger than wood. The entire hull is one piece of plastic. No leaks can occur. Since no ribs are necessary, the vessel is lighter than a wooden one. Also, it stays lighter. Wooden hulls absorb about 15 percent of their weight in water. The plastic will absorb less than 1 percent. Wooden boats of this type usually take a couple of months to build. A craft such as the one described here can be built in a week. No painting or caulking is necessary, and the plastic is resistant to corrosion. As a result, upkeep is reduced about 80 percent. Less time is spent on painting and repairing, and more time can be spent in sailing fun!

SUMMARY

A seagoing sloop can now be made almost entirely of plastic. The cost is half that of a wooden yacht. Nevertheless, plastic is lighter, stronger, and leakproof. The plastic boat is built in one eighth the usual time needed. Upkeep is reduced 80 percent, for plastic does not corrode and needs no painting or caulking.

Notice that the article is 220 words long while the summary is only 55 words, less than a third as long. Notice also that the summary omits such details as the name or length of the plastic boat. Instead it concentrates on essentials, the fact that a seagoing yacht can be built of plastic and the advantages of using this material.

● EXERCISE 1. Write a summary of the following article. Read the entire article before beginning your summary. Try to limit the summary to less than 100 words.

UNLOCKING EARTH'S TREASURE OF IRON

America's great industrial output is based upon a plentiful supply of steel made from our rich resources of iron. A few years ago, however, industry faced a limit to its production: lack of iron ore. Enough ore for only a dozen years or so remained.

Our deposits of rich ore were almost gone. We had, however, enormous deposits of lean iron ore—enough to last us for centuries. Unfortunately, this lean ore, called *taconite*, was held in rock so hard that it could not be mined. Even when this taconite was broken up by great effort, the particles of iron could not be separated from the very hard rock which held them.

The iron we needed so urgently was locked so tightly into the ground that we could not free it.

Then a key was found! Engineers developed a machine called a *jet-piercer*. This machine is an enormous blowtorch that spurts oxygen and kerosene and a jet of water. The tremendous flame causes the water to explode into steam. The combination of shooting fire and steam tears a hole in the hard ore, into which explosives can be lowered to blast the taconite apart.

Another problem still remained. How could the tiny particles of iron be separated from the hard rock? Research men ground the iron very fine, as fine as sugar or face powder. Then they ran a huge magnet over the ore. The iron particles were lifted out of the powder and they clung to the magnet! In this way the iron was separated from the waste rock.

Still the iron powder could not be used to make steel. The powder was so fine that, if dumped into a blast furnace, it would simply be blown out. The research men finally solved this problem by putting the powder into a slanting drum, adding water, and revolving the drum. The motion caused damp particles of iron to cling together and to form into balls the size of marbles. These marbles, given a heat treatment to harden them, could be used in blast furnaces. The treasure of iron had finally been unlocked from the earth by a key of flame.

● EXERCISE 2. Write a summary of the following paragraphs, bringing out the main points. The paragraphs have a total of 465 words. Your summary should be no more than a third as long.

American English is one of the most standardized languages in the world today. There are differences in words and expressions, and there are differences in pronunciation from one locality to another, but few of them are such as to cause us any real trouble in understanding one another. A person who lives in a place as far in the extreme southeast of the nation as Key West, Florida, can move to a city as far in the extreme northwest as Seattle, Washington, and not have the least bit of trouble talking to his new neighbors or understanding and being understood by them. In the same manner a person who lives as far in the northeast as Portland, Maine, can transfer to a new home, job, or school in a city as far southwest as Los Angeles, and not have any real language difficulties. We are so used to this fact and take it so much for granted that we hardly ever stop to think about it or appreciate it. And yet we should, because it is very important to us all, personally and as a nation.

Few other nations have so uniform a language. Even in England, for instance, where English was born and where it had been growing and developing for at least a thousand years before it came to America, you will find many dialects, which are sublanguages, or little languages within the big language, and these dialects differ so much from one another in the way words are pronounced or used that very often people speaking these different dialects cannot understand one another. This can happen in England, and it can also happen in almost any other country. Great national languages, like French, Italian, German, Russian, Chinese, are broken up into so many different dialects on their home soil that traveling around from one part of the country to another can be almost as difficult for the people who live there as it would be traveling in a foreign country whose language they didn't know at all.

But this does not happen in the United States. You can drive across the nation, you can move your home, your activities, your entire life to any part of the country that you want to without having any real language problems to face in doing so. It means that Americans as a nation are able to work together and play together; they are able to exchange ideas, and to share the same ideals; it has bound us more closely as Americans, and it helps us to have and build a strong, united nation. Our uniform language is in its own way as important a part of our national wealth and strength as are our oil wells and grain fields and vast industrial centers.[1]

● EXERCISE 3. Summarize one of the following.

1. A magazine article related to material your social studies class is studying
2. An encyclopedia article
3. A newspaper article or editorial
4. A chapter in a science book

LONGER REPORTS

A more challenging kind of report, which you will often be asked to write, requires you to gather and organize information from a number of different sources. In writing this kind of report, there are three basic steps:

1. Gathering information
2. Organizing the information
3. Writing and revising the report

Before you begin to search for information, however, you should have a good idea of what kinds of information to include and what not to include.

[1] Permission by Lothrop, Lee & Shepard Co., Inc. from *Our Language: The Story of the Words We Use* by Eloise Lambert. © 1955, by Lothrop, Lee & Shepard Co., Inc.

22b. Know your assignment.

Sometimes you will be asked to choose your own topic for a report. Then you face the same problems as in writing other kinds of compositions: finding a topic and limiting it. (See pages 417–18.) The best kind of topic to choose is one in which you are already interested and about which you wish to learn more.

Often your teacher will assign you a topic. Be sure you understand the assignment and know how long your report is to be. In a report, as in other kinds of writing, it is important to omit unnecessary details. Knowing your assignment will help you judge which details are necessary and which unnecessary.

For example, if you were asked to write a report on the duties and responsibilities of the governor of your state, you might tell how he supervises the work of various state institutions and departments and administers the laws passed by the state legislature. You would not describe how a candidate for governor campaigns for election, recount stories about past governors, or tell about the duties of other public officials such as mayors or congressmen.

Gathering Information

22c. Find sources of information about your topic.

Usually, the reference section of your library is the best place to begin gathering information. An encyclopedia or other general reference work will usually provide you with a good introduction to your subject. Depending on your subject, you may find additional information in more specialized reference books. (For a more detailed discussion of reference books, see pages 543–51.)

Reference books usually provide a more or less general introduction to a subject. For more detail, you must find books and magazine articles about it. To find books on your subject, you will be making use of the card catalogue (described on pages 541–43). Unless your subject is a broad one, it may be treated in *parts* of several books but not be the subject of a whole book itself. In this case, you will need to use the indexes of some of the books the card catalogue directs you to in order to find the information you need.

To find what has been written about your subject in magazines, consult the *Readers' Guide to Periodical Literature* (described in detail on pages 549–51).

● EXERCISE 4. Choose one of the following topics, and look up four sources of information about it. At least one source should be an article in an encyclopedia or other reference book; at least one should be a book (or part of a book) on the subject. Write your topic on a sheet of paper and list the four sources below it. For each, give title, author (if given), and number of pages devoted to the subject. If one of the sources is a periodical, give the name and date of the publication, as well as title and author of the article.

1. How the Declaration of Independence was written
2. The national park system
3. The history of Esperanto
4. The development of the internal combustion engine
5. Luther Burbank's contributions to agriculture

6. The early days of aviation
7. The invention of television
8. John Marshall and the Supreme Court
9. The pyramids
10. The Flemish school of painting

22d. Take notes on your reading.

You cannot hope to remember all the details of information that you collect without taking notes.

The most efficient way to take notes is to write them on cards or slips of paper, using a different card for each note. Early in your reading, you will find that the subject matter of your report falls into a number of general divisions or topics. As soon as you have three or four of these, you can use them as headings for your note cards. When you find information that would come under one of these headings, you write the heading at the top of the note card and write the notes under it. When you find useful material that does not fit under one of the headings, make up a new heading. The list of headings will form a working outline of your report. As you read and take notes, you will be continually revising the working outline. Every note card must have a heading showing the general subject. Following the notes, give the source: the title, author, and page number of a book; the name, date, article title and author, and page number of a magazine article.

Write notes in your own words. Occasionally you may need to quote the exact words used in the source, but it is much better to rephrase the information in your own words. If you do use an exact quotation, be sure to put quotation marks around it. Copying a writer's words without using quotation marks is completely unacceptable in a report or in any other writing.

Taking notes on cards or slips has a great advantage: when you come to write your final outline, you can arrange the cards in the order in which you plan to use them.

> *Salmon*
>
> *Great quantities of Pacific salmon (different from Atlantic salmon) are caught in the Yukon, Columbia, and Fraser rivers and in Puget Sound. Salmon are more valuable commercially than any other North American fish. Sold smoked, canned, frozen, as well as fresh.*
>
> *Compton's Pictured Encyclopedia*
> *Volume 13, pp. 28–29*

Sample Note Card

Suppose you are gathering information for a report on *Food from the Sea.* You have consulted an encyclopedia (see sample note card) and the card catalogue, where you found the titles of three library books that deal with your subject: *Conserving Natural Resources* by Shirley W. Allen, *World Sea Fisheries* by Robert Morgan, and *The Sun, the Sea, and Tomorrow* by F. G. Walton Smith and Henry Chapin. After reading the encyclopedia article, which gives an overall view of the subject, you decide that you will deal with the following three main topics in your report:

I. Need for seafood
II. Kinds of seafood
III. Utilizing our seafood resources

These topics are the beginning of a working outline.

On page 37 of *The Sun, the Sea, and Tomorrow*, you find this information: "The food that man lives by is roughly divided into carbohydrates and protein. The former gives us ready energy and the proteins are the body builders. . . . One of our greater difficulties in the face of a rapidly growing world population is to make more protein available to mankind. . . . Fish is a concentrated protein diet." [1]

This information deals with the first of the topics in your working outline—*Need for seafood.* On a note card you jot down this topic as a heading. Below it you record in your own words the information you want. Finally, you write the source of your information.

> Need for seafood
>
> Man needs protein. Fish is an important source of protein.
>
> The Sun, the Sea, and Tomorrow
> by F. G. Walton Smith and H. Chapin
> p. 37

[1] From *The Sun, the Sea, and Tomorrow* by F. G. Walton Smith and Henry Chapin. Reprinted by permission of Charles Scribner's Sons.

In another book you find other useful information as follows:

"Tunny. (Tuna.) A group of large and voracious species frequenting warm water, the largest of which (the bluefin tuna: *Thunnus thynnus*) reaches a length of 10 feet and a weight of over half a ton. . . .

"Tuna are caught in large quantities by the U.S.A. and Japan and in fairly large quantities by France and Spain."[1]

This information deals with the second of the topics in your working outline—*Kinds of seafood.* Since you will have additional cards dealing with other kinds of seafood, you will make the heading on your note card read "Kinds of seafood—tuna."

Kinds of seafood - tuna

Individual bluefin tuna run as large as 10 feet with a weight of over half a ton.

Japan and the U.S.A. catch the most tuna.

World Sea Fisheries
by Robert Morgan
p. 41

As you continue taking notes, you will follow the same procedure: (1) Write the heading at the top of the note card. (2) Write the information in your own words. (3) Write the source at the bottom.

[1] From *World Sea Fisheries* by Robert Morgan, published by Pitman Publishing Co.

● EXERCISE 5. Choose a topic for a report which you will later write. Be sure the topic is not too large to cover in one report. If necessary, review the material in the previous chapter on limiting your topic. (See pages 417–18.)

Find information about your topic in at least four different sources (including reference books), and take notes on cards or slips of paper. Prepare at least ten note cards on your topic. Each note should include a heading, the notes, and the source of information, including the page number. (If your teacher asks you to hand in your notes, prepare an additional card giving your name and the name of your topic and place it in front of the other cards.)

If you have difficulty in finding a topic, here are some suggestions. Some of these topics are too broad to cover in a short report and must be limited before you begin to take notes.

1. Ways in which an electromagnet is used
2. The sinking of the *Titanic*
3. Balloon racing
4. The preparation and use of cosmetics
5. How the U.S. astronauts reached the moon
6. The story of silkworms
7. The cause and cure of air pollution
8. New kinds of aircraft and what they do
9. The history of devices for telling time
10. Plant life in the desert
11. Fluoridation of water
12. Rain-making
13. The differences between a bird's eye and the human eye
14. The history of a game that interests you
15. The need for flood control

16. A particular fashion in women's clothing
17. The work of a landscape architect
18. The whaling industry today
19. Research in space medicine
20. Animals of the Arctic
21. How a play is produced
22. Air aces of World War I
23. The discovery of penicillin
24. The Lewis and Clark expedition
25. The cave drawings of Cro-Magnon man

Organizing the Report

22e. Organize your notes according to their headings.

Now that you have made notes for your report, you must prepare them for use. You may discover that some information is duplicated or that some facts do not fit your topic as you have limited it. Eliminate such notes. Next organize your notes by sorting the cards in piles according to their headings. You will then have in one pile all the information on one heading, or topic. If you follow these steps, your final outline will take shape, and you will have organized all the information for your report.

22f. Make a final outline based on your notes.

Study this final outline for the report on seafood.

FOOD FROM THE SEA

I. Need for seafood
   A. Lack of sufficient meat for two thirds of the world
   B. Fish as a source of needed protein

II. Kinds of seafood
  A. Fish
    1. Herring
    2. Salmon
    3. Tuna
    4. Halibut
    5. Cod
  B. Shellfish
    1. Oysters
    2. Clams
    3. Scallops
III. Utilizing our sea resources
  A. The sea as a potential food source
  B. Need to protect individual species of fish

● EXERCISE 6. Prepare a complete outline for your own report based on the notes written for Exercise 5. (To review outlining, see pages 425–29.)

Writing the Report

22g. Using your final outline and your notes, write your report.

You have gathered information, and you have organized your material in the form of an outline. As you write, observe the following suggestions.

1. Be sure you understand all the terms you use. If uncertain, look up the words in the dictionary.
2. As you write, keep in mind the basic parts of a composition: *introduction*, *body*, *conclusion*. (See pages 430–31.) Make your introduction interesting. It is important to catch your reader's attention at the outset.
3. Use your own words in writing the report. It is tempting to copy a passage from a book, but copying

is not writing. Introduce quotations only when they are particularly apt or striking.

4. Put every necessary detail into your report, but omit unnecessary items. Stick to your subject.

5. Give details in their proper order, using your outline as a guide.

6. At the end of the report, list the sources from which you got your information.

● EXERCISE 7. Write a first draft of your report. Be sure the report is in your own words and that it has an introduction, a body, and a conclusion.

Revision Checklist

CONTENT

1. Does the report contain enough information?
2. Are all the facts accurate?

CONSTRUCTION AND STYLE

3. Does your report have an introduction and a conclusion?
4. Do the title and opening paragraph arouse the reader's interest?
5. Is each paragraph constructed around one idea?
6. Are your sentences complete? Have you avoided sentence fragments and run-on sentences?
7. Are your sentences varied to avoid monotony?

FORM

8. Does your paper have a heading—name, class, and date?
9. Is there a title? Is it capitalized properly?
10. Are there one-inch margins at the left and right?
11. Is your name on each page of the report? Are the pages numbered?
12. Is the first line of each paragraph indented?
13. Are your sources listed at the end of the report?
14. Is the penmanship legible? Is the paper neat?

Revising Your Report

The first draft of any writing assignment is rarely free of errors. It is always wise to go over a piece of writing to locate any errors and correct them. Since a report may contain errors of fact as well as writing errors, you should be especially careful in revising it. In making your revisions, use the checklist above.

Here is the final copy of the report on seafood. Notice that the opening paragraph provides an introduction and the final paragraph a conclusion to the report. The body of the report is concerned with the different kinds of seafood available.

FOOD FROM THE SEA

The world does not raise enough cattle and sheep and other meat animals to provide food for all the people. Two thirds of the population of the earth is always underfed. The United Nations Food and Agricultural Organization estimates that we would have to increase our meat production by 50 million tons per year to obtain enough food—especially protein—for every living person. This just cannot be done. However, seafood is an important source of protein. We could provide more than enough protein food for the present population of the world if we increased our annual harvest of food from the sea.

Fish like herring, salmon, tuna, halibut, and cod make up most of our seafood. They provide both nourishment and variety at our dinner tables.

Herring provides more tons of food than any other fish. Norway has the largest annual herring catch—almost $1\frac{1}{2}$ million tons in a good year. Japan catches almost a million tons a year, while the United States ranks third with a catch of almost $\frac{3}{4}$ million tons. Herring is a very nutritious fish, and because of the huge annual catch, it is an important food.

Salmon and tuna are also important seafoods, particularly in canned form. Alaska, which provides half of the world's salmon, is the most important source of this fish. Ninety percent of all salmon caught in Alaska is canned. Fishermen of the United States and Japan catch most of the world's supply of tuna. A single bluefin tuna can run as large as 10 feet and weigh over half a ton.

Most halibut comes from fisheries in the United States and Canada. Sometimes a halibut is caught that is 7 feet long and weighs 300 pounds. Millions of pounds of cod, another important food fish, are taken each year from the Atlantic. We obtain much of our cod liver oil from this catch.

Shellfish also contribute to the world's food supply. Oysters, clams, scallops, lobster, and shrimp are highly prized seafoods and are enjoyed at many tables. In the United States alone, almost 90 million pounds of oysters are eaten each year. Although the United States harvests more oysters annually than any other country, Japan, Canada, and New Zealand also produce important catches. The United States, along with Japan, also leads in clam production; and together with France, our country leads in the production of scallops.

Mankind harvests about 30 million tons of food products from the sea each year. Since this is far less than one percent of the food resources in the sea, man can readily increase his take of seafood. However, great care must be used not to overfish any single species. Already, sardines and salmon have greatly diminished in number. Unless fishing is controlled by rules which make sure that enough fish of each kind are left to maintain their population, even the vast numbers of fish in the sea can be exterminated.

Sources *Compton's Pictured Encyclopedia*, Vol. 3
Conserving Natural Resources by Shirley W. Allen
World Sea Fisheries by Robert Morgan
The Sun, the Sea, and Tomorrow by F. G. Walton Smith and Henry Chapin

● EXERCISE 8. Write the final draft of your report. If your teacher says so, hand in your outline and first draft with it.

BOOK REPORTS

A book report gives two kinds of information: what the book is about and what you thought of it.

The first and usually longer part of a book report tells what the book is about. This should include only the book's highlights. If you are reporting on a novel, indicate the background of the story—time, place, main characters. Give a general idea of what happens and mention some of the main characters. Avoid getting bogged down in details. If you are reporting on a nonfiction book, summarize the important information given. If you are reporting on a biography, indicate why the person written about is important, and mention several of the chief incidents in his life.

The second part of a book report may be shorter than the first, but it is just as important. It gives your reaction to the book and shows how perceptively and intelligently you have read it. Give specific reasons for liking or disliking the book. Tell why others might share your opinion. A statement like *I enjoy this book because I am interested in horses* tells little about a book. The following sentence is a good beginning for a statement of opinion: *This book is clearly and vividly written and presents much interesting information about horses.*

When you write a book report, keep these guides in mind:

Guides

1. Give the title of the book and the name of the author. Underline the title when you write it.
2. When you tell what happened (or happens) in a book, decide on past or present tense and stick to it. Avoid shifting from present to past or past to present.
3. When you summarize a nonfiction book, be sure that you understand everything you describe and that your summary of complicated information is clearly written.
4. In your statement of opinion, tell how the book has influenced your thinking or ambitions. Use examples to support your ideas.

CHAPTER 23

Writing Letters

Friendly Letters, Social Notes, Business Letters

Receiving a letter from a friend is always a satisfying experience. It is interesting to learn what he has seen and done recently, what he thinks, and what has happened to people you both know. However, you will not receive many letters unless you reply to them.

When you begin to write a letter, you may think: But I don't have anything to say! A moment's thought will show that this is untrue. What do you want to learn from a friend's letter? What questions do you want answered? Probably he has the same kinds of questions to ask you.

FRIENDLY LETTERS

23a. In a friendly letter, write about the things that interest you and the person to whom you are writing.

Before you write a friendly letter, jot down your ideas. Include news that will interest your friend. Think of his last letter to you. Were there any questions or comments that need a reply? As you write, keep in mind the person who will receive your letter. You would not send the same kind of letter to a boy you met at summer camp as to your favorite uncle.

Study the following example of a friendly letter. Would you say that Bill is thinking of his friend Tom as he writes? Why? How would this letter be different if it were written to Bill's aunt?

1849 West Sixth Street
Los Angeles, California 90014
April 14, 1972

Dear Tom,

You asked what Carl and I have been up to lately. Well, Carl's taking care of a horse for a friend of his Dad's, but he's afraid to ride him. I said I'd ride him. You know me – no brains.

That horse bucked around the corral as if he'd been fed Mexican jumping beans. I stuck with him, though, until he reared straight up and went over backwards. Carl's Dad came running. He was mad, but all he said was that maybe we'd better put the horse back in the stable.

You asked what I'm doing for the Science Fair at school. Carl and I are preparing an exhibit showing the effects on rats of a poor diet and a well-balanced diet. We're working now on a chart comparing the two diets.

How about letting me know what you're doing?

Sincerely,
Bill

23b. **Choose stationery and ink that are appropriate for a friendly letter.**

Use letter stationery. White is always appropriate, though other colors may be used. *Never use lined paper.* If you can type well, type your letters. Do not type, however, if the result is usually a messy page of erasures and cross-outs.

Write in ink, never in pencil. In writing to close friends, you may use colored ink if you wish, but blue or black ink is more usual. (When writing on colored paper, avoid a colored ink that makes your letter difficult to read.) Avoid ink blots and erasures. Keep your writing neatly spaced and properly aligned; crowded lines that climb or stagger or droop give a bad impression. Make your margins wide; try to keep them equal on top and bottom as well as on the sides.

Try to estimate in advance how long your letter will be. A brief letter may require only one page. If you use folded stationery and the letter runs to two pages, do not write on the back of page one but skip over to page three. If the letter is longer than two pages, use the page order of a book; write the second page on the back of the first, and so on.

23c. **Follow generally accepted rules for the form of a friendly letter.**

The form of a friendly letter is not hard to master. Study the following instructions and example.

1. *Heading*

The *heading* tells when and where the letter was written. It consists of three lines, placed at the upper right

18 Shipwright Street
Annapolis, Maryland 20022
April 14, 1972

Dear Bob,

Sincerely yours,
Jim

Form for a Friendly Letter

corner of the page. The address of the writer is placed on the first two lines, and the date on which the letter was written is placed on the third. Note that a comma is used between city and state and between the date of the month and the year. The ZIP code number appears several spaces after the state and on the same line. There is no punctuation at the ends of the lines.

Two kinds of headings are appropriate in a friendly letter. The example shown on page 459 is in *block style*. That is, the second and third lines of the heading begin directly below the beginning of the first line. Another style that is often used for handwritten friendly letters is *indented style*, in which the heading looks like this:

2534 Polk Place
Portland, Oregon 97235
May 6, 1972

2. *Salutation*

The *salutation* begins at the left-hand margin and is placed a short distance below the heading. In a friendly letter, it is followed by a comma.

3. *Body*

The *body* of a friendly letter is the message, what you have to say. It may begin directly below the end of the salutation, or may be indented about an inch from the left margin. The first line of each paragraph that follows must be indented the same distance.

4. *Closing*

The *closing* for a friendly letter may be *Your friend, Sincerely, Sincerely yours,* or any similar phrase you like, except *Yours truly* and *Very truly yours,* which are used only on business letters. It is placed just below the final line of the letter, beginning a little to the right of the middle of the page, and is followed by a comma. Only the first word of the closing begins with a capital.

5. *Signature*

The signature in a friendly letter need be only your first name. Center it under the closing. Always write the signature by hand, even if you have typed the rest of the letter.

● EXERCISE 1. Make a list of experiences you've had in the last few days. Using this list as a basis, write a letter to a friend of your own age. Follow the instructions on the preceding pages concerning both content and form.

● EXERCISE 2. Using the list you prepared for Exercise 1, write a letter to a relative or to an adult friend. As you write, keep in mind the receiver of your letter. In class, discuss how your two letters differ.

Addressing the Envelope

The envelope of a letter should be addressed with care. The letter may not be delivered if the address is carelessly written. The ZIP (Zoning Improvement Plan) code number should always be included. There should always be a return address so that the post office may return the letter if your correspondent has moved.

Study the following instructions and example.

1. Place the return address in the upper left corner of the envelope.
2. Place the address of the person to whom the letter is going just below the middle and to the left of the center of the envelope.
3. If the letter is going to an adult, write a title before the name: *Mr.*, *Mrs.*, *Dr.*, and so on. Do not put a title before your name in the return address.

Susan Froelich
597 Spruce Avenue
Kansas City, Kansas 66143

Miss Astrid Addison
89 Kirkland Street
Cambridge
Massachusetts 02127

A Model Envelope

4. Write the state on a separate line, as in the example, or on the same line as the city. Put a comma after the city if the state is written on the same line. Place the ZIP code number several spaces after the state.

5. If you use *Post Office Box*, *Rural Free Delivery*, or *Rural Route* in the address, you may use abbreviations: *P.O. Box 351*, *R.F.D. 1*, or *R.R. 1.*

● EXERCISE 3. Using your ruler, draw the outlines of four envelopes. Then address the "envelopes," using the following information. Use your own return address for each one.

1. miss edna a burns 16 casita way
   omaha nebraska 68138
2. mrs h b byerley 111 orchid way
   st louis missouri 63149
3. miss ellen craig p o box 753
   butte montana 59601
4. dr n t bain r r 8
   winamac indiana 46996

● Exercise 4. Choose one of the following situations and write the letter it suggests. If you prefer to invent your own situation, you may do so. Address an envelope for your letter.

1. You are visiting relatives in another city, and they have taken you to see a World Series game. Write to your parents, telling them about the visit and the game.
2. A friend who lived nearby has moved some distance away. Give him recent news about your neighborhood and ask questions about his new home and neighborhood.
3. You are a radio "ham" and have been exchanging messages with a radio hobbyist in another town. Invite him to visit you and your family. Describe the members of your family and tell him about the fun he will have on his visit. If you like, tell him about other interesting hams you have contacted.
4. You are a 4-H Club member. At a recent 4-H convention you made friends with a member from another part of the state. Write your new friend, telling him (or her) about recent club activities and the exhibit you are preparing for the 4-H Club county fair.
5. You have recently attended a wedding. Write to a friend or relative, describing the events of the wedding: the ceremony, the reception, the behavior of the bride and groom and their parents, your own reactions.
6. Write to a friend who is in the hospital. Tell her that you went shopping and found two coats you like, but that you can't decide which one to choose. Ask her to make the choice for you. Describe the two coats and the hat and shoes that you would like to buy to go with each coat.

7. You have been elected social chairman of your club. Write to a friend or relative, telling about the preparations you are making for a club party.
8. Write to an older brother or sister at college. Tell about your own progress at school and ask questions about college life.

Folding the Letter

If your letter stationery consists of a folded page, fold it in half and insert it, fold first, into the envelope. If the stationery is a single sheet of the same width as the envelope, fold the bottom third up, then the top third down, and insert it into the envelope, with the last fold first. See the illustrations on page 473.

SOCIAL NOTES

23d. Write prompt, courteous social notes.

Social notes are written for a limited purpose, such as to extend or accept an invitation, or to thank someone for a gift or favor. Such notes generally follow the form of a friendly letter and are written on personal stationery. If they are brief, they may be written on correspondence cards.

Since you will have many occasions to write social notes, you should learn to write them properly.

The Thank-You Note

After receiving a gift or favor from someone whom you cannot immediately thank in person, you should write a thank-you note. Always write promptly. A delay gives the impression that you do not really appreciate the gift. A thank-you note will seem less like a duty letter if you write about something else as well, and if you give specific reasons for your gratitude.

Study the following thank-you note. Has Tony thanked his uncle properly?

641 Ardmore Avenue
Philadelphia, Pennsylvania 19153
June 3, 1972

Dear Uncle Harry,

Thanks ever so much for the model plane engine. I'm having a lot of fun with it. The other boys tell me that a Junior Wasp model like this is very dependable. It starts easily and runs with no trouble. I've been running it on a breaking-in block. It's surprising how much roar such a tiny engine has! I'm anxious to finish building my model. I know this engine will really make it zoom.

The folks gave me some fine birthday presents too, but I suspect that I'll remember this birthday most of all because of this mighty mite of an engine.

Your nephew,
Tony

A Thank-You Note

● EXERCISE 5. Write a thank-you note and address an envelope for one of the following situations, or choose a situation of your own.

1. An aunt, who lives in another city, has sent you a new dress (or sweater) for your birthday.
2. An uncle, who operates a ranch in another state, has sent you a .22 rifle (or a pair of skates) for Christmas.
3. Your grandmother, who lives in another town, has sent you ten dollars for Christmas.
4. An older cousin, who is with the army in Europe, has sent you a set of dolls in the native costumes of various countries.
5. A family friend, on a trip to Mexico, has sent you a fine, brilliantly colored blanket.
6. Your older brother, who has a job in another city, has sent you a radio for your birthday.

The Bread-and-Butter Note

Occasionally you are invited to visit friends or relatives who live out of town, and you spend several days with them. After you return home, you must write a note to your hostess—your friend's mother, or the adult who was really responsible for your comfort—to thank her for her kindness to you. This note, commonly called a "bread-and-butter" note, should be written promptly. Tell your hostess how much you enjoyed your stay and appreciated her efforts to make your visit pleasant. Mention some of the things she did for you. Put yourself in your hostess' place: wouldn't you like to hear that the trouble you went to, in order to make sure that a guest had a good visit, is remembered with a glow of pleasure? Your hostess will be interested, too, in what kind of trip you had returning home, so it is appropriate to mention that briefly.

Study the following bread-and-butter note. Notice that, like the thank-you note, it follows the form of a friendly letter.

34 Casa Grande Drive
Berkeley, California 94713
August 6, 1972

Dear Mrs. De Stefano,

Ever since I got home, I've been thinking about the wonderful week I spent with your family in Yosemite Park. The park had always been a sort of picture album place to me, and now I've got my own snapshots of it! Even more than the scenery I enjoyed camping with your family. Waking up in the morning to the smell of frying bacon and eggs, hiking up the steep trails and coming back to cool off with a swim in the river, sitting around the campfire singing and telling stories – I'll remember these things as some of the most fun I ever had. Thanks ever so much for having me as a guest.

Please tell Helen I'll send her some of my snapshots as soon as they are ready.

Sincerely yours,
Nora Davis

A Bread-and-Butter Note

● EXERCISE 6. Write a bread-and-butter note expressing thanks for the hospitality you received on a recent visit, or imagine that you were in one of the following situations, and write a bread-and-butter note.

1. A friend's family has taken you with them on a motor trip to a national park.
2. While your mother was ill in a hospital, you stayed with your grandmother. She lives on a big farm.
3. An uncle has taken you on a hunting trip and taught you to shoot a .22 rifle.
4. An aunt has taken you on a trip to New York City, where you visited the Empire State Building, the United Nations Building, and the Statue of Liberty.
5. You spent your summer vacation with your older married sister and her husband. They live in a nearby town and have two small children.

BUSINESS LETTERS

You may have already written business letters, possibly without realizing it. Perhaps you have ordered goods from a firm or requested information from an institution or government department. Later you will have occasion to write other business letters when you apply for a job or entrance to a school or when you request travel reservations and theater tickets. Such letters are mportant in our daily lives, and you should learn to write them clearly and correctly.

23e. Follow generally accepted rules for the form of a business letter.

Business firms use printed business stationery in two sizes: $8\frac{1}{2} \times 11$ inches, and (for brief letters) $5\frac{1}{2} \times 8\frac{1}{2}$

inches. You should use unruled white paper of standard typewriter size: $8\frac{1}{2} \times 11$ inches. If you type well, it is always advisable to type your business letters. If you do not type well, however, write carefully with pen and ink.

Make your letter neat and attractive. Center it on the page, leaving equal margins on the right and left sides and on top and bottom. Avoid ink blots, erasures, and crossed-out words. Write only on one side of the page.

The form of a business letter is somewhat different from that of a personal letter. One important difference is that a business letter always includes an *inside address*. Study the following instructions and example.

1. *Heading*

A business address always requires a complete heading: street address on the first line; city, state, and ZIP code number on the second line, with a comma between the city and state; date on the third line, with a comma between the day and the year. It is better not to abbreviate the month and the state.

Block style, not indented style, is always used in the heading of a business letter.

2. *Inside Address*

A business letter, for filing purposes, requires an inside address, which gives the name and the address of the person or the firm (sometimes both) to whom you are writing. A comma is used between the city and state, and the ZIP code number appears several spaces, or about one-quarter inch, after the state.

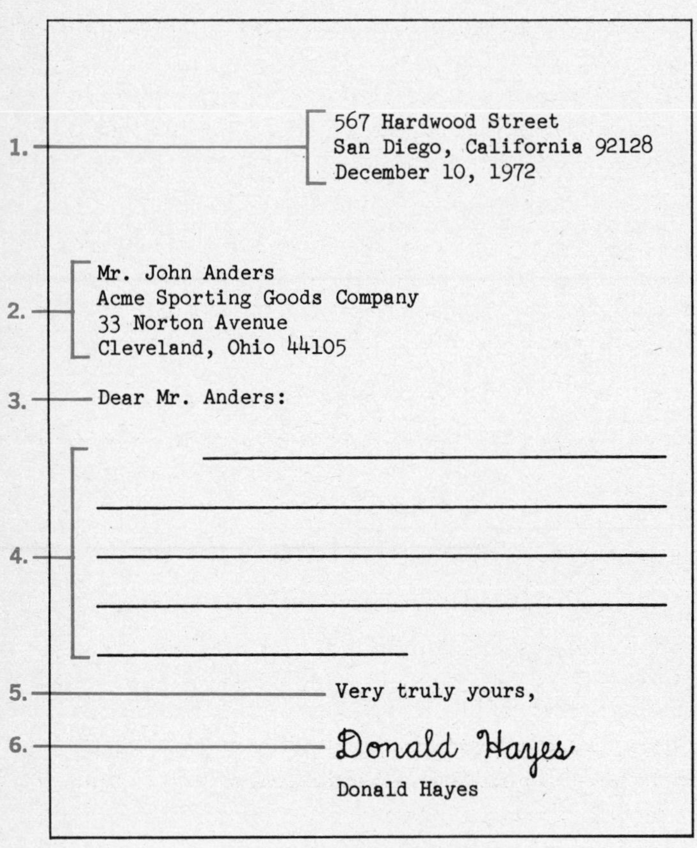

Form for a Business Letter

Place the inside address four typewriter lines below the heading and on the other side of the page, flush with the left-hand margin.

3. *Salutation*

The salutation is placed two typewriter lines below the inside address, flush with the left-hand margin.

It is followed by a colon, not a comma as in a friendly letter.

The kind of salutation you use will vary. Writing to a person whose name you have used in the inside address, it is proper to say *Dear Mr.* ——*:* (or *Dear Miss* ——*:* or *Dear Mrs.* ——*:*).

EXAMPLE Mr. S. E. Sorenson, Circulation Manager
Boys' Magazine
67 East Eighth Street
New York, New York 10037

Dear Mr. Sorenson:

If you are writing to a person whose name you do not know, but whose official position you do know, you say *Dear Sir:* or *Dear Madam:*

EXAMPLE Public Relations Director
State Oil Company
317 Bush Street
Dallas, Texas 75243

Dear Sir:

If, however, you are not writing to a particular individual but to a group or a company, the correct salutation is *Gentlemen:*

EXAMPLE Board of Trustees
Lafayette Elementary School District
56 La Mesa Drive
Lafayette, California 94549

Gentlemen:

4. *Body*

The first sentence of the body of a business letter begins two typewriter lines below the salutation; that is, the same distance that the salutation is below the inside address. This first line may be indented about an inch or the length of the salutation. The first lines of all paragraphs in the body should be indented the same distance. (If you are using a typewriter, indent five spaces.) Keep your left-hand margin straight; keep the right-hand margin as straight as you can.

5. *Closing*

The standard form for the closing of a business letter is *Yours truly* or *Very truly yours* or *Sincerely yours.* The closing should begin a little to the right of the middle of the page. Only the first word is capitalized. A comma follows the closing.

6. *Signature*

Directly below the closing, in line with it, sign your full name in ink. If you are typing the letter, type your name below your written signature. Never put a title (Mr., Mrs., Miss, etc.) before your handwritten signature.

Yours truly,
Margaret Nolan

Very truly yours,
John Anderson
John Anderson

7. *Envelope*

The return address and the address on the envelope of a business letter are written and placed exactly as they are on the envelope of a friendly letter. The "outside" address should be the same as the inside address.

8. *Folding the Letter*

If the letter is written on $8\frac{1}{2} \times 11$-inch paper, and is to be put into a long envelope, fold the sheet up a

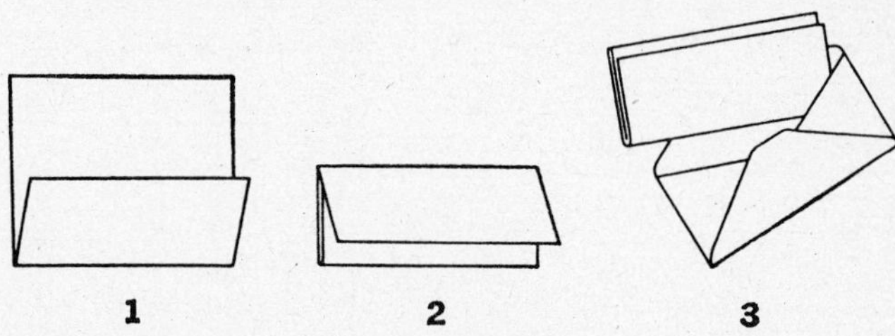

third of the way from the bottom, then fold the top third down over it. If the sheet is to go into a small envelope, fold the page up from the bottom to within a quarter of an inch of the top; then fold the right side over a third of the way, and fold the left side over it. Insert the letter into the envelope with the last fold at the bottom.

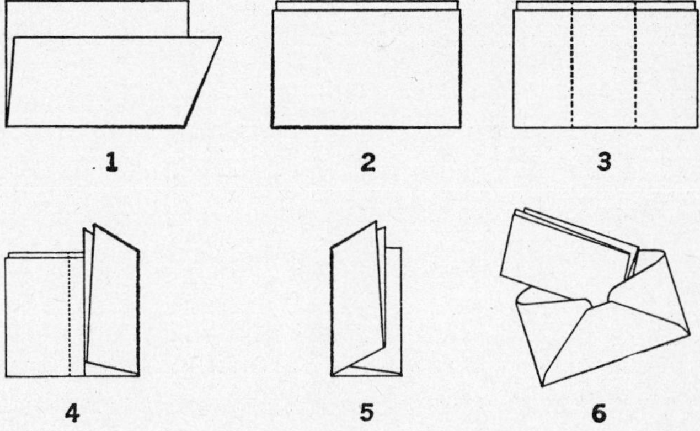

● EXERCISE 7. If your teacher agrees, have the class begin a collection of business letters from home.

Appoint a class committee to arrange a bulletin board display of these letters.

● EXERCISE 8. The following paragraph contains all the information needed for a business letter. Write the letter in correct form and arrangement on a sheet of business stationery. Address an envelope for it.

32 Berenda drive, Flagstaff, Arizona 86001 december 2 1965 Acme outfitting company inc p.o. box 289 milwaukee wisconsin 53248 gentlemen kindly send me your mail order catalogue on sporting goods and hunting and fishing equipment thank you yours truly jerry muller

23f. In a business letter, be clear, courteous, and brief.

If you buy something at the corner store and find, when you return home, that you have the wrong items—size 7 shoes instead of size 8, or pink thread instead of blue—you can quickly correct the error by walking back to the store. But if you order an item by mail, and forget to state the correct size or color, you will receive something you do not want. Obviously, it is important to make sure that a business letter furnishes all necessary information clearly and accurately.

It is also important to write courteously, especially when you are writing a letter of request. A crude or impatient letter will make a bad impression.

Many firms receive thousands of letters daily and would waste many valuable hours reading and answering unnecessarily long letters. Therefore, to ensure prompt service or consideration, a business letter should be brief and to the point.

Two common kinds of business letters are the *order* letter and the *request* letter.

The Order Letter

When writing an order letter, be sure to identify the merchandise you want by its catalogue number or the place you saw it advertised and by its price. State whether you are charging the merchandise or paying for it by cash, check, money order, or C.O.D.

◆ NOTE You will order many items of merchandise not by letter but by order blank. When you use an order blank, be sure to follow the directions carefully and fill in all the blanks. No covering letter is necessary.

● EXERCISE 9. Scan the advertisements in a catalogue, newspaper, or magazine. Select an item you would like to have, and write a letter ordering it. Exchange letters with a classmate. Examine his letter. Check to see whether (1) it follows the business letter form; (2) it identifies exactly the item wanted; (3) it states how the item is being paid for.

● EXERCISE 10. Choose one of the following situations for a business letter. Address an envelope.

1. You ordered a pair of rabbits, New Zealand Giants, from Beyer's Mail Order Mart, 88 H Street, Augusta, Georgia 30915. You received a set of "rabbit ears" antennae for a television set. Write a letter asking for a correction of the mistake.

89 East First Street
Kankakee, Illinois 60901
March 10, 1972

Standard Equipment Company
448 Westwood Boulevard
St. Louis, Missouri 63107

Gentlemen:

Please send me the binoculars, No. 791, which you advertised for $3.98, postpaid, in the February 17 issue of the Farm Gazette.

I am enclosing a money order for $3.98.

Very truly yours,

Richard Beam

Richard Beam

Model Order Letter

2. You ordered a cashmere sweater from the Chic Shop, 49 Sierra Road, Philadelphia, Pennsylvania 19154. When it arrived, it was the wrong size and color.
3. You ordered a first baseman's glove from Harold's Sporting Goods, Inc., 724 Freneau Parkway South,

Bangor, Maine 04401. Instead you received a catcher's mask.

4. You ordered (enclosing full payment) a pair of heavy mittens from Mercantile Mail Order Company, 97 West Ivy Street, Cleveland, Ohio 44153. You received twelve pairs of warm mittens which are the wrong color.
5. For your mother's birthday, you ordered an embroidered peasant blouse from Gift's Galore, 819 West Drive, Dubuque, Iowa 52018. In your letter you enclosed a money order. Your mother's birthday is five days off, and the blouse has not yet arrived.

The Request Letter

Occasionally you have to write a letter to get information, to ask for a pamphlet or a catalogue or samples. In such a letter you are, of course, asking a favor; be brief, clear, and courteous.

● EXERCISE 11. Write to a department of your city or state government, asking for free pamphlets or leaflets about the duties and services of the department. Address an envelope for your letter, but do not mail the letter unless you are seriously interested in the information. Remember: Your request is more likely to be granted if you are courteous in making it.

● EXERCISE 12. Write a letter for one of the following situations. Address an envelope, but do not mail the letter unless you are serious about your request.

1. Your class has been studying wildlife conservation. You would like some maps showing the great "flyways" on the continent of North America used

34 Addison Place
Boise, Idaho 83742
December 2, 1972

Air-Industry, Inc.
10 West Norton Avenue
Los Angeles, California 90037

Gentlemen:

Our eighth-grade class at Boonton Junior High School is studying the use of helicopters in farming operations. If you have any free printed matter, with pictures, describing your helicopters and how they are used on farms, we would very much appreciate receiving some copies.

Yours truly,

Martin Ames

Martin Ames

Model Request Letter

by migrating birds. Write for such maps to the Fish and Wildlife Service, United States Department of the Interior, Washington, D.C.

2. Your Boy (or Girl) Scout group wishes to visit a famous museum in your locality (or the Guggenheim Museum in New York City, New York, or the

Hearst Castle in San Simeon, California). Write for information about visiting hours and fees. Find out whether a reduced rate is possible for your group. Convince the management of the museum that your group is serious and responsible.

3. Write to the United States Government Printing Office, Washington, D.C. Ask if they have publications on a particular subject like national monuments. Tell why you are interested in this subject.

Checklist

FRIENDLY LETTERS AND SOCIAL NOTES

1. Jot down your ideas before you write the letter. Include news the other person might like to know. Answer any questions your friend may have asked in his last letter.
2. Use the correct form. Include your address and date in the heading. Place a comma after the salutation and closing.
3. Write a neat letter. Never use pencil.
4. In a note of thanks, be specific about whatever it is you are grateful for. Avoid the stiff and formal appearance of a duty letter.

BUSINESS LETTERS

1. Use the correct form. Use block style for the heading, not indented style. Include an inside address in the letter. Place a colon, not a comma, after the salutation.
2. Be careful to include all information necessary to understand or act upon your letter.
3. In an order letter, be brief and to the point.
4. In a request letter, make your request courteously.

PART SIX

Speaking and Listening

CHAPTER 24

Speaking

Announcements and Reports, Delivering a Speech, Evaluating a Speech

Everyone learns to speak early in life, and throughout a lifetime speaking continues to be one of man's most important activities. In informal situations speech is easy and natural. Learning how to speak well and comfortably before groups or in unfamiliar situations is an important part of every young person's education. This chapter will help you to perfect your speaking skills.

MAKING ANNOUNCEMENTS

If you were given the job of announcing a bit of information or an event to your classmates or to an assembly, could you do it well? For such a short speech, you will not need to make extensive preparation or elaborate notes. Nevertheless, you should write down the information you are to give and check it over to be sure it includes all the essential facts. Does your announcement tell what, where, when, who, why, and how?

24a. In making an announcement, be sure to include all the necessary facts.

Most announcements should include the following items: (1) the kind of event; (2) the time; (3) the place; (4) the admission fee, if any; (5) special features. The following example includes four of these items, omitting only the admission fee.

EXAMPLE The Stamp Club meeting that was scheduled for this afternoon has been postponed because of the storm. Instead, the Stamp Club will meet next Tuesday, December 10, at 3:05 in Room 27. All members and any other interested students are invited to be present for a program on "Stamps of New Nations."

Go over the facts of an announcement several times in your mind before you speak. If you are not sure that you will remember them all while you are speaking, carry a note card with the information written on it, and glance at it as you speak.

Use a normal rate of speaking, and make sure that you give your listeners time to take in what you are saying. Speak loudly enough so that everyone will hear.

● EXERCISE 1. Each of the following announcements omits essential items of information. What are these items? How would you correct the announcements?

1. Students in Miss Bergman's and Mrs. Novotny's classes who are going to the Science Museum tomorrow should be ready to leave at 11:15. The only expense will be money for lunch in the museum cafeteria.

2. The Junior High Glee Club needs more members. Even if you are not sure of your musical talent, why not come to a rehearsal and join the preparation for the Christmas program?
3. The eighth grade is having a Halloween party on Saturday, October 27, in the school auditorium. All eighth-grade sections are invited. Profits from the party will go to the Library Fund.

● EXERCISE 2. Prepare and deliver an announcement for one of the following events. Give all the necessary information. If you wish, the announcement may be about an actual event that will take place at your school.

1. An excursion sponsored by the Sea Scouts
2. The sale of your school newspaper
3. A 4-H Club meeting
4. Tryouts for a play
5. A Science Fair
6. A baseball game between the seventh and eighth grades
7. A class party
8. An openhouse at school for parents
9. A special assembly to hear a distinguished foreign visitor
10. A meeting of the Traffic Patrol to discuss the purchase of jackets for the squad

GIVING ORAL REPORTS

Throughout your school years you will be called on to give oral reports in your classes. Learning how to plan and deliver such a report is a skill that will be useful to you innumerable times.

24b. **Learn to prepare an oral report.**

Some instruction in preparing a written report is presented in Chapter 22. An oral report is prepared in much the same way, except that you do not write it out word for word. Instead, you may make some notes to help you remember your material as you speak.

(1) **Choose a topic that will interest your audience.**

If you are given a topic to report on, you have no problem of selection. If you are asked to choose your own topic, however, you must use some judgment. Select a topic that can be covered reasonably well in the time allotted for your speech. Make sure that it will interest your audience. A report on how to crochet a collar for a dress would probably fail to interest the boys; a report on how to repair a tubeless tire might bore the girls; a report on how to hang up your clothes properly would bore everybody. But a report on how to earn money after school or the landing of a spacecraft on the moon or the opening up of an ancient city buried under a lava flow would be likely to interest many of your listeners.

(2) **Gather material for your report.**

After you have a topic, your next step is to gather information on your subject. There are at least three sources for such material: (1) your own ideas and experiences, (2) other people who know something about your topic, and (3) books and periodicals. Consult all of these sources, and get as much information as you can. Write notes or brief summaries of the information you are accumulating.

(3) Prepare an outline.

From your notes, prepare an outline for your talk. (Refresh your memory on how to prepare an outline by looking at pages 419–29.)

Suppose that you have decided to give a talk in your science class on shooting stars. You have often observed shooting stars and have wondered what they are and why they occur. Having discovered that shooting stars are meteors, you go to the library (see Chapter 27, "The Library," page 537) and read articles on meteors in various reference works. On cards or slips of paper, you copy items of information you want to use. Study these notes until the material is familiar to you. From the notes, prepare an outline. The outline might have four main headings:

I. Time: when shooting stars, or meteors, are seen
II. Nature: what the characteristics of meteors are
III. Place: where and why shooting stars are seen
IV. Fate: final end of meteors dependent upon speed, size, and course

Under each of these headings you will arrange your material in logical order—the big ideas first, the details following them. Once you have settled on the content and structure of your report, you are ready to think about how you will deliver it.

(4) Write note cards to use as reminders when delivering your report.

Usually you will not write out a speech word for word and memorize it. Instead, you will read and reread your material and your outline until they are so familiar that you need only an occasional reminder to enable you to talk freely about your topic.

Prepare these reminders in the form of note cards. Your outline will provide you with the items to place on cards or slips of paper.

One useful way of preparing these reminder cards is to write one for each of the main ideas of your outline. You may include the subpoints under the main idea if they are few in number and detail.

Your reminder cards need not contain complete sentences; key words or phrases are often sufficient. Remember that the purpose of these cards is not to provide something for you to read aloud but merely to prod your memory.

A reminder card for the talk on shooting stars might look like this:

I. Time
   A. More after midnight than before
   B. More in the fall than in any other season
   C. Five per hour – 500 per minute

When giving your speech, you would start with this card. The items on the card are reminders. The main point tells you what this part of your speech is to be about; the subitems remind you of details to discuss. You might start your speech by saying:

We are all familiar with shooting stars, or meteors. Often, on summer evenings, we have seen silvery streaks dart across the dark blue of the sky. Most of us, however, are unaware that we can see more shooting stars after midnight than before, and that more are to be seen in the fall of the year than in other seasons. Usually, about five shooting stars per hour can be sighted. However, when meteor showers occur, sometimes as many as 500 meteors fall each minute . . .

In some cases it is wise to write full and exact details on a note card. If, for example, you want to give the ingredients of a recipe or the measurements of material needed to make a birdhouse or statistics on ships going through the Panama Canal, it is wise to write out the full details on a note card so that you can read them off when you need them.

In some talks you may want to use direct quotations from people whom you've interviewed. (Direct quotations will not only make your talk livelier but will give it the weight of authority.) Write out quotations exactly as given, so that you will run no risk of misquoting the person you interviewed.

If you are explaining a process to your audience, it may be helpful to have charts and pictures. You may also want to use the chalkboard to write figures and dates or draw illustrations. A reminder card can tell you when to use these visual aids.

You may need only a few reminder cards if the material of your speech is very familiar to you—perhaps just one for each main heading, and one or two additional cards with details to support some point requiring exact information. No rule can be set for how many cards you will need; prepare as many as you think you will require.

As you speak, hold the sheaf of cards in your hand. Glance at the top card, and talk on the subject it lists. Then move this top card to the bottom, uncovering the next topic of your speech. Continue this process until you have spoken on every topic listed on your cards.

As you practice your speech, practice using your note cards also. You should be able to use them smoothly so that they do not distract your audience from your words.

(5) **Plan an interest-arousing introduction and a strong conclusion.**

Sometimes it is helpful to write out an exciting first sentence, one that will arouse your listeners' interest. Memorize this sentence so that you will not have to read it but can look at your audience and speak it naturally.

Similarly, you may find it helpful to work out a strong ending statement for your talk; a sentence or paragraph that shows how your main ideas have led up to your conclusion. You may write this out on a card at which you can glance as you come to the end of your talk. You should not, however, spoil the effect of a good speech by reading the last part of it.

● EXERCISE 3. Plan a short talk on one of the following subjects or on a topic of your own which your teacher approves. Go through the steps of gathering material, outlining, and making reminder cards.

1. How Eskimos live
2. Modern whaling

3. Tree grafting: how to raise pears on an apple tree
4. What makes an airplane fly?
5. Housekeeping in New England in 1800
6. An interesting part of your city that many people don't know about
7. The Pony Express
8. A trip on a transcontinental railroad in 1870
9. A comparison of American football and English Rugby
10. Family customs among foreign national groups—the Japanese, the Mexicans, and so on
11. The invention of the typewriter
12. How man will use sunshine for energy
13. The kitchen of the future
14. Uses of closed-circuit television
15. The career of my favorite sports hero
16. Programs I'd like to see on television
17. Training a pet
18. A hobby that earns money
19. The cowboy's job today
20. Plant and animal life in —— (Choose a specific place, such as Yosemite Park, the Everglades, sand dunes near the Great Lakes, and so on.)

24c. Learn to deliver an oral report well.

An audience will judge your speech not only by how well prepared you seem, but by how you look and sound as you deliver it.

(1) Assume a natural but not a careless posture.

Stand straight, of course, and look at your audience. Do nothing which will draw attention away from your talk; for example, do not finger a necklace or chew gum or fidget. Try to be relaxed and natural.

(2) Speak loudly enough so that everyone can hear.

Your audience must hear your speech plainly. A talk that is not heard is wasted. An audience that must strain to hear becomes restless.

You can escape being monotonous by learning to vary your tone. Be expressive; where feeling is appropriate, let your voice reflect your interest, excitement, anger, or delight. Try to develop a voice that is pleasing, natural, and clear.

24d. Pronounce words correctly and enunciate carefully.

Part of the task of talking effectively involves speaking your words so that they can be understood by your listeners. Take care to speak correctly and distinctly. In many cases the meaning of a word varies with the way it is pronounced. Remember that your listeners will not see your words but only hear them. If they are mispronounced or if you mumble or run words together, your audience will have difficulty in following you.

1. *Vowel Sounds*

Each vowel in our language may be pronounced in different ways. In some words vowels or combinations of vowels have sounds that you might not expect from the spelling. Make sure you pronounce correctly the following words:

despite	opaque
draught	suite
drought	thorough
fertile	through
genuine	victuals

2. *Consonant Sounds*

As important as pronunciation is *enunciation*, the careful sounding of every syllable. Be especially careful with words that end in *–ing*, and words that contain similar consonants—*p* and *b*, *m* and *n*, *t* and *th*.

For practice, say the following groups of words aloud, taking care to make the consonant sounds clearly distinguishable so that no one in the room mistakes the word you used.

d–t		t–th	
do	to	tank	thank
dent	tent	taught	thought
din	tin	bat	bath
done	ton	tinker	thinker
dare	tear	mutter	mother
and	ant	ton	thumb
send	sent	ten	then
bed	bet	rat	wrath
wed	wet	tat	that
madder	matter	wetter	weather

b–p		v–f	
blank	plank	vendor	fender
bin	pin	veil	fail
bowl	poll	viewer	fewer
robe	rope	vault	fault
bunk	punk	veal	feel
Benny	penny	vision	fission

● EXERCISE 4. Practice reading aloud the following tongue twisters. Prepare yourself to read them to the class so distinctly that they are easily understood.

1. She said severely, "Son, shun the hot sun, or your poor back will burn pitifully."

2. She sells seashells at the seashore.
3. The tinker muttered thanks in a thin, throttled tone.
4. Jane's chuckles and antics jarred her ailing aunt and uncle.
5. The tank of thin tin was dank and dented.
6. In the still, chill silence of the church, Benny's penny clattered tinnily in the cup.
7. Chunks of junk smashed the vendor's fenders.
8. The mole delved twelve feet under the thin turf.
9. His mother muttered that wetter weather would wash his wrath away.
10. Penny's robe, belted with rope, was tugged snug at the throat.

3. *Omitting Sounds*

Take care not to omit sounds that belong in words. Below are listed some words frequently subject to this error.

asked (not ask' or ast)
geography (not g'ography)
library (not lib'ary)
midst (not mi'st)
poem (not po'm)
probably (not prob'ly or pro'ly)
slept (not slep')
strength (not stren'th)

● EXERCISE 5. Use five of the words listed above in sentences to be spoken aloud in class.

4. *Adding Sounds*

Take care not to add sounds to a word—either inside a word, or at the end. Do you make mistakes with any of these words?

arithmetic (not arith*uh*metic)
athlete (not ath*uh*lete)
barbarous (not barbar*i*ous)
chimney (not chim*b*ley or chim*u*ney)
column (not col*y*um)
corps (the *p* and *s* are silent)
elm (not el*u*m)
height (ends in *t*, not *th*)
scent (the *c* is silent)
subtle (the *b* is silent)
umbrella (not umbrell*er* or umb*e*rella)
vehicle (the *h* is silent)

● EXERCISE 6. Go around the class twice with the above list, with each student pronouncing a word.

5. *Changing Position of Sounds*

Be careful not to change the position of a sound within a word. Sometimes this error is based on the similarity of a word to another word that is almost like it in spelling. *Perspire* and *prescribe*, for example, have beginning syllables that are almost alike. *Perspire* is often mispronounced *prespire*, and *prescribe* is often mispronounced *perscribe*.

apron (not apern)
cavalry (not calvary)
children (not childern)
contradict (not conterdict)
modern (not modren)

● EXERCISE 7. Using all of the lists above, let a number of students write words on the board and call on other students to pronounce them.

● Exercise 8. Following is a list of frequently mispronounced words. Be prepared to read them aloud to the class. Use the dictionary if you are not sure of the correct pronunciation.

admirable	infamous
architect	jostle
bade	jubilant
champion	mischievous
favorite	museum
film	ogre
finale	partner
gape	remembrance
gesture	scythe
handkerchief	superfluous
hearth	theater
hurtle	toward
incomparable	tremendous
indict	yacht

6. *Running Words Together*

Another form of mispronouncing words is running them together when speaking. Telescoping words makes a wreckage of sense. Too often, for example, we run together the words of such a sentence as *I'm glad to meet you* into *'m gladdameecha.*

● Exercise 9. Translate the following mangled words into understandable language.

didja	gonna	woncha
gotcha	whereya	harrya
thankslot	lemetry	didjaseer
gimeyahan	whadideedo	wassamadawichoo
wachasay	begyaparn	wyncha

24e. Learn to speak with expression and meaning.

We give meaning to language not only by our choice of words but by the *feelings* we put into them—the tone of voice, the grouping of words, the emphasis, the variety of tone. The tone and emphasis we use can greatly influence the meaning our words convey. Differing emphases on certain words or syllables can convey different meanings and emotions.

You can increase the effectiveness of your speech by giving attention to your tone of voice and to the amount and kind of expression you use.

● EXERCISE 10. Study these sentences before reading them aloud. The class will discuss how well each person expresses the required feelings.

1. You are a parent with an active six-year-old daughter. Tell her, "Susan, put that puppy down!"
   a. Say it as if the mother dog, growling furiously, is getting out of her box to leap at Susan.
   b. Say it as if you know Susan is going to plead with you to buy the puppy and you don't have the money.
2. Someone has just walked through the living room with muddy feet, leaving tracks on the new rug. You ask, "Jimmy, did you just walk through the living room?"
   a. Say it as if you have told him countless times to wipe his feet before coming into the house.
   b. Say it as if you are overcome with grief to find your new rug so badly soiled.
3. A new dress has just been delivered to your house. Today is your birthday. You ask, "Mother, did you buy this dress for me?"

   a. Say it as if the dress is exactly what you have been hoping for, but you can't believe that your mother would be so extravagant.
   b. Say it as if you are bitterly disappointed.
4. Your brother has just got a new suit, and you remark, "Say, that's a pretty nice outfit!"
   a. Say it as if you are surprised at how nice it is.
   b. Say it as if you want to please him, even though it is not a particularly good-looking suit.
5. You have started on a long hike when you discover that your small brother is walking behind you. You tell him, "Andy, go home and go to bed."
   a. Say it as if he is feverish with a bad cold, and you are very worried about him.
   b. Say it as if you've told him repeatedly that he could not go along.

● EXERCISE 11. See how many meanings you can put into the following remarks by varying your tone and the words you emphasize.

1. I'll go now, if you don't mind.
2. I'd like some steak, too.
3. Bring all your money tomorrow.
4. I told you not to play with him.
5. You earned all that money yourself?
6. Did you say yes?
7. She will do the dishes, and you, Mary, will sweep.
8. Did you promise to help him, Dave?

EVALUATING A SPEECH

24f. Learn to evaluate another person's report politely and constructively.

Often, after a student has given a report, the class is asked to criticize the talk. The purpose of such an evaluation is to help the speaker improve and to help

24 e-f

others. Another purpose, too, is for the group to give recognition to the fine qualities as well as the weak points of the talk.

Be clear and definite. Whether praising a talk for its fine qualities or pointing out its weaknesses, always give reasons for your evaluation. Be generous with praise. When you see serious faults in a talk, it is wise to begin by discussing strong points, then going on to show how the talk might have been even stronger if certain faults had been corrected.

In the examples below, study the preferred comments. Why are they good examples of evaluation?

WEAK "I thought it was very interesting."

BETTER "His description of Mt. Rainier was very interesting because his details were so sharp that I could almost see the mountain trail." Or, "I liked his story of killing a whale because he built up so much suspense."

WEAK "The talk left me cold." Or, "I just couldn't follow it." Or, "He did not convince me."

BETTER "Her explanation was clear and easy to follow except in a couple of places, and I wonder if she left out some steps." Or, "He convinced me that fishing in the river should be limited for a while, but I'd like more proof that dumping factory waste into the river is the real reason why fish are scarce."

Do your part in helping the class to establish an atmosphere of kind and constructive helpfulness. Your class may decide to use an evaluation sheet like the one on page 499 for criticizing speakers. After a talk has been made, each listener rates the speech, and the sheets are collected and given to the speaker.

Remember:

1. Give praise when it is merited.
2. Avoid discussion of trifles.
3. Point out strengths as well as weaknesses.
4. Be definite and constructive.

● EXERCISE 12. Deliver the talk that you prepared in Exercise 3.

● EXERCISE 13. Write a paragraph evaluating a talk someone has given in class. Use the following evaluation sheet as a basis for your evaluation, but also give your opinion of the talk as a whole.

EVALUATION SHEET

Speaker . . . . Topic . . . .

	Very good	Good	Fair	Weak
Introduction				
Organization				
Conclusion				
Use of notes				
Posture				
Voice				
Pronunciation				
Other comments . .				

Critic . . . .

CHAPTER 25

Listening

Good Habits for Various Situations

Failure to listen well is a common fault. Many of us are victims of listening habits so lazy and careless that words often slip through our minds like smoke through a fishnet. We hear, but we do not listen with alertness. To listen well is a skill that many of us must make an effort to develop.

LEVELS OF ATTENTION

How well you listen is partly the result of how much work you put into listening. That effort depends upon how interested you are in what you are listening to and how important you think it is. When you hear popular music, you are likely to listen casually, with "half an ear." If you are listening to an exciting story, you listen intently to learn what comes next, though you make little effort to retain what you hear. If you are listening to directions on how to make a soapbox derby coaster, for example, you will listen alertly in an effort to fix details so sharply in your mind that you will remember them later.

25a. Listen with a kind of attention that is appropriate to the situation.

There are different levels of attention. Sometimes we listen casually for *entertainment*. Other times we listen carefully for the *general idea*. At still other times we listen painstakingly for *details*.

● EXERCISE 1. The following suggestions will help to make you aware of the many sounds you hear daily but pay little attention to.

1. For two minutes, the whole class will sit in silence and listen. Each student will list the sounds he hears. Compare the lists.
2. Make a list of sounds you hear in one of the following situations:

on the school bus	in a movie theater
at the zoo	at a carnival
lying awake at night	walking in the country
at a baseball game	in a tunnel

● EXERCISE 2. What kind of attention—casual, careful, or painstaking—would be appropriate for listening in the following situations?

1. You are in the audience at an orchestral program.
2. You are watching a TV drama.
3. You are watching a TV commercial.
4. Your mother is outlining the family's plans for today.
5. Your father is describing his day at work.
6. Your teacher is telling what the next science test will cover.
7. You and your friends are discussing what you will do during vacation.

8. The principal makes an announcement over the public address system.
9. A local businessman is speaking at an assembly.
10. The class is discussing a point that has come up in the social studies period.

Listening for Enjoyment

You probably spend many hours each week listening to radio and television. It is good to have the fun and relaxation that such entertainment provides. While very young people can be excused for lacking discrimination in their choice of programs, you owe it to yourself to cultivate your taste as you grow up and to develop a mature and sensitive appreciation of drama, music, and humor.

25b. Develop a discriminating taste in radio and television programs.

As you watch a program, ask yourself questions about it. Are you truly enjoying it? Are you getting anything worthwhile from it? Reading reviews of programs by thoughtful critics may give you some new ideas to think about. You should be learning to develop your own standards and to select wisely among programs.

● EXERCISE 3. Watch a show in a television series, and apply the questions below to it. Write the answers and bring them to class. Be prepared to explain your answers to the other students.

1. Did the central problem of the story make sense to you?

2. Did the story characters seem so real that you really worried about what happened to them?
3. Did the story hold your attention so firmly that you would have been disappointed if you had had to miss the ending?
4. Did the ending seem like a solution that was really earned by the chief characters, or did it seem merely tacked on by the author?
5. Was the acting convincing?
6. Was the dialogue natural?

Listening for Information

A large part of what we listen to is not only enjoyable—it is informative. Our daily life depends on people telling other people things that are useful for them to know. As students, much of your listening is done for the purpose of gaining information.

25c. Listen alertly and avoid distractions.

We all have listening faults. Sometimes we try to attend to two or more things at once: we converse while watching television, for example; or we whisper to a friend while a teacher is giving us an assignment; or we listen to hit records while doing homework.

The first good listening habit to develop is to give your full attention to whatever you are hearing. If the situation calls for alert listening, you should shut out all distractions and listen carefully.

● EXERCISE 4. What distractions normally interfere with attentive listening? Write down four situations in which it is important for you to listen carefully—at school, at home, and elsewhere. For each situation, what may interfere with attentive listening? How can you avoid or overcome these distractions?

● EXERCISE 5. Select two of the following persons. For each one, write a paragraph describing a situation in which he must listen carefully. Explain what possible distractions he must overcome.

1. a teacher
2. a judge
3. a nurse
4. a blind man
5. an actor
6. a doctor
7. a student
8. a reporter
9. a policeman
10. a parent

USEFUL TECHNIQUES

25d. Listen purposefully. Know what to listen for.

The basis of good listening is *interest* and *purpose*. You listen very attentively to something that interests you. You also listen attentively to, and remember vividly, information that will serve a purpose that you consider important.

When listening to a talk, ask yourself: *How can this information be of real help to me?* If you can determine ways in which the content of the talk is important to you, listening and remembering will be easier.

For example, you may be listening to a talk on how a particular club serves the community. You may not be very interested. The club has staged a benefit dance to buy a record player and records for a local hospital for the aged. To you, this is of no immediate concern. You could fog your mind in a daydream now, if you wished. But if you pay attention, you may discover that the club also sponsors recreation for young people, or that it contributes to summer vacations or advanced schooling for young people.

Sometimes you know what you are listening for—as when you listen to directions or assignments. At other times you should keep an alert, open mind—you may learn something unexpectedly useful.

● EXERCISE 6. What people would benefit from talks on the following subjects? Be prepared to tell why. How might you benefit from these talks?

1. Traffic control
2. Fire prevention
3. Home insulation
4. Tooth decay
5. Soil erosion
6. Weather prediction
7. Nutrition
8. Prevention of colds

● EXERCISE 7. Suppose the following people spoke in assembly programs at your school. What would be your purpose in listening to each?

1. A student from Iran studying at the state university speaks on "Schools in Iran and America."
2. The manager of a local department store talks on "How to Tell a Bargain from a Gyp."
3. A graduate of your school gives a talk on two years he spent with the Peace Corps in South America.
4. A professional violinist speaks on "What to Listen for in Music," illustrating points on the violin.
5. The head of a research laboratory gives a talk predicting the contributions of science to industry in the next twenty years.

25e. Listen actively.

Active listening means working at listening. When you have a purpose for listening to a lecture or discussion, you cannot listen with as relaxed and casual attention as you would to background music or a comedy, which you can forget without loss. If you intend to use the information you are hearing, you must be alert to grasp the ideas presented. You must select from among them the ones that you can use. You must retain them so clearly that you will remember them later when you need them.

(1) Listen for the general point of view.

Sometimes, while listening to a speaker, you want to know his general point of view on an issue. Is he (for example) for or against double sessions at school? Is he for or against a new recreation center in your neighborhood? You may already know the details of the issue. What you want to know is where the speaker stands, and why. In such situations, concentrate on grasping the central thought that the speaker is developing.

(2) Listen for a few main ideas.

On some occasions you will already know the speaker's general point of view, and you will listen to grasp the *main points* of his speech: the reasons why he supports one side of an issue rather than the other. If a speaker is not presenting an argument but giving information or relating an experience, you need to recognize the most important things he says. You must concentrate all your listening powers on following his talk, understanding the main ideas, and remembering them.

When listening for the main ideas of a speech, it is often helpful to pay special attention to the start and finish of the talk. A speaker often presents in his introduction the main points that he intends to develop; and, in his conclusion, he often sums them up. An able speaker makes an effort to emphasize his important ideas so that you can easily recognize them.

● EXERCISE 8. Let each student select a paragraph from one of his textbooks or from another nonfiction book. It should be a paragraph that has a clearly stated main idea. Draw lots to determine which students will read their paragraphs to the class; select six. The listeners will write down, in their own words, the main idea of what they have heard. Compare the answers.

(3) Listen for specific details.

On some occasions your purpose in listening to a talk will be to get specific details. Suppose, for example, that you are listening to a talk on how to start a model plane engine or how to decipher a secret code or how to tell edible mushrooms from poisonous ones. A general idea of the method will not be sufficient; you will want exact details.

● EXERCISE 9. This activity requires listening carefully to detailed information. Close your books and listen to the teacher.

The teacher will read the following instructions to the class. After he finishes, each student will write the directions from memory. When all have finished, the teacher will reread the instructions, and each student will check his paper for mistakes.

TEACHER: "This is what to do when someone has swallowed poison by mistake:

"If possible, phone or send for a doctor.

"Immediately dilute the poison in the victim's stomach by making him drink a lot of water or milk.

"If the poison container describes the antidote, and the antidote is available, give it at once.

"If no antidote is described, mix a drink of one part strong tea, one part milk of magnesia, two parts of crumbled burnt toast, and give it to the victim."

25f. Listen critically. Distinguish fact from opinion. Judge whether statements are backed up by evidence from dependable sources.

When you listen to a speaker, you do not wish to be fooled by trickery or unreliable sources of information. Ask yourself questions as you listen: Is this statement a fact or an opinion? If the speaker is presenting it as a fact, is he backing it up with proof from a dependable source or a trustworthy expert? Is he in a position to know what he is talking about?

In a dictionary you will find *opinion* defined as a "belief of something as probable, or as seeming to one's own mind to be true." A verifiable *fact*, however, is defined as "something that has occurred" or that "can be proven to be true." An opinion is a judgment about some event that may or may not be true. A fact, on the other hand, can be proved beyond doubt to be *true*.

Study the following examples. Can you see why two are opinions and two are facts?

OPINION The library facilities in this school are inadequate.

FACT In the library, there are ten books available for use in this assignment; in the school, there are 150 students who must do the assignment at once.

OPINION The referee is being unfair to our players!

FACT The referee has imposed three penalties on our players in the last five minutes.

● EXERCISE 10. If you heard the following statements, would you accept them as fact or interpret them as opinion? After each number on your paper, write *fact*, if you think the statement would be a fact, or *opinion* if you think it would be an opinion. Be prepared to explain each choice.

1. We ought to irrigate our desert lands with fresh water made from sea water.
2. A tornado in Kansas today wrecked fifty homes.
3. Sunbathing is harmful.
4. Stanford beat Santa Clara at football today, scoring 28 to Santa Clara's 14.
5. Fat men are always jolly.
6. TV Westerns are all alike.
7. Miss Currier gives too much homework.
8. A Ford gives the best value among low-priced American cars.
9. The Senior Orchestra has improved greatly this year.
10. Mrs. Townsend has been a good friend to my family.

● EXERCISE 11. Would you accept the following statements as being based on reliable sources? Write brief answers telling why or why not.

1. A woman on a sailing vessel brings bad luck (according to an old belief).
2. The dictionary defines *doff* as "take off."
3. The earliest dam known to archeologists, according to the *1955 Yearbook* of the United States Department of Agriculture, was built about 5,000 years ago.
4. The pharmacist at the local drugstore told us that strong antiseptics such as iodine are good for minor cuts but that they may be poisonous if they are swallowed.
5. Everyone knows that a ring around the moon means stormy weather.

PART SEVEN

Aids to Good English

CHAPTER 26

The Dictionary

Arrangement and Content of Dictionaries

When using most words, you rely upon your own experience as to their meaning, pronunciation, and general appropriateness. You have been accumulating this kind of experience about words since you first learned to talk. But no matter how extensive your experience with words, there will be times when it fails to provide the specific information you need. In such situations, you should turn to your dictionary.

Dictionary makers depend upon the experience of all users of English. A good dictionary tells you what meanings a word has had, how it is usually spelled and pronounced, what its history is, and, often, the kind of situation in which it is appropriate or inappropriate. Dictionaries are intended to back up and broaden your own experience. Travelers venturing into unfamiliar territory value the maps and notes of others who were there before. A good dictionary provides you with much the same kind of information about unfamiliar words. If you are not yet making sufficient use of the dictionary, this chapter will show you how to do so.

Since dictionaries differ one from the other in their methods of presenting information, a textbook can treat only the general features that dictionaries have in common. The best guide to the use of your dictionary is the introductory section that explains the arrangement of entries, the system of showing pronunciations, and special features of that particular book. If you are using one of the dictionaries specially prepared for students of your age, you will find everything you need to know carefully explained. If you use a larger dictionary, possibly at home or in the library, you will find a briefer but still adequate explanation in the front part. In either case, take the time to find out how your dictionary goes about the job of presenting information. Finding an entry will not be much help to you if you do not know how to interpret the information.

ARRANGEMENT

26a. Learn how to find a word in the dictionary.

The words in a dictionary are listed in alphabetical order. This does not mean simply that all words beginning with a particular letter are lumped together in one section. It means that words having *a* as a second letter come before those that have *b* as a second letter, and so on through all the other letters in the word. To find whether *force* or *form* comes first, you have to look at the fourth letter; to decide between *reconcile* and *reconciliation,* you have to look at the ninth. Running through the alphabet nine times is a lot of trouble. If you are still hazy about whether *q* come before *s,* or *m* before *n,* you will save yourself time and effort by getting it straight right now.

Two special problems should be kept in mind: abbreviations and entries of more than one word.

Some dictionaries explain abbreviations in a special section, but most dictionaries define them in the main part of the book right along with the other entries. In such dictionaries, abbreviations are entered according to the letters in them, *not* according to the complete words that they stand for. Thus, the abbreviation *pt.* (meaning *pint* or *part*) comes after *psychology*, even though both words that the abbreviation can stand for would come before *psychology*. In a dictionary, the abbreviation *St.* (for *saint*) comes after *squirt* and before *stab*. A name like *St. Denis*, however, would appear under the full spelling—*saint*.

Two or more words used together as a single word (*open season*, *prime minister*) are treated as though they were a single word. Thus *open shop* appears after *openly* because *s* comes after *l*.

● EXERCISE 1. Arrange the following words, phrases, and abbreviations in alphabetical order.

watermelon	statesmanlike
department	muddy
curtain	Mrs.
stateside	departmental
municipal	curtail
dept.	mudguard
st.	mt.
curvature	munificence
munificent	waterwheel
water moccasin	department store

You have to open a dictionary somewhere to find a word, but where you open it makes a difference. You can find *municipal* if you open at the *s*'s and leaf back to the *m*'s, but it would be better to open at the *m*'s in the first place. With a little practice you should be able to open near the place you want more often than not. This is how it's done.

1. *Divide the dictionary into thirds.* Think of your dictionary in three parts consisting of the following groups of letters:

abcde fghijklmnop qrstuvwxyz

The parts do not look equal because more words start with some letters than with others. However, if you will try these divisions, you will get three fairly equal sections. Your first object is to open to the third of the dictionary in which the word you want is to be found.

● EXERCISE 2. After the appropriate number, indicate in which third of the dictionary (first, middle, last) you would find each of the following words.

1. falcon	6. cryptic
2. recruit	7. stability
3. equation	8. pensive
4. opportunity	9. decimal
5. robin	10. fable

2. *When you have found the right third, find the letter you want.* As you get used to thinking of the dictionary in thirds, you will gradually come to know in what part of each third to look for particular letters. It helps to know that more words start with some letters than with others. For example, more words begin with *s* than with the letters *u*, *v*, *w*, *x*, *y*, and *z* combined.

● EXERCISE 3. With your dictionary closed on your desk in front of you, your teacher or another student in the class will call out a letter at random. Suppose he calls out *f*. You will then open your dictionary near the beginning of the middle third and call out the number of the first page you find that has words beginning with *f*. The winner can then call out the next letter for the class to find. If you are not clear about which letters belong in which third, it will help to have them written out in front of you.

3. *When you have found the right letter, begin looking at the guide words. Guide words* are printed in heavy type at the top of each dictionary page. The one on the left is the same as the first word defined on that page; the one on the right is the same as the last word on that page. Words that fall between guide words in the alphabet will appear on that page. A word that comes alphabetically before the first guide word will be found on a page toward the front, and one that comes after the second guide word will be found toward the back.

In using guide words, you will find it useful to have a general idea of the number of words beginning with a particular letter. If you are looking up *stanchion*, for example, and open to a page that has the guide words *size* and *skinner*, you can safely turn several pages at a time because you know that the *s*'s take up many pages. On the other hand, if you are looking up *yucca* and open to a page with the guide words *yawn* and *yet*, you had better turn one page at a time because it does not take long to get through the *y*'s. In general, look closely at the guide words on each page when you are close to the page you want, and turn several at a time when you are further from it.

● EXERCISE 4. Number your paper 1–15. Suppose the guide words *needy* and *neither* appear on a particular dictionary page. After the proper number, make a plus sign if the corresponding word would appear on that page. Write *before* if it would appear on an earlier page and *after* if it would appear on a later page.

EXAMPLES
1. nefarious
1. +
2. navy
2. *before*

1. negative
2. necessary
3. needle
4. nearsighted
5. neophyte
6. ne'er-do-well
7. newcomer
8. nobleman
9. neediest
10. necktie
11. negligent
12. Neanderthal
13. nemesis
14. New Zealander
15. negotiate

FINDING THE RIGHT MEANING

26b. Learn to find the meaning you want.

Most English words have a number of different meanings. Some common words, like *run*, for example, have thirty or more. When you go to the dictionary, you are usually interested in a particular meaning of a word—one that will fit into the particular sentence or situation in which you heard or read the word. Nevertheless, it is a good idea to scan all of the meanings given. By doing so you will form a general impression of the range of meanings that word may have. When you have read them all quickly, you can focus on the part of the entry that seems most closely related to the meaning you need.

Each separate meaning of a word is explained in a numbered definition. (Some dictionaries use letters within numbered definitions to distinguish between closely related meanings.) To see how this works, examine the following dictionary entry for the word *offensive:*

> **of·fen·sive** \ə-'fen(t)s-iv\ *adj.* **1** Having to do with attack; made or suited for attack; as, *offensive* weapons. **2** Causing unpleasant sensations; as, *offensive* smells. **3** Causing displeasure or resentment; insulting; as, an *offensive* remark that angered. — *n.* **1** The state or position of one who is making an attack; an aggressive attitude; as, to be on the *offensive.* **2** An attack. The army launched its *offensive.* — **of·fen·sive·ly**, *adv.*

Suppose you want to find the meaning of *offensive* in the sentence: *The boy was scolded for making such an offensive remark.* The first two numbered definitions do not fit this context, but the third does. What is more, the illustrative example provides a context very similar to the one you have in mind.

Now notice that for the last two meanings given, the numbers start with 1 again. The reason is that the first three numbered definitions are for one part of speech and the last two for another. In each case, the part of speech is indicated. Some dictionaries group meaning by part of speech, as in this example, while other dictionaries put closely related meanings together, mixing parts of speech. The following definition illustrates the latter method. Notice that the part of speech of each meaning is given at the end of the definition.

of fen sive (ə fen′siv), **1.** giving offense; irritating; annoying: *"Shut up" is an offensive remark.* **2.** unpleasant; disagreeable; disgusting: *Bad eggs have an offensive odor.* **3.** ready to attack; attacking: *an offensive army.* **4.** used for attack; having to do with attack: *offensive weapons, an offensive war for conquest.* **5.** position or attitude of attack: *The army took the offensive.* **6.** attack: *Our planes bombed the enemy lines on the night before the offensive.* 1-4 *adj.*, 5,6 *n.* **—of fen′sive ly,** *adv.* **—of fen′sive ness,** *n.*

Whichever dictionary you use, you will find meanings more rapidly if you know your parts of speech.

● EXERCISE 5. Below are three groups of dictionary definitions and ten sentences using the defined words. Number your paper 1–10. After the proper number, write the number of the definition giving the correct meaning of the word as it is used in the sentence.

fair \'far, 'fer\ *adj.* **1** Beautiful; as, this *fair* land of ours. **2** Light in color; blond; as, *fair* hair. **3** Frank; just; honest; according to the rules; as, *fair* play. **4** Distinct; easy to read; as, to write a *fair* hand. **5** Open to legitimate pursuit; as, a person who is *fair* game for ridicule. **6** Average; pretty good; as, to make a *fair* grade in arithmetic; to be in *fair* health. **7** Clean; without blemish; as, a *fair* name. **8** Clear; not cloudy or stormy; favorable; as, *fair* weather. **9** Likely; promising; as, to have a *fair* chance of winning. — *adv.* In a fair manner; as, to play *fair.* — **fair·ness,** *n.*

1. Larry is only a *fair* baseball player.
2. Miss Logan is quite *fair* in her grading.
3. Joan has a very *fair* complexion.

lead[1] (lēd), **1.** show the way by going along with or in front of: ***He leads the horses to water.*** **2.** be first among: ***She leads the class in spelling.*** **3.** be a way or road: ***Hard work leads to success.*** **4.** pass or spend (time) in some special way: ***He leads a quiet life in the country.*** **5.** go first; begin a game: ***You may lead this time.*** **6.** place of leader; place in front: ***He always takes the lead when we plan to do anything.*** **7.** right to play first: ***It is your lead this time.*** **8.** amount that one is ahead: ***He had a lead of 3 yards in the race.*** 1-5 ***v.***, **led, lead ing;** 6-8 ***n.***

4. Following this path will *lead* you straight to the main highway.
5. In the poem, Abou Ben Adhem found that his name *led* all the rest.
6. Mr. Blake *led* the boys to the old log cabin.

rank \\'rangk\\ *n.* **1** A row; a line; as, *ranks* of houses. **2** A line of soldiers ranged side by side; as, *rank* and file. **3** A group of individuals classed together; as, the *ranks* of the American farmer. **4** Relative position or order; standing. His *rank* was fifth in terms of size. **5** Official grade, as in the army or navy; as, to have the *rank* of general. **6** Position in regard to merit; as, a musician of the highest *rank*. **7** High position; as, a man of *rank*. **8** [in the plural] The whole body of private soldiers in an army; as, a man who rose from the *ranks*.

7. My uncle holds a high *rank* in the National Guard.
8. To the west was a *rank* of mountains.
9. The *rank* of soldiers executed a right turn.
10. Matisse is considered a modern painter of the first *rank*.

CONTENT

26c. Learn what different kinds of information a dictionary gives you about words.

So much information is packed into the typical dictionary definition that some of it is likely to be overlooked if you are not careful. The explanations below correspond to the labels on the sample column on page 523. Study the sample column and these notes in order to be sure that you do not overlook any of the information your dictionary has to offer.

1. *The entry word.* The word to be defined is called the *entry word.* It appears in heavy type. You use the entry word to locate a definition, to get the correct spelling of a word, and to find out how it is divided into syllables, if it has more than one syllable. Most dictionaries also indicate words that are capitalized by beginning the entry word with a capital letter. However, capitalization may be indicated in other ways, especially in dictionaries not specially designed for high school students. If there is more than one acceptable spelling of a word, the alternative is usually listed immediately after the entry word:

moustache *or* **mustache**

In most cases the first spelling listed is the one that most people prefer to use. You will never go wrong by using the first spelling given in any dictionary.

2. *Illustration.* Sometimes the best way to indicate the meaning of a word is through an illustration.

Cuneiform is such a word. The definitions tell you the meanings of this word; the illustration *shows* you cuneiform characters.

3. *Pronunciation.* The pronunciation of a word is usually indicated immediately after the entry word by means of special respelling, which is explained in detail on pages 533–35. The dictionary from which the sample column on page 523 was taken uses slant lines (\\) to enclose the pronunciation respelling, but many other dictionaries use parentheses to enclose the respelling. The sounds represented by the symbols in the pronunciation respelling are explained in a key that usually appears inside the front cover of your dictionary. A shorter key may appear at the bottom of each page or every other page. (For more about pronunciation, see page 532.)

4. *Definition.* The definition gives the meaning or meanings of a word. When a word has more than one meaning, each meaning is defined separately in a numbered definition. (Some dictionaries use letters to distinguish between meanings so closely related that they are defined in a single numbered definition.)

5. *Illustrative example.* For many words, and for different meanings of the same word, sample contexts are provided to show how the word is used. Don't overlook sample contexts. They often provide essential clues to the meaning of a new word. For example, a *hoax* is a kind of trick, but you cannot say that you have taught your dog a "hoax." Illustrative examples often provide the clues that will prevent you from making mistakes in usage.

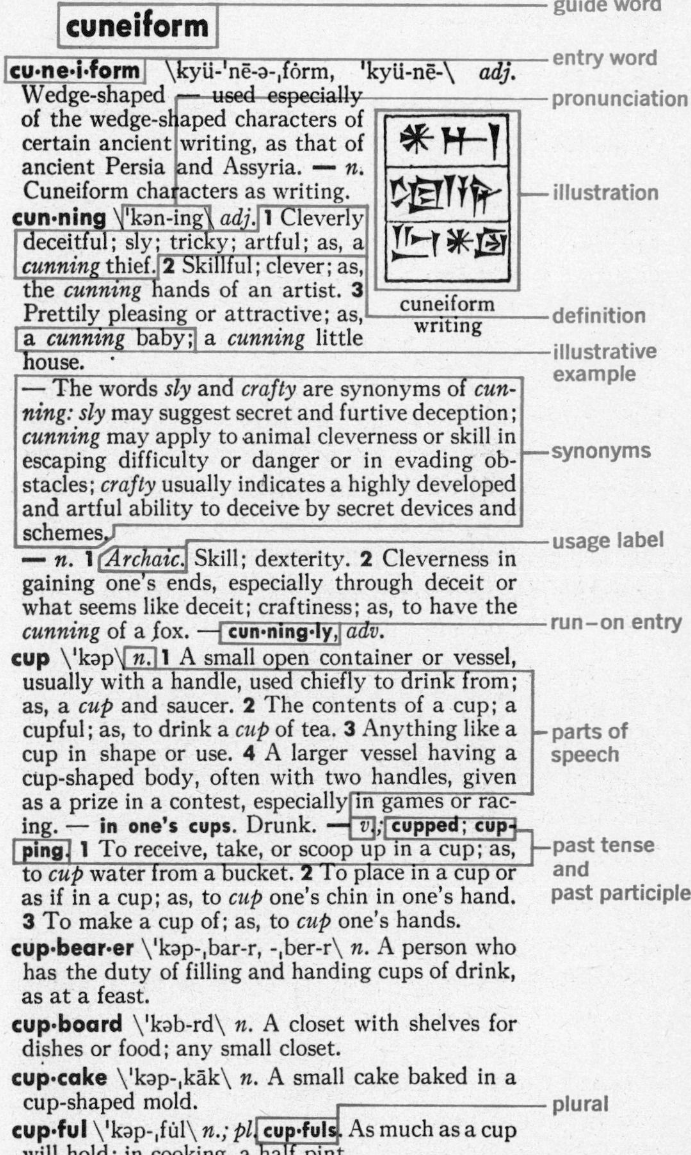

cuneiform

cu·ne·i·form \kyü-ˈnē-ə-ˌfȯrm, ˈkyü-nē-\ *adj.* Wedge-shaped — used especially of the wedge-shaped characters of certain ancient writing, as that of ancient Persia and Assyria. — *n.* Cuneiform characters as writing.

cuneiform writing

cun·ning \ˈkən-ing\ *adj.* **1** Cleverly deceitful; sly; tricky; artful; as, a *cunning* thief. **2** Skillful; clever; as, the *cunning* hands of an artist. **3** Prettily pleasing or attractive; as, a *cunning* baby; a *cunning* little house.

— The words *sly* and *crafty* are synonyms of *cunning: sly* may suggest secret and furtive deception; *cunning* may apply to animal cleverness or skill in escaping difficulty or danger or in evading obstacles; *crafty* usually indicates a highly developed and artful ability to deceive by secret devices and schemes.

— *n.* **1** *Archaic.* Skill; dexterity. **2** Cleverness in gaining one's ends, especially through deceit or what seems like deceit; craftiness; as, to have the *cunning* of a fox. — **cun·ning·ly,** *adv.*

cup \ˈkəp\ *n.* **1** A small open container or vessel, usually with a handle, used chiefly to drink from; as, a *cup* and saucer. **2** The contents of a cup; a cupful; as, to drink a *cup* of tea. **3** Anything like a cup in shape or use. **4** A larger vessel having a cup-shaped body, often with two handles, given as a prize in a contest, especially in games or racing. — **in one's cups.** Drunk. — *v.*; **cupped**; **cup-ping.** **1** To receive, take, or scoop up in a cup; as, to *cup* water from a bucket. **2** To place in a cup or as if in a cup; as, to *cup* one's chin in one's hand. **3** To make a cup of; as, to *cup* one's hands.

cup·bear·er \ˈkəp-ˌbar-r, -ˌber-r\ *n.* A person who has the duty of filling and handing cups of drink, as at a feast.

cup·board \ˈkəb-rd\ *n.* A closet with shelves for dishes or food; any small closet.

cup·cake \ˈkəp-ˌkāk\ *n.* A small cake baked in a cup-shaped mold.

cup·ful \ˈkəp-ˌfu̇l\ *n.; pl.* **cup·fuls**. As much as a cup will hold; in cooking, a half pint.

6. *Synonyms.* Synonyms are words that have similar meanings. Usually, words that are synonyms are alike in some senses and different in others. For example, *broad* and *spacious* are synonyms when the subject is a landscape. Yet we can describe humor as *broad* but not *spacious.* When a list of synonyms is given for an entry word, the list is often accompanied by an explanation of the special meaning of each word.

7. *Usage label.* Not all words entered in a dictionary are equally acceptable in all situations. A usage label is a mild warning that people use a word (or use a particular meaning of a word) only in certain situations. For example, the label *slang* indicates a word that may be used in certain informal situations but is likely to call attention to itself when used in other situations. Another label, *archaic,* indicates that a word was once common but is now rarely used. A third label, *dialect,* indicates that a word is used in only one part of the country. The introduction to your dictionary explains the meaning of all the usage labels employed by your dictionary.

8. *Run-on entry.* Many English words have companion forms that are closely related to them in meaning. Dictionaries include these words at the end of an entry as *run-on entries.* At the end of the adjective *bad,* for instance, you may find the notation "—**bad′ly** *adv.* —**bad′ness** *n.*" Although often no definitions are given in a run-on entry, a part of speech label is provided for each companion form. Some dictionaries also give the pronunciation for the companion form. (For more about companion forms, see pages 566–67.)

9. *Part of speech.* The part of speech of a word is indicated by an italicized abbreviation:

n.	noun	*adv.*	adverb
pron.	pronoun	*prep.*	preposition
v.	verb [1]	*conj.*	conjunction
adj.	adjective	*interj.*	interjection

Many English words can be used as more than one part of speech. For such words, a dictionary will indicate how the definitions are related to the part-of-speech labels. In some dictionaries, all the definitions for one part of speech are grouped together after the label, as on page 523. Other dictionaries provide numbered references to the definitions with the part-of-speech labels. The second method is used at the end of the following entry:

> **kick** (kik), **1.** strike out with the foot: *That horse kicks when anyone comes near him.* **2.** strike with the foot: *The horse kicked the boy.* **3.** drive, force, or move by kicking: *kick a ball.* **4.** act of kicking. **5.** win by a kick: *kick a goal in football.* **6.** spring back when fired: *This shotgun kicks.* **7.** recoil of a gun. **8.** *Informal.* complain; object; grumble. **9.** *Slang.* complaint; objection. **10.** *Slang.* excitement; thrill. **11.** *Slang.* the intoxicating effect of alcohol in a drink. 1-3,5,6,8 *v.*, 4,7,9-11 *n.*

[1] Unabridged dictionaries and those designed for older students distinguish between verbs like *wonder* in the sentence "I wonder" and verbs that require another word to show who or what is receiving the action; for example, *hit* in "The batter hit a home run." Such dictionaries label verbs like *wonder*, in the first example, *v.i.*, and verbs like *hit*, in the second, *v.t.* The abbreviation *v.i.* stands for *intransitive verb; v.t.* stands for *transitive verb.* Transitive verbs always have to have an object—a word showing who or what was affected by the action expressed by the verb.

A dictionary also provides the following information:

Origin. For some words, school dictionaries provide information about the history of a word, usually by indicating the language from which it was borrowed. Such information may appear near the beginning of the definition as in the example below, or at the end. In either case it is usually enclosed in brackets.

> **acre** \'āk-r\ *n.* [From Old English *aecer* meaning "field".] A measure of land equal to 160 square rods, or 4,840 square yards, or 43,560 square feet.

Encyclopedic information. A small number of dictionary entries deal with people and places. There are better places to find out about important people and places than in a dictionary—these are described in Chapter 27. However, if all you need is a general identification or location, the dictionary will usually provide it, as in the following entry.

> **Pierce, Franklin** (pirs), 1804–1869; 14th president of the U. S., from 1853 to 1857.

● EXERCISE 6. Number your paper 1–10. Write a synonym for each of the words below. If necessary, use the dictionary.

1. coax
2. development
3. distinct
4. diversity
5. final
6. find
7. gay
8. melancholy
9. perhaps
10. plain

● EXERCISE 7. Copy from your dictionary the usage labels for five of these words. Be prepared to explain what the labels tell you and how they would affect your use of the words.

1. afeared
2. corny
3. davenport
4. gabby
5. loco
6. lorry
7. ope
8. petrol
9. pone
10. raspberry

● EXERCISE 8. Copy from your dictionary a run-on entry for each of the following words.

1. celebrate
2. cold
3. fair
4. foolish
5. liquidate
6. mobilize
7. negative
8. rapid
9. reform
10. smooth
11. suppress
12. thin
13. turgid
14. water
15. weigh

● EXERCISE 9. Copy from your dictionary two definitions for each of the following words, each definition to be for a different part of speech. After the definitions, indicate the parts of speech by using part-of-speech labels.

EXAMPLE 1. flower a. The part of a plant that normally bears the seed, *n.*
b. To blossom; to bloom, *v.*

1. back
2. chance
3. holiday
4. Indian
5. maneuver
6. match
7. net
8. range
9. register
10. tag

● EXERCISE 10. Look up the following persons and places in your dictionary. Be able to tell what information the dictionary provides about them.

1. Ezra
2. Hecate
3. John Jay
4. Kyoto
5. Majorca
6. Maria Montessori
7. Nejd
8. Orinoco
9. Sergei Rachmaninoff
10. Tierra del Fuego

SPELLING

26d. **Learn to use your dictionary for spelling and capitalization.**

If you are not sure about the spelling of a word, you should look it up in the dictionary. Occasionally, it may be difficult to find. If you did not know the initial letters of *gnaw*, *knife*, and *pneumonia*, you might look for these words under *n*. Fortunately, most words in the dictionary are easier to find. The spelling of the initial sound of a word is much more regular in English than the spelling of sounds in the middle or at the ends of words. To find how most words are spelled, simply follow the principles of alphabetical order and let the guide words help you.

Variant Spellings

A dictionary occasionally gives two spellings for a word; *abridgment* and *abridgement*, *coconut* and *cocoanut*, *partisan* and *partizan*. Both spellings are correct, but usually a dictionary indicates which spelling is more usual by listing it first. Thus, *abridgment*, listed before *abridgement*, is given as the more common spelling in several dictionaries.

● EXERCISE 11. Copy from your dictionary a variant spelling for five of the following words. Be able to tell whether one spelling is more usual than another.

1. cantaloupe
2. demon
3. fantasy
4. frowsy
5. honor
6. judgment
7. likeable
8. mold
9. rickshaw
10. salable
11. savior
12. sulfa

Unusual Plurals

If the plural of a noun is formed in an unusual way, a dictionary will give the plural form with the abbreviation *pl.* preceding it. Notice the plural of *cupful* in the sample column on page 523. In this case, the plural *cupfuls* is formed in the usual way, but some people might use the incorrect form *cupsful.* Other plural forms given by a dictionary are the plural of *duty* (*duties*) and the plural of *deer* (*deer*). The correct form of the last word may be indicated by the notation "**deer** *n. sing. and pl.*"

Unusual Verb Forms

When a verb forms its past tense, its past participle, or its present participle in an unusual way, a dictionary will list these irregular forms. On page 523, the past tense and present participle forms of *cup* are given since the final *p* is doubled in these forms. The past participle form is not provided since this is the same as the past tense form. In the entry for *freeze*, a dictionary lists all three forms: *froze*, *frozen*, *freezing*.

Comparatives and Superlatives

When the comparative and superlative forms of an adjective are spelled in an unusual way, a dictionary provides these forms either near the beginning or end of an entry. Sometimes the abbreviations *compar.* and *superl.* are used. In the following entry, the comparative and superlative forms are at the beginning.

> **curly** \\'kər-lē\\ *adj.;* **curl·i·er; curl·i·est. 1** Curling or tending to curl; as, *curly* hair. **2** Having curls; as, a *curly* head.

● EXERCISE 12. Copy from your dictionary the unusual spelling forms (if any) for the following words. After the forms, write (*1*) if they are unusual plurals, (*2*) if they are unusual verb forms, or (*3*) if they are unusual comparatives and superlatives.

EXAMPLE 1. swim
1. *swam, swum, swimming* (*2*)

1. city	6. individuality
2. choose	7. mad
3. defy	8. needy
4. good	9. rise
5. index	10. rob

CAPITALIZATION

In English, proper nouns are capitalized while common nouns are not. You should be familiar with the rules for capitalization given in Chapter 12. If you are not sure about capitalizing a certain word, the dictionary might help you by printing the word either with or without a capital or stating whether or not the word is usually capitalized.

Sometimes a word should be capitalized in one sense but not capitalized in another. In such a case, the dictionary indicates which meaning requires a capital. For example, some dictionaries print *Mass*, meaning a religious ceremony, with a capital; but *mass*, meaning a large amount or number, appears uncapitalized. *Pole*, meaning a native of Poland, is printed with a capital; *pole*, meaning a slender piece of wood, is not capitalized.

● EXERCISE 13. Look up the following words in a dictionary to see when they are capitalized. Be able to explain why they are or are not capitalized in each usage. Your dictionary may not give capitalized uses for all the words.

1. cupid
2. democrat
3. devil
4. episcopal
5. japan
6. mercury
7. nativity
8. pope
9. senate
10. west

SYLLABLE DIVISION

A dictionary divides all words into syllables. *Cupbearer* on page 523 is divided into three syllables. Knowing the syllables of a word may help you spell the word. In addition, if you have to divide a word at the end of a line when you are writing, you must know the syllables to divide correctly. (See pages 280–81.)

If your dictionary uses small dots or dashes between the syllables of a word as on page 523, be careful not to confuse these marks with a hyphen. Look up a hyphenated word like *mezzo-soprano* or *open-minded* to be sure you can tell the difference.

● EXERCISE 14. Copy the following words, dividing them into syllables. Use the same method to indicate syllable division that your dictionary uses.

1. absolution
2. comma
3. endurance
4. extra
5. flexible
6. junior
7. penetrating
8. severity
9. socialize
10. underdog

PRONUNCIATION

26e. Learn to use your dictionary for pronunciation.

One of the most important pieces of information given in a dictionary is the pronunciation of a word. This information usually comes immediately after the entry word and is enclosed within slant bars (as on page 523) or within parentheses. Be careful not to confuse the pronunciation indication with the spelling of a word.

The Accent Mark

In words of two or more syllables, one syllable is always pronounced with greater force than the others. A dictionary indicates which syllable needs emphasis by using an *accent mark*. Most dictionaries use one of two kinds of accent marks: either the mark ˈ appearing before the syllable or the mark ′ placed after the syllable. Both marks appear well above the center of a letter. Look at the pronunciation indication for *cupboard* on page 523. Which of the two accent marks is used?

In a word of three or more syllables, a dictionary usually indicates two accent marks, one primary, the other secondary. The word *hippopotamus* has a primary accent on the syllable *pot* and a weaker accent on *hip*. Dictionaries generally show the secondary accent in one of three ways. When the mark (′) is used to indicate primary accent, the secondary accent is indicated by a weaker mark (′) or by two marks (″). When the primary accent (ˈ) is used, the secondary accent is a similar mark placed at the bottom of a syllable (ˌ). In the word *cupbearer* (page 523), where does the secondary accent mark occur?

● EXERCISE 15. Copy the following words, dividing them into syllables, and indicate the accented syllables. Use the kind of accent marks which are used in your dictionary.

1. aristocrat
2. detrimental
3. distribution
4. frugal
5. hornpipe
6. masquerade
7. Olympian
8. revolt
9. sarcasm
10. similarity

Pronunciation Symbols

A dictionary uses pronunciation symbols to indicate the pronunciation of a word. Most symbols are regular letters of the alphabet, but they are used more strictly than in ordinary writing. For example, the letter *c* can have several different pronunciations, as in the words *city*, *control*, and *cello*. A dictionary would indicate the beginning sounds of these words as *s*, *k*, and *ch*. To show the pronunciation of vowels, which is harder to indicate than the pronunciation of consonants, a dictionary uses *diacritical* marks—special symbols placed above the letters.

Indicating pronunciation is among the dictionary maker's most difficult tasks; and thus it is not surprising that dictionaries should vary in their use of symbols. In order to use the pronunciations given in your dictionary, you must become familiar with the symbols it uses. A key to these symbols usually appears inside the front cover and sometimes on each page as well. In addition, your dictionary probably includes a thorough explanation of its pronunciation symbols in the introduction. Study this explanation carefully.

In this chapter you will study several diacritical marks that are used by most dictionaries.

Long Vowels

To indicate a long vowel, a dictionary generally uses a diacritical mark called a *macron*—a long straight mark over the vowel. When a macron is used, the long vowel is said to have the sound of its own name.

EXAMPLES	main	\mān\
	mean	\mēn\
	mine	\mīn\
	moan	\mōn\
	immune	\imūn\

Notice the use of the macron in the pronunciations of *cuneiform* and *cupcake* on page 523.

Short Vowels

The vowels in the words *mat, head, bid, pot, could,* and *cut* are called short vowels. Dictionaries differ in their methods of showing the sound of short vowels.

One method uses a symbol called a *breve* (brēv) over the vowel. Another method is to leave short vowels unmarked.

EXAMPLES	mat	(măt)	or	\mat\
	head	(hĕd)	or	\hed\
	bid	(bĭd)	or	\bid\

Sometimes, when all that we say in an unaccented syllable is the sound of the consonant, the pronunciation indication in certain dictionaries may omit the short vowel altogether. This method is followed in the pronunciation of the last syllable of *cupbearer* on page 523.

The Schwa

Most recent dictionaries use an upside-down *e* as a symbol to represent the blurred, unclear sound of "uh." This sound occurs in the phrase *the men* (thə men) and in the following words:

minute (min′əte)
baron (bar′ən)
permit (pər mit′)

Most dictionaries use the schwa only in showing the pronunciation of unaccented syllables, but several dictionaries use this symbol in accented syllables and in one-syllable words. In the sample dictionary column on page 523, how is the schwa used?

● EXERCISE 16. Copy from your dictionary the pronunciation of the following words. Follow the practice of your dictionary in using parentheses or slant lines to enclose the pronunciation. Be able to explain all the diacritical marks used.

1. diet
2. erase
3. herringbone
4. matriarchy
5. nation
6. poverty
7. puny
8. revolve
9. seldom
10. sidesaddle

● EXERCISE 17. Follow the directions in Exercise 16.

1. appetite
2. collection
3. debatable
4. fraternal
5. gelatinous
6. heritage
7. major
8. Manila
9. radiator
10. slippery

● REVIEW EXERCISE. Use complete sentences in writing the answers to the following questions. If necessary, look the information up in the chapter.

1. Define

   a. synonym
   b. macron
   c. guide word
   d. schwa

2. Name three kinds of information about spelling that a dictionary provides.
3. After which of the following words would *father-in-law* occur in a dictionary?

   Fr.
   fatherly
   father
   fatherhood
   fatherland

4. What kind of information is given by the following terms: *slang*, *informal*, *archaic*?

CHAPTER 27

The Library

The Dewey Decimal System, the Card Catalogue, Reference Books

You can carry about in your head only a limited amount of information, but you can find out almost anything you want to know if you know where to look for it. Your best place to look for information is a library, whether it is your school library or a public library. To use a library efficiently, you must understand its system of arranging the books, magazines, pamphlets, and other materials it contains so that you can find what you want easily and quickly.

THE ARRANGEMENT OF A LIBRARY

Fiction

27a. Learn to locate books of fiction

In most libraries all books of fiction are located together in one section. The books are arranged on the shelves in alphabetical order according to authors' last names. For example, if you were looking for *The War of the Worlds* by H. G. Wells, you would go to the fiction section and find the books by authors whose last names begin with *W*. Among these, you could easily locate books by Wells. You might find a number of these and have to look along the shelf to find *The War of the Worlds*. To help you do this, the library arranges books by the same author also in alphabetical order according to the first word in the title, unless that word is *a*, *an*, or *the*. If the first word is *a*, *an*, or *the*, the second word of the title is used for alphabetizing. *The War of the Worlds* would come then in the *W* position.

◆ NOTE Books by authors whose names begin with *Mc* (like McDonald) are arranged as though the name were spelled *Mac; St.* is arranged as though spelled *Saint.*

● EXERCISE 1. Number your paper 1–10. After these numbers, write the authors and titles of the following books of fiction in the order in which they would be arranged in the library.

1. *The Light in the Forest* by Conrad Richter
2. *Bertie Comes Through* by Henry Gregor Felson
3. *Jane Eyre* by Charlotte Brontë
4. *Dirt Track Summer* by William Campbell Gault
5. *Boy Gets Car* by Henry Gregor Felson
6. *The Incredible Journey* by Sheila Burnford
7. *The Friendly Persuasion* by Jessamyn West
8. *Wuthering Heights* by Emily Brontë
9. *Rough Road to Glory* by William Campbell Gault
10. *Lassie Come-Home* by Eric Knight

Nonfiction

27b. Learn the Dewey decimal system of arranging nonfiction.

The Dewey decimal system is named after Melvil Dewey, the American librarian who developed it. Under this system, books are classified under ten headings, and each heading has a number. Books having the same number are placed together in the library. The numbers and headings are as follows:

000–099	General works (encyclopedias and other reference materials)
100–199	Philosophy
200–299	Religion
300–399	Social Sciences (economics, government, etc.)
400–499	Language
500–599	Science
600–699	Technology (engineering, aviation, inventions, etc.)
700–799	The Arts (architecture, music, sports, etc.)
800–899	Literature
900–999	History (including geography, travel books, and biography)

The number given to a book is known as the book's call number. To see how the Dewey system works, take as an example Arthur Zaidenberg's *How to Draw Cartoons*. Since the book is about art, its number will be in the 700's. Within this broad category, the numbers 740–749 are used for books on drawing and decorative arts. Books on freehand drawing are given the number 741. By means of a decimal the classification is narrowed further. The number 741.5 is given to books about drawing cartoons, and 741.5–Z is the call number for the book *How to Draw Cartoons.*

Biographies are arranged in alphabetical order according to the names of the persons written about, not according to the names of the persons who wrote the biographies. For example, *The Helen Keller Story* by Catherine Owens Peare will appear among the K's. The call number may consist of B, for biography, with K, for Keller, under it—$\frac{B}{K}$, or it may consist of 92 with K under it—$\frac{92}{K}$. Some librarians use the B; others use the 92, which is a short form of the Dewey number for biography—920; still others use 921.

● EXERCISE 2. Number your paper 1–10. Within which number range in the Dewey decimal system would you find each of the following?

EXAMPLE 1. A book on modeling in clay
1. *700–799*

1. A book about Greek philosophy
2. A book about travels in Arabia
3. A book about the development of the French language
4. A book about the Presidency
5. A collection of biographies of pioneer men and women
6. A book about baseball
7. A book about the early Christian church
8. A history of Portugal
9. A book about English poetry of the eighteenth century
10. A book about organic chemistry

THE CARD CATALOGUE

You can find out the call number of any book in the library by looking the book up in the card catalogue.

27c. Learn to use the card catalogue.

The card catalogue is a cabinet with small drawers which contain file cards arranged in alphabetical order. These cards represent the books in the library—fiction and nonfiction. For each book of fiction there are at least two cards, an *author card* and a *title card.* For each book of nonfiction, there are usually three cards, an *author card,* a *title card,* and a *subject card.* If the book is by two or more authors, there is an author card for each name.

Each card provides a different means of finding a book. If you are looking for a book by a particular author, you would look for the *author card.* If you know the title of the book but not the name of the author, you would look for the *title card.* If you need information about a particular subject (rockets and rocketry, for instance) but do not have a specific book or author in mind, you would look for a *subject card;* that is, you would look for cards with the word *ROCKETS* at the top.

Study the sample cards and explanation below.

1. *Name of author.* This information appears first on author cards, which are filed alphabetically under the author's last name. All books by one author are then arranged in the alphabetical order of titles. An author's birth date is often given after the name.

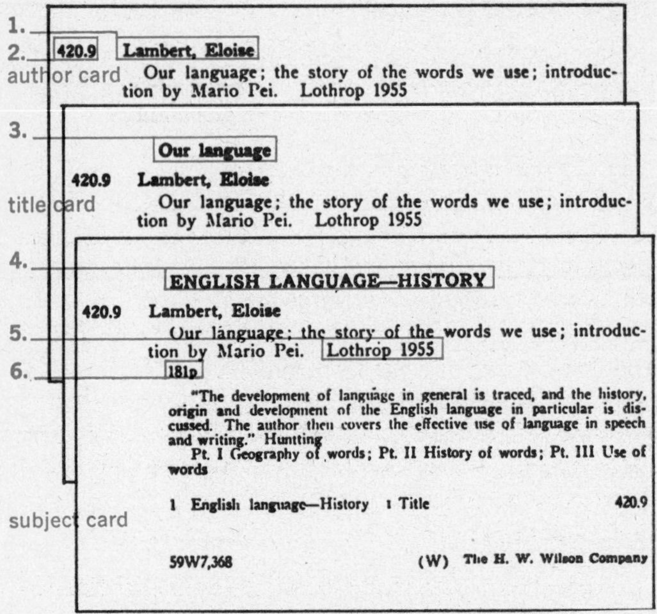

Principal Items of Information on a Card

2. *Call number.* This Dewey decimal number tells you where to find the book in the nonfiction section of the library.

3. *Title of book.* On title cards this information appears first. Title cards are filed alphabetically in the card catalogue according to the first word of the title, not counting the words *a*, *an*, or *the*.

4. *Subject.* The subject of a book appears first on subject cards. Like author cards and title cards, they are arranged alphabetically in the card catalogue.

5. *Publisher and date of publication.* The date of publication is an important guide if you want recent

information on a subject. If you are looking for facts about last year's baseball season, you would not choose a book published in 1955. The place of publication is often given before the publisher's name.

6. *Number of pages.* Occasionally this fact will be useful. Obviously a book about the history of the Supreme Court that is only seventy pages long does not give much detailed information.

7. *"See" and "see also" references.* Sometimes a subject card has a "see" reference or a "see also" reference sending you to another card in the catalogue. For example, if you looked up *Revolutionary War*, you might find a card saying, "See United States—History—Revolutionary War." If you looked up *Diving*, you might find the notation, "See also Skin Diving."

● EXERCISE 3. Using the card catalogue, list the call number, title, author, and date of publication of one book on each of five of the following topics.

1. Indians of the United States
2. Radar
3. Birds of Europe
4. Baseball
5. Florence Nightingale
6. South America
7. American poets and poetry
8. Jet planes
9. Color photography
10. Scientists

REFERENCE BOOKS

27d. Learn to use the reference books available in the library.

The section devoted to reference books is one of the most important parts of a library. These books contain information on a great many subjects or tell where such information can be found. Once you become familiar with the different reference books in your library, they will prove a valuable aid to your studies.

Encyclopedias

An encyclopedia contains articles on a wide range of subjects. These articles are written by experts and present information not only through words but through pictures, charts, and maps. Many articles, especially articles about cities, states, and countries, contain lists of facts and tables of figures. When you are writing a report, an encyclopedia article will give you a good overall view of the subject and may also suggest more detailed sources of information.

Three encyclopedias for persons of your age are:

Compton's Pictured Encyclopedia
World Book Encyclopedia
Collier's Encyclopedia

All these encyclopedias contain many volumes and arrange their articles alphabetically by subject. The guide letter or letters on the spine of each volume will help you to find information about a particular subject. Guide words at the top of each page will help you to find a specific article. Use them as you would use guide words in a dictionary. (See pages 516–17.) If you cannot find an article under a particular subject, look for similar subjects or for a larger subject that includes yours. For example, information on *jet planes* can probably be found in an article on *aviation.*

You can also find information in an encyclopedia by using the index. Most encyclopedias have indexes, but the indexes are not always located in the same place. For example, the index of *Collier's Encyclopedia* is the last volume, while the index in *Compton's Pictured Encyclopedia* is at the end of each volume. You can use the index to locate maps, charts, tables, and illustrations, as well as articles about a particular subject. Usually there is a guide to using the index at the beginning of the index itself.

The index in the last volume of the *World Book Encyclopedia* is in somewhat different form. It is a "Reading and Study Guide," which is arranged by subjects. Each subject is divided into a series of smaller subjects for which a list of articles available in the encyclopedia is given.

● EXERCISE 4. Look up two of the topics below in an encyclopedia and take half a page of notes on each of them. Below each group of notes, write the title of the article, the name of the encyclopedia, the volume number, and the number of the page on which you found the information.

EXAMPLE 1. The tourist industry in Hawaii

1. *300,000 tourists visit Hawaii annually. Busiest months are June, July, August, October, and December. The Hawaii Visitors Bureau, founded in 1903 and supported by the government and by businessmen, holds advertising campaigns to attract tourists. "Hawaii," World Book Encyclopedia, volume 8, page 99*

1. Soft-coal mining in the United States
2. The paintings of Rembrandt
3. Famous volcanoes

4. Cro-Magnon man
5. The Battle of Hastings
6. The origin of baseball
7. Penguins
8. The native tribes of Australia
9. How and where cricket is played
10. The invention of the Diesel engine
11. The statues on Easter Island
12. How to care for a pet
13. Ambergris, its origins and uses
14. The electron microscope
15. The population and industries of Maine
16. The building of the Appian Way
17. The ruins at Angkor Wat
18. Mesmerism
19. William Harvey's contribution to medicine
20. The first comic strips

Atlases

Atlases are reference books made up mainly of maps. Often they contain much other information, such as the population figures for cities, states, and countries; principal crops; natural resources; and major industries.

Atlases are of several kinds. Some contain maps for all the countries of the world. Others contain maps for a particular country only. Historical atlases show how countries have changed through the years, while economic atlases show such things as trade routes and natural resources. Several of the common atlases are:

Goode's School Atlas
Hammond's Library World Atlas and Gazetteer
Lord's Historical Atlas of the United States
Rand McNally Cosmopolitan World Atlas

Atlases will prove valuable in your history and geography courses. You should learn about the different kinds of information that atlases provide and become thoroughly familiar with at least one atlas.

● EXERCISE 5. Consult a world atlas and write answers to two of the following questions.

1. Name three national parks in California.
2. List three important geographical features (mountains, rivers, plains, deserts, lakes, etc.) of each of the following countries:
   a. Brazil b. Algeria c. England
3. List the countries which border on each of the following:
   a. Switzerland b. Venezuela c. Turkey
4. List four major products of each of the following countries:
   a. Bolivia b. Ethiopia c. Pakistan d. Iraq
5. In which country is each of the following places situated?
   a. Khenifra b. Jhansi c. Crewe d. Zutphen
6. List the following states in order of population beginning with the largest:
   a. Illinois c. Virginia e. Maine
   b. Alaska d. Ohio f. California

Almanacs

An almanac consists in large part of lists of miscellaneous information, including sports statistics, names of government officials, population figures, and birth and death rates. In addition, an almanac is a good place to find much recent information, since almanacs are published annually and give many facts about the preceding year. For instance, if you want a review of the important events of last year, you should consult this year's almanac.

The most widely used almanacs are *The World Almanac and Book of Facts*, the *Information Please Almanac, Atlas, and Yearbook*, and *The New York Times Encyclopedic Almanac*. The various kinds of information in an almanac are not organized alphabetically or according to any other kind of logical arrangement. The best way to find information is to use the index. In *The World Almanac* the index is at the front of the book, while in the other almanacs it is at the back.

● EXERCISE 6. Consult one of the almanacs mentioned above and write answers to two of the following questions.

1. Give the birth dates and birthplaces of the following persons: (Look up "Personalities, noted" or "Celebrated persons.")
   a. Bob Hope
   b. Mike Nichols
   c. Samuel Barber
   d. Tennessee Williams
   e. Dwight D. Eisenhower
2. Give the names of the Secretaries of State during the administrations of the following presidents:
   a. John Quincy Adams
   b. William Harrison
   c. Abraham Lincoln
   d. William Taft
   e. Warren Harding
3. Who won the Nobel Prize for physics in 1909? 1923? 1938? 1946? 1970?
4. Give the name of the author and novel that won the Pulitzer Prize for fiction in each of the following years:
   a. 1926
   b. 1928
   c. 1947
   d. 1955
   e. 1959
   f. 1972

Biographical Reference Books

A biographical reference book contains short biographies of famous persons. The following are among the most useful of these books. Find out whether they are in your library.

Who's Who, and *Who's Who in America*—useful for principal facts about living persons only.

Webster's Biographical Dictionary—very short biographies of famous persons, modern and historical.

Twentieth Century Authors, and *Twentieth Century Authors: First Supplement*—interesting short biographies of modern writers.

Current Biography—lives of persons currently prominent in the news. Published monthly.

THE READERS' GUIDE

To find a magazine article on any subject, you use a very valuable reference book called the *Readers' Guide to Periodical Literature*. Published twice a month (once a month in July and August), the *Readers' Guide* indexes articles in more than one hundred magazines. Every two years the issues are collected and published in a large volume. You can look up an article by its subject (like *hunting*) or by its author. To save space, the listings use abbreviations. If you are in doubt about the meaning of the abbreviations, you should consult the keys in the front of the *Readers' Guide*.

Study the following excerpt from an issue of the *Readers' Guide*. The marginal notes will make clear the information given.

subject entry

HUNTING
Gist of it; digest of the outdoor news; ed. by H. Moore. See issues of Outdoor life
Where to go fishing, vacationing, hunting, all over the world (title varies) P. A. Parsons. See issues of Outdoor life

division of main subject

Accidents and injuries
Dark tragedy; ed. by B. East. D. Mosher. il Outdoor Life 131:20-3+ F '63

name of magazine

Alaska
My Eskimo adventure. G. M. Daetz. il Outdoor Life 131:48-9+ F '63

Angola
Big lion of Mucusso. J. O'Connor. il Outdoor Life 131:17-19+ F '63

Canada
Ross and his rifle. D. Peck. il Outdoor Life 131:32-5+ Ja; 36-9+ F '63

title of article

Florida
Upland shooting down on Florida's Gold Coast. V. Kraft. il Sports Illus 18:52+ Mr 4 '63

author's name

Montana
Dark tragedy; ed. by B. East. D. Mosher. il Outdoor Life 131:20-3+ F '63

date of magazine

Ohio
Midwinter bird hunt. E. A. Bauer. il Outdoor Life 131:32-5+ F '63

volume number

United States
Hunting (cont) il Sports Illus 18:52+ Mr 4 '63
Hunting by air photos. L. Pringle. il Outdoor Life 131:50-1+ F '63
No more free hunting? A. Grahame. il Outdoor Life 131:14-15+ F '63

page reference

Wyoming
Rams were my bugaboo. C. Ormond. il Outdoor Life 131:28-9+ F '63

HUNTING dogs
Dogs. D. M. Duffey. See issues of Outdoor life

HUNTING with bow and arrow
Archery. G. H. Gillelan. See issues of Outdoor life

HURLEY, Richard J.
New revolution on the Potomac. Sr Schol 82:13T Mr 13 '63

author entry

Suppose you are writing an article about hunting and wish to include some information about hunting in Florida. The *Readers' Guide* (see excerpt above) would lead you first to the subject *hunting*, then to the subdivision *Florida*, and finally to an article by V. Kraft in the March 4, 1963, issue of *Sports Illus-*

trated. The entry for this article gives the following information:

An article about hunting in Florida called "Upland Shooting Down on Florida's Gold Coast" by V. Kraft may be found in *Sports Illustrated.* The article, which is illustrated (il), is in volume 18; it begins on page 52 and is continued on later pages (18:52+) of the March 4, 1963, issue (Mr 4 '63).

● EXERCISE 7. In the *Readers' Guide*, find an article listed under any five of the following subjects. Copy the entry for the article. Be ready to explain the information for the entry.

1. Scandinavia
2. Phonograph records
3. Lakes
4. Colleges and universities
5. Personnel management
6. Guided missiles
7. Elephants
8. Coal
9. Airplanes, military
10. Washington, D.C.

Summary List of Library Reference Tools

The card catalogue
Reference books
- Encyclopedias
- Atlases
- Almanacs
- Biographical reference books
  - Who's Who
  - Who's Who in America
  - Webster's Biographical Dictionary
  - Twentieth Century Authors
  - Twentieth Century Authors: First Supplement
  - Current Biography
- Readers' Guide

● REVIEW EXERCISE. Number your paper 1–20. Write the reference tool from the preceding list to which you would turn first to get information on the corresponding subject in the list below.

1. Latest developments in cancer research
2. History of the Nobel Prize
3. Source of the Mississippi River
4. Antarctica—climate, terrain, etc.
5. Motion Picture Academy Award winners in 1971
6. Title and author of a library book on outer space
7. Diplomatic career of James Russell Lowell, the American poet
8. Origins of jazz music
9. Titles of novels by Kenneth Roberts (1885–1957), an American writer
10. Population of Naples, Italy
11. Natural resources of the Rhineland in Germany
12. A list of magazine articles on a recent international crisis
13. The work of Grant Wood, American artist
14. Winners of the World Series since 1970
15. The title of a book in the library on the Revolutionary War
16. Height of Mt. Everest
17. Facts about the present Secretary of State
18. History of Italian opera
19. The life of a modern American poet
20. The biography of a person who has only recently become prominent in the news

CHAPTER 28

Vocabulary

Context, Word Analysis, Word Choice

The books you have read, the games you play, school subjects, hobbies—all your interests are reflected in your vocabulary. It is no surprise then that teachers and parents rely on vocabulary growth as one way of measuring success in school. Knowing many words, of course, does not make anyone a good student automatically. But hardly anyone does well in school without developing a good vocabulary.

Although there is no simple way to acquire a large vocabulary, there are ways in which you can learn and remember more of the words you encounter every day. This chapter will give you practice in using these methods. It will also introduce you to a number of words that are widely used in the books you will be reading this year and in the future.

To keep a record of your progress and to refresh your memory, set aside a section of your notebook in which to enter the new words you learn, together with a definition and a sentence or phrase illustrating their use. You can begin your vocabulary notebook with any words from the following diagnostic test whose meanings you are not sure of.

Diagnostic Test

Number your paper 1–25. After the proper number, write the letter of the word that is closest in meaning to the numbered word.

EXAMPLE 1. hamper a. build c. hinder
b. revise d. search

1. *c*

1. abashed	a. beaten	c. lowered
	b. ashamed	d. fallen
2. adept	a. skillful	c. proud
	b. bold	d. lazy
3. amity	a. boredom	c. anger
	b. hatred	d. friendship
4. belligerent	a. dull	c. swift
	b. warlike	d. gentle
5. crony	a. old woman	c. candy
	b. tower	d. friend
6. deluge	a. opinion	c. excitement
	b. illusion	d. flood
7. dexterity	a. sugar	c. handiness
	b. duplicate	d. kindness
8. fatigue	a. war	c. fatalist
	b. weariness	d. explosion
9. guffaw	a. laugh	c. loosen
	b. retire	d. drive
10. haughty	a. moderate	c. proud
	b. smiling	d. slow
11. humdrum	a. melodious	c. aggressive
	b. loud	d. dull
12. levity	a. simple lever	c. earnestness
	b. excessive speed	d. lack of seriousness

13. menace	a. army	c. song
	b. threat	d. rival
14. pallid	a. pale	c. sleepy
	b. excited	d. calm
15. pedagogue	a. teacher	c. politician
	b. learning	d. politics
16. primitive	a. undeveloped	c. violent
	b. prominent	d. religious
17. raze.	a. lift	c. destroy
	b. attack	d. repel
18. remorse	a. repetition	c. justice
	b. guilt	d. reason
19. revile	a. abuse	c. rebuild
	b. correct	d. bury
20. seraphic	a. telegraphic	c. angelic
	b. intelligent	d. serious
21. sinew	a. novelty	c. disappointment
	b. excitement	d. strength
22. tepid	a. unlucky	c. alone
	b. lukewarm	d. rushing
23. unique	a. special	c. uneven
	b. together	d. heavy
24. vehement	a. energetic	c. timid
	b. serious	d. laughing
25. visage	a. cage	c. face
	b. news	d. tang

LEARNING NEW WORDS

Occasionally we see or hear a word used alone, but most of the time we encounter words used in combination with other words. When the word is unfamiliar, these surrounding words often supply valuable clues to meaning.

28a. Learn new words from context.

The *context* of a word means the words that surround it in a sentence and the whole situation in which the word is used. The context of the words supplies the main clue to the meaning of *edible* in this sentence:

> The campers were told not to use toadstools in the stew because they are not edible.

Since the campers were warned against using the toadstools in a stew, it stands to reason that something *not edible* is something "not fit to eat." If you know that much about toadstools already, you can be even surer about your guess.

The situation itself provides the context clues that enable you to know that *pound* means one thing in a grocery store, another in a story about a dogcatcher, and still another in a British movie. Many common English words have different meanings. Keeping the situation in mind will help you in keeping them straight.

● EXERCISE 1. Number your paper 1–10. For each italicized word in the sentences below, write the letter of the definition that is closest in meaning. You will not need all the definitions in the list. Check your answers in the dictionary.

a. calm
b. peak
c. guidance
d. magic
e. pronounced
f. honesty
g. government
h. swung to hit
i. fearful
j. confused
k. without success
l. round of applause

1. Mr. Tompkins has been a loyal employee for twenty-seven years, and no one doubts his *integrity.*
2. The angry mob gathered at the palace to express their disapproval of the *regime.*
3. At twenty-four, Roy Jenkins is at the very *summit* of his athletic career.
4. The fortuneteller claimed that she had *occult* powers.
5. He is so *timorous* that he refuses to go to sleep in the dark.
6. Tired and unhappy, the baby *flailed* angrily at the bars of her playpen.
7. At the end of the play, the enthusiastic audience gave the actors a rousing *ovation.*
8. As he studied the puzzle, there was a *bewildered* look on his face.
9. The doctor spoke comforting words to *allay* the woman's fears.
10. The speaker *articulated* his words with care.

● EXERCISE 2. Follow the directions in Exercise 1.

a. aloneness
b. reduce
c. bravery
d. avoid
e. good luck
f. ambition
g. respect
h. get well
i. disaster
j. insult
k. joy
l. imaginary

1. The soldiers bowed to the emperor as a sign of *deference.*
2. The earthquake, a *catastrophe* causing hundreds of deaths and thousands of injuries, came unexpectedly.
3. Harold has a *fictitious* playmate, whom no one has ever seen.

4. Luke finds it extremely difficult to make friends because he has lived the greater part of his life in *isolation*.
5. After a successful operation, a patient usually remains in the hospital to *recuperate*.
6. With a roar the crowd expressed its *jubilation* at the football victory.
7. No person should attempt to *evade* his duties as a citizen.
8. If the railroad keeps on losing money, it will have to *curtail* its services.
9. Fred's only *aspiration* is to win a place on the baseball team.
10. Private Lewis showed such *valor* in battle that he was promoted to corporal.

Related Word Forms

28b. Learn the related forms of new words.

Some words can be used as different parts of speech without changing their spelling. The word *iron* can be a noun, an adjective, or a verb: a piece of *iron*, an *iron* bar, to *iron* a dress. More often, however, something is added or taken away from the word to change it from one part of speech to another. The ending *–ly* can be added to most adjectives to make them adverbs (*soft*, *softly*), and the ending *–ness* is often added to make them nouns (*softness*). You will study more about such changes later in this chapter. The main thing now is to be aware that a new word may have related forms that are just as useful as the one you have encountered. When you can learn two or three new words with no more effort than one, why not do it?

● EXERCISE 3. In the numbered pairs that follow, the first contains an italicized word used as a particular part of speech. The second part of each pair contains a blank in which a related form of the same word will fit. Number your paper 1–10 and supply the appropriate form. Use your dictionary if you need to.

EXAMPLE 1. an act of *valor*
a —— action
1. *valorous*

1. a *coherent* explanation
   to explain with ——
2. to *aspire* to something noble
   a noble ——
3. an *isolated* farmhouse
   to live in ——
4. to *evade* responsibilities
   an —— of one's duty
5. to *coerce* a person
   to get something by ——
6. a *futile* attempt
   to try —— to do something
7. the *tumult* of a battle
   a —— scene
8. the *validity* of an argument
   a —— reason
9. *appropriate* behavior
   to behave ——
10. a skillful *diplomat*
    skill in ——

Using the Dictionary

28c. Learn to find the meaning you want in your dictionary.

When you cannot guess the meaning of a word from context, you should go to your dict onary. Context is still important, however. Most words have a number of different meanings, and the best way of finding the one you want is to look for the definition that fits the context in which you originally encountered the word. Consider the following sentence:

> Your jokes are in poor taste, Harold, and we can dispense with any more of them.

Dispense has the following meanings: (1) to give; (2) to distribute; (3) to get rid of; (4) to get along without. By trying each of these meanings in place of the word *dispense* in the example, you can easily eliminate all of the choices except the last one—the meaning you want.

Which of these numbered meanings for *dispense* fits the following sentence?

> The Red Cross dispensed food and clothing to the flood victims.

Dictionaries often supply sample contexts to help you distinguish between the various meanings of a word (see pages 517–18). Such phrases can be very helpful in showing you how to use the new word in your own speech and writing.

● EXERCISE 4. The italicized words in the following sentences have a number of different meanings. Using your dictionary, select the meaning that best fits each sentence and write it after the proper number.

EXAMPLE 1. A candidate for the presidency is likely to be an *eminent* political figure.
1. *prominent*

1. The doctor said that there was nothing to be feared from the *benign* swelling.
2. The old man gave us a *benign* smile.
3. The professor's lecture *illuminated* the subject for us.
4. With the flick of a switch, he can *illuminate* the entire garden.

5. As we drove into the valley, a beautiful *pastoral* scene unrolled before us.
6. The minister attended to his *pastoral* duties.
7. Your argument seems *valid* and has convinced us all.
8. Since this is a *valid* contract, you will have to live up to it.
9. The manager's *bland* words calmed the angry customer.
10. I don't like this cereal because it is too *bland.*

● EXERCISE 5. The following two columns consist of a list of words and a list of definitions for these words. Number your paper 1–10. After the proper number, copy the letter of the definition that is closest in meaning. Refer to a dictionary when necessary. You will not use all the definitions in the second column.

1. chronic
2. appalling
3. sedate
4. forgo
5. prodigy
6. myriad
7. debonair
8. advent
9. decrepit
10. pewter

a. calm and serious
b. to climb rapidly
c. numerous
d. shocking
e. person having special abilities
f. arrival of an important event
g. give up
h. slowly falling
i. lively and gay
j. heavy silver-gray metal
k. law or principle
l. continuing for a long time
m. foolishly happy
n. feeble

● REVIEW EXERCISE A. The words in this exercise have been chosen from those you have studied so far. Number your paper 1–20. After the proper number, write the letter of the word nearest in meaning.

1. evade — a. run b. avoid c. trick d. lose
2. coerce — a. cooperate b. lag behind c. refuse d. compel
3. pastoral — a. finely made b. about rural life c. of the past d. richly perfumed
4. fictitious — a. handsome b. invented c. musical d. genuine
5. regime — a. airplane b. beating c. government d. regulation
6. malign — a. evil b. silly c. kind d. worthless
7. summit — a. dessert b. rebellion c. peak d. leap
8. illuminate — a. go as b. light up c. argue with d. seem like
9. valor — a. courage b. laziness c. wisdom d. vanity
10. tumult — a. disturbance b. accident c. motive d. hatred
11. bewildered — a. prepared b. bewitched c. confused d. lost
12. eminent — a. small b. permanent c. prominent d. clever
13. curtail — a. correct b. build c. finish d. reduce
14. timorous — a. unreliable b. afraid c. trusting d. royal

15. flail
   a. restore
   b. chase
   c. beat
   d. impress
16. integrity
   a. honesty
   b. loyalty
   c. misery
   d. treachery
17. recuperate
   a. lessen
   b. refill
   c. duplicate
   d. recover
18. coherent
   a. clear
   b. scrambled
   c. mistaken
   d. recent
19. aspiration
   a. relief
   b. slogan
   c. ambition
   d. notion
20. benign
   a. evil
   b. kind
   c. dangerous
   d. pale

PREFIXES, ROOTS, AND SUFFIXES

Some words can be divided into parts, and some cannot. Those that can be divided, like *housewife* and *unhappy*, often consist of parts that mean something separately. By learning how to divide words into their parts, you can sometimes discover additional clues to meaning.

The basic part of a word is called a *root.* A part added before the root is called a *prefix;* a part added after the root is called a *suffix.* Becoming familiar with the common prefixes and suffixes discussed in the following pages will provide you with helpful leads to finding the meaning of a large number of new words.

Prefixes

28d. **Learn how common prefixes change the meaning of words.**

The following common prefixes occur in thousands of English words.

PREFIX	MEANING	EXAMPLE
auto–	self	automobile
bi–	twice	biannual
circum–	around	circumference
con–	together	concord
de–	down	degrade
dis–	away or apart	disagree
ex–	out	expel
im–	not	impractical
mis–	wrong	misjudge
multi–	many	multiply
pre–	before	preview
semi–	half or partly	semiprecious

● EXERCISE 6. Number your paper 1–10. After the proper number, give the meaning of the italicized word in each of the sentences. Be prepared to tell how the prefix of the word helps determine its meaning. Use the dictionary if necessary.

1. The assistant principal *convened* the student council to draft a new student code of conduct.
2. An artillery shell completely *demolished* the hut.
3. He gave some *preposterous* excuse for not passing the test.
4. Our newspaper is a *semimonthly* publication.
5. Larry Chou was born on Formosa and was not brought to the United States until he was six years old; therefore, he is *bilingual*.
6. Some of the czars of Russia were cruel *autocrats* who were feared by the people.
7. To call Alvin a worker is a *misnomer* since he is always asleep with a broom in his hands.
8. Mr. Boscombe locked his cabin and departed on his *biweekly* trip for supplies.

9. She *depicted* the old man so vividly that her listeners could almost see him.
10. Mrs. Boone is a thorough housekeeper, and her apartment is always *immaculate.*

● EXERCISE 7. Follow the directions for Exercise 6.

1. Ferdinand Magellan, the Portuguese sailor and explorer, *circumnavigated* the globe..
2. The boy held a large, *multicolored* ball in his hands.
3. The mechanic had to *dismantle* the motor to find the faulty part.
4. Holding a lantern, he slowly *descended* the cellar stairs.
5. Because Mr. and Mrs. Harrison are a *congenial* couple, they rarely quarrel.
6. The theft of the jewels showed careful planning and must have been a *premeditated* crime.
7. We finally *dissuaded* Tom from writing "Mrs. Feeney is a meanie" on the blackboard.
8. Archimedes is supposed to have *exclaimed* "Eureka!" as he made an important discovery.
9. The Pueblo Indians have observed this custom since time *immemorial.*
10. The Whitmore Construction Company is building a group of *semidetached* houses on this block.

● EXERCISE 8. Follow the directions for Exercise 6.

1. Frank has become so efficient at packaging toys that he moves like an *automaton.*
2. The people, angry over years of misrule, *deposed* the unjust king.
3. Remember Shakespeare's *immortal* words: "This above all, to thine own self be true."
4. The Smiths own *extensive* lands in this valley.
5. Mrs. Slocum showed the class how to *bisect* an angle.

6. Is the prisoner truly sorry for his *misdeeds*, or is he only sorry he was caught?
7. Mr. Dobson publishes a *semiweekly* paper.
8. The prisoner was allowed to move freely within a *circumscribed* area.
9. Next year our city will hold its *bicentennial* celebration.
10. Douglass MacHenry Gardner, who donated the money for our new Civic Center, is a *multimillionaire*.

Suffixes

28e. Learn to recognize common suffixes when they occur in *companion forms*.

Sometimes adding a suffix will result in a word that is a different part of speech than the original word. For example, the suffix *–ly* added to the adjective *free* results in *freely*, an adverb. The suffix *–ly* occurs at the end of an adjective or an adverb but never at the end of a noun. Therefore, words ending in this suffix are never nouns. (When *–ly* occurs at the end of a noun such as *lily*, these letters are not a suffix but part of the basic word.)

There are many English words to which suffixes can be added. The new words formed by adding suffixes are *companion forms* of the basic word. Adding suffixes to the root *free* results in the companion forms *freedom* and *freely*. If you are on the alert for companion forms and learn some common suffixes, you will often be able to guess the correct meanings of new words. One fact to keep in mind is that the spelling of the root may change when a suffix is added. For example, when *–ly* is added to *gay*, the resulting word is not *gayly* but *gaily.* When *–ition* is added to *repeat*, the resulting word is spelled *repetition.*

Learn the following suffixes that occur in nouns.

SUFFIX	MEANING	EXAMPLE
–hood	condition	boyhood
–ness	quality	goodness
–ance, ence	state, act, fact	independence
–ation, –ition, –tion	action or state	celebration
–ity, –ty	quality	ability
–ment	result or action	employment

● EXERCISE 9. Number your paper 1–10. Form nouns from the following words by using the suffixes listed above; then give the meanings of the new words. In some cases, it will be necessary to change the spelling of the root. Check your answers with the dictionary.

EXAMPLES 1. kind
1. *kindness—the quality of being kind*
2. create
2. *creation—the act of creating*

1. replace
2. likely
3. articulate
4. accept
5. intense
6. man
7. fragile
8. aspire
9. improvise
10. friendly

The following suffixes occur in adjectives.

SUFFIX	MEANING	EXAMPLE
–ish	like or suggesting	boyish
–able, –ible	able	tolerable
–ous	having the quality of	religious
–esque	like	statuesque
–some	like or tending to	tiresome

28e

● EXERCISE 10. Number your paper 1–10. Form adjectives from the following words by using the suffixes listed on page 567; then give the meanings of the new words. Check your answers with the dictionary, and make changes if necessary.

1. lone
2. picture
3. harmony
4. devil
5. grace
6. girl
7. luxury
8. depend
9. meddle
10. riot

Learn the following suffixes, which occur in verbs.

SUFFIX	MEANING	EXAMPLE
–ate	cause to become	animate
–en	make or become	deepen
–fy	make or cause	fortify
–ize	cause to be	motorize

● EXERCISE 11. Number your paper 1–10. Form verbs from the following words by using the suffixes listed above; then give the meanings of the new words. Check your answers with the dictionary, and make changes if necessary.

1. captive
2. critic
3. strength
4. nausea
5. glory
6. active
7. civil
8. sweet
9. illumine
10. beauty

● EXERCISE 12. Each of the following sentences has a word with a suffix that you have learned in this chapter. Number your paper 1–10. After the proper number, find and copy the word and underline the suffix. Then write the meaning of the word. In some cases, you may be able to guess the correct meaning. In others, the root of the word may not be familiar to you, and you will have to look up the word in a dictionary. Check *all* your answers with the dictionary.

EXAMPLE 1. Gerry's arrogance has caused him to be disliked by many people.
1. *arrogance, state of being arrogant*

1. The beautiful scenery provided the artist with inspiration enough for fifty paintings.
2. The sentries in the prison camp were not allowed to fraternize with the enemy.
3. Job prayed to be relieved of his afflictions.
4. During the Christmas season, the store had a window display showing the Nativity.
5. The two countries formed an alliance to help each other in case of war.
6. The refinement of her manners is proof of her strict upbringing.
7. This company believes that it has an obligation to please all of its clients.
8. The coat of shellac guaranteed that the table surface would be durable.
9. Factories should not be allowed to fill our lakes and rivers with slag and other waste products that might contaminate our water.
10. *Carmen* is regarded as one of the most melodious of all French operas.

USING EXACT WORDS

28f. **Use the exact word in your speaking and writing.**

In English, many thousands of words are available to help you express exactly what you mean. If you use the same few words to describe many different people or things or actions or situations, you are not taking advantage of the variety of your language. Avoid the overworked word that is used in so many different contexts that it loses a precise meaning. *Good* is one such word. If you were to refer to someone as "a good man," would you mean that he is capable, kind, or dependable? If you were to say, "I had a good day," would you mean an enjoyable, a productive, or a tranquil day? *Good* might be the first word that occurs to you to describe a man or a day, but a moment's thought will usually supply a better word to express your meaning. Of course, the greater the stock of words at your command, the easier it will be for you to substitute a fresh, precise word for a trite one.

Using Adjectives to Describe

The English language is rich in adjectives. You should learn to use adjectives to express your meaning exactly. In talking about a book you enjoyed, for example, you might say it was *interesting*, but how much more expressive you would be if you called it *exciting* or *engrossing* or *stimulating!* Build your vocabulary by taking time to find the exact adjective to express your thought.

● EXERCISE 13. Each of the following sentences contains a vague or overworked adjective, in italics, which should be replaced by a more precise word. Number your paper 1–10. After the proper number, write the more precise adjective from the list preceding the sentences. You will not need all the words on the list.

Use the dictionary, if necessary, to check your answers and make corrections.

eccentric	customary	appalling
casual	burly	fluent
titanic	sallow	tangible
fragrant	devout	eligible
decrepit	insipid	boisterous

1. That rice pudding had a rather *flat* taste.
2. The *old* car drove slowly down the road.
3. The damage done by the hurricane was *shocking*.
4. The *large* man sat down at the table.
5. Paul is regarded as *odd* because he puts mustard on ice cream.
6. When we began to sing and shout, our counselor warned us that we were being too *lively*.
7. With a *great* effort, Samson tore down the pillars of the Philistine temple.
8. The foreman of the jury said that no *real* evidence of guilt had been produced.
9. No student who is failing one or more subjects is *qualified* for a student council position.
10. The roses were sweet-smelling.

● EXERCISE 14. Number your paper 1–6. After the proper number, write an adjective from the list below which conveys an idea appropriate to the sentence having that number. You will not use all the words in the list. Use the dictionary, if necessary.

diverse	feasible	abundant
latent	oratorical	excessive
resolute	homogeneous	pertinent

1. Mr. Henderson's system of programing students seems to work very well.
2. Martha has a stomachache because she ate too much dessert.

3. Once Ed has a goal in life, nothing will stop him from reaching it.
4. Your statement about housing conditions is very much to the point.
5. Carl has talent, but it needs to be developed.
6. All the men in this group are the same age and height, and all have the same interests.

Using Verbs to Express Action

Your ability to express yourself is directly dependent on your verb vocabulary. Verbs give action and color to your sentences. The following exercise includes a number of verbs that are important for you to know.

● EXERCISE 15. Number your paper 1–10. After the proper number, select and copy the verb which is appropriate in meaning for the blank. Change the tense if necessary to fit the sentence, and use your dictionary. You will not need all the verbs in the list.

soar	liberate	restore
saturate	carouse	obliterate
diverge	pollute	browbeat
confiscate	capitulate	wheedle
restrain	stray	elapse

1. Because Mr. Logan could not pay his taxes, the government —— his property.
2. The fighter was badly beaten but refused to —— to his opponent.
3. Realizing that the bird would die in captivity, the boy took it to the woods and —— it.
4. As the plane —— above the clouds, the earth disappeared from view.
5. Several hours —— before the weary hikers returned home.

6. He is extremely timid and allows a great many people to —— him.
7. Skillful detective work —— the stolen painting to its rightful owners.
8. The two hunters parted company when their paths ——.
9. Two centuries of wind and weather have almost —— the words carved on the stone.
10. Plump Mrs. Abercrombie was tempted to eat the strawberry shortcake with whipped cream, but she —— herself.

Using Adverbs to Modify Verbs

Because adverbs answer such questions as *How? When?* and *Where?* in connection with verbs, they are a very important part of your vocabulary. The exactness and vividness of your writing and speaking depend a great deal upon your using adverbs well. In the exercise which follows, there are a number of adverbs for you to learn if you do not already know them.

● EXERCISE 16. Number your paper 1–10. After the proper number, write an adverb from the list which answers the question. You will not need all the adverbs in the list. Use the dictionary, if necessary.

immensely	resonantly	superficially
covertly	scrupulously	rigidly
abruptly	urgently	elegantly
excessively	anonymously	ostentatiously

1. How did the conscientious bookkeeper keep his company's records?
2. How did the man who thought there were burglars in his house call for the police?
3. How did the opera star sing the low notes in his aria?

4. How did the audience like the actor's superb performance?
5. How did the newly engaged girl display her engagement ring?
6. How did the sleepy student check his homework for mistakes?
7. How did the little boy try to get a cookie from the cookie jar when his mother was in the next room?
8. How would a person stand if he were imitating a statue?
9. How does a doctor leave a dinner party when he receives an emergency call?
10. How does a woman dress if she spends much money on clothes and has excellent taste?

Synonyms and Antonyms

A *synonym* is a word which means nearly the same thing as another word. Sometimes a dictionary will define a word in terms of its synonym: one definition of *benign* is "kind." While words that are synonyms are close in meaning, they rarely have *exactly* the same meaning. At times you will be able to use one of several words in a sentence, but at other times only the exact word will do.

Pleasure, *delight*, and *joy* all have roughly the same meaning, yet each expresses a different shade of meaning. *Pleasure* is the most general of the three words; it covers a variety of situations, none of them very specifically. *Delight* indicates a sharp feeling of pleasure that lasts only a short time. *Joy* may indicate a deep and long-lasting happiness. In the following sentence, which of the three words fits most exactly?

> I receive great —— from my study of mathematics.

Pleasure fits, of course, but is not very specific. *Delight* does not fit very well because the feeling indicated in this sentence would seem to last for some time. The synonym that most exactly expresses the desired meaning is *joy*.

When you look up a word in a dictionary, you will often find several synonyms listed. Be sure you understand the exact meaning of each synonym. To help you to distinguish between synonyms, some dictionaries give *synonym articles*—brief explanations of how a group of synonyms differ in meaning. Your own reading will also help you. The more often you encounter a word in different contexts, the better you will be able to determine its meaning.

EXERCISE 17. Number your paper 1–10. After the proper number, select and write the synonym which best fits the sentence. Use your dictionary to learn the exact meaning of each synonym.

1. My jacket is made of a new (fabricated, artificial, synthetic) material.
2. Our (invincible, victorious, triumphant) army never has been and never should be defeated in battle.
3. The monks in several medieval monasteries kept (histories, annals, records) summarizing the important events of each year.
4. Medieval craftsmen had a special (fashion, technique, system) for making stained-glass windows.
5. The young mother fondly (fed, nourished, sustained) her baby.
6. You can imagine how (embarrassing, shaming, humiliating) it was to be spanked in front of all my relatives.

7. His (guess, conjecture, estimate) that there would be a test the next day was based on the fact that Miss Brown had assigned no homework that night.
8. Although the lawyer stayed within the law, he relied on (guile, cunning, fraud) to win his case.
9. Under the new government, many men were (dispossessed, deprived, divested) of their rights.
10. After studying the problem, Dr. Paley formed a working (theory, hypothesis, supposition), which he tested by experiment.

The antonym of a word is a word with the opposite meaning. *Bad* is the antonym of *good*, and *happy* is the antonym of *sad*. Sometimes an antonym is formed by adding a prefix meaning *not* to a word: an antonym of *wise* is *unwise*. Knowing the antonym of a word will often help you to understand the word's exact meaning (or at least one exact meaning). For example, knowing that *dexterity* is the antonym of *clumsiness* will lead you to a correct meaning for this word. A dictionary sometimes lists antonyms at the end of an entry for a word.

● EXERCISE 18. Antonyms for words in the first column below may be found in the second column. Number your paper 1–10. After the proper number, write the letter of the correct antonym. You will not need all the words in the second column. Use the dictionary, if necessary.

1. frustrate	a. tiny
2. contemptible	b. dawn
3. colossal	c. ornamental
4. impertinent	d. spiteful
5. upbraid	e. satisfy
6. twilight	f. wordiness

7. brevity
8. neutral
9. functional
10. random

g. biased
h. probity
i. orderly
j. eventual
k. admirable
l. courteous
m. remarkable
n. praise

SPECIAL VOCABULARIES

28g. Master the special vocabularies of your other school subjects.

Each of your subjects has special words that you must learn to understand important concepts. Some of the words are new, while others, which are used in everyday speech, have special meanings in a particular subject.

A textbook often calls attention to these new words by printing them in italics or in heavy type. Printing a word in a special way shows that it is important. Often a definition immediately follows the word. If not, turn to the back of the book to see if there is a glossary—a short dictionary of special words. There you will usually find a definition for the word. Always use a glossary when a textbook provides one. It is one of the most valuable features of a book.

● EXERCISE 19. The words below are used in mathematics books designed for students of your age. Write each word on your paper, and follow it by a short definition. Then write a short sentence using each word correctly. Look up any words you do not know in your textbook or in a desk dictionary.

acute	intersection	quotient
bisect	irrational	radical
diameter	numeral	radius
exponent	obtuse	rational

● EXERCISE 20. The following words are likely to appear in your social studies assignments. Follow the directions for Exercise 19.

History: blockade, capitalism, carpetbagger, depression, filibuster, gerrymander, initiative, recall, referendum, sharecropper, totalitarian, vassal
Geography: fjord, meridian, monsoon, plateau, precipitation, topography, tributary

● EXERCISE 21. The following words are likely to appear in your science assignments. Follow the directions for Exercise 19.

antibody	embryo	neutron
atom	friction	radiation
condensation	fulcrum	satellite
electron	nebula	spectrum

28h. Use the words from specialized vocabularies in your everyday speaking and writing.

Many words in a special field are often used outside the field. *Condensation* and *inertia* are often found in nonscientific books, while *exponent* and *radical* can be used by a political speaker as well as a mathematician. Learn the meanings of these words as used outside their fields. Use them in your own speaking and writing when they help express your ideas exactly.

● EXERCISE 22. The following words used in mathematics, science, and social studies have meanings outside these fields. Use these words appropriately in the blanks below. You will not use all the words.

blockade	fulcrum	obtuse
condensation	inertia	radical
diameter	initiative	satellite
embryo	intersection	vassal

1. Harold displayed great —— in forming a drama club and recruiting members for it.
2. Poland is considered a political —— of Russia.
3. The newspapers have called Alderman Tompkins "a —— of special interest groups."
4. George is so —— that he didn't get the joke even after I explained it.
5. The department store has been completely reorganized; you will discover some pretty —— changes when you go there.
6. The small firm of Rockefeller and Andrews was the —— of a gigantic corporation.
7. The fugitive ran up the stairs to the attic and ——d the entry by pushing a table against the door.
8. My father will meet us at the —— of Vernon Street and Third Avenue at two o'clock.

● REVIEW EXERCISE B. The words in this exercise have been chosen from all those you have studied in this chapter. Number your paper 1–33. After the proper number, write the letter of the word which is closest in meaning to the numbered word.

1. abundant	a. house	c. sloppy
	b. plentiful	d. crowded
2. affliction	a. aviation	c. report
	b. guardian	d. misery

3. appalling
   a. revealing
   b. annoying
   c. shocking
   d. rewarding
4. boisterous
   a. lively
   b. supporting
   c. treacherous
   d. weak
5. captivate
   a. rebuke
   b. capture
   c. charm
   d. release
6. concord
   a. sympathy
   b. conformity
   c. agreement
   d. boredom
7. covertly
   a. swiftly
   b. gaily
   c. badly
   d. secretly
8. decrepit
   a. decoyed
   b. feeble
   c. wise
   d. proud
9. deference
   a. pressure
   b. deceit
   c. respect
   d. loyalty
10. divest
    a. clothe
    b. deprive
    c. retreat
    d. amble
11. extensive
    a. large
    b. thin
    c. visual
    d. highly respected
12. feasible
    a. expensive
    b. fearful
    c. missing
    d. workable
13. flail
    a. shrink
    b. beat
    c. reveal
    d. forget
14. homogeneous
    a. alike
    b. different
    c. thoughtful
    d. respected
15. immaculate
    a. forgetful
    b. spotless
    c. cowardly
    d. intelligent
16. jubilation
    a. anniversary
    b. ceremony
    c. terror
    d. rejoicing
17. nativity
    a. birth
    b. citizenship
    c. ignorance
    d. innocence
18. nourish
    a. hate
    b. regret
    c. love
    d. feed

19. obscure
   a. magnificent c. unclear
   b. rosy d. quiet

20. ovation
   a. honor c. recipe
   b. action d. applause

21. premeditated
   a. deliberate c. foolish
   b. fiendish d. great

22. random
   a. close c. aimless
   b. emotional d. knowing

23. resolute
   a. reserved c. enduring
   b. determined d. miserable

24. restrain
   a. hold back c. dress up
   b. teach d. remember

25. rigidly
   a. stiffly c. cleverly
   b. stubbornly d. rudely

26. saturate
   a. wring out c. treat badly
   b. imitate d. fill completely

27. sedate
   a. noisy c. calm
   b. healthy d. honest

28. stray
   a. wander c. lonely
   b. direct d. puzzled

29. synthetic
   a. tiring c. careless
   b. expensive d. artificial

30. technique
   a. detail c. instruction
   b. method d. reason

31. titanic
   a. metallic c. backward
   b. huge d. alive

32. upbraid
   a. climb c. reverse
   b. misread d. scold

33. wheedle
   a. grow c. coax
   b. correct d. crawl

WORD LIST

The following list of 240 words should form the basis of your vocabulary study for the year. You have already encountered many of them in this chapter and should have written them in your vocabulary notebook. When you encounter a new word, add it to your notebook. Write a definition of the word, and then use the word correctly in a sentence.

abashed
abundant
activate
adept
adjacent
advent
affliction

allay
alliance
amity

analyze
anecdote
annals
anonymously
appalling
appropriate
aristocrat
arrogance
articulate
aspiration

attain
autocrat
automaton
badger

bayou
belligerent
benign
bewildered
bilingual
bisect

bland
boisterous
brevity
browbeat
bulwark
burly
canine
capitulate
captivate
carouse

casement
casual
catastrophe
ceremony
chronic
circumnavigate
coerce
coherent

colossal
concerted

conciliate
condole
confiscate
congenial
conjecture
consecutive
considerate
contaminate
contemptible
convene

covertly
crony
curtail
customary
debonair
decadence
decrepit
deference
deluge
demolish

depict

depose
descend
devout
dexterity
diplomat
dismantle
dispense
dissuade
diverge

diverse
divest
eccentric
edible
elapse
elegantly
eligible
eminent
encroach
enormity

ensue
evade
excessive
exclaim
extensive
facilitate
fatality
fatigue
feasible
fictitious

firmament
flail
fluent
forgo
fragile
fragrant
fraternize
frustrate
functional
futile

glorify
gracious
guffaw
guile
hamper
haughty
hibernate
hieroglyphics
homogeneous
humdrum

humidity
humiliate
hypothesis
illuminate
immaculate
immensely
immortal
impediment
imperative
impertinent

improvise
inanimate
incentive
incorrigible
indict
inquisitive
insipid
integrity
intensity
invincible

isolation
jubilation
juncture
latent
levity
liberate
malign
meddlesome
menace
misdeed

misnomer
multicolored
myriad
nativity
nauseate
neutral
nourish
nuclear
obligation
obliterate

obscure
occult
oratorical
ostentatiously
ovation
pallid
paragon
pastoral
pedagogue
permeate

pertinent
pewter
philanthropist
picturesque
pollute
posterity
prearrange
precocious
premeditated
preposterous

primitive
prodigy
punctual
quadruped
random
ravage
raze
rebate
recession
recuperate

regime
relevant
remorse
resolute
resonantly
responsibility
restore
restrain
revile
rigidly

riotous
sallow
satire
saturate
scrupulously
secluded
sedate
seraphic
sinew
soviet

sphere
stipulate
stray
substitute
successor
summit
superficially
synthetic
tangible
technique

tepid
timorous
titanic
transcend
tumult
twilight
unique
upbraid
urgently
valid

valor
vegetate
vehement
verify
vindicate
visage
vitality
wane
wheedle
whimsical

SUPPLEMENT

Topics to Write About

Topics to Write About

Have you ever had the frustrating experience of trying to write a composition but being unable to think of anything to write about? If you have, you are not alone, for while students are seldom at a loss for things to *talk* about, they are frequently at a loss for things to *write* about. Bring two teenagers together, and conversation is likely to flow effortlessly on a great many subjects, especially—to the despair of parents—if the conversation is on the telephone. But assign a composition to be written in English class, and students' minds frequently go blank.

The purpose of this supplement to the composition assignments in this book is to help you to find interesting topics. Help is given in the form of meaningful photographs and cartoons which can stimulate your imagination and your powers of invention.

DESCRIBING AN ACTION IN A SNAPSHOT SENTENCE

Take a good look at the picture below (figure 1).

Can you see exactly what has happened? You can probably see that the pole this unfortunate pole-vaulter was using has broken and left him in a dangerous situation. Actually, he landed safely. The picture was taken during a track meet at the University of Wisconsin.

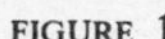

FIGURE 1

Now suppose that you have been assigned to write three things about this picture: (1) A one-word title, or caption; (2) A title, or caption, of several words—this title may be a phrase or a brief sentence; (3) A one-sentence description of the action in the photograph. A one-sentence description like this is called a "snapshot sentence." Newspaper editors become skillful at writing interesting and entertaining captions. Writing a snapshot sentence not only is fun, but it will also give you excellent practice in fitting a number of facts or ideas into one smooth sentence—an important composition skill.

For the picture of the pole-vaulter whose pole has broken, one student wrote the following:

(1) one-word caption—crack*down!*
(2) multi-word caption—"I feel a headache coming on!"
(3) snapshot sentence—As the pole-vaulter flung himself upward in an all-out effort to break the record, the new, lighter pole, straining under his weight, snapped in the middle, leaving him upside-down in midair.

Plan your snapshot sentences carefully. How many elements in the picture can you include in one sentence? How can you phrase these elements so that they are not strung out with *ands?* For example, an inferior form of the snapshot sentence about the pole-vaulter would be, "The pole-vaulter was trying for a record, and he flung himself upward in an all-out effort, and the new, lighter pole strained under his weight and broke in the middle and left him upside-down in midair."

Before writing composition 1, review the writing of complex sentences, rule 18b, pages 341–50, and the selection of words in description, rule 19e (2), pages 381–85.

● COMPOSITION 1. For each of the pictures (figures 2, 3, 4, and 5) on pages 590–92, write (1) a one-word caption, (2) a multi-word caption, and (3) a snapshot sentence.

● COMPOSITION 2. Write a snapshot sentence describing an action you have seen recently, perhaps on your way to school or at an athletic contest. Make your sentence clear enough so that when your classmates read it, they will see exactly what you saw.

FIGURE 2

FIGURE 3

FIGURE 4 ↓

FIGURE 6

← FIGURE 5

DESCRIBING A PERSON

When you describe a person, you give two kinds of information. The first kind describes his appearance—what he *looks* like. The second kind describes his personality—what he *is* like.

Take a long and careful look at the man in the photograph (figure 6) above.

In class, discuss the answers to the following questions:

1. If you were writing a description of this man's appearance, which features would you mention? Why? What words would you use to describe them?
2. What kind of work does this man do? Was the photograph taken after work or before work?
3. In what kind of mood is this man? Try to guess what he is thinking about.
4. While it is often unfair to judge someone's personality and character solely by his appearance, we all have a natural tendency to judge by appearances. Look at the picture and explain what kind of person you think this man is. Would he be an interesting person to know? Why do you think so? Is he a leader or a follower? a competent worker? a good husband and father? What other personal qualities does his appearance suggest?

● COMPOSITION 3. Write a paragraph that summarizes your impressions of the man in figure 6. If you wish, give him a name and tell where you think he lives. Include some description of his appearance.

● COMPOSITION 4. Examine carefully the two photographs (figures 7 and 8) on page 595.

Select the one that interests you and write a description (100–150 words) of the person, including details of both appearance and personality. We often tell anecdotes about someone to show what kind of person he is. You may wish to invent a brief story, an incident involving your subject, to illustrate one of his revealing characteristics.

FIGURE 7

FIGURE 8

WRITING A STORY FROM A PICTURE

A photograph may suggest a story in which the photographed event occurs. A person with an active imagination can make up a story from almost any picture. The pictures on pages 596–97 were chosen because they suggest stories.

Not only can a picture suggest a story involving the persons, place, and actions it shows, but it may also remind you of a personal-experience story that you could write about. As you study the pictures on pages 596–97, let your imagination work freely either to invent a story based on the picture or to plan a story about an experience of your own that the picture reminds you of. As

FIGURE 9

Bob Peterson, LIFE Magazine © Time Inc.

FIGURE 10

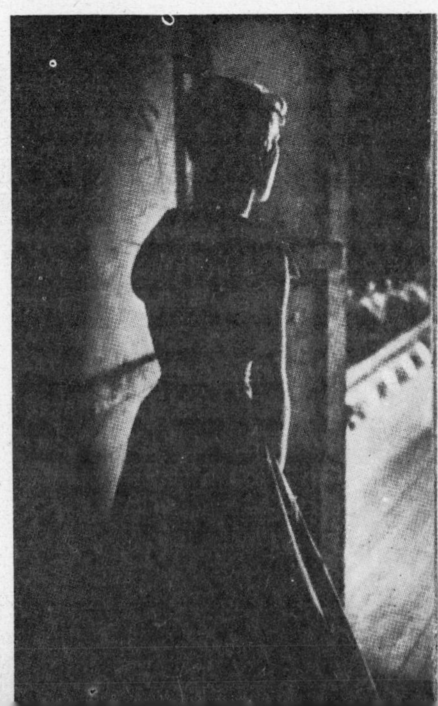

FIGURE 11

FIGURE 12

you plan your story, turn back to Chapter 19 and review what is said about planning a story and about the basic parts of a story (pages 361–67). After you have written a plan, but before you begin writing, review "Writing Vivid Stories" (pages 367–74) and "Dialogue" (pages 374–77).

You will probably want to name the characters in your story, and you will want to make the time and place clear. A personal-experience narrative will be written in the first person, but you may use either first or third person for a story invented from one of the pictures.

● COMPOSITION 5. Select one of the photographs (figures 9, 10, 11, or 12) on pages 596–97, and plan and write an interesting story suggested by it.

● COMPOSITION 6. Write a short story about one of the persons in figures 6, 7, or 8. Your story should be an imagined event in the life of the person, told in much greater detail than was the incident invented for the character sketch you wrote in composition 4.

CARTOON IDEAS TO WRITE ABOUT

A cartoon is a drawing with a message, for cartoonists are interested in ideas. A cartoon may help us to crystallize our thinking about a serious subject, or it may simply give us a good laugh at ourselves.

Study the cartoon (figure 13) on page 599, and prepare to discuss answers to the following questions:

1. What important fact about our world does this cartoon reflect? State this fact in a sentence.
2. What problems do underdeveloped nations present to nations like the United States?

Drawing by Arnold Roth from VISTA, May–June 1968, pp. 64–5.

FIGURE 13

3. Do developed and underdeveloped nations differ in their degree of civilization only, or do they differ in other ways?
4. How has the increased speed of travel during the last fifty years, represented here by the airplane, affected relationships between nations?
5. There have always been differences, great contrasts in some instances, between nations. Why can these contrasts no longer be permitted?
6. What can be done to solve the problem referred to in this cartoon?

● COMPOSITION 7. Write a paragraph in which you describe and explain the world problem symbolized by this cartoon (figure 13). State the problem in your first sentence—the topic sentence—and then develop the paragraph by giving additional details in the form of facts, examples, and reasons.

Both of the cartoons (figures 14 and 15) on pages 600 and 601 make the same point. Although the cartoons picture mice and ducks, their purpose is obviously to remind us of an important fact about ourselves. What do you think this fact is? How could it be the cause of friction among us?

● COMPOSITION 8. Write a sentence stating the fact about human beings that you think the cartoons (figures 14 and 15) express. Use your sentence as the topic sentence of a paragraph and develop it by giving examples of its truth from everyday life.

FIGURE 14 *"Look, Mother, Angels!"*

FIGURE 15 "*Boy, what a day, huh?*"

The two cartoons (figures 16 and 17) on pages 602 and 603 are about protests and protesters.

Study the cartoons and prepare to discuss answers to the following questions:

1. In what ways have protests become important in life today?
2. Against what things have popular protests been raised?
3. Who seems to be doing most of the protesting?
4. What varying forms do protests take?
5. To understand figure 16, you need to know the conditions under which Francis Scott Key wrote the "Star-Spangled Banner." Explain why it might be called a protest song.

FIGURE 16 "*Writing another of your little protest songs, Mr. Key . . . ?*"

FIGURE 17 *"It's a protest song I just made up: 'My son says I'm stupid and funny,/But he uses my car and my money./He . . .' "*

6. Does the cartoonist sympathize with protests and protesters? Explain.
7. In figure 17 does the cartoonist sympathize with the father or with the son? The cartoon is humorous. Is it also serious? What point about many youthful protesters is the cartoonist trying to make? Do you agree with him?

● COMPOSITION 9. Select either figure 16 or 17 and write a paragraph explaining the idea it expresses and giving your reactions to the idea. If your teacher approves, you may prefer to write one paragraph on the idea and a second paragraph on your reactions.

FIGURE 18 *"I'd like to point out that there are people trying to listen to a message of importance in here."*

FIGURE 19 *"Sure, I'd like to have children someday, but I wouldn't want to be—well, you know—a parent."*

● COMPOSITION 10. Study the cartoons (figures 18 and 19) on page 604, and decide what the central idea is in each. Select the cartoon that expresses an idea you could write about. Take time to think of as many implications, or ideas, as you can. Plan and write a composition that will treat the general subject of the cartoon. Use your own experiences as examples. State your own opinions—not necessarily those of the cartoonist.

IDEAS IN PHOTOGRAPHS TO WRITE ABOUT

Photographs, like cartoons, express ideas. The idea expressed by a photograph, however, is usually not so explicit as the idea expressed by a cartoon. When you and your friends look at a cartoon, you all get nearly the same idea from it. When, on the other hand, you look at a photograph, you may get many ideas, all suggested by the same picture but varying according to what each of you sees. In other words, a photograph, unlike a cartoon, is subject to many interpretations.

Cartoons and photographs may be frivolous or serious in tone. In fact, the same photograph may be considered amusing by one person but far from amusing by another.

Carefully examine the picture (figure 20) on page 606. We are so used to our bodies that we rarely think about what tremendously complex and marvelous machines they are. In a moment of exasperation we may say, "I wish I had three hands" or "You need eyes in the back of your head." What advantages would there be in having six hands? What disadvantages? If you could have one or two more eyes, where would you like to have

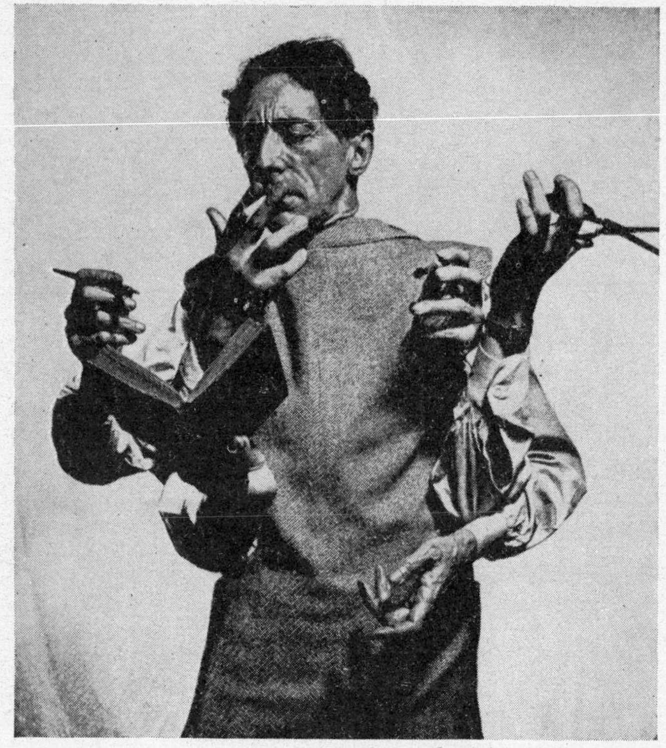

Copyright by Philippe Halsman.

FIGURE 20

them placed? Can you think of other changes in, or additions to, the human body that you think would offer interesting possibilities?

● COMPOSITION 11. Write an entertaining composition based on the picture of the man with six hands. Explain specific advantages and disadvantages that six hands would provide. How would the addition of four hands change our daily lives? the appliances and ma-

FIGURE 21

chines we use? the games we play? At what points on the body would you place the additional arms?

The photograph (figure 21) on this page is serious. Study it and prepare to discuss answers to the following questions:

1. The flowers are obviously symbols. What do they symbolize?
2. What general idea do the guns symbolize?

3. Characterize the people who are putting the flowers into the gun barrels. What is significant about them?
4. Write in one sentence the meaning of this picture. Do you agree with the idea the picture expresses?

● COMPOSITION 12. Write a composition (100–150 words) in which you express and develop one or more ideas suggested by figure 21. Give your reactions to the idea and support them with reasons.

The photographs (figures 22, 23, 24, and 25) on pages 609–11 express some serious ideas for you to write about. Study the photographs and decide what idea each presents.

● COMPOSITION 13. Select one figure (22, 23, 24, or 25) that you think you would like to write about, and then plan and write a composition based on it. You may state and explain the meaning of the photograph and give your reactions to it, or you may, if you prefer, write about an idea of your own that the picture brought to mind.

FIGURE 22 →

Andreas Feininger, LIFE Magazine © Time Inc.

FIGURE 23

FIGURE 25 →

FIGURE 24

Andreas Feininger, LIFE Magazine © Time Inc.

Tab Key Index ▶

GRAMMAR

USAGE

MECHANICS

CORRECTION SYMBOLS

ms	error in manuscript form or neatness
cap	error in use of capital letters
p	error in punctuation
sp	error in spelling
frag	sentence fragment
ss	error in sentence structure
k	awkward sentence
nc	not clear
rs	run-on sentence
gr	error in grammar
w	error in word choice
¶	You should have begun a new paragraph here.
t	error in tense
^	You have omitted something.

Index

Index

PICTURE CREDITS

Page 588, Edwin Stein; 590, World Wide Photos; 591 (top), Edward Lettau; 591 (bottom), Frank Dandridge, PIX; 592, Wolf von dem Bussche; 593, Fritz Henle; 595 (top), Eve Arnold, Magnum; 595 (bottom), Photograph by Ken Heyman; 596 (left), Bob Peterson, LIFE Magazine © Time Inc.; 596 (right), W. Eugene Smith; 597 (top), Bruce Roberts from Rapho Guillumette; 597 (bottom), Copyright © 1968, Martin J. Dain, All Rights Reserved; 606, Copyright by Philippe Halsman; 607, Bernie Boston, Washington Evening Star Photo; 609, Jim Theologos; 610 (top), Andreas Feininger, LIFE Magazine © Time Inc.; 610 (bottom), Andreas Feininger, LIFE Magazine © Time Inc.; 611, John Bryson from Rapho Guillumette

5 6 F 7 G 8 H 9 I 0 J 1